MW01137101

The Emperor Commodus

To Mary, Patrick and Joseph. For you, always.

The Emperor Commodus

God and Gladiator

John S. McHugh

Pen & Sword
MILITARY

First published in Great Britain in 2015 by
Pen & Sword Military
an imprint of
Pen & Sword Books Ltd
47 Church Street
Barnsley
South Yorkshire
S70 2AS

ISBN 978 1 47382 755 4

A CIP catalogue record for this book is available from the British Library

Typeset in Ehrhardt by
Mac Style Ltd, Bridlington, East Yorkshire
Printed and bound in the UK by CPI Group (UK) Ltd,
Croydon, CRO 4YY

Pen & Sword Books Ltd incorporates the imprints of Pen & Sword
Archaeology, Atlas, Aviation, Battleground, Discovery, Family History,
History, Maritime, Military, Naval, Politics, Railways, Select, Transport,
True Crime, and Fiction, Frontline Books, Leo Cooper, Praetorian Press,
Seaforth Publishing and Wharncliffe.

For a complete list of Pen & Sword titles please contact
PEN & SWORD BOOKS LIMITED
47 Church Street, Barnsley, South Yorkshire, S70 2AS, England
E-mail: enquiries@pen-and-sword.co.uk
Website: www.pen-and-sword.co.uk

Contents

Synopsis

The notorious emperor Commodus is synonymous with extravagance, megalomania and infamously fighting as a gladiator in the coliseum of ancient Rome. Both mad and bad, his advisors, fearing for their lives, arranged for him to be strangled by his own wrestler in the baths of the imperial palace. However he was emperor for fifteen years, a reign whose duration alone suggests that he could not have been all of these things and survived. This book is a complete re-evaluation of this tumultuous period of Roman history as Commodus struggled with the crises he inherited from his vaunted father, the philosopher, Emperor Marcus Aurelius. The Roman Empire was suffering from the dual canker of a devastating plague that was destroying whole armies and emptying cities, whilst years of almost unceasing warfare had left large areas of the empire pillaged. The finances of the empire buckled under the strain.

Commodus, according to the senatorial historian Cassius Dio, inherited a kingdom of gold and left it one of iron and rust. This account challenges this view which has been unquestionably accepted by many historians and film-makers. Faced with an unstable political structure and a financial system on the brink of collapse, a system that rewarded a small aristocratic elite, he attempted to transform the empire in order to create an imperial government based on an autocratic monarchy supported by a professional cadre of imperial freedmen and officials rather than rely on an increasingly disloyal and self-serving group of senatorial nobles. Deprived of their access to imperial privileges, gifts and promotions, a small group of aristocratic families repeatedly conspired to murder the very man they publicly praised and from whom they sought access to high office.

Commodus rejected the values of the old republic that Augustus had hidden his new imperial and monarchical government behind. Commodus saw himself in the role of a supreme patron, ruling for the good of all. Fighting as a gladiator in the grounds of the imperial palace from a young age, he increasingly associated himself with the demigod Hercules. Both had prodigious physical strength and excelled as huntsmen and warriors; both repeatedly faced death and survived and both sought the divine through their deeds in helping mankind. Commodus' appearance before the baying crowds in the coliseum was an empathetic expression of his understanding of mankind's resilience in a world of chaos and sudden death in a time of deadly plague. To the Romans chanting his name, he had transcended the mortal to become their 'Roman Hercules', fighting to preserve the empire, to preserve the future, to create a new golden age. This the Roman populace readily accepted, their emperor had after all virtually rebuilt their city after its destruction in a devastating fire. Yet one small elite group of aristocrats resented the threat to their status, power and influence. They recalled their privileged golden age during the reign of Marcus Aurelius, and in order to justify their murder of his son, they decried Commodus' actions as those of a madman, a tyrant and a serial debaucher, and so had him assassinated. The consequence? Nearly a hundred years of barbarian invasions, bloody civil wars and the transformation of the empire into the very system that Commodus had tried to create.

This book is designed to be accessible to the general reader and also for those with a more detailed knowledge of the period. It is a unique biography of the emperor; none has ever been published in English, the only other biography was written by F Grosso in Italian in 1964. This work has never been translated into English. Two recent books on Commodus are both thematically based, whose authors explicitly state that their works are not meant to be a comprehensive, chronological or holistic approach to his reign. Both are highly academic analytical works that are aimed at a narrow but specialized audience. *Commodus: An Emperor at the Crossroads* written by O Hekster is not widely available and mainly focuses on the emperor's presentation of himself as the god Hercules rather than an overview of his life. *The Emperor Commodus: Gladiator, Hercules or Tyrant* by G Adams is essentially a detailed commentary on the three main ancient sources that record the reign of Commodus and an evaluation of their 'anti-Commodian' nature. Historians and publishers have focused on his predecessor and father Marcus Aurelius and his eventual successor Septimius Severus. The important reign of Commodus which marked a turning point in Roman history, has been virtually ignored. *The Emperor Commodus: God and Gladiator* is unique in evaluating his reign as a whole against new research that has taken place on the nature of politics in imperial Rome. The actions of the emperor are placed into the political, religious and social context of ancient Rome drawing upon a wide range of recent academic research. However, the old assumptions are rigorously questioned, as are the ancient senatorial sources. Yet the intention is to paint a picture of a man who daily faced sudden death, a man betrayed by his own mother, sister and brothers-in-law. A man who rose above the hostility of the elite that he was a member of to attempt to create a new Rome. A man who was betrayed by the woman he loved. In Commodus we find a very human face, a man of ready emotion: fear, anger, passion, love. He was a man looking for loyalty, and yet was betrayed by those closest to him.

List of Maps and Photographs

Maps

Photographs

1. Commodus as a youth in the Museum of Cologne, Germany.
2. Bust of Commodus in the National Museum of Rome, c. 180.
3. Emperor Commodus in the Kunsthistorisches Museum.
4. Bust of Commodus in the Vatican Museum in Rome.
5. Emperor Commodus.
6. A Young Hercules wearing a lion skin and carrying a club, now lost.
7. Head of a statue of an emperor (probably Commodus).
8. Statue of Commodus.
9. Emperor Commodus.
10. Portrait of Emperor Marcus Aurelius.
11. Portrait of Co-emperor Lucius Verus.
12. Faustina the Younger.
13. Marble bust of the Empress Bruttia Crispina.
14. Bust of Commodus as Hercules in the Capitoline Museum, Rome.
15. Commodus as Caesar.
16. Æ Sestertius
17. A clipeus dated to the early 180s.
18. A sestertius struck under Commodus in 180.
19. Coin struck in 185 AD to celebrate the crushing of the revolt in Britain and restoration of the province after the invasions of 180.
20. Coin depicting Commodus' head. Struck 186 AD.
21. Rome mint. Struck AD 191–192.
22. A sesterces of 192 AD.
23. Bronze medallion of Commodus as the god, Janus.
24. Bronze medallion from 192 depicting Commodus as Hercules.

The Roman Empire (c180 AD)

Oceanus Germanicus

Sarmatia

Germania

Armenia

Mesopotamia

Pontus Euxinus

Pontus

Cappadocia

Syria

Cilicia

Arabia

Bithynia

ASIA

Galatia

Iudaea

Phrygia

Lycia

Mare Aegaeum

Aegyptus

Dacia

Moesia inf.

ILLYRIUM

Moesia sup.

Thracia

Macedonia

Epirus

Achaia

Mare Adriaticum

Pannonia

Dalmatia

Noricum

ITALIA

Cyrenaica

Raetia

Germania sup.

Gallia Cisalpina

Roma

Sicilia

MARE INTERNUM

Germania inf.

Belgica

GALLIA

Narbonensis

Corsica

Mare Tyrrhenum

Africa proconsularis

Lugdunensis

Sardinia

Numidia inf.

Aquitania

Baleares

Numidia sup.

Africa

Britannia

Oceanus Atlanticus

Gallaecia et Asturia

Terraconensis

HISPANIA

Lusitania

Baetica

Mauretania

Central Districts of Imperial Rome

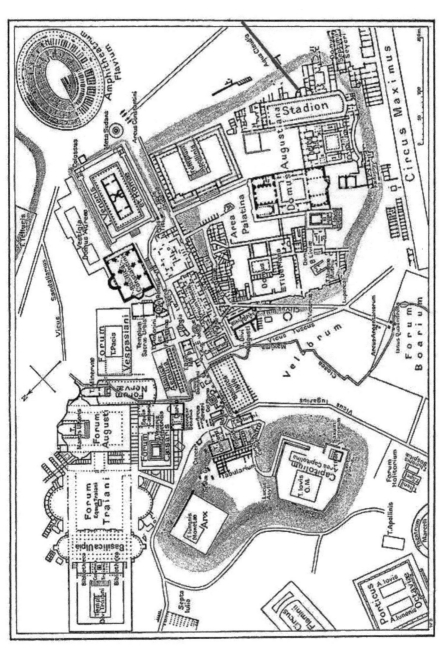

Map of Imperial Rome

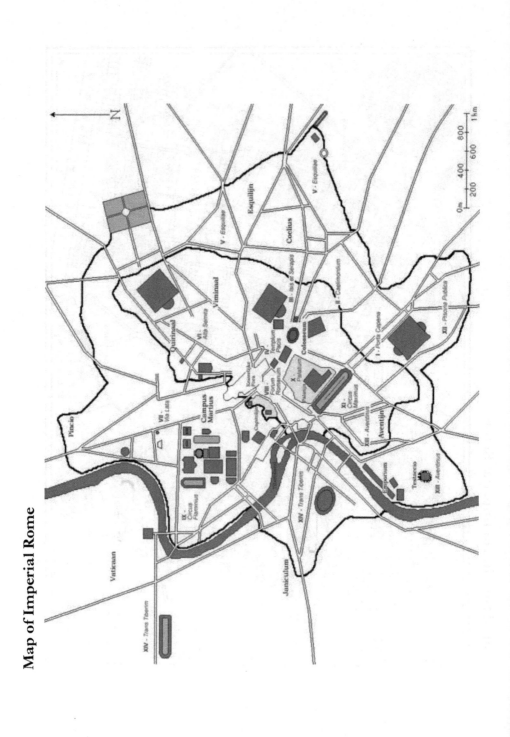

Introduction

The Roman Empire by the time of Commodus had benefited from an extended period of political security. On the assassination of Domitian in 96 AD, the Senate chose Nerva as emperor, knowing full well that, at the age of 65 and having no children, his reign would be short. However, the emperor lacked the support of both the army and the Praetorian Guard. He was virtually forced to adopt the commander of the German legions, Trajan, as his heir. From the reign of Nerva onwards, emperors were adopted by their predecessors, due mainly to the lack of male offspring rather than an act of deliberate policy. This adoption was legally binding in Roman law but was not a new concept; Julius Caesar had adopted his nephew Augustus, then named Octavian. Augustus later adopted his wife's son by a previous marriage, Tiberius. Commodus' father, Marcus Aurelius, succeeded his adoptive father, the Emperor Antoninus Pius, in 161 AD. Marcus Aurelius ascended the throne with Lucius Verus who had also been adopted by Antoninus Pius in a complex agreement with the ruling Emperor Hadrian. Their joint rule was cemented by Verus' marriage to Marcus Aurelius' daughter Lucilla in 164, whilst Marcus Aurelius had been married to Faustina, the daughter of Antoninus Pius. The empire had prospered under years of peace but this was shattered by two unrelated events; the outbreak of the plague and huge barbarian invasions in late 166 or early 167 AD across the Danube into Pannonia.

The 'Antonine Plague' had been brought into the empire by soldiers campaigning under Lucius Verus in the East against the Parthians. After the successful completion of the war in 166 the legions returned to their normal stations around the empire carrying the disease with them:

> It was his fate to seem to bring a pestilence with him to whatever provinces he traversed on his return, and finally even to Rome.[1]

Lucius Verus, whose full title was Lucius Ceionius Aelius Commodus Verus Antoninus, was not classed by the ancient sources as either one of the five good emperors of the Antonine dynasty (Nerva, Trajan, Hadrian, Antoninus Pius and Marcus Aurelius), or a bad emperor (Commodus), as 'he did not bristle with vices, no more did he abound in virtues'.[2] On his return to Rome he brought with him skilled slaves, musicians and performance artists who were highly valued in the elite aristocratic households in Rome. In order to avoid the plague which was rife in the densely populated streets and apartment blocks of the imperial capital, Verus built a huge new palace complex on the outskirts of the city. Here he carried out imperial business, sometimes without consulting his co-emperor and lived the high life;

> He built an exceedingly notorious villa on the via Clodia, and here he not only revelled himself for many days at a time in boundless extravagance together with his freedmen and friends of inferior rank in whose presence he felt no shame, but even invited Marcus.[3]

No doubt the young Commodus was a visitor and watched Verus duelling as a gladiator using the wooden training swords or partaking in his other passion, chariot racing. Surrounded by his freedmen Geminas, Agaclytus, Coedes and Eclectus, the emperor attended to the business of empire. These freedmen were the true professional bureaucrats whose skills and experience were vital to the smooth running of imperial government. They were often brought into the imperial household as slaves, earning their freedom through years of loyal service. Yet they were stigmatized by their low social status as ex slaves and their influence jealously resented by the noble elite in the senate.

In contrast to Verus, Marcus Aurelius surrounded himself with the noblest and 'best' men of the senate in addition to philosophers and men of learning. The great man of letters, M Cornelius Fronto, had been the tutor of both emperors as children and remained a close friend (*amicus*), whilst Fronto's own son in law, Aufidius Victorinus, would remain an intimate of both Marcus Aurelius and his son, Commodus. Other members of this inner core of imperial advisors or *consilium* included the senatorial philosopher Gnaeus Claudius Severus who married Marcus' daughter Annia Faustina; Marcus Ummidius Quadratus Annianus, the nephew of the emperor who adopted a son of Claudius Severus; M Acilius Glabrio who could trace his ancestry back to Republican Rome; the Quintilii brothers, Maximus and Condianus who would name their children after each other. They had shared their consulships together, two being available every year, and would die together. These elite aristocrats would be joined by new men who would be ennobled through being granted the consulship by Marcus Aurelius, who, in his need for skilled and experienced military commanders, would promote men such as Helvidius Pertinax and Tiberius Claudius Pompeianus to this inner circle.

The aristocracy of Imperial Rome was completely reliant on the emperor granting them honours, wealth, magisterial office and privileges in order to retain and justify their exalted status. The ultimate imperial gift or *beneficia* was the consulship itself, which ennobled the man's family and his descendants. There were two 'ordinary' consuls appointed every year by the emperor who gained the honour (*dignitas*) of having the year named after them. Their name was preserved forever in the state records. The emperor could also appoint 'suffect' consuls on the prearranged resignation of the ordinary ones; this allowed the emperor to draw upon a greater reservoir of suitably qualified men who could be appointed to the imperial provinces or command of the legions.

One of the greatest threats to the emperor were senatorial commanders (legates) using their position to lead a military revolt against his rule. It was crucial that these men be totally loyal to the emperor. This aristocratic elite expected to be treated as an equal by the emperor despite the paradoxical situation that they could not command the same access to official posts, wealth, power or influence. Just as the emperor was the ultimate patron, each senator was also a patron who would need access to privileges, posts, honours and gifts from the emperor to retain and extend their own network of friends (*amici*) and clients. This complex relationship was based upon the customs and tradition of *amicitia*, reciprocal bonds of friendship, where gifts and *beneficia* were bestowed by an *amicus* or patron on the expectation that it would be returned at a future time and date.[4] However, the emperor's superior position made it impossible for this reciprocal relationship to be based on that of equals and yet it was expected by the senatorial aristocracy that the language of equality be used otherwise the social status inferred was that of a lesser relationship that existed between patron and client. This would insult the honour and dignity of the senatorial nobility by inferring social inferiority. In return for his *beneficia*, the emperor expected loyalty (*fides*) and public expressions of gratitude (*gratia*) from the recipient. Access to the emperor was of paramount importance in persuading him to grant such favours. Those people who held this privileged position were firstly his own family, secondly the friends of the emperor (*amici Caesaris*, who were traditionally high status members of the senatorial class) and thirdly, the officials of the imperial household including lower status equestrians and imperial freedmen. The best occasions to solicit the emperor were either the morning greetings (*salutatio*) in the palace or through a prestigious invitation to the imperial banquets. Here a couch near the emperor was a mark of the highest honour.[5] The emperor retained stability through developing bonds of patronage, securing the loyalty of his *amici* through distribution of imperial *beneficia* and other grants, allowing his *amici* to build their own networks of *amicitiae* and clients whose own loyalty to the emperor was indirectly secured. Marcus Aurelius was a master at this role with members of the senatorial elite having access and influence over imperial decisions, gifts, offices and other privileges.

From 166 onwards the plague ravaged the empire killing the poor and the wealthy elite without distinction. Rome itself suffered severely, the dead were carried away on carts and wagons. Even the famous doctor Galen left the capital and retired to Pergamum in Asia Minor. Yet worse was to come. Barbarians started to cross the Roman frontier. The barbarian incursions, firstly by the Langobardi and Obii who were displaced by other tribes far beyond the borders of the empire. This raid of approximately 6,000 warriors in 166 AD was later followed by an attack on Dacia in 167 with the loss of the valuable gold mines. The movement of tribes in central Europe pushed in others like a row of dominoes towards the Roman frontier. In 168 a tidal wave of Quadi and Marcomanni, whose lands lay across the Danube facing the Roman provinces of Upper and Lower Pannonia, streamed into the empire demanding land on which to settle. Appalling damage was done; the legionary fortress at Carnuntum was burnt to the ground. Other fortresses in these provinces, and the neighbouring provinces of Noricum and Raetia, suffered a similar fate. The two emperors mobilized their army and proceeded north only to receive news that some of the tribal kings were suing for peace after the defeat of the Quadi and the death of their king by Roman forces. At some point the Praetorian Prefect Furius Victorinus was lost along with a significant part of his army. Our sources are unclear in explaining whether this was due to enemy action or the impact of the plague which is recorded as wiping out whole armies. The emperors proceeded to the Danube allotting experienced administrators along the way. Arrius Antoninus was made curator of Ariminum and Helvidius Pertinax given a procuratorship responsible for the grain supply (*alimentia*) in order to secure the logistical support for the army. With the approach of winter and the end of the campaigning season the emperors decided to return to Rome but Lucius Verus was taken ill and after three days died, probably of the plague. The imperial funeral rites were carried out in Rome, and then with apparent unseemly haste Marcus Aurelius remarried Verus' wife, his daughter Lucilla, to the new man Claudius Pompeianus whose military skills the emperor would repeatedly call upon. Lucilla however was horrified by the match; she, the daughter of an empress and ex-wife of an emperor, forced to marry a man of no noble ancestry whatsoever, Pompeianus lacked the necessary *nobilitas*. Despite the complaints of her mother, Faustina, the marriage vows were exchanged. Lucilla's resentment would continue to grow and fester.[6]

The records from 169 of the VII Claudia legion stationed in Upper Moesia show the plague continuing to spread through the legions along the whole of the Danube. Calpurnius Agricola, the Governor of Dacia, perished either in battle or of the disease at this time. Soldiers were summoned from across the empire to replace losses and prepare for an offensive, in particular from the eastern provinces and new legions were raised. Even gladiators and provincial police units were drafted. The financial impact of the plague and the war was immense. The Roman offensive of 170 across the Danube under the watchful eye of the emperor met with unmitigated disaster. Twenty thousand troops were slain and the victorious Quadi and Marcomanni advanced unchecked through the Julian Alps to lay siege to the city of Aquileia on the borders of Italy itself. Italy had not been invaded for hundreds of years. Upper Moesia and Dacia were also invaded by the Jazyges and the Roman commander slain. The Costoboci overran the Balkans and penetrated deep into Greece whose cities had long since allowed their walls to fall into various states of disrepair. They were unceremoniously sacked and plundered, their populace slaughtered. Cities hastily tried to reconstruct their ancient walls but were warned by the emperor that they needed to seek imperial approval beforehand, even in times of extreme peril; precedents that undermined imperial authority could not be allowed.

In this time of crisis Marcus Aurelius turned to his most gifted and experienced generals, allocating posts not on senatorial status and nobility but military ability. Valerius Maximianus, a man whose father had been a mere priest in the colony of Poetovio in Pannonia, but a successful general in the war against Parthia, was ordered to cut the supply route to the barbarians to the south in Greece by patrolling the Danube. He would also secure supplies for the Roman soldiers stationed along the river itself. Pompeianus was ordered to throw the barbarians out of Italy and secure its alpine borders. Pompeianus chose as his junior commander his old client and *amicus*, Pertinax. Marcus Aurelius meanwhile made Carnuntum in Pannonia on the Danube his headquarters where he would remain for the next three years.

Unremitting warfare was to follow. In 171 the Quadi and Marcomanni, heavily encumbered with loot, plunder and captives they had seized in Northern Italy were trapped by Roman forces as they attempted to recross the Danube. They were destroyed and the captives released. The soldiers requested the usual monetary reward (donative) for such victories but Marcus Aurelius refused on the grounds that he could only afford it by increasing taxes on their own parents and families. The financial crisis had already started to bite. Disturbing news now came from Spain where Moors had crossed the straits of Gibraltar from North Africa and were plundering the undefended provinces in the region. The emperor's *amicus*, Aufidius Victorinus, was despatched with soldiers from the successful campaigns in Greece to deal with the Moors.

Following a policy of divide and rule, certain tribes were offered peace terms and others alliances in order to separate them from the Marcomanni and Quadi. Thirteen thousand Roman captives were returned, more were promised to be handed over later. Roman deserters were returned to await their fate whilst some barbarians were settled within the empire probably to replace losses caused by the plague; however those settled in Ravenna attempted to revolt and so the emperor ended this policy. The Cotini however, pretending to seek terms from the Romans, attacked a delegation led by the *ab epistulis*, an imperial secretary responsible for correspondence with the emperor, Tarrutenius Paternus, from which he managed to extricate himself but with great loss of life. Paternus would eventually exact his revenge as Praetorian Prefect.

The campaigning season of 172 started with another Roman offensive. Again the Romans suffered a number of reverses. One of the two Praetorian Prefects, Macrinus Vindex, was killed in battle. Marcus Aurelius would have replaced him with Pertinax, but he was now ineligible having been promoted to senatorial status for his successful campaigns in Italy and the Alps along with Pompeianus. The office of Praetorian Prefect was held by men of equestrian status as their close physical proximity to the emperor and responsibility for the imperial bodyguards made them a potential threat, so men of the high status senatorial class were not chosen in case they claimed the throne themselves. The elitism of the senatorial aristocracy is exemplified by the criticism the emperor and Pertinax received from the 'best men' in the senate, despite the fact his consulship was the just reward for saving Italy and the senatorial nobilities' estates from plunder and devastation.

When Pertinax as a reward for his brave exploits obtained the consulship, there were nevertheless some who showed displeasure in view of the fact that he was of obscure family, and they quoted this line from tragedy: 'Such things accursed wars bring in its train.' Little did they realize that he (Pertinax) would be emperor as well.[7]

In Egypt a group of tribesmen based around the Nile delta rebelled and nearly captured the vast metropolis of Alexandria itself. The emperor gave permission for the senator Avidius Cassius to enter the province with his Syrian legions to crush the rebellion, which he did effectively and efficiently. He also appears to have used this as an opportunity to build up support for himself amongst the equestrian officials. Senators for this very reason were banned on pain of death from entering this rich province that was the breadbasket of the city of Rome itself. Avidius Cassis would later rebel against his friend Marcus Aurelius, the province of Egypt being amongst the first to offer its allegiance to the usurper. The year finally brought a significant but unlikely victory. The famous rain miracle probably took place in 172 AD. A Roman army had advanced deep into the territory of the Quadi but became surrounded by larger numbers of enemy forces in an ambush. The Roman soldiers were becoming exhausted from almost continuous fighting and fatigue caused by their wounds but most of all the soldiers suffered from heat and thirst. The soldiers locked shields and stood in line awaiting their end:

When suddenly many clouds gathered and a mighty rain, not without divine interposition burst upon them ... when the rain poured down, at first all turned their faces upwards and received the water in their mouths: then some held out their shields and some their helmets to catch it; and they not only took deep draughts themselves but also gave their horses some to drink ... And when the barbarians now charged upon them, they drank and fought at the same time; and some becoming wounded actually drank down the blood that flowed into their helmets along with the water. So intent, indeed, were most of them on drinking that they would have suffered severely from the enemy's onset, had not a violent hail storm and numerous thunderbolts fallen upon the ranks of the foe. Thus in one and the same place one might have beheld water and fire descending from the sky simultaneously; so that while those on one side were being drenched and drinking, the others were being consumed by fire and dying.[8]

Presumably the Quadi held the higher ground and so were hit by the lightning strikes. The soldiers on both sides saw this as divine intervention, the Romans elated by the favour they had been shown by Jupiter, the Quadi dismayed that the gods had snatched victory away from them. The ensuing battle was a foregone conclusion. Marcus Aurelius was awarded the title 'Germanicus' by the senate, a title also conferred upon his young son Commodus who was present in the imperial headquarters at Carnuntum. The youthful image of the young Commodus appears on a medallion with the Caesar acquiring the name 'Germanicus'.[9]

The winter saw a battle on the frozen Danube. A large Roman force was pursuing a retreating army of Jazyges who were used to fighting on ice. The Jazyges turned to face their pursuers, and rushed forward to engage the Romans on the frozen river, their horses, also trained to manoeuvre on ice, moved to outflank the Roman line. The Romans closed ranks and turned to face their attackers who assailed them on all sides. The soldiers lay down their shields on the ice, resting one foot on the shield for grip they withstood the enemy charge, grabbing hold of the bridles of the enemy horses or their opponent's spear or shield and pulled the enemy soldier towards them to engage in close combat where the shorter Roman sword, the *gladius*, would provide a greater advantage than the enemies' long sword used for slashing. The barbarian soldiers or cavalrymen often lost their footing by this action and were pulled to the ground, often bringing the Roman soldier down on top of them. A gruesome and desperate wrestling match then ensued with each punching, stabbing and biting their opponent. The Romans with their armour and better training usually won this duel; the Jazyges force was utterly destroyed.[10]

The Naristae, an ally of the Quadi, were defeated by the individual heroics of Valerius Maximianus who had been reposted from the Danube securing the supply route to fortress stationed along its banks. An inscription raised in his honour in Numidia during the reign of Commodus records that the general slew the king of the Naristae in single combat. He was decorated by the emperor; receiving a horse, phalerae and arms as well as appointment to an elite double strength cavalry regiment, the Ala I Ulpia Contariorum at Arrabona.[11]

The war had now become one of guerrilla warfare; the barbarian tribes using hit and run tactics, disappearing into the forests and mountains. The Romans too adapted to this, breaking up the legions into smaller units of men, *vexillationes*, which were used to occupy enemy territory in a slash and burn strategy. The Column of Marcus Aurelius records the grim reality of this tactic; it shows villages burned, the inhabitants brutally slain, including women and children, and the survivors chained and being led off to the slave markets. The Quadi and Marcomanni, worn down by this attrition, sought and were granted peace terms. These terms were remarkably similar to those offered later by Commodus in 180 AD to the same tribes and yet Commodus received condemnation in the ancient sources for being too lenient on the defeated barbarians.

By 177 AD the tribes had recovered and breaking the terms of their recently signed treaties, attacked the empire again. Marcus Aurelius was now bent on a war of annihilation; it is even possible he wished to convert the territories occupied by these warring tribes into Roman provinces. An inscription dated to 179 AD on a high bluff found at Trencin in modern Slovakia records the winter quarters resplendent with bathhouse of a vexillation of legionaries hundreds of miles from the Danube:

> To the victory of the emperors (Marcus Aurelius and Commodus), dedicated by 855 soldiers of the second Legion of the army stationed at Laugardio. Made to order of Marcus Valerius Maximianus, legate of the Second Adiutrix legion.[12]

Commodus would take a leading role in this 'Second Marcomannic War' alongside his father whilst Valerius Maximianus would be rewarded for his long and loyal service with a governorship of peaceful Numidia, and Commodus would ennoble him with the suffect consulship of 186. The career of this illustrious general of low birth is completely omitted from the histories of the pro-senatorial writers of the time but can be pieced together from inscriptions put up in his honour around the empire.

To the senatorial historian Cassius Dio, the reign of Marcus Aurelius was 'a kingdom of gold'.[13] Modern historians have followed his lead contrasting the father's reign to that of his son. We need to be less accepting of the prejudices of the ancient primary sources and question their inherent bias. Cassius Dio, Herodian and the senatorial source of the Historia Augusta, Marius Maximus, seek to justify the murder of Commodus by members of the same senatorial elite. Herodian, probably not a senator, but an eyewitness to the events he describes produced his work with his audience in mind, the educated elite of the empire. The philosopher, Emperor Marcus Aurelius, dealt with the crises and problems he faced adeptly and with great ability and intelligence relying heavily on the advice and support of the aristocratic senatorial classes but at the same time promoting men of lesser status to positions of great power and prestige due to the emergency of war. The empire faced during his reign almost unremitting war with the prosperous lands of Italy and Greece threatened and ravaged. The provinces south of the Danube were left desolate wastelands and banditry was starting to become endemic in large areas of the empire as the provincial forces were withdrawn to the war zone. Spain also faced incursions by the Moors. The plague was killing thousands every day, not just in Rome but across the empire. The army suffered grievously from losses caused by this disease and in war itself. The finances of the empire were already becoming stretched with reducing revenues as the plague led to reduction in trade and agricultural production, but also there was a massive increase in costs with new legions being created and the army needing to be fed and supplied. The emperor had to resort to selling the precious objects, trappings and ornamentation in the imperial palace. He refused however to ask the Roman elite to pay more in taxes. Finally in 175 AD the spectre of civil war arose when Avidius Cassius rose in revolt taking the whole of the east with him. This was the kingdom Commodus inherited from his father in 180 AD. A kingdom of gold?

Chapter One

Born to the Purple (161–177 AD)

‘I was born both man and emperor.’ So Commodus announces to the assembled legions in Herodian's dramatic account of his accession to the throne on the northern frontier of the empire. Commodus was 'born to the purple'; the first emperor to be born to a living emperor and he could trace his line back through adoptions to the Emperor Nerva (96–98 AD). Emperor Antoninus Pius was his biological grandfather through his mother Faustina, and he was the scion of the noble senatorial family, the Annii who were ennobled through M Annius Verus' consulship of 97 AD. Commodus' later coinage emphasizes his *nobilitas*. He was proud of his lineage which raised him far above the other nobles in the senate, whilst the senatorial sources attempt to discredit his status and question his legitimacy by repeating the rumour that he was the product of an adulterous relationship between his mother and a gladiator.[1] His childhood was a continual preparation for his future imperial role and we see few glimpses of him being allowed the freedom to behave as a child should, and even then to the dissatisfaction of the senatorial source:

> … he was adept at certain arts which are not becoming in an emperor for he could mould goblets and dance and sing and whistle, and he could play the buffoon and gladiator to perfection.[2]

Marcus Aurelius, his learned father, ensured his son had the best education an empire's wealth could afford.[3] The traditional education of an aristocratic child was in Latin classics and grammar, followed by Greek language and literature and finally law, rhetoric and philosophy. His father, when present, educated him himself. However in his father's prolonged absences Commodus had a range of gifted tutors, Onesicrates, specialist in Greek literature, Antistius Capella in Latin and Ateius Sanctus in rhetoric.[4] Galen mentions Pitholaus as his tutor and a further possible tutor was Julius Pollux of Naucratis whose Onomasticon was dedicated to the young Commodus.[5] The Onomasticon was a type of Greek thesaurus arranged according to subject matter. The dedication refers to Commodus as Caesar, so must have been made before he was proclaimed Augustus in 175 AD.[6] The tutors were evidently well paid for their work but the prospect of further substantial rewards deriving from close proximity to the emperor and his Caesar were likely.

T Ateius (probably correctly named Aius) Sanctus had previously held the post of *ab epistulis graecis* in charge of the emperor's letters and correspondence to the Greek speakers of the empire and a highly influential and powerful post. Being an established orator he was appointed Commodus' teacher of oratory by 176 AD at the latest. His was able to use this position to successfully gain promotion to responsibility for one of the two imperial financial departments as 'procurator of the *ratio privata*' as well as an *a rationibus* (a financial official) and indeed he may have continued to hold these posts whilst being tutor. He was then probably promoted to be Prefect of Egypt in 179/80 AD and adlected or promoted to the senate by Commodus when sole emperor. Evidently Sanctus' skills and teaching had been and continued to be appreciated by both father and son. Rhetoricians, poets, grammarians and philosophers of provincial cities, especially the Greek east had, after the emperor's *amici*, the easiest access to the emperor and it was from these posts that many of the emperor's assistants and secretaries were drawn as the drawing up of imperial letters and receipts was the most common form of contact between emperor and his subjects. Direct access to the emperor brought power and influence, particularly if you were also tutoring the future emperor. Marcus Aurelius gave thanks in his own philosophical work, the *Meditations*, for being able to find such talented tutors for his children. These were clearly able men who were themselves talented administrators in their own right.

The ancient sources however denigrate the intelligence and ability of Commodus despite the gifts of his tutors. Dio Cassius refers to him being 'guileless' and 'his great simplicity ... made him the slave of his companions'. Dio states that his mother, Faustina, also felt her son was 'simple minded'. Furthermore the writer of the *Historia Augusta* states that his 'teachers in all their studies profited him not the least'. The *Historia Augusta* is a notoriously unreliable source that places events out of context so that the real meaning is confused or presents rumours and slanders as factual information. Yet these opinions are contradicted by his father who in his *Meditations* gives thanks that his children were neither stupid nor deformed. A number of events also seem to contradict this view of Commodus' intelligence. Julius Pollux was a famous sophist and he decided to dedicate his work to the emperor's son rather than the emperor himself. Each address in his dedication is in the form of a letter and urges on Commodus the importance of this branch of study. Later Pollux wrote an '*epithalamium*' or wedding hymn at Commodus' marriage ceremony in 178 AD which impressed the groom with the charm of his voice. Pollux was rewarded with the chair of Greek rhetoric in Athens. Another Greek sophist, Adrian of Tyre left his native city at the age of 18 and became a student of Herodes Atticus in Athens where he was later granted the chair of rhetoric by Marcus Aurelius. Aurelius returning from his tour of the East with his son Commodus in 176 AD listened to Adrian speak on the topic of

'Hyperides heeds only the argument of Demosthenes, while Philip is at Elatea'. Marcus Aurelius was so impressed by his oration that Adrian was granted a range of imperial benevolences, including imperial financial support in Athens, precedence at games, priesthoods, immunities from taxation, gold, silver, horses and slaves. Adrian was then later promoted, probably by Commodus, to the higher chair of rhetoric in Rome winning such recognition that even those who knew no Greek rushed to hear him speak. In his eighties and lying on his deathbed the Emperor Commodus wrote a letter to the dying Adrian apologizing for the failure to appoint him to the post of '*ab epistulis Graecis*' as the emperor's advisor and assistant for affairs in the Greek east. Adrian died crying tears of gratitude hugging the letter to his chest. Not only does this suggest that the role of '*ab epistulis Graecis*' was the highest and most prestigious post for a Greek sophist as he had direct access to the emperor himself, it also infers that Commodus was learned in both Latin and Greek and also took an intellectual interest in oratory and philosophy throughout his life. These actions of the emperor contradict the views of the senatorial sources that refer to Commodus as simple-minded and guileless. Commodus continued in his 'moral studies' throughout his life and it is only with the overthrow of his chamberlain Cleander in 190 AD that Herodian states that he abandoned these pursuits in order to focus on the physical 'pleasures' of chariot racing and gladiatorial combat. It was only now that, according to Herodian, men of learning and scholarship were driven from the court. This may be due to the fact these men were linked to the fall of the Greek Cleander.[7]

Commodus was born on 31 August 161 AD in the imperial villa on the coast at Lanuvium where his mother's father was born. His mother Faustina probably chose this location as she knew it well and knew the cool breezes off the sea would be a welcome distraction from the hot summer weather. Astrologers were summoned who cast a horoscope for him and his twin, Titus Aurelius Fulvius Antoninus, which were both pronounced favourable. His twin brother was also known as 'Verissimus', a pet name denoting perhaps a favourable status in the affections of his parents but Marcus Aurelius' letters to Fronto describe a dotting affection towards all his children. Coinage, used to promote imperial propaganda, celebrate the twins' birth showing the infants under a star with the legend 'SAECULI FELICITAS'. However, Antoninus would die in 165/166 AD after just being named Caesar with his brother Commodus, being 4-years-old. His elder brother Hadrianus had already died in 162 AD. Being the sole male survivor of the dynasty may have nurtured a belief in the young man that he was divinely protected. A statue dated to 166 AD found at Tivoli and now in the Museum of Fine Arts in Boston depicts a young Hercules strangling two snakes. The face and hairstyle of the demigod bears remarkable similarity to that of the young Commodus suggesting an early association with the deity he was later to closely identify himself, a belief seemingly condoned by his father who must have sanctioned the statue. However the statue may have been carved later in the sole reign of Commodus to associate himself from an early age to Hercules or it could be a depiction of his twin brother, Fulvius Antoninus, made to mark their naming as Caesar. A number of statue bases discovered at Sabratha in North Africa dating to 164–166 AD celebrate Marcus Aurelius' children on a marble panel showing the family in procession. It was already evident to provincials that Commodus and his brother were intended to be potential heirs to the throne. Another statue base from Athens dated between 166 and 176 AD was presented to Commodus by the entire city, perhaps on his visit to Athens in 176 AD with his father.[8] Commodus' image does not appear on the coinage again until 177 AD, perhaps reflecting the fear of all parents that their son would not live to see adulthood, a fate befalling the vast majority of Roman children. A further son of Marcus Aurelius, M Annius Verus, was born in 162 AD, and would be made Caesar with Commodus in October 166 but die when Commodus was 8-years-old in 169 AD leaving him the sole male heir. These deaths would clearly have some impact on the young Commodus, however he did have four surviving sisters: Faustina (b151), Lucilla (b150), Fadilla (b159) and Annia Cornificia (b160) and later Sabina, born around 170 AD. Their roles would be to cement the loyalty of influential senatorial families to his father with Lucilla married to the co-emperor Lucius Verus in 161 AD and Faustina was married in 159 AD to aristocrat Gnaeus Claudius Severus, a close advisor and *amicus* to Marcus Aurelius. Therefore Commodus would have grown up with his two sisters Fadilla and Cornificia as well as his twin and younger brothers until their deaths. His older sisters Lucilla and Faustina would have left the imperial palace and joined the household of their husbands. Commodus perhaps did not have the opportunity to develop close bonds and Lucilla's later actions demonstrate no filial loyalty. It is interesting to note however that Fadilla remained a loyal confidant of Commodus having free access to him and warning him of a rising against his freedman Cleander that was taking place outside his palace. Cornificia's husband Marcus Petronius Sura Mamertinus was involved in a conspiracy against Commodus leading to his execution along with their son but she herself was spared, suggesting she was either not involved in the plot or Commodus still felt some loyalty to his sister as he had no hesitation in ordering the exile and then execution of Lucilla when she organized a widespread conspiracy against him. Likewise Sabina's husband Lucius Antistius Burrus was also executed for involvement in a conspiracy in 188 AD but she was allowed to remarry, albeit to an obscure equestrian.[9]

Commodus was born on the same day as Emperor Caligula (Gaius) and this fact was significant to our senatorial sources that saw a mirror between the actions and death of the two emperors. There is a great deal of similarity between the actions and events of Commodus and his predecessor Caligula. In his *Meditations*, a book in all probability Commodus read under his father's tutelage, Marcus Aurelius comments:

> Reflect continually on the fact that all things as happen now, also happened before, and on the fact that they will happen again. The whole dramas and the comparable scenes which you know from your own experience or from history of the past, place these before your eyes, such as the whole court of Hadrian, the whole court of Antoninus, and the whole court of Philip, Alexander, Croesus. All these were similar only the actors were different.[10]

Commodus would have been taught the lives of such famous 'actors' from the past and surely Commodus would have been drawn to the life of one such actor whose birthday he shared. Indeed key events in his life appear marked to coincide with key events in Roman history. Commodus was invested with the Toga Virilis at Sirmium on 7 July 175 AD, the day Romulus, the founder of Rome, disappeared from the earth to ascend to the heavens. Clearly the date was deliberately chosen by his father to enhance the prestige and mystique of his son but the choice of date would certainly have an impact on his 14-year-old son who would later portray himself as the refounder of Rome.

Commodus' full name was Lucius Aurelius Commodus, named in honour of his father's co-emperor Lucius Verus who had been called Commodus himself before being made Augustus.[11] Verus, unlike the more austere and stoic Marcus Aurelius, had a poor reputation due to 'the excessive licence of his life', being devoted to pleasure, he appears carefree yet also clever. Verus enjoyed both hunting and wrestling.[12] As with many aristocrats he relished chariot racing supporting the 'greens' as well as holding gladiatorial contests to entertain his guests at banquets. In the very early years of Commodus' life Verus was in the East successfully campaigning against the Parthians. He returned to Rome a victorious general being awarded a triumph on 12 October 166 AD, the first for nearly fifty years. It was at Verus' insistence that Marcus Aurelius' surviving sons were made Caesars.[13] This appears to have been the start of a strong bond of affection between the two. The triumphal ceremony was unusual as it included not only Lucius and Marcus Aurelius but also their children, including Commodus aged 5, and his younger brother Annius Verus aged 3.

This event would have impressed the young boys especially as both were given the title of Caesar at the request of Verus. At the forefront of the triumphal procession came the senate led by the magistrates of Rome without their lictors accompanied by ranks of trumpeters announcing Rome's victory. White bulls escorted by their attendants were led behind towards the Temple of Jupiter for sacrifice. Next came immense carts full of the spoils of war including gold, silver and other precious objects. Then came the insignia and weapons of the conquered Parthians followed by captured nobles, princes and generals. The adoring and cheering crowds overawed by the immensity of the loot and large numbers of prestigious prisoners then had the opportunity to acclaim their emperors, Marcus Aurelius and Verus, who were dressed to resemble Jupiter, the supreme god. They would have been carried in a chariot and worn a tunic embroidered with palm trees with red make up on their faces, carrying a sceptre. All these accoutrements were associated with Jupiter creating the impression of their near divine status. A slave stood behind each of the triumphators holding a gold wreath above their head reminding them that they were not gods themselves; 'Look behind you, remember you are only a man', would be whispered regularly in their ears.[14] Commodus, Lucilla, Verus' wife, and the rest of the imperial family then came behind observing the acclamations of the adoring crowd who would throw flowers as they passed and marching behind them; the massed ranks of the legions clad in togas without their weapons but wearing the laurels of victory. The ceremony had begun early in the day on the Campus Martius on the west bank of the Tiber and then as they had approached the city limits (*pomerium*) the whole Senate met them. The generals would formally relinquish their commands allowing them to enter Rome. The procession advanced along the via Sacra to the Forum, past the Circus Flaminius and Circus Maximus and then up the Capitoline Hill to sacrifice the bulls at the Temple of Jupiter. Marcus and Verus were awarded civic crowns of oak leaves by the senate at the same time for 'saving the lives of fellow citizens' by the judicious conduct of their campaign and each received the title 'Father of their Country', *pater patriae*. The 5-year-old Commodus must have considered his father and Verus gods incarnate. After the triumph, games were held where Marcus and Verus appeared in their triumphal robes and no doubt Commodus and his brother sat next to the two emperors to watch the games. Verus 'was fond of circus games no less than that of gladiatorial spectacles' unlike Marcus Aurelius, who would often use the time to read, listen to and sign documents much to the disgust of the crowds.[15] The Coliseum held approximately 50,000 screaming Romans whereas the Circus Maximus held 250,000. The games were where the ordinary people of Rome met the emperors and the imperial family and feasted upon a spectacle of blood. A late Christian source uses his own experiences to describe the addiction of the games:

When they had arrived and sat down in what seats they could, the whole place was boiling with pleasures of the most savage kind. Alypius closed the doors of his eyes, and forbade his mind to pay any attention to all this wickedness. Would that he could have stopped his ears! For at one moment in the fight, a gladiator fell, and a great clamour arose from the whole populace, and beat against him … and he opened his eyes and was more severely wounded in his soul than the gladiator whom he longed to see had been in his body … The noise entered his ears and unlocked his eyes … it saw the blood, it drank in it savagely, nor did it turn away, but fixed its gaze and glutted itself on the fury … taking pleasure in the wickedness of the fight and becoming drunk on its bloody pleasure … He watched, he cheered, he burnt, he took his madness away with him, to stir him up to come again.

We do not know whether Commodus attended these games, however when he did, just like Alypius, he must have drunk it all in, revelling in the adulation of the crowd who acknowledged their emperors who made all this possible. It is reassuring to know that at these games Marcus Aurelius was so concerned at the injuries sustained to a young child who fell whilst performing as a rope dancer, that to prevent this happening again he ordered mats to be placed under all future performers. Coins were then issued celebrating the glory of the triumph and the celebratory games.[16]

Verus' returning army had also brought back with them from the East a hidden scourge, the plague, which was to blight the remainder of Marcus' reign and also that of his son. In Rome the dead were removed from the city by the cartload including many of the noblest senators.[17] In these circumstances it is likely that the imperial family would have taken up residence in one of the imperial villas on the outskirts of Rome. It was perhaps for this reason Verus constructed a new villa for himself and his household on the Clodian way which ran north-west of Rome through Etruria. The villa was probably near modern Acqua Traversa.[18] Verus packed his new palace with the riches he had brought back from his war against the Parthians including skilled slaves who were musicians, mimes, jesters, jugglers and actors, the most famous being Maximus whom Verus renamed Paris and Agrippus Memphius whom he renamed Apolaustus meaning 'enjoyable'. Paris was the favourite actor of the emperor Nero whose birthday Verus shared.[19] On completion of the villa Marcus Aurelius visited for five days, holding court in the day and attending lavish banquets in the evening.[20] It is likely the young Commodus would also have attended and enjoyed the exotic entertainment from the Greek east, mimes, music, dances, wrestling and gladiatorial contests.

Whilst Verus and Marcus Aurelius remained around Rome the rumblings of war resounded on the northern frontier as 6,000 Langobardi and Obii burst into Pannonia. These were ably dealt with by the Roman forces stationed there and their leader, the King of the Marcomanni, Ballomarius, sued for peace.[21] In 167 AD Verus and M Ummidius Quadratus, Marcus Aurelius' nephew started the year as consuls with the young Commodus probably being present at their inauguration.

The year was spent dealing with the repercussions of the plague and the famine. Laws were passed dealing with the disposal of the dead to attempt to stop the spread of the disease, funerals were modified and measures taken to reduce the potential for popular unrest amongst desperate inhabitants of the city. Religious ceremonies were performed to purify the city, including the Feast of the Gods, where the statues of the gods were placed on banqueting couches in public places around Rome and served offerings on a table. Pestilence and disease was seen as a sign of divine disapproval and as arbiters of the divine, emperors could be seen as personally responsible for public misfortune.[22] At the start of 168 AD the loss of life in Rome meant the Praetorian guardsmen were finding it difficult to find prospective brides and so Marcus Aurelius, eager to cement the loyalty of his bodyguards, announced to the assembled units that prospective fathers of potential brides would gain the same privileges from the birth of a grandson as they would from the birth of a child of their own. It may also have been the case that the Praetorians were blamed for bringing the plague back from the East where many had accompanied Verus and so were becoming increasingly unpopular in the city and its surrounding area.[23]

Much of the second half of 167 AD would also have been used to organize the imminent military campaign on the northern frontier raising both funds and new legionaries. The Marcomanni and the Victuali had threatened to invade the empire unless they were admitted. The two emperors set off north at the start of 168 AD clad in their military cloaks after a formal greeting by the senate, accompanied by a large entourage of *amici* and advisors. Some of these Commodus would inherit as his *amici* on the death of his father. They included Aufidius Victorinus whom Commodus would make Prefect of Rome and Tiberius Claudius Pomeianus who would earn rapid promotion from Marcus Aurelius in these campaigns, helping to defeat the initial force of invaders and ultimately becoming Commodus' brother-in-law and closest *amici*. This was to be the last time Commodus was to see Verus as he was to die on his return journey at Aquileia in 169 AD. On Verus' death his household was subsumed into that of Marcus Aurelius who freed many of the slaves he inherited but also retained many who were too valuable to lose, some being attached to the household of the young Commodus. Many of these would become senior advisors to Commodus and wield immense power. Marcus Aurelius probably did not want to lose the talents of these able and skilled individuals yet did not have vacancies in his own household. Furthermore the 7-year-old Commodus would have jumped at the chance to retain a link to Verus. The sources criticize the power and influence many of these freedmen had held under Verus just as they would under Commodus. Both men recognized ability above nobility of birth and for that they were condemned: 'Verus' freedmen, furthermore, had great influence with him … namely Geminas and Agaclytus' and 'Verus had other unscrupulous freedmen as well, Coedes and Eclectus and others'.[24] According to the writer of the *Historia Augusta*, Marcus Aurelius dismissed them all apart from Eclectus who later slew Commodus. Dio states that Commodus 'became a slave of his companions' meaning the imperial freedmen, who 'refrained from no form of mischief' as 'some members of the imperial household interfered and tried to corrupt the character of the young emperor'; these were the 'parasites at his table' and the men who 'measured happiness in terms of their bellies and their depraved vices'. Here we see reflected the prejudices of the senatorial class who felt nobility of birth should guarantee them both power and influence which came from access to the emperor.[25] It is these men whom the senatorial source of the *Historia Augusta* refers to in his invective against the members of the young Caesar's household:

> The more honourable of those appointed to supervise his life he could not endure, but the most evil he retained, and, if they were dismissed, he yearned for them even to the point of falling sick and when they were reinstated through his father's indulgence, he always maintained eating houses and low resorts for them in the palace. (HA. Commodus 5. 6–7)

The use of the Latin *popinas et ganeas* for low-class eating places of the common populace is used in the source to emphasize the low-born nature of these advisors and companions as opposed to the highly educated tutors selected by his father. These tutors however were well rewarded by both Marcus Aurelius and many were promoted by Commodus himself during his reign as were many of the freedmen, much to the anger of the aristocratic senatorial class.

Before his death Verus gave his freedman Agaclytus in marriage to Fundinia, the widow of Marcus Annius Libo, the consul of 128 AD, much against the wishes of Marcus Aurelius who refused to attend the wedding.[26] This is the only known example we have of a freedman being allowed to marry someone from the senatorial class and hence Marcus Aurelius' disapproval at the marriage. Fundinia however was a distant cousin of Verus and so Marcus Aurelius did not have the right to intervene.[27] It does demonstrate the power of some of these freedmen. Commodus later married the son of Fundinia and Agaclytus, the equestrian L Aurelius Agaclytus, to his sister Sabina after the execution of her first husband for conspiracy in 188 AD. Commodus was clearly maintaining the bonds established with the household of Verus. This is evident in the significant careers of a number of Verus' household that passed to Commodus.

After his manumission from the household of Verus, Apolaustus took the name L Aelius Aurelius Apolaustus Memphius Aurelius in honour of the emperor who gave him his freedom and he is commemorated in numerous honorific inscriptions from the cities of Italy demonstrating the power he retained in the imperial household.[28] Later he would be executed by Commodus in 189 AD having being closely associated with the fall of the imperial freedman Cleander. Another influential figure in Commodus' rule was his mistress Marcia. Marcia is probably identified with Marcia Aurelia Ceionia Demetriade, the possible daughter of Marcus Aurelius Sabinianus Euhodius whose name suggests that she had belonged to the household of Verus (full name Lucius Ceionius Aelius Commodus Verus Antoninus). A statue to M Aurelius Sabinianus Euhodius from Anagnina in Italy records him as a patron of that city. The inscription also records that his daughter was awarded the status of a *femina stolata* which was usually given to a free woman who had given birth to free children.[29] Marcia is not recorded as having had any. She became the mistress of the influential senator M Ummidius Quadratus, after she was transferred to the household of Marcus Aurelius' sister on the death of Verus, Annia Cornificia, the mother of Quadratus, a future conspirator. She was then acquired by Commodus on Quadratus' execution in 182 AD. Eclectus was explicitly retained by Marcus Aurelius on the dissolution of Verus' household probably because his knowledge and skills were already well recognized by the emperor who had no wish to dispense with his invaluable talents. Eclectus appears to have risen through the imperial posts to become the *cubicularius* (bedroom attendant) of Commodus upon the execution of Cleander in whose fall Eclectus probably had an influential, if not pivotal role as he did in the murder of Commodus himself. The artist Paris also seems to have been retained as he appears to have retained influence at court and significantly was a friend of Adrian of Tyre.[30]

Marcus Aurelius returned to Rome with the body of Verus and attended to the funeral rites of his dead colleague and public mourning would have been announced. The senate would have met the sad procession on the outskirts of the city dressed in the dark *toga pulla*, probably accompanied by the members of the imperial family. The funeral would have proceeded a few days later with servants wearing the portrait masks of Verus' illustrious ancestors followed by the body wearing the civic crown he had so recently been awarded. Marcus Aurelius would have given a eulogy praising the character, deeds and ancestry of his colleague accompanied by songs and music. The body would then be cremated, the ashes placed in a funeral urn and carried by either Lucilla or the emperor himself to be buried with his father in the Mausoleum of Hadrian. Verus was pronounced a god on a vote of the senate and worshipped by priests in Rome who had previously been enrolled to worship the deified Antoninus Pius, emphasizing the divine heritage of Verus, Marcus and his sons. Presumably the Temple of Antoninus Pius and Faustina would have been used whilst some of the names of the new priests are known from inscriptions. These included an *amicus* of Marcus Aurelius, Aufidius Victorinus, whom Commodus would later appoint to important posts in his regime.

It is significant that in the later years of his reign Commodus changed his name on the coins he issued, retaining his association with Lucius Aelius Aurelius Verus, but omitting reference to his father. The coins of 191 drop 'Marcus' and 'Antoninus' referring instead to himself as Lucius Aelius Aurelius Commodus. Even at 30 years of age the emperor still remembered and honoured the name of Verus. Although heavily stylized and idealized it is remarkable how closely the statutes of the Emperor Commodus resemble those of the Emperor Verus even allowing for similarities in the style of hair and the heavy beard that were popular amongst the Roman aristocracy at the time.

Verus' death presented Marcus Aurelius with the problem of finding a husband for his widowed daughter. Allowing her to remain unmarried would invite problems as the Augusta would attract the interest of uninvited suitors and the chance of a political scandal, especially if the emperor was absent in the north dealing with barbarian unrest. Without waiting for the traditional period of mourning to lapse and against the wishes of his wife Faustina and Lucilla herself, he married her to his general and *amici* Claudius Pompeianus. The unseemly haste probably had something to do with the personality of Lucilla herself. There had previously been stories circulating in Rome that Lucilla felt her proper station and status was being undermined by the closeness of the relationship between her ex-husband and his sister Fabia whom Lucilla 'could not endure' . She appears to have been a 'prickly' character who was overly concerned with the symbols of status and power. A R Birley in his life of Marcus Aurelius postulates that her father's concern was that she might be used by 'some unscrupulous and ambitious person for their own ends', and events in the reign of her brother Commodus were to suggest that it was she who was unscrupulous and her father's urgency in arranging her marriage before the traditional period of mourning was over was astute objective character evaluation. Dio, a source with no love of Commodus, refers to Lucilla as 'no more modest or chaste than her brother, Commodus, detested her husband, Pompeianus'. Lucilla was horrified to be married to a man of such low station and her attitude reflects the arrogance of her class. Claudius Pompeianus was probably in his early fifties at the time of their marriage, as he was alive twenty-four years later, and is described in the sources as 'advanced in years'. Indeed in terms of the average Roman life span, he was. Lucilla, born in 150 AD would be only 19. This however was not the issue: 'Claudius Pompeianus was the son of an *equites* (a Roman knight), a native of Antioch whose birth was not sufficiently noble since Marcus' daughter was an Augusta (empress) and the daughter of an Augusta.' He had however served with distinction in the Parthian War with Verus and was rewarded with adlection to the senate and made suffect consul in 162 AD. The attainment of the consulship ennobled a senator and his family. Pompeianus had then helped to defeat the invasions across the Danube by the Lombards in

166 AD and served the emperors in following years with such skill that he had been chosen by Marcus Aurelius to join his *consilium* as an *amicus*. To Lucilla, focused on rank, precedence and status, this was not enough. With her mother, Faustina, she must have forced a compromise from her father who, whilst not backing down on the marriage, did allow Lucilla to keep the privileges of an Augusta. She could still take her place in the imperial box in the theatre and have the ceremonial torch carried before her in public. She would also have the imperial *vexilla* (flag) carried with her in procession as well as the *fasces laureati* (the bundle of rods associated with the magisterial power of office). Lucilla, her precedence and status preserved, accepted these terms for the time being with bad grace. At this time many of the imperial properties, probably including the one in which Commodus resided, were emptied of many of their furnishings, statues and paintings. The imperial treasury was straining under the financial demands of war including the recruitment of new soldiers. Furthermore the plague had also reduced revenues with a reduction in trade and food production, a problem that would continue to blight the reign of Commodus. The *Historia Augusta* refers to a sale of the contents of the palaces taking place in the Forum of Trajan. Eutropius states it lasted two months, giving an indication of the volume of imperial possessions sold which included imperial robes, the empress' and emperor's silk gold embroidered garments, goblets, jewellery, flagons, wine. It is doubtful, as Eutropius claims, that the gold raised would pay for the rest of the war which was not to end until 180 AD otherwise he would not have had to continually debase the coinage. Assessors were also sent to three provinces in Gaul to examine their accounts which presumably were also in deficit as the plague spread across the empire.[31]

The heavy mortality of the plague from 166 AD onwards led many of the elite to leave Rome for safer climes. Amongst these was the physician Galen who had already come to the emperor's attention treating many leading senators in the capital. However in 169 AD Marcus Aurelius had summoned him to Aquileia to attend upon the health of the emperors in the cold damp climate of the north. The summons must have filled the Stoic with horror at finding himself in a catch-22 situation. He would have to travel to the war zone which was as far removed from the civilized environment of Alexandria and Rome and the warm climate of his native Pergamum as it could be, or refuse the direct command of the emperor. Luckily Galen, a devotee of Asclepius, received an answer from his god. In a letter he informed the emperor that Asclepius had appeared before him in a dream who told him that in no circumstances should he travel north. The emperor believed his fellow Stoic and ordered Galen to return to Rome and be Commodus' personal doctor. A task he fulfilled from 170 AD onwards. He would remain the court physician for Marcus Aurelius, Commodus and later the Emperor Septimius Severus writing most of his treatise whilst in Rome.[32] After the departure of Marcus

Aurelius to the Danube in response to a massive invasion by the Marcomanni and their allies, Galen saved the life of Commodus who was close to death by providing a miracle cure. After leaving the wrestling school (*palaestra*) Commodus was 'seized by a hot fever'. Galen took his pulse and diagnosed inflammation, whilst Commodus' tutor Pitholaus expressed surprise that inflammation of the tonsils could alter the boy's pulse. Galen decided that the gargling concoction which had been prescribed by other physicians was too strong and prescribed a gargle of honey and rose water. By the third day of his illness Commodus' fever had almost passed when the noblewoman Annia Fundiana Faustina, called in to check on his health; she was surprised to find him much improved and praised Galen. Galen also mentions that Cn Claudius Severus, an *amicus* of Marcus Aurelius, was also left in charge of Rome during the emperors' absence as well.[33] The account is interesting for it shows, firstly, the access that even distant members of the imperial family had to the corridors of power, Annia Fundiana Faustina being a cousin of Marcus Aurelius and the daughter of the consular senator M Annius Libo and married to the future consul of 176, T Vitrasius Pollio.[34] Secondly it shows the interest the young Commodus took in the physical pursuits, in this case wrestling, an activity espoused by the dead Verus.

Medical attention was however the undoing of Commodus' brother, M Annius Verus, who died in an operation at the imperial villa near Praeneste (Palestrina) to remove a cyst behind his ear in 170 AD just before the departure of his father for the war on the Danube. Marcus Aurelius allowed himself five days of mourning but still conducted business, probably related to the upcoming campaigns. Not wishing to interrupt the games of Jupiter Optimus Maximus that were then taking place in Rome he ordered statues to be decreed by the senate for his dead son, one of which was to be carried in procession in the Circus Maximus. It was also decreed that the dead Caesar's name should be inserted into the song of the Salii, the leaping priests of Mars whose ritualistic dancing opened military campaigns.[35] Marcus Aurelius then headed north. It is difficult to know what the 9-year-old Commodus made of these events and the stoical reaction of his father, however the birth of his sister Sabina would have changed the mood in the imperial household that remained in the capital.

For the next two years the emperor would remain away campaigning. On many an occasion Roman forces came close to calamity. The whole northern frontier of the empire was threatened on the Upper Rhine, Pannonia, the Lower Danube and Dacia. The Roman offensive against Marcommani was met with disaster resulting in the death of Marcus Aurelius' Praetorian Prefect, Marcus Vindex.[36] The *ab epistulis Latinis* (the official responsible for imperial correspondence with the Latin speakers of the empire), Tarrutenius Paternus, was sent on a mission with a force of soldiers to the Cotini on the pretext of forming an alliance but fell into a prearranged trap with his army and suffered grievously.[37] In Dacia, Claudius Fronto was killed fighting the Iazyges but blame was attached to his procurator, Pertinax, who was dismissed from his post.[38] The *Historia Augusta* states that 'through the machinations of certain persons he (Pertinax) came to be distrusted by Marcus and removed from this post'.[39] It is hard to see why Pertinax would have come to the attention of the emperor or made powerful enemies as his career up until this point had not been unusual or particularly distinguished. He was the son of a freedman and had at first pursued a career as a teacher of Greek grammar. Later, looking for greater challenges, he decided upon a military career and received his first military appointment as a chief centurion through the recommendation of his father's patron Lollianus Avitus, a former consul of 144 AD. From this post he was appointed prefect of a cohort in Syria where he fought in Verus' war against Parthia and winning promotion, he was sent to Britain as tribune of a legion. Then transferred to Moesia he became a *praefectus alae* (commander or tribune of a unit of cavalry). His next appointment was to the *alimentia* in Northern Italy distributing grants of grain and money to the poor. It was not unusual for promotions on the *cursus honorum*, the ladder of magistracies and offices, to vary between military and civic responsibilities. This was not an issue in times of peace but in times of nearly unceasing warfare it diverted experienced and able military officers away from the posts where they were badly needed. From the *alimentia* he achieved his first major appointment to commander of the fleet on the Rhine and then to his post in Dacia.[40] This career record was the steady path worn by many aspiring equestrians before him, promotions managed by powerful patrons working on behalf of their client in return for future favours to be drawn as and when required. The patrician Lollianus Avitus was the most powerful landowner and senator in the area of Liguria where Pertinax's family had settled but the future Emperor Pertinax appears to have rejected his father's patron for Claudius Pompeianus:

> Pertinax had received just enough education to enable him to gain a livelihood. This had brought him into association with Claudius Pompeianus through whose influence he had become a tribune of the cavalry, and had reached such a height that he now was actually the emperor of his former patron. (Dio 74.3.1–2)

Clearly Pertinax had been a tutor in Pompeianus' household and having been granted his first post as a centurion through the patronage of Lollianus Avitus and subsequent promotions including the post in Britain he developed bonds of patronage to Pompeianus. He also made some powerful enemies. After Pertinax had ascended the throne on the assassination of Commodus, Lollianus Avitus' son, Lollianus Gentianus, tried to humiliate the new emperor in the senate as he was angered and embittered that a man of low birth was now emperor whilst he himself was of noble birth, and now answerable to a former client of his father's.[41] Behind Pertinax's fall from grace we can perhaps see the poisonous working of court politics. Lucilla now saw an opportunity for revenge not just against Pertinax who was to blame for the death of her husband's *amicus* Fronto, but also a chance to undermine her husband who was now the patron of Pertinax. The Lolliani and Lucilla now used their influence to engineer the dismissal of Pertinax.[42]

Pertinax's career was now saved by his patron Pompeianus who had been given the job of clearing barbarians from Rhaetia and Noricum and preventing an invasion of Italy. Pompeianus chose his client Pertinax as one of his subordinates and the two worked closely together, both sharing the accolades of success with coins celebrating a 'German victory'. Marcus Aurelius was now willing to listen to Pompeianus' defence of his client with both generals distinguishing themselves. Pertinax was enrolled in the senate but his responsibilities on the front meant it would be years before he had the opportunity to enter the senate house itself. Clearly a close bond developed between the two generals and Pompeianus continued to promote Pertinax within the emperor's *consilium* until the emperor was won over. The emperor recognized that Pertinax had been the victim of an unjust plot and in recompense adlected Pertinax to the rank of Praetor without actually holding the post and he gave him the command of the First Adiutrix Legion stationed in Upper Pannonia. His continued military prowess was rewarded with a suffect consulship in 175 AD and entry into the emperor's *consilium*.

Whilst the Costoboci ravaged the Balkans and Northern Greece until defeated by *vexillationes* under Vehilius Gratus, the Chauci crossed the Rhine only to be thrown back by Didius Julianus commanding the legio XXII Primigenia in Upper Germany. Julianus was then promoted to the governorship of Gallia Belgica, a post he retained for five years. This was unusual as there was a significant danger that a governor in charge of a large numbers of troops might use his influence to undermine loyalty to the emperor in preparation for a bid for the throne himself. However desperate times required proven commanders in the places of greatest need. Julianus defeated a serious sea born attack upon his province and the emperor made him a suffect consulship at the same time as Pertinax.

By 171 AD Marcus Aurelius had moved his headquarters to Carnuntum on the Danube. The physical proximity of the emperor to the war zone and the promotion of talented and experienced commanders irrespective of birth gradually turned the tide of war in favour of the Romans. Some of the barbarian tribes sent envoys to Marcus Aurelius to sue for peace. However the turning point came towards the end of the campaigning season when a barbarian horde, laden with booty from the plundered provinces, was caught as they were attempting to cross the

Danube. This victory was commemorated in the coins of the following year showing Marcus Aurelius crossing a bridge with his soldiers. The emperor took the name 'Germanicus' which he shared with Commodus. The reduction of the barbarian threat in the alpine areas around Northern Italy had allowed the emperor to summon his family to the imperial headquarters at Carnuntum. A dedication discovered at Lilybaeum in Sicily offers a prayer for the safe return of the emperor and his children.[43] On it Marcus Aurelius is not given the title 'Germanicus' suggesting a date late in 171 or early 172 AD. A dedication from the precinct outside of Carnuntum supports the case that Commodus was present with his father to receive the title 'Germanicus' and the acclamation of the assembled legions.[44] An inscription from Marsala with reference to the *liberi* (children) of Marcus Aurelius and dedicated *pro salute et reditu* shows the emperor presenting his son to the soldiers.[45] Herodian states that Commodus' father would bring him with him when he was just a small boy and entrust him to the care of the army. Marcus Aurelius was thinking of the succession, winning the loyalty of the army to his son, associating him with their victory and calling him a fellow soldier. Commodus would have stood at the side of the emperor on a raised platform built on the parade ground outside the legionary camp surrounded by the emperor's *consilium* and *amici*. Marcus Aurelius would have addressed the assembled soldiers and then received their shouted acclamations. Marcus Aurelius was also making a point to the powerful senators and advisors who stood behind him: the young 9-year-old boy standing at his side was his intended successor and the army recognized this. Commodus received this, his first acclamation, on the Ides of Hercules which can be dated to 15 October 172 AD.[46] The symbolism and identification of Hercules with himself was to resonate throughout his reign and perhaps started at this point in his life.

Commodus may have remained in Carnuntum to observe the peace envoys from the Marcomanni who agreed to provide hostages, as well as agreeing to the surrender of all Roman prisoners and deserters, a restriction to their right of assembly, a ban on all trade with the empire and a ten mile exclusion zone along the north bank of the Danube. These terms were very similar to those Commodus himself imposed to permanently end the northern war, terms that he has been heavily criticized for. The focus of the war now turned towards the Quadi, Sarmatians and Jazyges on the Hungarian Plain and so the imperial headquarters were moved to Sirmium.

A remarkable event, preserved in Philostratus' work, *The Life of the Sophists*, took place at Sirmium in 173 AD which yet again demonstrates the political manoeuvring and machinations of imperial court life.[47] The participants were all powerful individuals who had the ear of the emperor. The victim was Herodes Atticus, Marcus Aurelius' old tutor and a rich Greek senator, orator and sophist who held considerable land in both Greece and around Rome. He had however managed to insult Sextus Quintilius Condianus (son of Sex Quintilius Condianus, the consul of 151 AD) and Sextus Quintilius Maximus, the consul of 172 AD (son of Sex Quintilius Maximus consul of 151). Their fathers were both the *amici* of the previous emperor Antoninus Pius as well as Marcus Aurelius and continued to hold important military commands on the Danube. So influential was this family that Marcus Aurelius used to call them 'my Quintilli' and when Sextus Quintilius Condianus the younger became ill he let the imperial physician Galen treat him. Whilst carrying out his duties as pro-consular governor in Greece, Sextus Quintilius Maximus, supported by his cousin, was insulted by Herodes Atticus who had the temerity to argue with them over the outcome of a musical competition at the Pythian Festival. Atticus then made the mistake of making a joke at their expense, referring to them as Trojans as their family originated from Alexandria Troas near Troy. The Quintilli took immense offence, with their *dignitas* insulted, they used Herodes Atticus' dispute with powerful figures in Athens to destroy him. A case was made by the leading Athenians: Demostratus, Praxagoras, Mamertinus and many others, no doubt at the behest of the Quintilli, who accused Herodes Atticus and his freedmen of behaving as tyrants towards the citizens of Athens. Herodes Atticus made a counter petition against his accusers which was presented before the proconsul but the defendants managed to escape and headed north for an audience with the emperor, rapidly followed by Herodes Atticus. However Atticus' fate had already been sealed. Faustina, the emperor's wife, supporting the Quintilli, entreated her husband to find in favour of Demostratus and his fellow plaintiffs. It was also alleged that Herodes Atticus was involved in a conspiracy with Verus, when he was alive, to overthrow Marcus Aurelius. To cement Marcus' favourable view towards them Faustina regularly got her 3-year-old daughter, Sabina, to fall at the feet of her father imploring him to save the Athenians and thereby demonstrating admirable awareness of current affairs for a 3-year-old. When the two parties arrived in the city, both lodged near the imperial headquarters whilst waiting for the summons to appear before the emperor. Marcus Aurelius however regularly enquired that the Athenians had all they needed in the mean time, whilst Atticus received no such benevolent enquiries. Tragedy now struck Atticus. He had taken lodgings in a tall tower which was struck by lightning killing two servants, mere children whom he looked upon as his own daughters. Shortly after this the summons arrived for him to appear before the emperor. The distraught Atticus had to make his case first before the emperor, his *amici* and the Praetorian Prefect, Marcus Bassaeus Rufus. A water clock was started marking the time allotted for his presentation of his case. Losing all self-control Atticus unleashed invectives upon the emperor, crying out, 'you sacrifice me to the whim of a woman and a three-year-old child.' Bassaeus Rufus, fearing a violent attack upon the person of the emperor, drew his sword. Atticus cried out that he invited death and with that left the court. It would have been interesting to see the look of satisfaction on the face of the Quintilli. The Athenian Demostratus and his colleagues now presented their case 'with honey eloquence', wishing they had died in the plague rather than suffer under the tyranny of Herodes Atticus. Unsurprisingly the emperor found against Atticus but now found himself in a difficult situation as he was bound by bonds of *amicitia* to his friend and old tutor yet he was also obliged to give justice. His solution was to pass a lenient sentence on Atticus, sending him into temporary exile at Oricum in Epirus but severely punishing his unfortunate freedmen. Imperial clemency was extended to the freedman Alcimedon, whose daughters had been killed by the lightning bolt and so had been punished enough. A solution worthy apparently of a philosopher. If Sabina had been present at court it is likely the 12-year-old Commodus would also have been present. The politics of the imperial court would have provided him with an education in survival, more important and relevant than the lessons of his learned tutors. Commodus was probably present at Sirmium as his young sister was evidently present to be used as an unwitting vehicle for her mother's machinations. In January 175 AD Commodus was enrolled into all of the colleges of priests which was a formal step towards entering public life. The event was commemorated on a series of coins issued at this time.[48] At some point though he returned to the warmer climate of Italy where, according to the *Historia Augusta*, the young Commodus whilst staying at the imperial villa at Centumcellae, ordered the bath keeper to be thrown into the furnace for preparing a bath for him that was too cold. The slave ordered to carry this out however threw a sheep skin into the furnace instead in order to make Commodus believe he had done so by the terrible stench that the burning skin produced.[49] The biographer of the *Historia Augusta* cites this as an example of the latent cruelty of the youth that was to become evident during his rule. It is however surprising that neither Herodian nor Dio, both hostile to Commodus, refer to this in their accounts. In fact Dio explicitly states that for all his faults Commodus 'was not naturally wicked' and only in later life was he led into 'lustful and cruel habits'.[50] The biographer, imitating the style and approach of his more famous predecessor Suetonius, panders to the desire of his readers for salacious details of each emperor's life, so presenting rumour and gossip as fact. The villa at Centumcellae is located 80km north-west of Rome on the coast of Etruria. Commodus seems to have enjoyed coastal locations as they may have reminded him of his childhood stays at Lanuvium, which remained one of his preferential locations when not residing in Rome itself.[51]

Commodus and his household remained in Italy for a considerable period of time until in May 175 AD the young Caesar received an urgent summons from his mother and father on the Danube. The commander of the eastern armies, Avidius Cassius, had raised a massive revolt and the horrors of civil war were about to descend upon the empire endangering all that Marcus Aurelius had fought for but also endangering the life of Commodus himself. Rome had erupted in panic and the emperor was forced to send Vettius Sabinianus, governor of Lower Pannonia, to Rome with a special force to 'protect the city' and Commodus himself. Avidius Cassius had developed close links with many senators in Rome and Vettius Sabinianus' role would have been to ensure the revolt did not spread to the empire's capital. A great deal of preparation would have been needed to ensure the success of this revolt over a significant period of time and Avidius Cassius would have been waiting for the right opportunity to strike. Cassius could trace his descent from his father, who had been Prefect of Egypt, to the Seleucid King of Syria, Antiochus IV Epiphanes, and through his mother to the ancient Roman aristocratic family of the Cassii. His father, C Avidius Heliodorus, was the *ab epistulis* of the Emperor Hadrian who gained promotion to the prefecture of Egypt from 137 to 142 AD. It was there that Cassius was probably born,[52] as in a papyrus discovered at Oxyrhyncus he refers to Alexandria as his 'fatherland' but grew up on the family estates in Syria around Cyrrhus.[53] After serving on the Danube Avidius Cassius quickly rose to prominence during the Parthian War capturing the Parthian capital Ctesiphon. His reward was to be chosen as suffect consul by Marcus Aurelius in 166 AD and then he was given the strategic province of Syria to govern. A revolt by herdsmen (Bucoli) in the Nile Delta in 172 AD was crushed by Avidius Cassius after being granted special permission by the emperor to enter the province as senators were banned from Egypt due to its important position as the grain basket of Rome. This was probably too good an opportunity to miss and Cassius now started to strengthen his bonds with key officials in the province. The Prefect of Egypt, Calvisius Statianus, was probably suborned at this time and rapidly joined the revolt in 175 AD which increased the pressure on Marcus Aurelius as Rome faced shortages of grain. It was probably this news that led to unrest in the city requiring the presence of Vettius Sabinianus. Although it was May of 175 AD that Marcus Aurelius was informed of the revolt through a letter from the loyal governor of Cappadocia, Martius Verus, it is evident from the Oxyrhyncus papyrus that Statianus recognized Avidius Cassius as emperor as early as April or March. The seven legions in Syria, Arabia and Palestine promptly declared for Cassius as did the major cities in these areas including Antioch which he made his headquarters. His royal origins and close marriage connections with a powerful group of Lycian nobles through his son-in-law Claudius Dryantianus, as well as his military renown from the Parthian War and the bonds of obligation he had developed over the previous years, can account for the level of support he commanded in these provinces. He had also developed close ties to leading figures in Rome itself as after the death of the usurper, Marcus Aurelius did not imprison or execute the senators linked to the revolt but asked the senate as a whole to try them. The emperor also ordered the court records from the trial of Calvisius Statianus to be destroyed as they clearly implicated important senators at Rome whom Marcus Aurelius would either have to execute, an act he refused to do, or exile them, so alienating their families, *amici* and clients.[54] Dio also hints at another cause of discontent amongst the nobility and the army on the Danube which would have contained many soldiers from the eastern provinces of the empire; that of the continuation of the drawn out Northern War. In a speech which Dio makes Marcus Aurelius deliver to the assembled soldiers on the Danube, the emperor exclaims:

> Now if the danger were mine alone, I should have regarded the matter as of no moment … but since there has been a public secession, or rather rebellion, and the war touches all alike, I could have wished, had it been possible, to invite Cassius here and argue before you or the senate the matter at issue between us; and I would have gladly yielded the supreme power to him without a struggle, if this had seemed to be for the good of the State. (Dio 72.24.3)

The issue that Dio refers to was not over who should be emperor but some other matter of which Dio gives no further clues. However many of the assembled soldiers, many from the eastern provinces now in revolt, would have been fighting this war since 166 AD and longed to see their families again. Nor had these soldiers received the usual distribution of financial bonuses usually granted on significant victories. Historians have wondered how Cassius could have so miscalculated in thinking the eastern legions at his disposal could defeat the battled-hardened armies on the Danube under the emperor's command. Yet many of these soldiers had come from the east and Cassius had probably received reports that their morale was low. Cassius, announcing that he would end the 'Northern War' calculated that in battle many of these soldiers would either mutiny or refuse to fight their old comrades. News of the revolt, which the emperor had attempted to keep from the soldiers, had become public knowledge and caused unrest amongst the soldiers fighting on the Danube. It would perhaps not be surprising to find some of the assembled equestrian and senatorial commanders also weary of the war that was financially crippling, which offered no real opportunities of individual financial reward in the forests and swamps north of the Danube. Added to this was the continued death toll caused by the plague. Would Avidius Cassius not try to further sow the seeds of discontent by offering to end the war should he attain the imperial purple? This was not a revolt that broke out on the spur of the moment but something planned, prepared for and propagated over many years.

The one major and disconcerting surprise in this revolt was the role of Faustina, the emperor's wife, whom he clearly dearly loved, and Commodus' mother. Two of our main sources are both clear that she was deeply involved in prompting Avidius Cassius to aspire to the throne. Such an outcome would inevitably have led to the murder of her own son Commodus! Avidius Cassius had two sons of his own, Avidius Heliodorus and Avidius Maecianus, the former would be exiled to an island after the failure of the revolt and the latter executed. Avidius Cassius would not allow Commodus to live, as to do so would endanger the lives of his own children and the end of his line. Faustina, it would appear, was hedging her bets as she was concerned over the health of her husband and so had been in communication with Avidius Cassius offering some form of alliance or marriage on the death of her husband, in order to consolidate her own position of power, probably fearing her loss of status in the imperial court.[55] Marcus Aurelius had clearly been unwell as Dio records. The emperor's own *Mediations* are full of references to the nearness of death.[56] Faustina was present to witness the deterioration in her husband's health as she had just been awarded the title 'Mother of the Camp'.[57] Dio suggests it was Faustina who duped Avidius Cassius, encouraging him in his aspirations for the purple as she felt Commodus was too young to be emperor. Commodus, aged 13, had not yet been awarded the toga of manhood which formally recognized the transition from childhood to adulthood. The *Historia Augusta* states that Faustina was in despair at this time worrying incessantly over her husband's health.[58] However there are suggestions that in fact it was Avidius Cassius who duped Faustina. Avidius Cassius had long been planning the revolt and seized upon Faustina's concerns over the health of the emperor to draw her unwittingly into the plot. There is little evidence that she was planning to murder the emperor but was perhaps planning ahead should he die, yet her naivety was exploited by Cassius. Cassius himself, probably notified of the emperor's poor health in Faustina's secret correspondence with him, instigated the rumour that Marcus Aurelius had died, announcing to the eastern legions that Marcus Aurelius had already been deified by the Senate.[59] With this, as on cue, the seven legions in the eastern provinces, including Egypt, acclaimed him emperor. On hearing the news Herodes Atticus sent a letter to Cassius later celebrated for its brief and succinct summarizing of the usurper's actions: 'You are mad.'[60] However the situation soon began to unravel for Cassius. The governor of Cappadocia and commander of two legions, Martius Verus, remained loyal and sent Marcus Aurelius the news of the revolt which reached him in May at Sirmium on the Danube.

Marcus Aurelius heard the message from Verus with dismay, having at first attempted to keep news of the rising from the assembled armies on the Danube, many of whom had fought with Cassius in the war against Parthia. Moreover, rumours were circulated causing unrest amongst the soldiers. The letters of Fronto describe the morale of both the soldiers and the officers and generals as 'thoroughly bad'. The emperor was able to restore their loyalty after addressing the assembled legions but he was greatly concerned over the loyalty of Rome and senators with ties of friendship or obligation to Avidius Cassius.[61] The governor of Lower Pannonia, Vettius Sabinianus, was sent with a force of loyal soldiers to Rome to protect the city.[62] The senate declared Avidius Cassius a public enemy and confiscated all his lands. In order to remind the populace of the city of their loyalty to the imperial family Commodus, still wearing the *toga praetexta* of childhood, distributed largesse to the people in the Basilica of Trajan.[63] In effect this reminded the people of Rome of their status as clients to their patron Marcus Aurelius and his family. This was commemorated on coins showing Commodus seated holding out his right hand with the personified figure of Liberalitas standing before him holding an abacus and cornucopia whilst a member of the populace holds up a fold in his toga to catch the falling coins.[64] The cornucopia was a traditional symbol of wealth and plenty. Behind Commodus stands a figure who could be the Prefect of the City, T Vitrasius Pollio, or Vettius Sabinianus. The coins proclaim the loyalty of the armies, something usually done when their loyalty was problematic. Other coins show Commodus on the obverse whilst on many of the reverse sides Commodus is associated in various guises with military victory. Marcus Aurelius wished to promote his own victories and link these in the minds of the army and populace with his son. The range of denominations, including the gold *aureus*, and lesser value silver *denarius* and *sestertius* ensured this propaganda message reached the largest possible audience. The Basilica of Trajan was built to provide a prestigious covered space for law courts, commerce and to add weight to the dignity and presence of the emperor. The hall itself measured 117m x 55m with semicircular apses at either end. It was the traditional venue for the distribution of imperial largesse. As the citizens approached Commodus they would have to pass through a central nave surrounded at ground level by colonnades of grey Egyptian marble with an upper colonnade of green Carystian marble. Clerestory windows, 25m above them, sent down shafts of light that was reflected from gilded bronze tiles.[65] Gilded statues lined the external colonnades of the basilica and forum representing horses and spoils of war. A more lavish, prestigious and spectacular building could not be imagined and provided the setting for Commodus' entry into public life. One issue of coins distributed at this time shows Commodus seated on a raised dais holding a coin counter. The young Caesar is also associated with Jupiter Conservator, the protector of the empire. A propaganda message resonant in coinage throughout the reign of Commodus.[66]

Marcus Aurelius immediately summoned his son to join him on the Danube, primarily to secure the safety of the young Caesar but secondly to assure the loyalty of the army. He left Rome on 19 May and the journey north probably took him two or three weeks. The emperor had decided to carry the ceremony of the *tirocinium fori* admitting Commodus to the ranks of Roman citizens and also making him *princeps iuventutis*, leader of the knights, before the assembled troops rather than in the traditional location at Rome. The emperor commended his son to the armies. These ceremonies had been delayed until 7 July to coincide with the Nones of July, the day Romulus, the founder of Rome, had ascended into heaven. Marcus Aurelius was asking for the protection of the armies for his son but also announcing that Commodus was his heir and successor. The day would also resound for Commodus himself who assumed manhood under the protection of Rome's founder and he who would later style himself the re-founder of Rome, supplanting Romulus himself. A multitude of coins were issued celebrating this event proclaiming Commodus' designation as the heir of Marcus Aurelius and coins of their joint reign would carry images of both Castor and Romulus; Castor being seen as a role model for princes whilst Romulus publicized Commodus as heir designate.

Whilst preparing his armies for the war against Cassius, Marcus Aurelius received the news from Martius Verus, the loyal governor of Cappadocia that Avidius Cassius was dead. A centurion by the name of Antonius had found Cassius on foot and charged him on his horse striking him in the neck. The wounded Cassius attempted to escape but a decurion finished him off. Cutting off his head, both assassins proceeded to the emperor with their booty, no doubt expecting to receive an immense reward from the emperor. There is no suggestion in any of the sources that Marcus Aurelius had ordered the murder. Yet there can be no doubt he was relieved at the bloodless termination of the civil war, but he was said to be greatly upset by the death of Cassius. Orders were given for the severed head to be buried.[67] We are not told of the reward given to the assassins; however the emperor made a clear distinction based on rank in his punishment of the supporters of the usurper. Senatorial supporters of Cassius were referred by Marcus Aurelius to be tried before their peers in the senate with the emperor instructing that any found guilty should escape the death penalty as he had promised never to put a senator to death in his reign.[68] However punishment for those of non-senatorial status was swift and final. C Calvisius Statianus, a key figure in the revolt, was exiled as he was senator. The equestrian governor of Egypt was executed, as was Avidius Cassius' son Maecianus. However Cassius' youngest son Heliodorus was exiled whilst his daughter Alexandria and son-in-law Druncianus were given freedom of movement and entrusted to the protection of their uncle by marriage, perhaps identified with the Lycian senator Claudius Titianus. He also encouraged the prosecution of 'certain people' who had insulted Cassius' surviving relatives thereby placing them within the protection of the emperor's friendship.[69] Marcus Aurelius also exiled other children of Cassius' but did return estates in Italy to the family.[70] He pardoned many of the cities in the east apart from Antioch, Cassius' headquarters, which had been particularly vocal in its support of the usurper. The emperor removed the city's privileges, abolishing their right to hold games or hold public assemblies or meetings.[71] A law was passed prohibiting a governor governing a province where they had been born as clearly Cassius had drawn immense strength from his clients within Syria and utilized family bonds and friendships. The two legions in the east that had remained loyal to Marcus Aurelius the Legio XV Apollinaris and XII Fulminata, were rewarded with the titles 'Loyal and True' and 'Sure and Steadfast'.[72] The clear implication was that the other eastern legions had been quite the opposite. However with many soldiers from the eastern armies still serving on the Danube the emperor's hands were tied, yet he did execute many centurions in Cassius' armies rather than disgrace whole legions. When Martius Verus entered Syria from Cappadocia to take control of the disloyal province, Cassius' *ab epistulis graecis*, Prudens, was captured along with the traitorous correspondence with senators and officials across the empire. The emperor ordered its contents burned.[73] Such evidence of widespread conspiracy was a political minefield. Not only would such material implicate and embarrass Faustina and so himself, he would also be forced to remove powerful figures in Rome and across the empire alienating their families and also their own clients and friends. This was a step he was unwilling to take, unlike his son.

The gods clearly smiled upon Marcus Aurelius for the death of Avidius Cassius was not the only good news he received on the Danube. His generals had won victories over a range of barbarian tribes as well.[74] It was at this time he was awarded the title 'Sarmaticus' (Conqueror of the Sarmatians). Over 100,000 captives were returned to the Romans indicating the extensive nature of the damage caused to the empire by the war and 8,000 Sarmatian cavalry were provided by the defeated tribe of whom 5,500 were stationed in Britain, a sign of unrest in the province.[75]

The emperor decided to use the opportunity that peace provided to extinguish any smouldering embers of insurrection in the east as well as reaffirm the loyalty of the provincials to himself and his son and successor. The motives behind the imperial tour are evident in a series of coins issued which clearly name Commodus as heir, the message now being directed towards those provinces that had sided with Cassius.[76] This would be an educational experience for his son as well as introducing the eastern subjects of the empire to their future emperor, building bonds of loyalty after the recent insurrection. The members of the imperial party were carefully selected to enable the emperor to draw upon a variety of expertise and knowledge of the eastern provinces. Pertinax and Claudius Severus were certainly with him, men whom Marcus Aurelius clearly valued, the emperor's opinion of Pertinax being restored by his campaigning with Claudius Pompeianus in preventing Italy being invaded.[77] Claudius Severus, married to Annia Aurelia Galeria Faustina, the sister of Commodus, came from a noble family which had strong connections with Marcus Aurelius. He held his second consulship in 173 AD with Claudius Pompeianus as his colleague. Claudius Severus possessed connections and influence in both Ancyra and Paphlagonia, areas which the imperial party planned to pass through. Pertinax's patron, Claudius Pompeianus, also accompanied the imperial party. Married to Commodus' sister Lucilla, he was a vastly experienced military commander but more importantly a patron of Antioch, the city of his birth. He would be able to offer the emperor advice on the internal politics of the city which had been at the heart of Avidius Cassuis' revolt. The presence of Faustina and Lucilla would have added a certain edge to collective decision-making of the group who would act as the emperor's advisors, the *concilium principis*. The Quintillii brothers (joint consuls of 151 AD) were not only members of this *concilium principis* but were also natives of Troad and so familiar with Asia Minor, whilst their sons (Maximus, the son of Condianus and Condianus, the son of Maximus) were left in command of the two Pannonian provinces on the Danube. The eminent senatorial legal expert Arrius Antoninus was ordered to take over the province of Cappadocia from its loyal Governor Martius Verus, now engaged in Syria eliminating the last embers of revolt.[78] Antoninus probably accompanied the emperor until he reached his designated province. Basseus Rufus as Praetorian Prefect and advisor will also have been present and large numbers of the guard as well. Commodus would inherit these men as his *concilium principis* on his father's death and so the emperor would have been hoping emotional bonds of loyalty and mutual respect would develop between them and his son. The experienced general M Valerius Maximianus was sent on ahead with a squadron of Marcomanni, Quadi and Naristae who had recently signed peace terms with Rome. The purpose of this force, in the words of an inscription discovered at Diana Veteranorum, was 'to punish the Oriental rising'. Clearly Cassius' revolt had been widespread and still considered a potential threat to the emperor despite the death of its leader, his son and the capture of the remainder of his family.[79] Avidius Cassius also appeared to have many senatorial supporters in Rome itself as Marcus Aurelius was forced to write to the senate whose members had seized the opportunity of the failed revolt to accuse rivals of complicity in the revolt and were clearly wanting a death sentence passed on the accused, so eliminating rivals to their own power and influence. The emperor instructed the senate that sentences were to avoid the death penalty:

But also on behalf of those in Rome (for even there many of the senators had been convicted of openly favouring the cause of Cassius) he sent a message to the senate asking them not to pass any harsh decree, his exact words being as follows, 'I implore you the senate to keep my reign unstained by the blood of any senator.' (Epitome of Dio: cf Joan Antioch: LXX. 30.1 as noted in Loeb translation p51).

Marcus Aurelius also ordered the records of the case against Calvisius Statianus, the rebel Governor of Egypt, to be burnt.[80] Later in 182 AD when Commodus was sole emperor Manilius, Cassius' *ab epistulis Latinis* (responsible for correspondence to Latin speakers) and *amicus* was captured along with letters to important personages written in Latin. No doubt in return for his life Manilius offered to inform on Cassius co-conspirators but like his father, Commodus ordered these letters to be burnt and refused to grant Manilius an audience.[81] These actions reflect the problem of how to deal with Faustina's complicity in the uprising. Publication of the letters would be a major embarrassment to both husband and son alike and could add fuel to the malicious rumours spread around Rome concerning Commodus' fitness to rule and allegations of questionable parenthood. These rumours would have been spread by supporters of Cassius wishing to question the validity of Marcus Aurelius' plans for the succession.[82]

Accompanying the emperor would be a vast army of imperial freedmen and slaves to provide not only for the needs of the imperial family, but also many administrative officials, powerful figures in their own right. These would include the *ab epistulis Graecis* and the *ab epistulis Latinis* in charge of the emperor's Greek and Latin correspondence, the *a rationibus* responsible for the finances, the *a libellis* in charge of private petitions from individuals, the *ratio privatae* responsible for the private estates of the emperor and the *ratio patrimonium Caesaris* with responsibility for the imperial estates, the *a cognitionibus* in charge of the legal proceedings of the imperial court of law and legal advisor. Each of these administrators would have required lesser officials to report to them as departmental heads. Aurelius Papirius Dionysius is the earliest example of a lawyer who was *a libellis* and then *a cognitionibus* under Marcus Aurelius. He was promoted to the highest equestrian prefectures of the *annona* in charge of the grain supply for Rome and Egypt.[83] Papirius Dionysius may have accompanied Marcus Aurelius in the tour of the east and would continue to hold high office in the reign of Commodus. Another imperial official, Tiberius Claudius Vibianus Tertullus is known from inscriptions in Ephesus and Pergamum to have been *ab epistulis Graecis* in about 173–5 AD and *a rationibus* sometime in 177–80 AD before becoming *praefectus vigilum* (Prefect of the Vigiles in Rome).[84] Commodus' tutor probably accompanied the imperial party, T Aius Sanctus, who was *ab epistulis Graecis* a little earlier and then procurator of the *ratio privata* and then after being made *a rationibus* he was given the prestigious post of the Prefecture of Egypt probably in 179/80 AD and under Commodus adlected to Senate.[85] These powerful individuals would have used the opportunity of the presence of the future emperor to ingratiate themselves, becoming his *amici* and thereby hoped to preserve their positions or improve upon them.

As the imperial party crossed Asia Minor and approached the Taurus Mountains tragedy struck; Faustina died. The sources agree that her death was sudden. The

Historia Augusta is clear that she succumbed to an illness, however Dio, unsure of the causes initially suggests gout but then maliciously suggests suicide as she feared she would be convicted for her 'compact' with Cassius.[86] Faustina had clearly survived the fall of Cassius; otherwise she would have been condemned long before she was allowed to enter the rebellious provinces in the east. Furthermore all the sources agree that the emperor was left devastated and grief-stricken by her death and so it seems very unlikely her husband would have prosecuted her for involvement in the conspiracy. In his *Meditations* Marcus Aurelius' dedication to her is moving:

Such a fine woman, so obedient, so loving, so simple. (*Meditations* 1.17.18)

However her actions and political manoeuvrings suggest otherwise. It has been suggested that she died in childbirth based on a passage in the *Meditations*, and the fact that she had already given birth to at least 14 children and was 45-years-old would indicate that there would have been a great risk of complications.[87] However no other source suggests this as a reason for her death. What the sources don't record is the affect of her death on her children, including Commodus, and we are only left to imagine how the loss of a mother at the age of fourteen would impact upon the young man.

The senate decreed her divine honours, ordering a temple to be erected to her with a new order of Faustian girls created to honour her. Silver images of Faustina and the emperor were erected in the Temple of Venus and Roma and an altar set up where all brides married in Rome were to sacrifice. Furthermore a golden statue of Faustina was also to be carried in a chair into the theatre at the start of performances and placed in the imperial box where she sat when the emperor was present. The village of Halala where she died was renamed Faustinopolis and created a colony with a temple dedicated to her.[88] A series of dedicatory coins were issued at this time in which Faustina was given the title *sideribus receta* meaning 'received among the stars'. The coins show her veiled holding a sceptre being carried aloft on Juno's peacock towards the heavens.[89] Despite his Stoical beliefs Marcus Aurelius was clearly carried along on a wave of grief, the eulogy he delivered to his children, close advisors and assembled troops must have been both moving and poignant.

Gratefully leaving Halala the emperor progressed through the Cilician Gates to winter in the city of Tarsus. There Marcus Aurelius received a letter from Herodes Atticus complaining that the emperor no longer wrote to him after their altercation in court at Sirmium. The emperor replied, describing the loss of Faustina and his own poor health, but indicating that when he visited Athens he would like Atticus to initiate him into the Eleusinian Mysteries.[90] This would bestow a great honour upon Atticus and also signify his return to the imperial favour. Whilst in

Tarsus Marcus Aurelius visited the young sophist Hermogenes to listen to him speak. Suitably impressed he rewarded him with 'splendid presents'.[91] Although Commodus' presence in this instance is not recorded, it is likely his father would not have allowed this opportunity to have passed without his son listening to the oratorical skills of someone of similar age, Hermogenes being only 15 at the time.

The business of empire however continued. It was probably at this time that Marcus Aurelius, after consulting Commodus as Caesar and his *consilium*, issued a decree prohibiting senators serving as governors in their native province.[92] Syria and the East remained unsettled to the extent that Herodian directly compares the emperors' military and political ability in dealing with the inhabitants of the northern territories and beyond with his dispositions whilst travelling through the eastern provinces (Herodian 1.2.5). The Northern War had nearly brought the empire to its knees and yet this historian compares Marcus Aurelius' and Commodus' actions in the eastern provinces to the conflict he had been fighting almost continually with the northern tribes since the early 160s. The east was far from pacified. On departing Tarsus the emperor refused to visit the cities of Antioch and Cyrrhus as they were closely associated with Avidius Cassius, Cyrrhus being his home whilst Antioch had been made his headquarters.[93] However on his return journey Marcus Aurelius was persuaded to make a brief visit to Antioch, pardoning the citizens. This was probably on the advice of Claudius Pompeianus who was himself born in the city and was counted as one of its patrons. Antioch was too powerful a city with a population of over half a million to be allowed to continue to be disaffected and so a potential power base for any future usurper. Commodus himself, perfectly aware of continued unrest in the area, in 181 AD rescinded his father's punishments imposed on the city thereby hoping to gain Antiochenes' gratitude and loyalty in return.

The emperor and his Caesar continued southward pardoning the communities that rebelled but executing centurions in the units that had joined Cassius' revolt. The loyalty of the army was paramount. Commodus would have been introduced to the assembled legions by the emperor much in the same manner as he had before the assembled armies on the Danube at the start of Cassius' revolt. Passing through Palestine however the emperor was horrified by the rebelliousness of the Jewish population in the province. The Emperor Hadrian had brutally suppressed a Jewish revolt in this area barring Jews from entering the holy city of Jerusalem. This had not been forgotten or forgiven.[94]

Reaching Alexandria in Egypt, a city that had strongly supported Cassius, the emperor surprisingly treated both its citizens and its previous governor with great leniency. Calvisius Statianus, the rebel governor of Egypt, was merely banished to an island and he pardoned the Alexandrians. Avidius Cassius' surviving son, Heliodorus, was brought to trial and also treated with great clemency, being merely banished but allowed to retain half of his father's estates. The probable reason for this was the emperor's admiration of Greek learning based in the city. The city had been founded by Alexander the Great and his General Ptolemy had founded a renowned university in the city as well as building the greatest library in the ancient world. Marcus Aurelius, no doubt accompanied by Commodus, visited the stadia, temples and listened to philosophers. They both would have revelled in this centre of learning. Commodus' later actions demonstrate a major influence of Greek and Hellenistic attitudes towards religion, in particular eastern Greek perceptions of their rulers as deities and their worship of them as divine. Whilst at Alexandria a delegation from the Parthians arrived and negotiations resulted in ratification of a peace treaty.[95] As Caesar, Commodus would have been present and this experience would have been used by his father to train his young son in the realities of power politics; Parthia being the only other super power.

In the spring of 176 AD the imperial party started the long journey home. One of his sisters though had remained behind in Alexandria although which is not mentioned.[96] The fact that Lucilla gave birth to a son in early 177 AD suggests she was excused the arduous journey overland to be permitted to travel by sea when the storm season had passed. Lucilla herself would have been looking to escape the presence of her husband whom she continued to detest. Pertinax departed from the group at this point to take up responsibilities on the Danube having been appointed Governor of Moesia. When the emperors entered Antioch they were greeted with celebratory games for *epheboi*. These were dedicated to Commodus, the people of the city reasoning that the forgiveness of Marcus Aurelius was not within their grasp. This appeal to Commodus seems to have had the desired effect because as sole emperor Commodus initiated a large building programme placing the city in his debt.

The party travelled through Asia Minor to Miletos where they granted permission for the games held in the city, the Didymeia, to be renamed the Didymeia Kommodeia. The provincial cities hoped to gain the *gratia* of the 'rising sun' in the expectation of returned favours when he became emperor. On arriving in Symrna the emperor waited three days in the expectation of a greeting (*salutatio*) from the famous sophist Aelius Aristides. All local notables would have been expected to greet the imperial personages each morning. This was also an opportunity to pass on petitions and requests. Philostratus refers to 'throngs' of people at these occasions and also the presence of the Quintilii brothers at the emperor's side. When Aristides failed to appear the Quintilli were delegated the task of arranging a meeting the next day and the sophist had the honour of being escorted to court by two of the emperor's closest *amici*. Asked about his delay in paying a visit to the emperor Aristides explained that he had been distracted by his studies. The emperor, suitably impressed, asked for Aristides to give a speech to which the sophist asked for his students to be present. The following day, on a topic of the emperor's choosing, Aristides was granted an audience, along with his students before the imperial party.[97]

From Smyrna, as promised to Herodes Atticus, Marcus Aurelius crossed the Aegean to Athens for initiation into the Eleusinian Mysteries. The *Historia Augusta* states that he entered the sanctuary unattended and suggests that he wished to be purified by entering the cult to 'prove he was innocent of any wrong doing'.[98] Only those who were considered pure were allowed to enter the cult. Clearly malicious gossip at the time was suggesting the emperor had in fact murdered Faustina. What the biographer of the *Historia Augusta* often did was to dress up gossip, slander and rumour as truth to titillate his audience in the manner of Suetonius' biography of the first twelve emperors. What both Dio and the *Historia Augusta* fail to mention is the presence of Commodus whose own initiation is recorded in an inscription from the time. The initiator is recorded as a certain Julius and the priest L Memmius who had initiated Verus fourteen years earlier.[99] Herodes Atticus' presence is not recorded at all. Perhaps the presence of the Quintilii deterred the philosopher from making an appearance.

A Christian writer in Athens by the name of Athenagoras describes composing a 'defence of the faith which he addressed to the emperors Marcus Aurelius Antoninus and Lucius Aurelius Commodus, conquerors of Armenia, (Media, Parthia, Germany,) Sarmatia, but, greatest of all, philosophers'. It is doubtful he would have been granted an audience with the emperors and, bearing in mind the Roman hostility towards this new religion, would he have truly wanted one? It seems that the dedication written at the start of his work is an imagining of his recital to the court. Athenagoras addresses the emperors as 'in every way, by nature and by upbringing, good, moderate, beneficent and deserving of kingship'.[100] It is refreshing to see Commodus described in this way, as both a philosopher and moderate, as a counter point to our main sources who want to airbrush his positive accomplishments out of history. The school of rhetoric and philosophy at Athens was world renown and Marcus Aurelius, undoubtedly with Commodus, used this opportunity to listen to a number of orators and philosophers. One, Adrian of Tyre who the emperor had previously appointed to a chair in Athens, had received some criticism from one of the emperor's *amici*, Claudius Severus, and he was summoned and given a topic to speak upon. The emperor was so impressed he showered lavish gifts upon him. Later, Commodus as sole emperor would remember his oration and appoint him to the higher chair of rhetoric in Rome and then close to death, appoint him to the post of *ab epistulis Graecis*. Teachers were then appointed by the imperial visitors to the various chairs of each branch of philosophy: Platonist, Aristolean, Stoic and Epicurian at Athens, each with a salary paid for by the emperor, and various honours were given to the Athenians themselves.[101]

In late autumn 176 AD the imperial party set sail for Italy but encountered a violent storm. They did however make it safely to Brundisium. Once in Rome Marcus Aurelius addressed the people, undoubtedly with Commodus at his side. When he referred to his many years away from the city the crowd cried out and held up four fingers on each hand. Public addresses, and the imperial presence at the games, were one of the few opportunities for the people to express their grievances or make demands of the emperor. Dio provides a remarkably detailed account of what happened. The crowd were clearly using their numbers to pressure the emperor into providing a gratuity or *congiarium* of eight gold coins to each citizen worth 800 *sesterces*. The emperor, perhaps remembering the questionable loyalty of elements at Rome during the revolt of Avidius Cassius gave in and with a smile said 'eight' in reply. This was another learning experience for Commodus as he began to appreciate the power of the crowd to threaten the imperial regime, a lesson he would remember. The amount his father had granted was larger than any previous distribution of *congiarium*. Marcus Aurelius needed to reaffirm the loyalty of the populace of the city, including the elite. In order to placate the equestrian and senatorial classes, the emperor cancelled all debts owing to the public or state treasury and the imperial *fiscus*, the revenues that went directly to the imperial treasury. All outstanding debts from the previous forty-five years, but not including the fifteen years of Hadrian's reign, were cancelled and all records of these debts were publicly burnt in the forum so that these remittances could not be overturned.[102] This was an astounding decision as the empire was financially in a poor state. The years of war and the loss of tax revenues due to deaths from the plague had severely reduced the income available to the state. This is reflected in the continual reduction of the precious metal content of coinage during the years of Marcus Aurelius and led to such desperate acts as publicly auctioning imperial property in the forum to pay for the Northern War. Add to this the financial disruption caused by the rebellion in the east and we can see that the emperor, well aware of the empire's precarious financial position and the cost of the games he announced, was prioritizing political stability over financial.

Marcus Aurelius had clearly been planning to raise his son to the position of joint emperor since the revolt of Avidius Cassius. The rapid promotion of his son was an attempt to secure his own position against this rival as well as securing the succession and the Antonine dynasty. Commodus' return to Rome was celebrated on an issue of coins with the legend *Adventus Caes(aris)*. For the first time in the imperial coinage of the reign of Marcus Aurelius the image of Hercules appears, a medallion carrying the name of Commodus shows an image of the demi god, whilst a gem, possibly from this year, depicts the young Commodus with a Hercules lion skin. Hercules was a popular divinity on the coinage of all the Antonine emperors apart from Marcus Aurelius. However four *aurei* and a *sesterces* of the co-emperor, Lucius Verus, carry the figure of Hercules. The newly empowered Commodus clearly wished to associate himself with the man he had admired as a young boy.[103] A triumph was announced for the successes in the German and Sarmatian Wars which were to be held on 23 December. Wishing to associate Commodus with these victories the emperor asked the senate to grant his son *imperium* or magisterial authority so he could take part in the triumph. Furthermore he decided to appoint his son one of the ordinary consuls for 1 January 177 AD and as such needed the senate to excuse Commodus from the legal provisions of the *lex annalis* which would make Commodus, at 15 years of age, the youngest consul in history.[104] As his partner in the consulship the emperor chose Marcus Peducaeus Plautius Quintillus, his daughter Fadilla's husband and nephew of Verus. This was clearly a great honour for Quintillus. Commodus must have had some influence on the choice of his co-consul and it seems apt that he chose a relative of his idol, Lucius Verus. Both Plautius Quintillus and his sister Fadilla would remain loyal advisors to Commodus during his reign, Quintillus being rewarded with the honour of a second joint consulship with the Emperor Commodus. Interestingly Quintillius' mother, Ceionia Fabia, had tried to interest Marcus Aurelius in marriage after the death of Faustina, however her advances were rejected, and the emperor took a mistress instead.

The triumph was held on 23 December 176 AD with the emperor running at the side of the triumphal chariot in which his son was seated, controlling the reigns. This sight, before the assembled thousands in the Circus, would have left no doubt as to whom the emperor had chosen as his heir.[105] Coins were also issued to commemorate their joint triumph with the legend *De Germanis, De Sarmatis*. Then the imperial family withdrew to the palace at Lanuvium on the coast, the place of Commodus' birth, only to return to Rome a few days later for Commodus' formal entry into the consulship when he was awarded tribunician power.[106] The promised largesse was then distributed to the people and the games held. The so-called 'panel reliefs' that survive from the triumphal arch of 176 AD built to celebrate Marcus Aurelius' triumph show two scenes in which Commodus' image once was carved but was obliterated after his death by a vengeful senate. The first shows Commodus riding in his father's triumphal chariot and the second shows him sat behind his father on a podium distributing money and largesse to the people. A *sesterces* of 177 AD shows Marcus Aurelius and Commodus seated on a platform announcing *liberalitas*, denoting imperial generosity. Commodus is identified by his round, beardless head and shorter height. It was probably at this time that the senate voted to build the famous Column of Marcus Aurelius rather than the later date postulated by the late Roman historian Aurelius Victor. Firstly

Commodus does not appear at all on the column itself but he was involved in the war from 178 AD and secondly Dio fails to mention the dedication of the column when mentioning the honours voted to the deceased Emperor Marcus Aurelius by the senate when he does refer to the erection of a golden statue of the emperor to be set up outside the senate house. Other coin issues present the young Commodus as the embodiment of success and prosperity by associating him with Salvus, the goddess of health and wealth; whilst another, an *aureus* from 177 AD, shows him with Castor who with his twin Pollux, were regarded as the helpers of mankind.[107] At this time Lucilla gave birth to a son who was named Aurelius Commodus Pompeianus. At some point after these events Marcus Aurelius again fell ill, only to cured by Galen through a treatment Galen declares in his *On Prognosis* to be 'genuinely remarkable'. This illness hastened the emperor to grant Commodus the title Augustus and all remaining imperial titles apart from 'Pontifex Maximus', the high priest of the College of Pontiffs. Commodus was now joint emperor with Marcus Aurelius just as Lucius Verus had been.

The actions of Marcus Aurelius clearly show that he intended his sole surviving son to succeed him. However the revolt of Avidius Cassius and his own poor health accelerate the process. Previous emperors from the reign of Nerva had adopted their successors but this had been forced upon them by circumstance, having no surviving male children to succeed them. Marcus Aurelius would have counted himself as fortunate that he had. When he had ascended the throne in March 161 AD, having been adopted himself by Antoninus Pius with Lucius Verus, he demanded that Verus be recognized as his co-emperor by the senate. Failure to do so could have led to a dynastic crisis. Furthermore Marcus Aurelius, at the time of his ascent to the throne, had no male offspring as all had died young; Commodus and his twin not being born until 31 August 161 AD. Although Faustina would have been clearly pregnant there was no guarantee that the babies would survive to adulthood nor that they would be male. Once Commodus entered his early teens it was clear he would probably survive to manhood and so to adopt another as his successor would have condemned his own son to an early grave. There are no clear, direct references to Commodus in Marcus Aurelius' work *Meditations*. However there are a number of passages which do give an insight into Commodus' upbringing and may indeed refer to him. Marcus Aurelius writes: 'If you can, convert him by teaching, if not, remember that kindliness was given to you for this very thing …' and 'if he makes a mistake, teach him with kindliness and point out what is being overlooked; if you fail blame yourself, or not even yourself …' and finally, 'kindness is invincible … what can the most insolent do if you continue to be gentle with him and quietly show him a better way at the very moment that he tries to do you harm'.[108] If indeed these passages do refer to the young Commodus they demonstrate Marcus Aurelius to be a loving, doting father and Commodus a headstrong, strong-willed child. Clearly this father would not endanger his only son.

Marcus Aurelius has been severely criticized by historians, both ancient and modern, for abandoning the so-called Antonine 'system' for selecting successors based on the abilities of the most able candidates and instead opting to revert to a dynastic model by choosing Commodus. Oliver Hekster and G Adams have however conclusively demonstrated that in fact there was no system of adoptive selection by the Antonine emperors.[109] Indeed most of these 'adoptive' emperors were themselves relatives of the ruling emperor: the exceptions being Trajan whose command of the legions on the Rhine forced the childless Nerva to adopt him and the adoption of Lucius Ceionius Commodus by Hadrian whose daughter was betrothed to Marcus Aurelius, probably Hadrian's intended long-term successor.[110] On Ceinonius' death Hadrian adopted Antoninus Pius as Marcus Aurelius was seen as too young at the time to inherit the throne. Antonius Pius was Marcus' uncle, and the proposed marriage to Ceionius' daughter was broken off for Faustina, Antoninus' daughter, whilst Antoninus Pius formally adopted Marcus. To ensure a smooth uncontested succession for Antoninus Pius, Hadrian had his elderly brother-in-law Julius Servianus and his grandson commit suicide. This would not have been necessary if the dynastic and family principle to succession had been widely rejected. Furthermore the conspiracies by leading members of Commodus' own family on his accession only make sense if they believed they had a right to the throne through their dynastic links to Marcus Aurelius. After the murder of Commodus, his brother-in-law, Marcus Peducaeus Plautius Quintillus was killed by Septimius Severus and Lucilla's son, Tiberius Claudius Pompeianus, by Caracalla. This also would have been unnecessary if their links to the previous imperial dynasty were not considered a potential threat.

The contemporary historians themselves stress the lineage of Commodus on his accession and on his death. Herodian has Commodus addressing the soldiers on the Rhine on the death of his father stating: 'Fate has given the empire to me as his successor, not as an adopted heir like my predecessors ... but as the only one of your emperors born in the palace.'[111] Whether Commodus actually gave this speech is immaterial as Herodian's readers would clearly have recognized the claims made in it. The army and people demanded hereditary succession. After the fall of Commodus and then the end of the Severan dynasty, attempts were made throughout the third century to found new dynasties to the extent that when the senate chose Balbinus and Papienus as emperors the army and people of Rome demanded Gordian the Third be made emperor in succession to his father and grandfather.[112] On inscriptions Commodus models himself as *nobilissimus omnium princeps*; the most noble of all emperors.[113] In commenting on his death, Dio states 'He lived thirty-one years and four months: and with him the genuine line of the Aurelii ceased to rule'.[114]

Chapter Two

The Rising Sun (177–180 AD)

The emperors' most important role, as perceived by their subjects was answering petitions or *libelli*.[1] As joint emperor Commodus would now be expected to attend the morning *salutatio* where petitioners would attempt to pass their requests to the emperors. The imperial palace on the Palatine was approached from an entrance in the forum via a series of ramps built up the hill. As the petitioner entered the great palace of Domitian they would be ushered into the large vestibule to await a summons. Pliny describes hordes of people waiting at the gates.[2] On entering the basilica the emperor would be sat in an apse guarded by the Praetorians and surrounded by his advisors, the Prefects of the Guard, as well as an *ab epistulis Graecis*, *ad epistulis Latinis* and *amici* drawn from the most prominent senators and equestrians. The emperor was then to be saluted first by the Praetorian Prefects, also by his *amici* and the *principales officiorum*, officers of the court, and then the senators and followed by the equestrians or knights present.[3] Many petitioners would be patrons who wished to gain the *gratia*, gratitude of an *amicus* or client to obligate them to himself or his family. Petitioners were probably divided into three categories based on status with the first smaller, elite cohort having the best opportunity to pass on their requests.[4] The emperor was expected to pass on gifts, grant requests or promotions as *beneficia* or gifts whilst in return the emperor expected loyalty. This was not an equal role as the leading senators were obligated to the emperor on behalf of their own *amici* or clients, yet Marcus Aurelius played it to perfection, treating senatorial petitioners with respect and feigned equality. Commodus was ultimately to reject this by presenting this relationship for what it was: the emperor a benevolent autocrat whilst the rest of the petitioners mere subjects.

The only other opportunity to meet the emperor face-to-face was through invitation to an imperial banquet. This was only granted to close *amici* and was seen as a great honour. Vespasian thanked the Emperor Caligula for an invitation to such a banquet before the senate.[5] Such a convivial environment permitted a more private and intimate conversation with the emperor and with it a greater chance of having a request granted. Those with the greatest and closest access to the emperors could wield immense power as they had his ear on more occasions. These powerful figures were often the centre of complex networks of client patronage based on access to opportunities and gifts that the emperors alone could provide. The emperors' *amici* and court officials exploited these opportunities to the full, influencing imperial decisions, procuring promotions and appointments for clients and their own *amici* as well as receiving and distributing *beneficia* including imperial properties.[6] It is perhaps with heavy irony that the philosopher Epictetus laments the hardships endured by the *amicus Caesaris*; the friends of Caesar, having to lose sleep owing to attendance of the morning *salutatio* added to the humiliation of dining at the emperor's table as a social inferior.[7] However in the same work he also elaborates on the advantages of being an *amicus* of the emperor:

> What could anyone imagine you want? You are rich, you have children, a wife and many slaves; Caesar knows you, you have many friends in Rome, you can perform your duties and know how to return kindness with kindness and injury with injury.[8]

The threat of such power is resonant in that last phrase. Pliny the Younger records the fear he felt by taking a case against 'the most powerful men in the senate and even friends of Caesar'.[9] Pliny's own patron was Julius Servianus, an *amicus* of the emperor Trajan. This was a reciprocal relationship as Servianus on Pliny's behalf got the *ius trium liberorum*, a privilege granted to Roman citizens who had three or more children that excused them from public charges and obligations. Pliny himself later became an *amicus* of the Emperor Trajan and received from the emperor through numerous petitions adlection to the senate for his *amicus* Voconius Romanus, citizenship for his doctor, full citizenship rights for a freedman of Antonia Maximilla, and for himself appointment to augur or priest. Commodus had entered the dangerous world of power politics.

We have two accounts from the ancient sources of emperors at work. Firstly Suetonius, himself an *ab epistuli* of Hadrian describes Vespasian's routine:[10]

> ... he would rise early, before dawn even, to deal with his private correspondence and official reports. Next he would admit his friends and receive their greeting while he put on his shoes and dressed himself. Having attended to any business that had come up he would first take a drive and then return to bed for a nap – with one of his several mistresses who he had engaged after Caenis' (his wife) death. Finally he took a bath and went to dinner where he would be in such a cheerful mood that members of his household usually chose this time to ask favours of him.

Note that Vespasian would admit his *amici* before the official business of the morning *salutatio* where they would attend on him offering advice at his side.

The second account comes from Dio, an *amicus* of a number of the Severan emperors, where he describes Septimius Severus' routine:

> the emperor rose before dawn and walked in the grounds speaking and listening on matters of government, then he passed judgement in court unless there was a major religious festival on. He gave equal time to both the prosecution and defence using a water clock seeking legal clarification from his legal advisors until mid day. Then he went riding and did gymnastic exercises followed by a bath. The emperor then had lunch with his sons or alone and then slept. Any outstanding matters were then dealt with in Greek and Latin whilst walking in his gardens and then he had another bath followed by a banquet with his household.[11]

Clear similarities exist in their working days and a significant proportion of their time was reacting to events or responding to letters and in passing judgement in court cases. Imperial administration was not proactive nor given to future planning, it was primarily given to micromanagement on an immensely time-consuming scale. Marcus Aurelius sometimes spent eleven to twelve days listening to one court case and emperors must also have received a vast number of official reports, letters and *libelli* or petitions from both prominent individuals, governors and provincial cities on a daily basis.[12] A small number of these have been preserved in the legal digests and inscriptions for the joint rule of Commodus and Marcus Aurelius. However, on his death, the senate declared Commodus a public enemy, *damnatio memoriae* (damning his memory), requiring that all references to his name or actions be removed from the public record including inscriptions and public documents. Consequently records of legal judgements and decrees preserved on inscriptions passed by Commodus as sole ruler are almost non-existent; however some passed as co-emperor with his much esteemed father were preserved.

One such rescript from Commodus and Marcus Aurelius is preserved in the *Digest* of Roman law written in reply to a legal enquiry from Scapula Tertullus, probably the proconsular governor of Africa. The emperors respond to the advice on the correct legal treatment of a madman of high social standing who in an alleged state of insanity murdered his wife. It is clear both emperors read the letter as the reply states: 'But since we have learned from your letter.' The emperors instruct Scapula to assess whether the murderer at any time becomes lucid, to ascertain the permanence and nature of his madness and, if they come to the conclusion that he is insane, to keep in custody. However if they find him to be sane then the governor is requested to refer back to the emperors for judgement. In the meantime the governor is to investigate how the madman's guardians could allow him to commit the crime when he was already declared to be insane.[13] Such detailed invention in one case in one province is indicative of the micromanagement of the empire and an indication of the volume of such inquiries from administrators across the empire. The constant referrals to the Emperor Trajan by Pliny whilst he was governor demonstrate clearly the extent to which central government was involved in affairs of individuals or cities.

A typical enquiry is provided by a referral to the emperors by Aufidius Victorinus, an *amicus* of Marcus Aurelius and governor of two Spanish provinces responsible for dealing with an incursion of Moors from North Africa, involving the freeing of slaves. The resulting 'law of liberty' ensured slaves freed in a will did obtain their freedom whatever legal obstacles were raised at the time of the will. Slave dealers had clearly been purchasing the slaves of the deceased, ignoring caveats in the will that manumitted them.[14]

Another case referring to the emperors in 177 AD involved a senator from Sparta whose wife had left a large legacy to her two sons, but instructed that they could only inherit the bequest on the death of their father, a senator. The senator proposed that he could emancipate his sons immediately so they could inherit but this would make him in legal terms dead and also this would leave his children beyond his legal control. The emperors found in favour of the father's suggestion.[15]

Two murder cases are recorded as being referred to the emperors. A father, finding his married daughter in bed with her lover, attacked them both, killing the lover and severely wounding his daughter. The *lex Cornelia* allowed for justifiable homicide if both adulterers were killed. The emperors ruled that as the father had intended to kill his daughter as well, he should be pardoned.[16] Following on from this a husband was pardoned for killing his wife as he had caught her also with her lover. Other legal judgements attributed to Commodus recorded in the *Digest* include pronouncements on tax law, trial procedures and reinforcing the rights of former masters over their freedmen who could be sold as slaves if the freedmen did not observe their legal and customary obligations to their former owners.[17]

The Northern War broke out again in 177 AD with the Quintilii cousins (sons of the two brothers who had accompanied Commodus and Marcus Aurelius to the east) having only some limited success.[18] Marcus Aurelius was acclaimed Imperator for the ninth time and his son for the second but the situation on the frontier continued to deteriorate. The war was having some unforeseen consequences: many troops who had previously been employed policing the countryside and roads had been drawn away to the war beyond the Danube causing an increase in lawlessness in the provinces. Runaway slaves, who previously would have been rounded up by units of troops were now free to loot and plunder provincials and the rural estates of the wealthy. These groups had been augmented by deserters from the war to the extent that the experienced General Valerius Maximus had previously been sent to Lower Moesia as procurator to deal with bandits and brigands. This unrest was clearly widespread as Didius Julianus had been appointed to deal with unrest in the neighbouring area of Dalmatia[19] and Pertinax was transferred from Lower Moesia to Dacia.[20] These concerns led to a proclamation by the emperors demanding that governors of provinces, local magistrates and militia were duty-bound to assist slave owners in hunting down runaway slaves and give them up if found, rather than, it is to be assumed, selling them for a profit. This law also stipulated that if the runaways were knowingly harboured by the landowner where they were captured then the landowner was also to be punished. Any person who captured a runaway was to publicly bring him forward and local magistrates were to ensure captives were kept in secure custody to prevent escape.[21] Another rescript from the time describes a landowner by the name of Julius Donatus who, hearing of the approach of bandits and brigands, fled his villa but was wounded in making his escape. Donatus was tended by his own slaves and relatives but subsequently died.[22] The problem of runaway slaves and deserters would not be solved by these actions and would escalate to full-blown war during the reign of Commodus.

Losses caused by the near perpetual war against the northern barbarians, desertion and the plague led to a massive shortage of available men for the army leading to a massive increase in the price of gladiators provided by professional trainers (*lanistae*) for spectacles throughout the empire as many had been conscripted into the army. This had a major impact on the elite of the empire who often had to provide shows as part of their religious or magisterial duties. A petition was sent to the emperors from the council of the Three Gauls on behalf of one of their number who had been chosen to be a priest for the following year. Facing financial ruin this wealthy man declared himself to be bankrupt citing the enormous costs of the gladiatorial shows he had to organize as part of his priestly responsibilities. The emperors instructed the procurator of the province to supply the priest with condemned criminals for the Gallic festival at a cheap price of six gold pieces a head to use as gladiators. The priest was overjoyed, but I am sure the same cannot be said for the criminals. The emperors also founded the *Collegium Silvani Aureliani*, a collegium for gladiators dedicated to the god Silvanus who was closely linked to Hercules, the patron of gladiators. If a gladiator reached retirement they dedicated their weapons to Hercules and often had his image inscribed on their weapons. Silvanus was believed to be Hercules' mythological grandson. Later the statue of the collegium was restored in the sole reign of Commodus, the inscription exclaiming that the health of the emperor guaranteed the happiness of the gladiators: '*salvo Commodo, felix familia*', and the procurator tasked with restoring the statue added the epithet 'Commodianus' to his name. This post was originally a lower-ranked post but Commodus' interest in gladiatorial combat, along with the shortage of trained men for the arena caused by the continual fighting, meant the post was upgraded and would be highly valued as the post holder could gain the emperor's attention.[23]

This imperial decision to use criminals in gladiatorial contests may have had an unfortunate consequence for Christians living in the Gallic provinces. Eusebius details the martyrdom of a significant number of Christians at the festival games in Lungduum. 'At the beginning of the festival there, at which there was a heavy attendance as all the (Gallic) provinces gather together for it …', the governor interrogated a man accused of being a Christian under torture. Before the gladiatorial combats criminals would be executed, tortured or given to wild animals to be eaten. Eusebius writes that Christians who had been denounced and refused to renounce their faith before the governor were condemned to death as criminals and fed to beasts in the amphitheatre, roasted on an iron chair or gored by a bull. One such man, having been led around the amphitheatre with a placard announcing 'This is Attalus, the Christian', was returned to prison, the governor having been informed at the last moment that Attalus was a Roman citizen. An enquiry was sent to Rome as the governor sought advice on how he should treat him. The imperial reply allowed for Attalus to renounce Christianity or be executed. Attalus refused to recant and the sentence was carried out.[24]

Miletus in Asia Minor also sent a request to the emperors concerning a religious festival and its associated games. Both emperors appear to have addressed the senate with the issues raised but what is also evident is that an imperial oration had the force of law:

> Having received your message about the festival, we thought it fitting to consult the sacred assembly of the senate, to gain its agreement to your request. There were many other matters to speak to it about too. Since, therefore, it did not ratify individually each item which we raised, but its decree was instead a joint, collective one about the matters which we had spoken to it that day, we have attached to this answer for your information the section of the speech delivered by us relevant to your request.[25]

Clearly both emperors were present at the session and both were actively involved in the day's business. The fact that the extract from the imperial speech was sent to Miletus as legal assent suggests that the imperial oration itself became law. Roman legal writers often quote as a source of law an imperial oration not the senatorial decree ratifying it that was passed after the imperial speech.[26] It is also evident that the emperors controlled the agenda for the meeting and chaired it. The emperors spoke first and then would ask the leading members of the senate to discuss the proposals starting with the two serving ordinary consuls, other leading magistrates and then the leading aristocrats in the senate; junior members of the senate who had not held a magistracy or were not from the noble families would in all probability not be called to speak.[27] The leading senators themselves wanted the emperor to speak first on proposals, stating his opinion, so allowing subsequent senators called to speak to agree to the imperial proposals without offending or antagonizing the emperor by contradicting him or expressing opinions that might result in the senator falling out of favour.

Clearly these were not the only petitions sent to Rome complaining at the cost of gladiatorial shows. A senatorial decree, introduced at the emperors' request, was passed encompassing the whole empire which fixed the price at which gladiators could be bought.[28] Two inscriptions of this decree have been found, one from Sardis in Asia Minor inscribed in marble and the other from Italica in Spain inscribed on a bronze tablet. The inscription from Italica also preserves a speech from an unnamed senator responding to the imperial proposals;

> Moreover, although many think that everything which our mighty emperors have proposed to us should be proposed in one succinct motion, nevertheless, with your permission, senators, I shall deal with each point individually, taking over from the most sacred oration the very same words to clarify the motion, so that there be no room anywhere for misinterpretation.[29]

It is evident that one or both emperors had given an oration to the senate. However what this speech does suggest is that some degree of genuine discussion and debate took place within the senatorial meeting, as the inscription records the senator quoting extensively from the imperial proposals. The senator also describes the gratitude felt by the Gallic provinces at the introduction of the law.[30] It is hard to imagine a delay between the emperor's oration to the senate and the senatorial debate that allowed news of the proposals to travel from Rome to Gaul and then back again. The senator must therefore have been from Gaul himself and as such, saw himself as a representative of the views of the Gallic aristocracy to the law fixing the cost of gladiatorial games. By proposing this law the emperors were providing *beneficia* and favours to the ruling elite and in return they expected loyalty and service. They also wanted to ensure the games were provided to entertain the people as 'bread and circuses' were the essential requirement to retain the loyalty of the people across the empire and not just in Rome.

An inscription from the Bagradas Valley in Africa records a petition sent to both Commodus and Marcus Aurelius from the tenants (*coloni*) of imperial estates in the area who were being forced by the lessees of the land (*conductores*) to provide more cash, labour and work days than they were legally obliged to do. The *conductores* were being supported by the imperial procurator as soldiers were used against them when they complained. The inscription fails to detail what the imperial reply was, however the procurator clearly ignores it as the *coloni* were forced to send a second petition at a later date as it addresses only Commodus, Marcus Aurelius presumably having died in the meantime. This second approach clearly had the desired effect as the *coloni* were able to inscribe the imperial response in stone. Commodus' response is referred to as 'the sacred subscriptio of our lord, the most sacred emperor, which, when it had been given to his libellis, Lurius Lucullus …' and here the text is lost. Any written document addressed to the emperor was termed a *libellus* and it was the custom of emperors to dictate their response to an official of equestrian rank, *a libellis*. The response was then written under the original document as a *subscriptio*. The inscription preserves Commodus' *subscriptio*:

> Imperator Caesar M Aurelius Commodus Antoninus Augustus Sarmaticus Germanicus Maximus to Lurius Lucullus and others. The procurators having regard to my rules and customs will see to it that nothing is exacted from you in contravention of the standing regulations.

Written in another hand is added: 'I have written it. I have checked it'.[31]

From this it is clear that the reply was dictated to the *libellis* and then checked and authenticated by the emperor. This was the common practice of emperors as preserved in other inscriptions and papyri.[32] However the *Historia Augusta* accuses Commodus of laziness and carelessness 'in signing libellis that he answered many petitions with the same formula, while in very many 'epistulis' (letters) he merely wrote the word "farewell".'[33]

In 178 AD the legal status of women was augmented by the Senatus Consultum Orfitianum named after one of the two consuls of that year. This law gave precedence to a woman's children in a will, over and above the other relatives, including her brothers and sisters. Whether this was introduced at the instigation of the emperors is not indicated.[34]

In all these inscriptions it is clear Commodus was as much part of the decision-making process as his father yet the contemporary sources refer only to Marcus Aurelius passing legislation and running the imperial government. Statue bases from this period from across the empire show that provincials considered both emperors to be equals in both authority and status. Ten are dedicated by cities celebrating the commencement of joint imperial power and the continuation of the dynasty whilst two citizens of Osilipo are an expression of loyalty to the new emperor. The ancient written sources wished to disassociate the 'bad' Emperor Commodus from the 'good' Emperor Marcus Aurelius. After all, Dio was a part of the senatorial class that opposed Commodus, as was Marius Maximus whose lost work probably constituted the main source for the life of Commodus in the

Historia Augusta. The murder of Marcus Aurelius' son had to be justified and the senatorial elite who constituted the reading audience for the histories of Cassius Dio and Herodian would need to justify their actions, ridding Rome of a tyrant. Otherwise people would pose the question: in whose interests were they acting when they conspired, plotted, murdered and celebrated the death of the legitimate emperor? 'This attitude can be seen in the work of the great jurist Ulpian in the reigns of Caracalla and Severus Alexander who clearly knew of legal rescripts of Commodus but chose not to cite them although they are referred to in the legal works of contemporary jurists Callistratus, Papinian, Marcianus and Modestinus.

Our knowledge of legal decisions from his reign as sole emperor is hampered by the fact that his name was removed from all public inscriptions after he suffered *damnatio memoriae* after his death. Furthermore the great fire of Rome in 190 AD also destroyed the state records and much legislation passed under his auspices. The absence of laws bearing his name in the *Codex Justinianus* may be due to the fact that the lawyers derived from the senatorial class were antagonistic to the emperor and so censored his name from legal pronouncement, which would also hold true for the record of laws in the *Digest*. Other emperors who were despised by the senatorial class were similarly associated with a significantly reduced number of legal records, for example those preserved from the reigns of Nero and Domitian, whilst there are no records for Caligula (Gaius).One late source, Eusebius, does refer to an imperial decree issued by Commodus, sanctioning the use of the death penalty on servants and slaves, who inform on their masters accusing them of being Christians or 'other such matters'. This legislation does not appear in the *Digest* or *Codex*.[35]

In 178 AD an earthquake devastated the city of Smyrna and Aristides, as patron of the city and an *amicus* of Marcus Aurelius, wrote to the emperors describing the devastation and requesting funds for its rebuilding. Normal procedure would have been for the city itself to send an embassy to the emperors but clearly an *amicus Caesaris* would have far greater influence than dignitaries from a distant province. Marcus Aurelius read the petition and wept as Aristides 'lamented its fate ... in such moving words that the emperor frequently groaned at other passages in the petition, but when he came to the words: "She is a desert through which the winds blows" the emperor actually shed tears over the pages and in accordance with the impulse inspired by Aristides, he consented to rebuild the city'.[36] Dio, without referring to the role of Aristides, provides more detail. A senator of praetorian rank was assigned to manage the rebuilding work and monies were also made available to other cities in the area as well.[37]

Another important inscription from the town of Bansa in Africa dated to 6 July 177 AD commemorates the awarding of citizenship to the family of Julianus by the emperors at the request of the procurator of the province of Tingitana, no doubt his patron. The text refers to imperial freedman Asclepiodotus checking the register of Roman citizenship granted by previous emperors. The granting of citizenship was witnessed by the two emperors and twelve members of the *consilium* or advisory council named in order of precedence.[38] Although membership of the *consilium* could vary depending on the matters to be addressed and limited by the absence of prominent figures on other duties around the empire, these men were the friends of Caesar and as such had a great deal of personal contact and access to the emperor. These were amongst the most powerful men in the empire in 177 AD;

M Gavius Squilla Gallicanus: from an aristocratic family from Verona. His father was probably M Gavius Squilla Gallicanus, the consul of 127 AD. He was chosen as the ordinary consul of 150 AD by Emperor Antoninus Pius. He had been proconsul of Asia and his son was probably Marcus Gavius Cethegus Cornelius, the ordinary consul of 170 AD. He was an *amicus* of Fronto, Marcus Aurelius' tutor, and his son was also tutored by Fronto.

M Acilius Glabrio: from an ancient aristocratic family dating back to the Republic and the Punic Wars. Probably no other family in Rome could trace their line back so far apart from the Calpurnii Pisones and Cornelii Scipiones Orfiti. The family was granted patrician status probably in the reign of Domitian. He was the ordinary consul of 152 AD. It was probably this same man, rather than a son, who was suffect consul in 173 AD and had the great honour of sharing a further ordinary consulship in 186 AD with the Emperor Commodus. He is described as 'the most nobly born of all the patricians as he traced his descent from Aeneas the son of Venus and Anchises' and for this reason Pertinax allegedly offered him the throne on the murder of Commodus.[39]

T Sextius Lateranus: a member of one of the oldest aristocratic families had been given the honour of sharing the ordinary consulship of 154 AD with Lucius Verus, the adopted heir of Antonius Pius, along with Marcus Aurelius.

C Septimius Severus: his family originated from Lepcis Magna in the province of Tripolitania in modern Libya. His brother P Septimius Aper was suffect consulship in 153 AD whilst C Septimius Severus was awarded the suffect consulship 160 AD by Antoninus Pius and then made a governor of one of the German provinces. A priest of the prestigious *quindecimviri sacris faciundis* and so entrusted with care of the Sibylline oracles and foreign religious rites in Rome, including the cults of Isis and Sarapis. Appointment to such a post would come as a gift from the emperor. His cousin was L Septimius Severus, the future emperor, he was termed an 'uncle' to L Septimius Severus in the *Historia Augusta*, probably due to helping to nurture his career. It was probably through C Septimius Severus' influence that Marcus Aurelius adlected L Septimius Severus into the senate. In 173 AD he was chosen by lot in the senate to be proconsul of the senatorial province of Africa and he selected L Septimius Severus to accompany him as a legate to gain valuable experience. On his return to Rome L Septimius Severus was made a tribune of the plebs as one of the emperor's candidates, which guaranteed selection, whilst his brother Geta was made legate of the Legion I Italica and probably served under Pertinax on the Danube from 175 AD. C Septimius Severus as an *amicus* of the emperor could use his influence to promote the interests of his family members.

P Julius Scapula Tertullus: probably an ex consul of approximately 163 AD to whom as proconsular governor of Africa the emperors wrote a rescript in reply to his enquiry concerning the legal status of an insane man who had killed his wife.

T Varius Clemens: from the Celeia in the province of Noricum. He had extensive military experience in a series of military posts and then he held five procuratorships in imperial service including commanding in the war in Mauretania the early 150s AD, Beligica and the two Germanies. Chosen then by Verus and Marcus Aurelius to be *ab epistulis Latinis* with responsibility for all imperial correspondence to and from the Latin speaking elements of the empire and accompanied the emperor in the war zone on the Danube. For his services he was probably adlected to the senate and rewarded with a suffect consulship.

M Bassaeus Rufus: rose from peasant origins through outstanding service in the army to Prefect of the Vigiles, the city of Rome police. In 168 AD he was appointed Prefect of Egypt, but on the death of Victorinus, the Prefect of the Praetorian Guard, Bassaeus Rufus was recalled and appointed in his place. At the emperor's side and witnessing Herodes Atticus' rant in court at Sirmium, Bassaeus Rufus had drawn his sword intending to end Atticus' diatribe permanently, but was restrained by Marcus Aurelius. The Praetorian Prefects were the only officials allowed into the emperor's presence armed with a sword. He accompanied Marcus Aurelius to the East after the failure of Cassius' revolt and was decorated in 176 AD for his services in the war against the barbarians. He had retired or died by August 178 AD.

P Taruttienus Paternus: was a legal expert who had written a work entitled: *De re militari*. This seems to have been a work on the legal analysis of the implications of a range of laws on the army and soldiers. He is first attested as *ab epistulis Latinis* to Marcus Aurelius in 171 AD on the Danube. The Cotini, under the pretext of allying themselves with the Romans against the Marcomanni and Quadi, lured Paternus with a large force of soldiers into an ambush and, in the words of Dio, 'handled Paternus very roughly'. Patrernus' reputation was not severely damaged as, if he was not already Praetorian Prefect in 177 AD with M Bassaeus Rufus, he was about to be.[40] On his promotion Paternus, probably using his influence with the emperors, managed to arrange for the promotion of an *amicus* of his own, Vitruvius Secundus as *ab epistulis Latinis*.[41] The Praetorian Prefect's role had developed during the empire from responsibility for the emperor's safety to other roles as well, commanding armies, controlling access to the emperor, administrative responsibilities and providing legal advice at imperial trials and, in the absence of the emperor, hearing cases themselves and passing judgement. An example of this being an enquiry passed on to the prefects Macrinus Vindex and M Bassaeus Rufus in 169–72 AD by an *a rationibus* (a high-ranking imperial official mainly concerned with finances) concerning interference with imperial flocks in the Abruzzi. The prefects wrote to the local magistrates in Saepinum ordering them to cease 'less it be necessary to examine the case and exact punishment for what has been done, if it is so'.[42]

Next are named high ranking equestrians. Sex Tigidius Perennis: he had probably been appointed *praefectus annonae* ensuring efficient food and supplies for the army on the Danube. He was to replace M Bassaeus Rufus as Praetorian prefect. Dio describes him as highly ambitious for office but 'privately he never strove in the least for either fame or wealth, but lived a most incorruptible and temperate life'. Herodian describes him as an Italian with a fine military record.[43]

Q Cervidius Scaevola: was an eminent legal expert who had helped Marcus Aurelius review and restore old laws and introduce new ones. Scaevola was of the *amici* offering advice to the emperor in the audience hall of the palace on the Danube when adjudicating on the case of the Spartan senator of praetorian rank, Brasidas. He is not attested as holding any office until 175 AD when he was appointed to the Prefecture of Vigiles, the urban cohort in Rome. He later produced his extensive legal works *Digesta*, *Responsa* and *Quaestiones*.

Q Larcius Eurupianus: who rose to the consulship under Commodus only to be executed in 191 AD.

T Flavius Piso: who is later recorded as Prefect of Egypt in 181 AD replacing Titus Aius Sanctus, Commodus' tutor who was appointed in 179 AD.

Despite early successes by the Quintilii cousins, the situation on the Danube had deteriorated to the extent that the emperors felt their own presence was required to restore the situation. Archaeological evidence shows the forts at Intercisa and Gorsium to have suffered severe damage around 178 AD and the titles 'Germanicus' and 'Sarmaticus' disappear from the coinage.[44] Marcus Aurelius, appreciating that their absence from Rome would be for a considerable amount of time decided to bring forward the marriage of his son. Bruttia Crispina was chosen as the bride. She was the 14-year-old daughter of the consul of 153 AD, Bruttius Praesens. This powerful senator was an *amicus* of Hadrian, Antonius Pius and Marcus Aurelius and his father had previously been twice consul and was a friend of Pliny. The consulship of 180 AD was allocated to Bruttius Praesens to honour the arrangement; the consulships of 179 AD had already been awarded to Commodus and Martius Verus. It was also probably decided at the time to give Gn Julius Verus the other ordinary consulship of 180 AD but he was to die before taking the post. He was replaced by Sex Quintilius Condianus (son of one of the Quintilii brothers, Sex Quintilius Condianus con 151 AD) as a reward for his campaigning on the Danube. The marriage ceremony was simple, the imperial wedding described as being 'in the manner of ordinary citizens'.[45] At the ceremony the wedding hymn was composed and delivered by Julius Pollux of Naucratis who had previously dedicated his new work, the *Onomasticon*, to Commodus. Pollux so impressed the groom he was promoted to the chair of rhetoric in Athens as a gift.[46] The event was celebrated on coins and largesse was again distributed to the people.

By this time there was no difference between the private wealth and revenue (*fiscus*) of the imperial family and revenues derived by the state managed by the senate,[47] however Marcus Aurelius formally requested additional funds to pay for the renewed conflict 'not because such funds were not already at the emperor's disposal, but because he was wont to declare that all funds, both these and others, belonged to the senate and to the people' and he went on to declare the imperial palaces themselves the property of the senate.[48] Marcus Aurelius believed that his imperial position rested on patronal ties to his aristocratic supporters whose social status required them to be treated as equals and not clients of the emperor.[49] Merely taking the necessary funds from the senatorial treasury would humiliate the senatorial class by exposing the hard realities of the situation: the very nature of the imperial system was based on inequality with the emperor the font of all *beneficia*, whether it be entrance to the equestrian or senatorial orders, magistracies, gifts or favours while the senators were cast as clients. After all the system and language of *amicitiae* was based on the reciprocal exchange of *officia* and *beneficia* but what could a senator offer in repayment?[50] The emperor would expect a beneficiary's loyalty (*fides*) and gratitude (*gratia*) but there is clearly no equality in this relationship.[51] In other words all senators, equestrians and people of the empire were clients of the emperor. This is what Marcus Aurelius and his predecessors (Caligula excepting) had attempted to hide behind the language of equality and *amicitiae* but it was this facade that Commodus chose to abandon after the failed plot of 182 AD.

The emperors now made the formal declaration of war by throwing the spear kept in the Temple of Bellona into the ritually designated enemy territory.[52] The emperors set out on the second German expedition on 3 August 178 AD. Some experienced generals and *amici* of the emperors were already campaigning. The Quintilii brothers were probably advising their sons who were the governors of the two Pannonias. Pertinax had been moved from Lower Moesia to Dacia. Accompanying the emperors to supplement their *consilium* went the two Praetorian Prefects, Perennis and Paternus, Paternus seeking to avenge his humiliating defeat in 171 AD. Also present was Bruttius Praesens, Commodus' new father-in-law, his brother-in-law Claudius Pompeianus, Junius Maximus and Vitruvius Pollio. Pollio, a patrician, was married to Anna Fundania Faustina, cousin of Marcus

Aurelius; he had accompanied the emperor on previous campaigns on the Danube from 168 AD. In 175 AD he was in Rome guarding Commodus at the start of Avidius Cassius' revolt, depicted on coins standing behind Commodus as the young Caesar distributing *liberalitas* to the people.[53] His outstanding military service was rewarded by the erections of two statues to him, one in the Forum of Trajan and the other at the Temple of Antoninus and Faustina. His loyalty during Cassius' revolt was further rewarded with the ordinary consulship of 176 AD. A member of the imperial family and a proven general with experience of campaigning beyond the Danube, his advice would be vital in the coming war. He died sometime before 180 AD of natural causes. The other senator of vast military experience was Junius Maximus, an *amicus* of the co-emperor Verus; he had campaigned with him in the east against the Parthians and gave a victory address to Marcus Aurelius on Verus' behalf.[54]

The imperial party probably arrived at their headquarters on the Danube too late in the campaigning season to have any impact upon the course of the war for that year. However time was used to plan for the campaigns of the following year and make some surprising appointments. The vastly experienced general Pertinax was transferred from Dacia to be Governor of Syria.[55] There must clearly have been continued unrest in Syria which had been ongoing since the revolt of Avidius Cassius; otherwise it is difficult to understand why a man with proven military ability would be transferred from Dacia which faced barbarian incursions. At about this time the estates of a certain 'Depitianus, a senator, who had participated in the Cassian frenzy', were confiscated and taken over by the imperial *fiscus*. This Depitianus is identified as Dryantianus, the son of Avidius Cassius who was allowed to retain half his father's property.[56] We are not told how or why this man died but confiscation of property was often exacted as punishment for *maiestas* or treason. It needs to be noted as well that Manilius, Cassius' *ab epistulis Latinis*, was still at large only to be captured a few years later in the reign of Commodus (see note 81 of Chapter 1). To survive undetected for that amount of time must have required some kind of support network from adherents of the usurper. The loyalty of Syria was continuing to cause the emperors concern. Egypt had also been a centre of Cassius' revolt. T Aelius Sanctus, probably to be identified as Commodus' teacher of rhetoric and whose loyalty could not be questioned, was appointed Prefect of Egypt having been *ab epistulis Graecis* a little earlier, then a procurator of the *ratio privata* followed by the post of *a rationibus*. The post of *a rationibus* was one focused on financial responsibilities and so the men appointed to this post had no literary or legal expertise. Furthermore the post did not involve regular contact with the emperor unlike the posts of *ab epistulis* or *a libellis*. Consequently an *a rationibus* was viewed as a lower-ranking post than that of *ab epistulis* or *a libellis*. For this reason the career of Aelius Sanctus appears unusual and reflects the urgent need of a reliable pair of hands in this province. He was later adlected to the senate by Commodus for his services. Furthermore the only example of a man of literary background like Sanctus being appointed to the post of *a rationibus* comes from this time. Ti Claudius Vibianus Tertullus' career is recorded in inscriptions from Ephesus and Pergamum. He was *ab epistulis Graecis* in about 173–5 AD and then *a rationibus* sometime in 177–80 AD before becoming Prefect of the Vigiles in Rome.[57] These unusual careers reflect not only the precarious loyalty of elements in ruling the elite of Syria and Egypt but also the crisis precipitated by falling imperial revenues and increased outlay. These problems required a man who could investigate lost revenues from the Greek-speaking eastern provinces disrupted by Cassius' revolt and a man of proven loyalty. In the prolonged absence of the emperors it was also vital to ensure Rome itself was secure. Gaius Aufidius Victorinus, a fellow student of Fronto with Marcus Aurelius and *amicus* of the emperor, was appointed city prefect.

Britain also was causing concerns. In 173 AD Marcus Aurelius had sent 5,500 defeated Sarmatians to the province, no doubt to bolster the troops facing increased incursions from beyond Hadrian's Wall. As veterans they were settled at Ribchester in Lancashire but remained under special supervision as their loyalty was clearly doubted.[58] Q Antistius Adventus, an experienced commander who had previously been given a special command in the Alps countering a barbarian invasion was replaced probably by another general of extensive experience, Ulpius Marcellus.[59]

Another decision made was to appoint M Valerius Maximianus to command First Legion Adiutrix as well as adlecting him to the senate to reward previous loyal service.[60] Plans were being drawn up by the emperors and their *consilium* for the strategy to be implemented in 179 AD and clearly M Valerius Maximianus' role was crucial. Paternus was also to be given a large force to strike deep into enemy territory where fighting was already taking place, probably a smaller Roman force being used to draw the Marcomanni or Quadi out of the forests.[61] A Roman victory would allow the occupation forces to build fortifications to control the surrounding areas in a war of extermination.

Fighting broke out as planned at the start of the campaigning season in 179 AD drawing the barbarians and their allies out of their mountain hideouts. Paternus advanced with the main body of troops from Pannonia meeting the barbarians in a day long battle. As fighting was so physically intense battles normally only lasted a few hours before one side broke. However it appears the barbarians did not retreat but were destroyed in their entirety. Paternus had his revenge; clearly no prisoners were taken.

Some tribes now perceived that the tide was turning in favour of the Romans and they started to seek terms. The ambassadors from the Jazyges met the emperors, probably at Vindobona, modern Vienna, on the Danube. The ambassadors asked for release from the previous treaty restrictions. The emperors decided to rescind some of the previous terms to earn some goodwill. The Jazyges were informed that more terms would be rescinded once they joined the war against the Marcomanni and Quadi, which they appeared willing to do as long as the Romans continued the war to the destruction of these two tribes rather than come to terms with them as before. This fitted into the Romans' plans perfectly. As the Romans occupied enemy territory, the Jazyges in the words of Dio 'proved most useful', probably by attacking territory the Romans had not occupied.[62] Late in 179 AD the emperors released their allies from many of the previous restrictions imposed upon them, apart from those prohibiting the occupation of islands in the Danube or the use of boats on the river and they were still forbidden from holding markets or assemblies. One major concession was to allow the Jazyges to pass through the Roman province of Dacia to meet with their cousins, the Roxolani.[63] The Buri had also sent envoys but declined the terms offered and instead decided to pursue the war. The Romans' main targets for this year were the Quadi and Marcomanni.

Other tribes in north of the Danube also broke from the Quadi, Marcomanni and Buri, sending embassies to seek terms. However each was treated differently, depending on their past transgressions. The less fortunate tribes were allowed only temporary exemptions from tribute. Some more fortunate tribes were granted permanent exemption from tribute and taxes: these taxes must be on goods traded across the border of the empire. Some tribes were allowed to become Roman protectorates with guarantees of support and their leaders granted Roman citizenship.[64] Another group totalling 3,000, the Naristae, broken by defeats and attrition, were allowed to cross the Danube and were settled on Roman territory.[65] This divide and rule approach rewarded those tribal leaders who had shown loyalty in the past but, more importantly, isolated the Marcomanni, Buri and Quadi. For these total conquest and subjugation was planned: their envoys returning empty-handed from their audience with the emperors.[66] The ancient sources are clear that Marcus Aurelius planned to end the war once and for all by incorporating the territory of these tribes into two new Roman provinces of Marcomania and Sarmatia. The less reliable *Historia Augusta* states Marcus Aurelius 'turned his attention to completing the war' and 'had he lived longer he would have made these regions provinces'. The writer of the *Historia Augusta* adds that Marcus Aurelius previously wished to carry this out in 175 AD but was thwarted by the revolt of Avidius Cassius.[67] This is reflected in Dio who laments that 'if Marcus had lived longer he would have subdued the entire region' and the fact that the troops building forts in the occupied territories were also building bath houses, suggests they were intending to remain in the region for a considerable time.[68] A medallion of this year found in Cyprus shows a bust of both emperors on the obverse whilst the reverse carries the slogan *propaga/toribus/imperii* which Birley and Hekster convincingly argue translates as 'one who enlarges the empire'.[69]

Whether annexation of these territories was in fact advisable is now starting to be questioned by modern historians, although the ancient sources are united in their condemnation of Commodus' abandonment of this project after the death of his father.[70] Frank McLynn suggests the northern frontier of these new provinces would lie at the Sudeten Tatra Mountains covering parts of modern Bavaria and Slovakia. A frontier line defined by mountains is far more defensible than one defended by a river, however a vast salient would have been created by the incorporation of these provinces that would be exposed on three sides and so vulnerable to invasion from the Lazyges, now Rome's supposed allies, to the east. This would have precipitated the need for further expansion. The war was also financially draining on the already stretched resources of the empire, especially with the plague ravaging the army and the population at large. Roads and towns would also need to be built and a provincial administration created.[71]

The Marcomanni and Quadi were now subjected to a war of annihilation. Twenty thousand soldiers, mostly auxiliaries supplemented by vexillations of legionaries were stationed in forts north of the Danube. Their job was to prevent the pasturing of livestock, tilling of the soil or collection of food.[72] The panels from the Column of Marcus Aurelius, although based on actions earlier in the war, give an indication of the brutality of the occupying forces. The panels show villages burnt, women and children cut down as they try to escape, beheadings, and imploring captives are dragged away in chains surrounded by weeping women. There are no similar scenes on Trajan's column. These barbarians had repeatedly broken treaties, disputed Roman dominance and threatened Italy itself. There was to be no clemency, they had to be utterly defeated and exterminated.[73] The Romans started to receive large numbers of enemy deserters and also many who had been captured during the invasions of Roman territory. Normally the Romans retreated from enemy territory in the winter months but an inscription discovered on the top of a cliff at Trencin in Slovakia dated to the winter of 178/9 AD records the presence of Valerius Maximus with a vexillation of legionaries from the Second Adiutrix to which he had been transferred. The inscription reads:

Made by 855 legionaries of the Imperial victory, who are stationed in Laugaricio. Made under the supervision of Maximus, legate of the Second Legion.

The Quadi broke and sought to move en masse to the territory of the Semnones, the cousins of the Suebi. Roman troops however barred the roads preventing their departure.[74] Dio is clear that the emperors' primary aim was punishing the tribes by avenging previous Roman defeats and restoring Roman honour. Honour was restored by vengeance, a concept widely accepted in the ancient world. Trajan built his monument on the banks of the Danube following his successful campaigns against the Dacians to 'Mars the Avenger' at Adamklissi in Bulgaria following Dacian defeats of Roman armies in the past.[75] It was Tacitus who famously said: 'The Romans create a wasteland and call it peace.' However merely blocking the roads would not prevent the migration of all the Germans and Herodian is explicit that some did manage to escape from Roman occupied land to their neighbours: 'There were some who had fallen back for the time being and retreated in fear at the presence of the emperor.' Herodian is also clear that the Marcomanni, Quadi and Buri were not yet completely subdued.[76] For this reason both emperors remained in their headquarters on the banks of the Danube over the winter of 178/9 AD despite the presence of the plague.

In March 180 AD Marcus Aurelius fell ill. He was 58–years–old and had suffered from almost continuous boughts of illness all his life, most recently when Galen had performed a miraculous cure on him whilst in Rome in 177 AD.[77] The illness was not sudden but the emperor realized that his chances of recovery were slim.[78] Marcus Aurelius summoned his son to him and according to the *Historia Augusta* urged his son to continue the campaign. Commodus apparently was concerned about catching the illness, remembering the demise of Verus from the plague whilst returning from the front and wanted to leave as soon as possible but he delayed for a few days. The late Roman historian Aurelius Victor provides Commodus' response: 'For when he was being advised by his father in his will not to allow the barbarians, who were now exhausted, to regain strength, he had responded that, although negotiations could be completed over a period of time by a live man, nothing could to be completed by a dead man.' Wanting to hasten death the emperor then refused food and water, until after six days, he summoned his *amici* and Commodus.[79] Commodus had clearly remained with his father to comfort him and also be ready for the necessary religious and political actions on his death. Dio however repeats malicious gossip from an unnamed source who suggests his doctors poisoned him, even though he was already ill with the disease, in order to curry favour with Commodus. Marcus Aurelius himself seems to have suspected nothing as he commended his son to both the soldiers and his *amici*.[80] Dio's own account does not appear to make sense, nor is it repeated in Herodian or the more salacious *Historia Augusta*, both of whom clearly attribute Marcus Aurelius' death to disease. Dio appears to have not questioned the biased nature of his own senatorial sources and most modern historians agree that Marcus Aurelius died of natural causes. It is doubtful any of our sources had access to what was actually said by the emperor on his death bed, but in the rhetorical tradition, the dying emperor is made to give a speech to his assembled *consilium*.[81] The emperor lived for another day and a night, his last password to the Praetorian tribune in command of the night watch in the palace being: 'Go to the rising sun; I am already setting.'[82] A fitting, loving tribute by a father towards his son.

Commodus is considered ill prepared for his new role as sole emperor in both the primary and secondary sources. Having spent most of his time as joint emperor on the Danube it is claimed that he would have neither had little experience of politics in Rome itself nor the business of running the empire, a task undertaken predominantly by his father as 'senior' emperor. Admittedly he had not held the offices of the *cursus honorem* but since 175 AD he had been wielding the supreme power of imperial office, being the designated successor of the reigning emperor. What could he learn from a praetorship or post of aedile? Such junior posts with little power were often handed out as part of the imperial *beneficia* as a reward for loyal service or at the request of an *amicus* of the emperor. Putting aside the bias of our written senatorial sources who wished to disassociate the father from his son, it is clear from legal rescripts and inscriptions that contemporaries across the empire considered Commodus to have an important role in the decision-making process. Commodus had accompanied Marcus Aurelius on a tour of the eastern provinces from 175 AD where he would have been part of the imperial *consilium*. The governance of the empire did not stop as the imperial party passed through these provinces that had so recently supported Avidius Cassius, as is evident from the composition of the group of prominent advisors who travelled with them. The sources record audiences with both prominent provincial representatives and foreign dignitaries. On his return to Rome Commodus is recorded as fully involved in legal decisions, and again on the Danube, the business of empire would have continued against the backdrop of renewed warfare. Most of the prominent members of the senate were present as part of the imperial *consilium* providing Commodus with the experience of working with these key players in politics of imperial Rome and they continued to form his own *consilium* on the death of his father. All his life he had been preparing for his role as emperor and for the last five years he had gained valuable experience in carrying it out.[83]

Chapter Three

The Turning Point (180–182 AD)

ommodus, now 19, was already Augustus and had previously received all the powers necessary to take control of the empire. For this reason there is no evidence of any formal vote of imperium by the senate. However the acclamation of the army was vital if Commodus was to commence his reign as sole emperor on a sound footing. The *consilium* carefully planned and choreographed Commodus' introduction to the assembled troops: the formal *adlocutio*. The new emperor's *amici* were judged 'the best men of the senate'.[1] These were the senatorial elite whose family had been ennobled by their distant ancestors holding numerous consulships. It was this elite group who saw men such as Pertinax as social inferiors as he had only recently attained this office.[2] Of the *amici* present on the northern front were Vitrasius Pollio (husband of Marcus Aurelius' cousin Fundania Faustina), the two Quintilii cousins and Bruttius Praesens, Commodus' father-in-law. All of these were from the established senatorial aristocracy. Also present were two men who had recently attained this status through service to Marcus Aurelius: Claudius Pompeianus despised by his wife Lucilla for this reason, and Valerius Maximus. Pompeianus' lineage was 'not sufficiently noble' since he was married to an Augusta who was the daughter of an Augusta.[3] Pertinax was absent in Syria and the noble Gaius Aufidius Victorinus was attending to his duties as Prefect of Rome. The two Praetorian Prefects, Paternus and Perennis would also have formed the new emperor's *consilium* on the Danube.

Herodian refers to most of the senatorial nobility being present at the headquarters on the Danube and from this we can assume that Commodus' sons-in-law were also present.[4] His admiration for Marcus Aurelius getting the better of him, Herodian praises the deceased emperor for marrying his daughters to leading senators who were not 'patricians of ancient lineage, nor men noted for their accumulation of wealth'.[5] He is incorrect in his assessment. Apart from Claudius Pompeianus and Antistius Burrus, the remaining sons-in-law were all from the senatorial elite. L Antistius Burrus, like Pompeianus, was not of aristocratic lineage. He was the son of an African senator from Thibilis who had not attained the consulship but served as legate, quaestor and governor of Arabia Petraea. He was married to Sabina, Commodus' sister, at some point before the death of Marcus Aurelius. Burrus was perhaps granted this honour based on the distinguished service of his father and his relative, Antistius Adventus who had served in the Parthian War as well as on the northern frontier dealing with the Marcomannic invasion of the Alpine area and Britain.[6] Commodus was also to grant him the honour of sharing the consulship of 181 AD with him which would have been his first appointment as sole emperor to this office. He was a man held in high esteem. Cn Claudius Severus, married to Commodus' sister Annia Faustina and son of Marcus Aurelius' *amicus* and fellow philosopher of the same name, had mentored Commodus in Rome before he was rushed to his father on the Danube on the news of Cassius' revolt and had accompanied him on the tour of the east. He was descended from a Greek family probably ennobled in the reign of Trajan, whilst Severus himself had been ordinary consul in 167 AD and 173 AD and chosen as *pontifex*, a much sought after priesthood. A son by his first wife was adopted by Marcus Ummidius Quadratus Annianus, the consul of 167 AD and nephew of Marcus Aurelius.[7] Marriage to Annia Faustinas and the adoption of his son, Marcus Claudius Ummidius Quadratus, was a singular honour and repaid by Claudius Severus through years of loyal service. M Peducaeus Plautius Quintillus was married to another of Commodus' sisters, Fadilla. He was the nephew of Verus through his sister Ceiona Fabia, and had been joint consul with Commodus in 177 AD. M Petronius Sura Mammertinus, whose grandfather was Emperor Antoninus Pius' Prefect of the Praetorian Guard whilst his father was consul in 150 AD, was also a relative of Marcus Aurelius' tutor and *amicus* Fronto and married to Cornificia. Commodus would make him ordinary consul of 182 AD. From the members of the *consilium* of 177 AD preserved on the inscription from Bansa in Africa we can assume that three were too old or infirm to travel to the Danube (M Gavius Squilla Gallicanus consul 150 AD; M Acilius Glabrio consul 152 AD; T Sextius Lateranus, consul 154 AD). C Septimius Severus is not recorded after 177 AD nor is P Julius Scapula Tertullus although his son would become consul in 195 AD, presumably having been promoted through the various magistracies of the *cursus honorum* by Commodus. Another *amicus* recorded on the inscription, M Bassaeus Rufus, had either died or retired whilst Perennis and Paternus were still members of the imperial *consilium*. Q Cervidius Scaevola would have been in Rome carrying out his official duties, whilst T Flavius Piso and T Varius Clemens may have been present but the sources omit their names, as they do Valerius Maximus. Piso was soon to be promoted to Prefect of Egypt, one of the most prestigious posts in an equestrian's career, only surpassed in status by the office of Praetorian Prefect.

The days after Marcus Aurelius' death were spent planning for the funeral and the formal *adlocutio* from the assembled legions.[8] Marcus Aurelius' body was returned to Rome to rest in the Mausoleum of Hadrian alongside those of Verus and Antoninus Pius, his adoptive father. In an extraordinary and unique meeting the senate and assembly, sitting jointly, granted numerous honours to the dead emperor: Marcus Aurelius was deified, given the names 'Pius' and 'Divus' and a golden statue was set up inside the senate house itself.[9] Coins were issued commemorating this event. A temple to the divine Marcus Aurelius, now lost, was also decreed and built by his son. The fact that Commodus remained on the Danube rather than accompanying the body of his father on its return journey suggests he looked to complete his father's designs and carry out the campaigns planned over the previous winter. Commodus' advisors then made preparations for Commodus' formal address to the troops. A tribunal was built on the parade ground outside the legionary fortress. The emperor attired in his imperial regalia marched to the altar alone and performed the traditional sacrifices to gain the favour of the gods. The emperor had already been enrolled in the priestly colleges and as such controlled all religious and sacred matters and was seen as gatekeeper and interpreter of the divine will.[10] The auspices were pronounced as favourable and so the emperor ascended the tribunal, followed by his fathers' *amici*, the army's most experienced commanders who had themselves led the assembled troops to victory: Paternus, Claudius Pompeianus, the two Quintilii cousins and Valerius Maximus. Surrounding Commodus as he gave his address to the troops they were publicizing their ascent and support for the emperor as well as forming a visual reminder of the continuity of rule and command from father to son.

Herodian's record of Commodus' speech contains a number of clichés which regularly appear in the ancient sources in contexts such as these. However these stock reminders of shared experiences, loyalties and dangers would no doubt have been included on the advice of his *consilium* to appeal to the veterans before him. The references to his own noble ancestry would have reinforced his right to rule, an ancestry which is referred to in all the sources as being unique, being born both a man and emperor and now the son of a god. There is no reference to ending the war in the speech; Commodus looks forward to further victories, extending Rome's frontiers to the very oceans themselves. The assembled army would then have acclaimed him, saluting him as *imperator* and together given their oath of loyalty. As was traditional at the start of a new reign Commodus ordered a donation to be distributed to the army and then he retired to the palace. The coins that were distributed showed an important change in the image of Commodus. Gone is the beardless youthful representation of the co-emperor, to be replaced by an older, bearded face that represented his maturity and also stressed the similarity to his bearded predecessors on the imperial throne. The Antonine dynasty was set to continue.[11]

Commodus, at this time, had no intention of withdrawing from the occupied provinces or abandoning the war as he is accused in the sources.[12] According to the *Historia Augusta* the Marcomanni, Quadi and Buri would have been crushed and the occupied regions beyond the Danube made provinces if Marcus Aurelius had been able to campaign against them for another year.[13] These tribes were however far from being completely conquered.[14] His son did wage war against them for another campaigning season employing the same troops and generals as his father, and no doubt utilizing his agreed strategy formulated over the winter when his father was alive. Yet the barbarians were not conquered nor was the area ready to be created into provinces. One of Marcus Aurelius' concerns on his deathbed as described by Herodian, was the fact the Germans had not been completely subdued and some had retreated beyond the borders of the two proposed provinces awaiting the opportunity to attack again.[15] What is clear is that Commodus remained on the Danube from the death of his father on 17 March 180 AD until returning to Rome on 22 October; in other words the whole of the campaigning season of 180 AD. Later historians preserve a tradition of Commodus fighting with distinction against the Germans during this interval of time: Commodus 'himself fought successfully against the Germans' whilst the Christian writers, seeming to hold a more positive perspective of his reign record that 'he conducted a successful war against the Germans'. The coins of Silandus in Lydia issued to commemorate his victory depict Commodus symbolically represented by Zeus throwing thunderbolts towards a Germanic warrior. An inscription recording the career of the equestrian officer Ti Plautius Felix Ferruntianus records that having served in the Marcomannic War under Marcus Aurelius as commander of a vexillation from the Third Augusta Legion, he was promoted to a procuratorship in the logistics office, as *procurator ad solaminia et horrea*, but then recalled to active service when war broke out again to serve as prefect of the *ala I Thracum veteranorum sagittariorum* based in Lower Pannonia. The inscription records that this later post was under an emperor whose name is erased, who could only be Commodus as sole emperor as he, unlike his father, suffered *damnatio memoriae*. The officer served in the Northern War under the command of Commodus as sole emperor and clearly for a significant period of time.[16] This is supported by a close reading of Dio. Commodus' campaign of 180 AD was directed against the Buri, probably as the Marcomanni and Quadi were being defeated by the continued war of attrition in their territories. Envoys from the Buri arrived at the imperial headquarters asking for terms but Commodus refused as they still remained strong and remained a potent threat to the security of the empire. He then launched an offensive against them which must have been very successful as the Buri again requested terms, only to be again refused. Towards the end of the campaigning season Commodus was satisfied that the Buri were exhausted and, receiving their envoys, granted peace terms. Hostages were taken from the Buri who would have been leading tribal leaders or their children, and they were prohibited from entering a five mile strip of land along the border of the province of Dacia. Thousands of Roman captives were returned as well as 15,000 prisoners from unspecified 'others', probably the Alani.[17]

Whilst campaigning against the Buri, Commodus would have received worrying news from Britain. The tribes north of Hadrian's Wall invaded the Roman province 'to do much mischief and cut down a Roman general together with his troops ... Commodus became greatly alarmed and sent Ulpius Marcellus against them'.[18] It may have been the legate of the Sixth Legion Victrix based in York who was cut down, as an inscription records a vexillation from the Second Legion Italica reinforcing the Sixth. More probably this commander was Ulpius Marcellus' replacement as governor with his bodyguard who were the unlucky victims of the invasion, necessitating Marcellus' urgent return.[19] Damage, as evidenced by burnt timbers to the forts at Halton, Chesters, Rudchester and Corbridge can be attributed to this invasion.[20] Ulpius Marcellus had experience of the province having replaced Antistius Adventus as governor of Britain a few years earlier, but he had himself been moved on and was probably returning to Rome when he received the imperial instructions to return.[21]

Herodian refers to a *consilium* summoned by Commodus where the emperor sought advice on the continuation of the war after the emperor had supposedly been suborned by 'some of the imperial household' who urged him to return to the pleasures of Rome. This desire to return to the pleasures of the capital seems doubtful as Commodus had been present on the Danube commanding armies since August 178 AD. What access Herodian and Dio had to what was discussed in the *consilium* has to be questioned. Both Herodian and Dio seem deliberately unaware of more pressing political and military issues that would have concerned both the emperor and his *amici*. Herodian has Commodus express concerns of a coup in Rome in his absence by members of wealthy nobles in Rome.[22] Commodus would remember the instability caused by Avidius Cassius' revolt in 175 AD and the need of his father to secure the capital in case wealthy nobles rose in support of the usurper. It had been two years since Commodus had been in the city and Herodian later in his work emphasizes the importance of a new emperor returning to Rome immediately upon ascending the throne.[23] In 182 AD the emperor's fears were to be realized when members of the imperial family and some of the most prominent senatorial nobles formed a conspiracy to murder him. Commodus' actions however suggest this was not the major topic of discussion at the *consilium*, for the emperor remained at the front 'for a time', that time being the ending of the campaigning season in October. Of more concern to the emperor may have been events in Britain. Dio famously compared the reigns of Marcus Aurelius to that of his son: 'our history now descends from a kingdom of gold to one of iron and rust.' This idealized view of Marcus Aurelius' reign is reflected in all the sources but it does not stand up to close scrutiny. The German tribes were still a threat on Rome's borders and the two proposed provinces were far from being pacified, the empire was financially stretched with the treasury empty, leading to debasement of the coinage since 169 AD. The east had recently risen in revolt with clear evidence linking Avidius Cassius to leading senators in Rome and the emperor's wife herself implicated. The loyalty of Syria remained questionable. One of Commodus' first acts was to rescind the punishments his father had placed on Antioch in order to reduce the risk of rebellion. Plague continued to ravage the empire, reducing revenue and recruits for the army. In 178 AD a 'sudden mortality at Socnopaiou Nesos in Egypt reduced the tax payers by about one third in two months'.[24] The soldiers campaigning on the Danube were drawn from across the empire, and had been fighting almost continually over the previous decade, many having left behind wives and children. Areas of the empire were also starting to suffer from banditry caused by desertion and runaway slaves as many army units had been drawn to the war zone and away from the interior. Finally the province of Britain was now suffering major incursions. Commodus had inherited many problems on the death of his father. It is therefore more surprising that Commodus remained on the Danube to attempt to fulfil the promises he made to Marcus Aurelius than returning to Rome earlier.

Dio's account compresses the events of 180 AD to create an impression of Commodus abruptly drawing the war to a close in order to return to Rome: 'after making a truce with the barbarians he hastened to Rome'.[25] Commodus had indeed made a truce with the barbarians, but only the Buri initially and not the Marcomanni or the Quadi. Dio refers to a separate delegation of envoys from the Marcomanni, who sent only two of their chief men and two of inferior rank to the emperor before he returned to Rome. Dio seems to suggest that this was meant as an insult to the emperor; however what it really suggests is a division amongst the elite of the tribe with some wanting peace with Rome and others wishing to continue the war. Commodus followed a policy of divide and rule, came to terms with the 'peace party' but continued the war against those elements that remained hostile to Rome. These groups probably joined with the Quadi and the war against them continued into 181 AD. That the Quadi later had to provide 13,000 soldiers to the Roman army as part of their peace terms rather than a 'smaller number' from the Marcomanni suggests that they were being punished for continuing the war when most of the barbarian tribes had come to terms.[26] What was clear from the terms offered to the Marcomannic and Quadi chiefs was that Commodus had abandoned plans for creating two new provinces beyond the Danube.

Herodian can be used to supplement the account in Dio. Commodus, at the end of the campaigning season sent letters to all of his commanders providing them with detailed instructions on the continuation of the war against the Quadi when the new campaigning season began and allocated commands to experienced trustworthy commanders. The Quadi who had escaped the efforts by Marcus Aurelius to prevent their departure from the occupied territories were to be the focus of war for 181 AD as Herodian refers to the commanders' orders being 'to check the incursions of the barbarians'. These commanders 'soon either reduced most of the barbarians by force of arms or easily persuaded them to form treaties of alliance by offers of large subsidies'. The clear inference here is that the fighting continued into 181 AD. The tribal kings required gold to distribute to their sub kings in charge of the war bands in order to retain their loyalty otherwise rivals might lead groups into the empire in search of plunder. Herodian praises Commodus for realizing this.[27]

When Commodus left for Rome in late September 180 AD the army on the Danube became volatile with soldiers demanding a return to Rome for the expected triumph and the associated pleasures that they could enjoy in the capital or permission to return to their home stations and their families.[28] The fact that these soldiers remained campaigning during 181 AD has to be put down to the discipline imposed upon them by their commanders but Commodus will have been sent reports of this unrest and realized that the legions might revolt if the war continued beyond 181 AD. It was probably at this point the Quadi came to terms, being offered the more stringent but similar terms as those given to the Marcomanni chiefs.

The treaties imposed on the Marcomanni and Quadi followed the principles in the earlier treaty of 175 AD imposed on them by Marcus Aurelius. Roman troops were to leave the occupied areas north of the Danube but the barbarians were forbidden from entering a band of territory ten miles deep on the northern bank. They were therefore unable to use boats on the Danube which they could use in an invasion. They also had to hand over their weapons which, to a Germanic warrior who believed swords to be imbued with mystical powers and were even given names, was meant to insult their standing as warriors. All Roman deserters were to be returned as well as captives taken since 177 AD. A hundred thousand captives had been returned on conclusion of the peace treaty in 175 AD which reflects the devastation caused in the provinces bordering the Danube. Thirteen thousand Quadi and a smaller number from the Marcomanni were to be enlisted in the Roman army. Only one tribal assembly was permitted each month at an allotted place in the presence of a Roman centurion. Both tribes were forbidden to make war on the Jazyges, the Buri or Vandals. The reasoning behind this was the usual consequence of defeat led to the weakened tribe often being forced by the neighbouring tribes to leave the territory they occupied, precipitating further wars as such a mass movement of populations, placed pressure on bordering tribes causing further conflict. Acting like a row of dominoes, further incursions penetrated Roman frontiers. Furthermore the Jazyges were now allies of Rome and had entered into this alliance on the proviso that Rome would support them against future aggression by the Quadi and Marcomanni. An annual amount of grain was to be provided by both the Quadi and Marcomanni;

however Commodus later released them from this requirement, probably as their territories had been devastated by the Roman tactics of slash and burn and also as reward for their good conduct.[29] Commodus also made arrangements for improving the fortifications along the Danube and Rhine. A series of inscriptions from the bank of the river in Pannonia Inferior attests to the building of rectangular watchtowers and guard posts in Lower Pannonia to prevent the secret crossing by 'brigands', in other words barbarians. This work would continue from 182 AD until after 185 AD. A further legion was allocated to the area to help police the region and deter these small raids.[30] Recent archaeological excavations have discovered a new artificial frontier built 30 km east of the previous frontier limes complete with a ditch and bank topped with a wall walk and wooden palisade running for 382 km. In Raetia a stone wall was also erected replacing a wooden one. The suggested date for this massive enterprise has been conjectured to be the 180s and was probably constructed to replace the previous fortifications which had fallen into a state of disrepair. The fort at Aalen in Germania Superior forming part of the Raetian Limes was rebuilt in the time of Commodus. The fort was built to hold the largest cavalry unit in Western Europe, *Ala II Flavia Miliarria*, a double strength unit of 1,000 men. The fort at Ellingen, Roman Sablonetum, also in this province, had its wooden walls replaced by stone, as were all forts in both Upper and Lower Germania. At Oescus in Moesia Inferior a temple to 'Fortuna' was built at this time, some 30m long with a Corinthian portico, whilst in Dacia Alba Julia, home to the Thirteenth Legion Gemina and the town of Apulum was elevated from a *municipia* to a *colonia*, whilst Napoca was made a *colonia* by Commodus. Inscriptions honouring Commodus have been found in both Scythia Minor and other parts of Moesia Inferior. Archaeological evidence has been found for extensive refortification along the whole of the Danube at this time.[31] Archaeological evidence points to the increased erection of villas of the Italian type at the end of the second and early third centuries in the Pannonias whilst parallel activity can also be seen in Moesia Inferior.[32] Commodus, as claimed in the sources, did not abandon the northern frontier but appears to have put structures in place to restore peace and prosperity as indicated by the return of the wealthy elite to the area whose prosperity was based on land ownership and agricultural production.

There were a number of strategic considerations, both for and against, the abandonment of his father's planned provinces but the Danube frontier of Raetia, Noricum and the Pannonias remained secure for the next seventy years until the disastrous reigns of Valerian and Gallienus. This is a remarkable achievement of both Marcus Aurelius and Commodus. Economic prosperity returned to the regions south of the Danube with increased Romanization.[33] Commodus was the first emperor to take the title *invictus* or invincible; the Marcomanni and Quadi would clearly agree with this title. The complete defeat of these tribes as well as the Buri had clearly avenged previous Roman defeats and Roman honour had been restored. The resultant treaties had been made from a position of strength and the enemy humiliated. Commodus never placed Germanicus or Sarmaticus on his coins as he acknowledged that these victories were mostly based on his father's work. He did however issue two sets of coinage at this time, one for deification of Marcus Aurelius and the other to commemorate victory in the war of 180 AD where he was hailed as *Adventus Augusti Fortuna Redux* meaning 'With the advent of a new Augustus, Fortune returns'.[34]

It is academically futile to discuss whether Commodus was correct in making his decision to withdraw from territories of the Marcomanni and Quadi north of the Danube. Yet it is evident that his judgement was based on sound analytical thinking. All the sources however reiterate it was a decision Commodus made against the advice of his *consilium* and under the influence of 'parasites' attached to the imperial household.[35] Herodian appears to be referring to the group of imperial freedmen whom Dio refers to as the *Caesarei*. These would be imperial freedmen appointed to posts such as the *cubicularius* who was a chamberlain or *nutritor* in charge of the imperial bedchamber. Freedmen were given posts that equestrians also had access to; these included the offices of *a libellis*, *a rationibus* and *ab epistulis*. Their power lay in almost unrestricted access to the emperor as with access came opportunities to influence imperial decisions and attain *beneficia* for their own clients and *amici*. The first century poet Statius illustrates the power and opportunities proximity to the emperor provided by acknowledging the influence gained by being available 'always to attend the side of the emperor'.[36] These were ex slaves and, as such, were considered by the equestrian knights and senatorial classes to be of far lower social status than themselves. The senator Pliny, writing in praise of the rule of the Emperor Trajan, commends him for restricting the opportunities and status of his freedmen; he writes, 'the chief sign of an insignificant emperor is great freedmen. As most "weak" emperors were the slaves of their freedmen, by their advice they were ruled, by their agency they both listened and made pronouncements. By their agency they awarded praetorships, priesthoods and consulates which were even petitioned for from them.'[37] Under Caligula, Claudius, Nero and Domitian, all considered 'bad' emperors, as Commodus was, freedmen held considerable power. However by the very nature of their responsibilities they held considerable power and influence even under 'good' emperors.[38] What was different was the visibility and public recognition that these 'bad' emperors gave to their freedmen, men who had gained their posts through ability, expertise and loyalty and did not owe it an accident of birth.

The influence of Commodus' *cubicularius* Saoterus, from Nicomedia, grew during the year 180 AD, to the extent that senatorial sensibilities were shocked when this freedman sat in the triumphal chariot on Commodus' return to Rome, probably holding the golden wreath above the emperor's head and repeating the line 'Remember you are mortal.' It was commented upon with disgust that Commodus openly kissed Saoterus in the procession and afterwards in the theatre.[39] The Roman custom was to allow a social inferior to kiss your hand but a social equal was kissed on the cheeks. To ignore such social mores and publicly treat a freedman as an equal was seen as scandalous by the Roman elite. It does however reflect the influence Saoterus had on the new emperor. Another freedman whose influence was steadily growing was Cleander, who is described in a letter sent by Commodus to Athens in 186 AD as 'my nutritor entrusted with the care of my bedroom and my person'. (AE 1952 6) He was born in Phrygia, brought to Rome as a slave porter, sold into the imperial household of Verus and on Verus' death freed by Marcus Aurelius. Commodus appears to have inherited many of Verus' old household and so he entered the future emperor's service.[40]

Despite the rise of Saoterus, the senator Claudius Pompeianus remained the most senior of the emperor's advisors which suggests the absence or death of Claudius Severus who was from an aristocratic senatorial family, unlike Pompeianus.[41] According to Herodian, Pompeianus argued that withdrawal from the provinces would only encourage the barbarians to launch further invasions of Roman territory and was dishonourable. It would be highly surprising that Pompeianus would have called the emperor's potential actions dishonourable to his face. Furthermore Paternus' victory and the victory over the Buri, as well as the occupation and destruction of the lands of the Marcomanni and Quadi would suggest Rome's honour had been restored and previous defeats avenged. With the benefit of hindsight it is evident that the barbarians were not encouraged to invade Roman territory by the withdrawal from the occupied territories. It is also doubtful whether all of the *amici* in the *consilium* would have been unified in their opposition to withdrawal. Verus in 166 AD opposed Marcus Aurelius' plans for the continuation of the war and Avidius Cassius may have appealed to dissention amongst the senatorial elite by promising an end to the war in 175 AD.[42] This is what Marcus Aurelius is referring to when he recalls 'the issue' that existed between them.

Commodus left the Danube in late September and was greeted enthusiastically in the cities he passed through: 'Making his appearance through festive crowds, he was hailed as the darling of the people when they saw him.' Such was the eagerness of the people and senate of Rome to meet him they travelled a considerable distance from the city to be amongst the first to greet him.[43] The passing of the emperor had an immense impact on the provincial population. One of the best accounts comes from a century after Commodus but it does illicit the enthusiasm and near hysteria that this event caused:

All the fields were filled with crowds not only of men rushing to see, but with herds of animals leaving their remote pastures and forests; the peasants vied with each other in reporting what they had seen to all the villages. Altars were lit, incense thrown on, libations poured, sacrificial victims slain.[44]

The ritual of *profectio* or *adventus* would be repeated in every city the emperor passed through as the leading citizens of each city hailed him before their gates. As he passed through the city streets the banners of the various *collegia* would be hanging aloft, as well as images of the local gods and musicians played as the emperor passed. It was expected that this ritual be performed by the leading citizens and especially from the elite of the capital itself, each would try to gain the emperor's *gratia*. It was also expected that the emperor and his bodyguard would allow the leading citizens access to him so he could listen to their requests. The popularity of Commodus and his decision to end decades of war is recorded in Herodian's account of Commodus' *adventus* as he approached Rome as the populace emerged like a tidal wave from the city wishing to give 'a sincere expression of their emotions' bringing garlands of flowers and bay leaves. The whole senate left Rome and travelled a considerable distance in order to meet him on the road. The reasons for their enthusiasm were, according to Herodian, twofold. Firstly many were impressed with his illustrious ancestry being a descendant of emperors and patricians. Secondly his youth and appearance engendered admiration. Commodus is described as strikingly tall, muscular and handsome, his hair was so fair that he allegedly put gold dust in it, something Verus is said to have done and clearly a stock criticism. He is described as having 'more handsome looks and a better physique than any other man in his day'.[45] He was well proportioned, which you would expect as a man who trained as a gladiator yet according to the scurrilous writer of the *Historia Augusta*, his expression was 'dull'. This writer goes on to refer to a growth in his groin which was probably a hernia as his enemies called him 'ruptured'.[46] The enthusiasm and festivity engendered by the passing of the emperor had another reason consciously ignored by our ancient senatorial sources: the return of peace. There was in fact a tradition recorded by the late Christian writer Eusebius that the ending of the Northern War was welcomed by large sections of the population.[47]

On entering Rome on 22 October Commodus sacrificed at the Temple of Jupiter on the Capitoline, and then sacrificed at other temples around the city giving thanks for his victories. He then went to the senate, delivering a speech that Dio appears to have been unimpressed with. Dio was born in 163/4 AD and so in 180 AD would have been too young to have been enrolled in the senate; however Augustus had established the right of the children of senators to listen to senatorial sessions to gain experience of the procedures.[48] Dio describes the speech as full of trivialities, stories and lofty 'pratings'.[49] He recounts hearing Commodus describe how he had saved the life of his father who had fallen from his horse into a quagmire. It is unlikely the emperor would have made up such a story as many in his audience would have known the veracity of the account having served Marcus Aurelius themselves. Commodus showed due respect to the august body by, in the words of Herodian, gratefully acknowledging the senate.[50] The teenage Dio, listening to the emperor, would have been impressed at the time. However his views would have been changed by subsequent events and influences when he came to write his account of the vicissitudes of these years some twenty-six years later. From the senate Commodus addressed those troops of the Praetorian Guard who had remained in Rome during his two year absence as his safety depended on their vigilance and loyalty. He then retired to the imperial palace on the Palatine. The triumph was then held a few weeks later, described as *triumphus felicissimus Germanicus secundus* and the emperor was hailed *imperator* for the fourth time. The honour and status given to Saoterus during the triumph would have shocked those senators who had not been with the emperor campaigning on the Danube. Coinage was issued commemorating the triumph and significantly Commodus changed his praenomen from Lucius to Marcus having in 180 AD added Antoninus to his name, all in memory of his father but also stressing the continuity of his reign. On his arrival in Rome Commodus would have received welcoming news from North Africa where the Moors had caused considerable trouble, even invading southern Spain leading to the dispatch of Aufidius Victorinus to restore the situation. On 13 October, Canarta, the King of the Baquatar, made a treaty with the Governor of Mauretania Tingitania to become a client king.[51] The problem of Moorish incursions however was far from solved and extensive refortification of the Mauritanian frontier with the construction of forts and towers has been dated to between 183 to 185 AD.[52]

Commodus retained the same composition to his *consilium* as he had inherited from his father as these were men whose experience both he and Marcus Aurelius had drawn upon since 177 AD. These were considered the 'best men of the senate'.[53] 'For a few years he paid full respect to his father's friends, acting in every case on their advice.'[54] On the advice of Pompeianus, a native and patron of Antioch, Commodus had already rescinded Marcus Aurelius' penalties imposed on the city. It was probably at this time that the emperor accepted the honour of becoming *panegyriach* of the Eleusian Mysteries. He also became the first emperor since Hadrian to accept Athenian citizenship after ascending the throne.[55] This was meant to honour the city of Athens as the emperor retained fond memories of his visit to the city with his father, listening to the debates of the philosophers and his own initiation into the mysteries.

The problems caused by the plague would have been brought to the emperor's attention with its financial impact on imperial revenues. An inscription from Virunum in Noricum from 182 AD mentions the death of a whole family from the disease whilst a list of worshippers of Mithras from the same town shows five of the thirty-five worshippers dying in the first half of 184 AD. Furthermore analysis of leased land, issues of army diplomas, general documentation, inscriptions, brick production and coin production show a dramatic decline in volume over this time.[56] Later in his reign Commodus was forced to look for alternative sources of revenue to supplement the depleted income from more traditional taxes. However the senatorial elite in his *consilium* would not have urged an increase in taxes on the land and wealth of their own class and so the issue was ignored apart from the continued debasement of the coinage, a policy already initiated by Marcus Aurelius. Since 169 AD the currency had been devalued by reducing weight of the denarius from 3.85g to 3.35g and by reducing its purity from 79 per cent precious metal content to 76 per cent. However both weight and purity varied considerably throughout the reign of Commodus. Coin issues of late 180 AD and 181 AD, the vehicle used for imperial propaganda, proclaim victory, with images of the goddess Roma seated holding the incarnation of victory and a spear. Other images include trophies of arms next to captives and images of the emperor with laureate and cuirass.[57]

Although the Roman frontier bordering the territory of the Marcomanni, Quadi, Buri and Iazyges was now secure, problems continued on the borders of the Roman province of Dacia. Twelve thousand Dacians had been driven off their land by neighbouring tribes and now looked to invade Roman Dacia. The governor of the province, Vettius Sabinianus, who had been rushed to Rome to secure the safety of Commodus in 175 AD at the start of the revolt of Avidius Cassius, settled this displaced group peacefully in the province itself. Such an act would have required the emperor's permission.[58] The situation however descended into full-blown war as the tribes outside the province invaded leading to Dacians within the province joining their ranks. Lucius Pescennius Niger and Decimus Clodius Albinus are recorded as both winning fame fighting against 'barbarians beyond Dacia' and as both are mentioned together it would suggest they were the commanders of the two legions in the province, the Fifth Macedonica and Thirteenth Gemina.[59] The *Historia Augusta* says the Dacians were conquered and the provincial rebels crushed by the legates in the province. Commodus' fifth salutation as *imperator* on coinage can be attributed to the successful conclusion of this war in late 182 AD with coins carrying the image of Mars, the god of war, advancing right carrying a spear and trophy. A senatorial dedication by the consul of 182 AD, Q Tineius Rufus, offered in Greek to the Egyptian *theoi synnaoi kai symbomoi* for Commodus' safety and victory may refer to this conflict.[60] Sabinianus appears to have been moved to the governorship of Pannonia at the start of 182 AD, after completing the unsuccessful settlement of the 12,000 Dacians. Didius Julianus, after suppressing bandits as Governor of Dalmatia from 176–180 AD, was appointed Governor of Germania Inferior where he had previously fought against the Chauci. An inscription from the praetorium in the fortress at Cologne records that rebuilding work was completed during his governorship. The forts at Valkenburg and Zwammerdam were probably reconstructed at this time as well as forts along the coast to defend against further incursions by the Chauci. Commodus and his advisors were clearly drawing upon experienced and talented commanders in making their appointments. The situation in Britain was being restored by the harsh disciplinarian Ulpius Marcellus but it was not until 184 AD that Commodus took the title *Britannicus* on his coinage. The coins of 181 AD carry the legend *Magnificentia* and new coin types appear defining the new reign of Commodus where victory and peace are stressed (coins extol *Securitas Publica*, *Felicitas*, *Libertas*, *Annona*, and *Aequitas*). This would coincide with the successful conclusion of the war delegated to his commanders on the Danube and in Dacia and celebrated by games held in Rome.

The security of Egypt, the breadbasket of Rome, was always placed in the hands of loyal and efficient equestrians. Senators were not even allowed to enter the province without the personal permission of the emperor. The last such request was granted by Marcus Aurelius to Avidius Cassius to enable Cassius to use his Syrian legions to crush a revolt of herdsmen and bandits in the Nile Delta. The future usurper had carried out this job efficiently but he had also used this as an opportunity to build up a foundation of prominent supporters. The province was one of the first to renounce Marcus Aurelius for Avidius Cassius. Commodus would have been aware of the importance of Egypt yet he appears to have doubted the abilities of the equestrian governor who lacked the necessary experience or prominence. The Prefecture of Egypt was the second most prestigious appointment at the apex of the equestrian career, the prefecture of the guards providing greater opportunity to influence imperial decisions, whilst those of the *vigiles* and *annona* were not quite as prestigious. His old tutor Sanctus had probably been replaced by an otherwise unknown Titus Flavius Piso. Decimus Veturius Macrinus was surprisingly appointed to the post of Egyptian Prefect in July of 181 AD. He appears to have little previous experience and little to commend him for such rapid promotion. He had been governor of the minor imperial province of Tingitana. One suggestion provided by Birley for this unusual appointment, which he bases on the fragment of an inscription, is that Veturius in fact held a higher office as governor of both Tingitana and Mauretania at the same time. Another suggestion is Veturius had already had a prestigious career dealing with Moorish incursions or dealt effectively with a disputed succession in a client kingdom as recorded on an altar at Volubilis which Veturius dedicates to the spirit of the Emperor Commodus (the name later chiselled away) dated to 13 October 180 AD. A certain Canarta is described as *principe constituto gentis Baquatium*. It appears Canarta was chosen to lead the Baquates and was enrolled as an honorary adopted son of the emperor. As arbiter in such a dispute Veturius must have held a very senior post. After his tenure as Egyptian prefect was ended in 183 AD there are no surviving records of posts he held until he reappears when the Emperor Didius Julianus appointed him as a third Praetorian Prefect at the same time as Septimius Severus sent him letters appointing him to the same post. The fact these two aspirants to the throne would fight for the friendship of this man suggests he continued to hold high office, prestige and influence in the remaining reign of Commodus. In Syria the continued hunt for supporters of Cassius' revolt led to the capture of Manilius, the usurper's *ab epistulis Latinis*. The emperor refused to listen to the captive's entreaties even though he offered to name prominent supporters of Cassius. Instead, following the policy of his father and, no doubt, the advice of his senatorial *amici*, Commodus ordered all the correspondence publicly burnt without reading any. Many senators in Rome would have been greatly relieved. Commodus though had nothing to gain by reminding the world of the involvement of his mother in the conspiracy. Continued fear of unrest in the province of Syria and the continued influence of Commodus' *amicus* Pompeianus is shown in the building of massive public baths in Antioch named the Commodianum, a Temple to Olympian Zeus and Xystos with seats and colonnades. The Temple of Athena was also restored and money provided for a reorganization of the Olympic Games in the city and other festivals.[61]

From his actions it is evident that there was a great deal of continuity between the father's policies and the son's reflecting the continued advice of Marcus Aurelius' old advisors, a manner of government Herodian characterizes using the word 'restrained'. The ordinary consular list demonstrates this continuation of the power of Marcus Aurelius' *amici*. Commodus shared the consulship of 181 AD with his brother-in-law Burrus and that of 182 AD was given to another brother-in-law, the noble Marcus Petronius Sura Mamertinus; the other post being allocated to the otherwise unknown Q Tineius Rufus. In 182 AD Commodus would have allocated the consuls for the next year: his father's old friend and *amicus*, Aufidius Victorinus, was given the honour of a second consulship which he was to share with the emperor whilst a suffect consulship was to be given to M Egnatius Postumus, also from an aristocratic senatorial family. Members of the imperial family only held the ordinary consulship on seven occasions between 180 and 193 AD, allowing greater opportunity to honour and reward other members of the senatorial nobility: these included Cassius Apronius (consul 184 AD), Atticus Bradua (consul 185 AD), Lucius Septimius Severus (consul 190 AD) and Quintus Tineius Sacredos (consul 192 AD). All were members of prominent noble families or distinguished commanders. The emperor also sent his father-in-law, C Bruttius Praesens to Urso in Spain as *curator rei publicae* probably to restore damage caused by the Moors in their incursions during the reign of Marcus Aurelius. Appius Sabinus was made *corrector* of the free cities of Africa and the eminent senator Ti Claudius Candidus was made *logistes* of Nicomedia and Ephesus, probably managing the vast amount of funds allocated to rebuilding work caused by the earthquake. Candidus had been responsible for the logistics on the resumption of the war on the Danube by Marcus Aurelius and Commodus and would continue to have an illustrious career, eventually serving the emperor Septimius Severus. Commodus held banquets in the evenings inviting members of these senatorial elites so they could have access to him and, to cement the connections between his brother-in-law and the imperial family, a relative of Pompeianus was betrothed to Lucilla's daughter.[62]

The influence of the senatorial aristocracy however was under increasing challenge from the growth in power and influence of Saoterus. The imperial freedmen and slaves were, unlike the senatorial and equestrian magistrates and *amici*, the real professional bureaucrats of the imperial administration providing whatever specialist skills the emperor needed.[63] It is no wonder that Commodus began to rely so heavily on his *cubicularius* and other freedmen. Commodus granted the ex slave a fictive status as a man of free birth through the *ius aureorum anulorum*, no doubt at the freedman's request in an attempt to raise his status in the eyes of the social elite.[64] Dio records that Saoterus' influence became so great that he obtained from the senate the privilege of celebrating some games and erecting a temple to Commodus in the city of Nicomedia.[65] Coins from the city confirm that the request also permitted a priesthood to be created with associated games, a *neocorate*. This request therefore was more likely to have come first to the attention of Commodus who then referred the issue to the senate. Talbert questions whether Saoterus' influence must have been brought to bear on the emperor in order to be granted the right to have the issue presented to the senate.[66] The simple answer is he had influence over both. Saoterus, through his access to the emperor would have become a powerful patron himself with members of the senate who weren't themselves *caesari amici* (friends of the emperor) or had patrons who were.[67] These aspiring and ambitious senators would have sought the patronage of the *cubicularius* hoping he would use his imperial influence to gain *beneficia* for themselves or their own clients. Personal contact with the emperor was vital in having requests and petitions granted and the *cubicularius* was in an ideal position to channel imperial *beneficia*; he could even refuse admission to the emperor's presence.[68] The senatorial friends of the emperor saw themselves as the rightful brokers and mediators of imperial patronage enabling them to build up their own extensive network of *amici* and clients. Senators would therefore be keen to support Saoterus in the senate to gain his *gratia* and so hope to obligate him into returning the favour at a future date. This was how a complex reciprocal network of relationships built up and was embedded in Roman society.[69] Even the gods required sacrifice as repayment for their *beneficia* whether it be for good luck, prosperity or survival in a storm. The senatorial writers express intense dislike at the humiliations suffered by fellow senators who had to seek *gratia* from imperial women, freedmen or slaves to advance their careers. There were two types of relationship in Roman society: that between equals as expressed in the language of *amicitiae* phrased in the bonds of friendship, and that of patron and client based on the social inferiority of the client. The sources themselves try to avoid the use of the words 'client' and 'patron' as it was perceived as degrading and humiliating for the social inferior.[70] The Roman poet Martial describing canvassing during the early Principate gives some indication of the humiliations suffered by proud senators seeking the highest offices of state:

> If you wish to be consul, you must lose your sleep, run around, kiss hands, rot away at other men's doors, say and do many undignified things, send gifts to many and daily tokens to some. And what is the result? Twelve bundles of rods, sitting three or four times on the tribunal, giving circus games, and distributing dinners in baskets.[71]

Seeking such *gratia* from a freedman deemed of lower social status than an equestrian or senator of long noble ancestry was seen as a social inversion as patronal favours had to be accepted or bribes given to a man who was once a slave. Such senators would have to treat with Saoterus using the language of *amicitiae* inferring social equality, yet they would have felt that it was the social superior who was being placed in the inferior social position of client. Epitectus who was the slave of Epaphroditos at the court of Nero wrote that senators, forced to cultivate such patrons, became 'the slave of slaves'.[72]

Resentment at the power of Saoterus amongst the senatorial and equestrian elite grew as it did against Commodus who allowed such men to wield such a great influence that they became powerful patrons themselves in competition to the noble senatorial families.

Within the imperial family itself resentments also grew, based on social status and court precedence. Animosity between Commodus' wife Crispina and his sister, Lucilla, escalated at this time. Crispina herself may have been pregnant, which would have weakened Lucilla's position in the imperial family further. Lucilla, once married to an emperor and herself the daughter of an empress and an emperor with noble lineage, felt she deserved greater precedence than a woman from a senatorial family. A daughter of an emperor could play a crucial role in the stability of the throne and play a pivotal role in the succession, so family relationships had great political significance. Massive political prestige derived from blood relationships to the emperor and imperial relatives could offer ideal rallying points for groups of disenchanted aristocrats to coalesce around, and promote an alternative emperor and successor. If the daughter of the emperor entered into a relationship with any aristocrat, the threat to the emperor was potentially grave indeed.[73]

Marcus Aurelius was aware of this and, no doubt to try and mollify Lucilla when he forced her to marry the low-born Pompeianus, he allowed her to keep all the insignia of her previous imperial position, that of an Augusta even though Verus had died. Commodus also agreed to this arrangement, allowing her to take a prominent seat in the imperial box in the theatre and, when moving around the city or provinces, have the imperial fire carried before her as well as the imperial *vexilla* (flag) and the twelve *fasces laureati* carried by lictors. Herodian though understood that Commodus had to grant precedence to his own wife once they married, yet Lucilla considered this an insult to herself and her status. Her marriage to Pompeianus was in 178 AD so it seems surprising that this should be cited as a main cause of Lucilla's conspiracy in 182 AD. However Herodian is clear that she had repeatedly complained to Commodus over a period of time but her brother clearly ignored: 'her continual, bitter complaints about her rights of precedence' and if, as the coinage suggests, Crispina was pregnant, she would have feared that her sister-in-law, as mother of a future emperor, would always take precedence over her.[74] Dio adds another reason for Lucilla's actions: hatred of her husband.[75] Pompeianus, much older than her, was the first consul in his family and he was a provincial from Syria. Commodus had probably refused her a divorce and with her brother's removal, she could gain her freedom from the husband she detested. All of the ancient historians name Lucilla as being central to the plot. She had taken a lover, Quadratus according to Dio, but Herodian names him Claudius Pompeianus; both would be involved in the conspiracy. Perhaps Lucilla used her charms on both. Quadratus is to be identified as the son of the Cn Claudius Severus, adopted by the nephew of Marcus Aurelius, M Ummidius Quadratus who is described as a young noble.[76] Claudius Pompeianus is identified as Claudius Pompeianus Quintianus, most likely the son of her husband's brother or her husband's son through an earlier marriage. As Herodian speaks of him as a young man, he was probably the former. According to Dio, Claudius Pompeianus Quintianus was betrothed to Lucilla's daughter at the same time as Lucilla was having an affair with him. He was also an *amicus* of the emperor, being invited to imperial banquets and accompanying the young emperor in 'youthful escapades'.[77] It seems very surprising that a man who had access to imperial *beneficia* and about to be connected in marriage to the imperial family would jeopardize all in a high risk conspiracy. Perhaps he had designs on the throne and his delusions were fed by Lucilla. The *Historia Augusta* does describe him as a fool and Herodian as 'an extremely rash youth'. The plotters must have considered who would be Commodus' successor. Ummidius Quadratus had the greater claim being a member of the imperial family. This link could have been further reinforced through marriage to the Augusta Lucilla. One wonders what Lucilla's plans were for her own child that she had conceived with her husband. Plans had been already drawn up to distribute largesse, probably to the Praetorians. Herodian's text suggests it had already been distributed which places question marks over the loyalty of one if not both the Praetorian Prefects.[78] Quadratus, supported by Lucilla no doubt, then persuaded a number of leading senators to join the plot including some of Commodus' *amici*. Dio records that Marcus Aurelius' two *amici*, the Quintilii brothers, Condianus and Maximus, had made it widely known that they were 'displeased with existing conditions'. The conditions being referred to must have been the exalted status, power and influence of the freedman Saoterus. No doubt other leading senators had similar misgivings and joined the plot. The sources are unclear when the assassination attempt was carried out but the title 'Pius' assumed by Commodus on 7 January 183 AD fixes the plot to late 182 AD.[79]

It was decided to murder the emperor as he entered the amphitheatre where Claudius Pompeianus Quintianus would wait in the shadows of the arches, presumably letting the bodyguards past, and then jumping out, stab Commodus with a dagger he had concealed under his cloak. The darkness would also allow him to advance on the emperor unseen and the narrow entrance would limit the ability of the emperor to avoid the blows and restrict the ability of his bodyguards to rush back to help him, as the passage would be blocked by people running to escape. The fact he was wearing a cloak suggests the attack took place in the winter months as wearing a cloak during the heat of summer would have drawn attention to himself. The plan worked perfectly until the moment the excitable youth jumped out, as, instead of stabbing the surprised emperor immediately, Quintianus shouted out; 'See! This is what the senate has sent you.'[80] The delay allowed Commodus to take 'precautions' and the imperial bodyguard had time to seize the assassin leaving the emperor physically unharmed. Quintianus was arrested and no doubt tortured and executed along with Quadratus. Lucilla was exiled to Capri where she was later put to death. The unknown Norbana and Norbanus, Paralius and his mother were also put to death. These were evidently not from the senatorial class and were perhaps *amici* or clients of the nobles involved. The words of the assassin made clear the key role of leading members of the senate in the conspiracy which the senatorial sources tried to play down.[81] Immediately Commodus ordered an investigation into the conspiracy led by the Praetorian Prefect, Paternus, according to the *Historia Augusta* and Perennis in Herodian.[82] It may be that Commodus appointed both prefects to investigate the conspiracy or he appointed Paternus initially but after his fall, Perennis was ordered to take over. The conspiracy was clearly widespread yet surprisingly few people were uncovered and punished immediately after its failure. This may be down to Paternus, who is accused in the *Historia Augusta* as also being involved in the plot, seeking to prevent his own unmasking.[83] Our two main sources, Dio and Herodian, do not implicate Paternus at all in Lucilla's conspiracy; in fact Dio vehemently denies it. If Paternus had been involved, it is surprising that the plot had not been successful, as those involving Praetorian Guards tended to be, for example the murder of Caligula. However David Potter points to the wording in the *Historia Augusta* which is unusually adamant in confirming that Paternus actively hindered the investigation into the conspiracy and was 'believed' to be actually involved. Potter suggests the senator Marius Maximus may have been present at the senatorial trial of the newly adlected senator and a witness to the evidence presented against him. The bodyguards that seized Quintianus may have been the *equites singulares* who were the personal Germanic bodyguard of the emperor not under the command of the Praetorian Prefects.[84] However the conspirators chose a very public area to attempt the murder, the Flavian amphitheatre. If a Prefect of the Guard was involved then the conspirators would have had access to the palace itself with its vast corridors and rooms allowing for a greater opportunity of success. Why choose a time to strike when the emperor would have been accompanied by guards if the conspirators had access to a less public environment where guards would not have been so close? Paternus' actions preceding his arrest also suggest he had no idea that he was under suspicion as he would not have allowed himself to be isolated as he was.

As the investigation progressed both Paternus and Perennis became increasingly aware of the hatred that Saoterus was held in by the leading senators and that this was undermining the stability of Commodus' rule. Being the highest ranking equestrians they must also have sympathized with the views of senators towards the *cubicularius* and looked for an opportunity to remove a rival to their own power and influence. They planned to have Saoterus murdered but their choice of assassins seems surprising, the *frumentarii*. These were soldiers employed as spies and assassins; in Rome they would have been based in the *Castra Peregrina* and reported to the *Princeps Peregrina* who reported directly to the emperor. In this instance this officer appears to have taken his orders from the Praetorian Prefects.[85] The murder of the emperor's favourite could be easily traced back to these commanders. The two prefects provided Saoterus the honour of escorting him from the palace to one of the nearby temples where they carried out a sacrifice. Having removed him from the confines of the palace at a prearranged time and the sacrifice completed, Saoterus set off towards his villa unaccompanied. The *frumentarii* lying in wait between the temple and the *cubicularius'* villa murdered him. Commodus was more angered by the murder of his *amicus*, Saoterus, than he was by the attempted assassination of himself by his sister and leading *amici*.[86] Paternus no doubt hoped to blame senatorial co-conspirators whom he had failed to apprehend yet Perennis, described by the historian Dio who appears to admire him, was 'ambitious' and this ambition 'made him chiefly responsible for the ruin of his colleague Paternus'.[87] Although chiefly responsible, there are clear indications that he did not act alone; Cleander was also involved. Perennis appears to have implicated Paternus in the plot against the emperor, probably using the murder of Saoterus as evidence and deflecting blame from himself. The arrest of a Praetorian Prefect was always fraught with difficulty. When Caligula suspected his prefect, Macro, of treachery he transferred him to the Prefecture of Egypt, to remove his control of the Praetorians and then arrested him. Paternus was therefore promoted to the senate and to persuade the prefect to give up his secure position in joint command of the guards with almost unlimited access to the emperor, he was adlected into the senate with the status and rank of an ex consul. This is recorded in a fragmentary inscription referring to Paternus receiving *ornamenta consularia*. This is the earliest case of *adlection inter consulares* from equestrian status and was an immense honour. Indeed there are few examples from the third century and almost all were already senators.[88] The next few days allowed Perennis time to consolidate his control over the guard and then, Commodus accused Paternus of plotting against him and intending to make the noble senator P Salvis Julianus emperor, Julianus' son being betrothed to Paternus' daughter. Commodus' *ab epistulis*, Vitruivius Secundus, who was a close *amicus* of Paternus, was also arrested. All were then executed. The problem with executing powerful individuals was the enmity of their family and *amici* that this act engendered and so these were also accused of conspiracy, so removing a potential threat. Salvius Julianus was a powerful senator, his father being an eminent jurist who was in the *consilium* of both Hadrian and Antoninus Pius, whilst he had been an *amicus* of Marcus Aurelius. He also commanded the legions in Upper Germania and is stated as 'enjoying the devotion of the soldiers'. Dio's denial of Salvius Julianus' involvement in conspiracy appears to actually suggest he was aware of a plot against Commodus but did not actively support the conspirators:

> He had refused to make any rebellious move, both because of his own probity
> and because of the goodwill that he bore to Marcus even after that emperor's
> death.[89]

If Julianus had been aware of the plot he may have decided to wait upon events. Furthermore being aware of a conspiracy against the emperor and not informing him was treason itself. Communication between Rome and governors of the provinces was through the department controlled by the *ab epistulis*. It can also be conjectured that it was Lucilla's conspiracy that he was aware of, rather than the alleged one involving Paternus. Salvius Julianus' son was also a close *amicus* of Commodus who, according to the writer of the *Historia Augusta*, Commodus tried to lead into 'debauchery' and failing to do so, Commodus plotted against him.[90] Causes seem to be simplified in the sources to mask the true involvement and motivations of alleged conspirators. The son, Commodus appears to have not punished, perhaps in recognition of their old friendship or it was felt he was innocent of any knowledge or involvement.

Perennis, now sole prefect, took charge of the investigations that Paternus had failed to make significant progress in. The two Quintilii brothers, Sextus Qiuntilius Condianus and Sextus Quitilius Maximus, were arrested, tried and executed together using strangulation. An arrest warrant was issued for the arrest of their respective sons who Dio suggested 'even if they were not planning any rebellion, they were nevertheless displeased with existing conditions'.[91] One of the sons who was in Syria escaped, Sextus Condianus, the son of Maximus. He feigned death by falling from his horse and having previously drunk blood, vomited it up. Carried to his room he later made his escape whilst a ram's body was placed in his coffin. Dio, who was in the neighbouring province of Cilicia accompanying his father who was governor there, records him changing his appearance and clothing whilst wandering the province.[92] What Dio fails to include is what Condianus was doing whilst trying to evade his pursuers. Those details are provided by the *Historia Augusta*: 'he made his escape in order to raise a revolt.' The situation may have necessitated the sending of Aquilius Felix to the province. He is described as a centurion of the *frumentarii* and a notorious assassin of generals and senators, Condianus being both. The heads of persons resembling Condianus were sent to Rome but none were identified as belonging to that of the conspirator. Their state of preservation cannot have helped in this process. However Condianus disappears from history so at some point Felix must have got his man.[93] The fact that Condianus was already in Syria at the time of the conspiracy suggests that the province, which had a history of rebellion and unrest, was to be suborned in support of the conspirators. Suspicion would immediately fall upon the governor of the province and the legates of the legions. The governor was Marcus Aurelius' *amicus*, Helvius Pertinax, whose rule of the province is criticized for its greed as he sold military appointments and exemptions from service. The exemptions were probably from the costly magistracies in the local cities with their obligation to provide games. The *Historia Augusta* states that Pertinax received orders from Perennis to retire to his father's farm in Liguria.[94] Pertinax had failed to capture Condianus and his loyalty, already under suspicion, was again questioned. Septimius Severus, the future emperor, and commander of one of the three Syrian legions was also dismissed from his post, and, although we do not know the names of the other two legates, we can assume they suffered the same punishment. The *Historia Augusta* names Severus as legate of the Fourth Scythia legion stationed near Massilia before his dismissal, but this must be an error as the legion was based in Syria at the time. Syria had been the heartland of Cassius' revolt and Commodus and Perennis could take no risks. Unrest in the province is suggested by the punishment of two other senators from Syria, Aemilius Juncus from Tripolis who was exiled and Velius Rufus, the consul of 178 AD from Heliopolis who was executed. The hunting down of the supporters of Condianus by Perennis and his agents is referred to in the *Historia Augusta*:

> Not a few provincials, for the sake of their riches, were charged with crimes by Perennis and then plundered or even slain; and some, against whom there was not even the imputation of a fictitious crime, were accused of having been unwilling to name Commodus as their heir.[95]

We can infer that against most of these alleged conspirators there were allegations of crimes, probably by informers or *delatores*. It was customary from the time of Augustus amongst the ruling classes to leave bequests to the emperor in wills in repayment of imperial *beneficia* in the past and this act became symbolic of a subject's loyalty and goodwill. When Gaius Fuffius Geminus was charged with *majestas* (treason) in the reign of Tiberius, he took his will to the senate in which the emperor was named as co-heir, so proving his loyalty.[96]

Egnatius Capito and D Velius Rufus Julianus, probably suffect consuls from 182 AD, were also executed at this time as was Vitrasia Faustina. The Egnatii were a noble senatorial family with senators going back over seventy years. Vitrasia Faustina was the daughter of Annia Fundiana Faustina, a distant relation of Commodus and Titus Pomponius Vitrasius Pollio, a senatorial general of Marcus Aurelius who had probably died before 180 AD as he disappears from our sources. Vitrasia Faustina appears from inscriptions to have lived in Cales in Spain where she paid for repairs to the Temple of the Great Mother. There is no record of a marriage or offspring but she may have become involved in the conspiracy at the prompting of her brother Titus Fundanius Vitrasius Pollio, another young senator of noble descent. Another ex consul, Atiliuis Severus, was also exiled. Crispina, the emperor's wife, is erroneously included in the list of casualties of the failed plot by Dio who was absent in Cilicia at the time of the coup attempt and the epitomizer of Dio's work condensed the material as well as drawing upon events out of chronological sequence to attempt to illustrate Commodus' character. Crispina was still alive in 187 AD as she was honoured in an inscription of that year and also another dating her survival to at least 191 AD.[97] She did however fail to produce the heir Commodus desired; stillbirths and infant deaths were so common an occurrence that any mention of them would be omitted in the sources. T Claudius Pompeianus retired to his estates on the outskirts of Rome, humiliated by the fact he was seen as being unable to control his wife and his position as an *amicus* of the emperor fatally undermined. His son with Lucilla was allowed to have a political career and he was eventually seen by Commodus as his potential successor, attaining the offices of state, the *cursus honorum*, culminating in the consulship of 209 AD. He was to be murdered by the Emperor Caracalla, being the last surviving relative of Commodus.

There are two clear causes of this plot. Firstly Lucilla's resentments that grew from her forced marriage to Claudius Pompeianus and, what she considered, a reduced status after Commodus' marriage to Crispina. The key conspirators all had links to her. These conspirators then drew on senatorial resentments created by Commodus' elevation of the freedman Saoterus' social and political position, hence Perennis' and Paternus' desire to remove Saoterus in order to restore positive relations between the emperor and the senatorial elite. Whether Paternus himself was involved in the coup is open to conjecture and some doubt, but his removal necessitated the removal of Salvius Julianus, his *amicus* and potential threat. The sources are clear that both Perennis and Cleander were behind the fall of the Praetorian Prefect. These sources also try to create the impression that the conspiracy was led by Marcus Aurelius' old *amici* and the senatorial elite. Of the old emperor's *consilium* only the Quintilii were involved, victims of the political machinations they had been weaving since 175 AD when they had undermined Herodes Atticus with the help of Faustina at the emperor's court at Sirmium. Pompeianus retired, his position destroyed by the actions of his wife and kinsman, whilst Pertinax had conspicuously failed to hunt down a potential usurper. However many of Marcus Aurelius' old *amici* continued to serve Commodus and win promotion. Pertinax himself was to become governor of Britain and Urban Prefect and shared a second consulship with the emperor in 192 AD; Aufidius Victorinus continued to hold the urban prefecture and was awarded the consulship of 183 AD; Valerius Maximianus was to serve as a legate in Numidia and be awarded a consulship in 186 AD;[98] Acilius Glabrio was honoured with another consulship in 187 AD which he shared with the emperor, as did Crispina's brother and Bruttius Praesens' son in 189 AD and so did the son of Herodes Atticus in 185 AD. Commodus' brothers-in-law continued to be members of his *consilium*.[99] What perhaps we see is the resentment of young noble senators at having to seek *beneficia* from freedmen and the anger of their parents, senators, who had already achieved high office but now had to petition such low-born men on behalf of their children or their *amici*.

All the sources agree that the effect of this conspiracy on Commodus was enormous. Perennis took full credit for the efficiency with which he dealt with the investigation of the conspiracy and potential unrest in Syria. He had gained the emperor's trust to the extent that a colleague was not appointed to the Praetorian Prefecture as was usual practice. Dio's sympathetic account of Perennis, unlike the hostility shown him by Herodian and the *Historia Augusta*, praises the prefect for guarding Commodus in complete security. Perennis was now preeminent. The effect on Commodus is more marked with the words of his potential assassin striking deep into his psyche:

> The wound he received was to his feelings, by what was said. He never forgot the sound of his assailant's words.[100]

Commodus became increasingly reliant on men who had earned his trust as he became more concerned for his own personal safety. The main threats to an emperor were the conspiracies of those in close proximity to his person and those holding military commands. The freedmen and *equites* owed their position to Commodus' patronage alone, unlike the senatorial *elite*, and so these men of lowly status would, in the emperor's eyes, prove more loyal than some of the senators from the leading aristocratic families.[101] The hostility in the senatorial sources is derived from this shift within the imperial government. Commodus increasingly saw himself as holding the divine favour of the gods having survived childhood, unlike his eight brothers; the revolt of Avidius Cassius and his sudden departure from Rome and now the conspiracy of his own sister and other prominent senators. The first innovation to his coinage can be dated to this time with the word 'Pius' added to his title. The timing of this addition is not coincidence. He was not suddenly linking himself to his predecessor Antonius Pius, but rather contrasting his own link to the favour of the gods in contrast to the impiety of Lucilla and her fellow conspirators.[102]

It has been suggested that the emperor also attempted to associate himself with the mystical cult of Mithras at this time in order to increase his popularity with the army, many of whom worshipped this eastern god. A Mithraeum was built in 180 AD in the Castra Peregrina with its first priest being the equestrian A Caedicius Priscianus, who was also a priest of the *domus Augusta*. However as Hekster suggests, the building of the Mithraeum would merely be a response to the demands of the soldiers who were held temporarily in the camp until their orders had been completed. The appointment of Priscianus does not prove any link to the religious policy of the emperor. The *Historia Augusta* records Commodus' desecration of Mithraic rights by murdering a man but this act is not mentioned in either Dio or Herodian. The rites included the testing of an initiate with an imaginary killing. This act of impiety would be in complete contradiction to his title 'Pius'. Nor does Mithras appear on any imperial coinage or statues, as later the image of Hercules would in abundance. The fact he granted the construction of a Mithraeum in his imperial residence at Ostia does not prove he himself was an initiate; rather members of the imperial household were.[103]

Chapter Four

Commodus and Perennis (183–185 AD)

The emperor now felt vulnerable and, deciding attack was the best form of defence, he decided to sow conflict within the aristocracy by reintroducing the charge of *majestas*. The *Lex Julia majestas* probably dated from the time of the civil war at the end of the republic and covered acts of treason against the Roman state. As the emperor was the embodiment of the Roman state this included acts of conspiracy against Commodus himself. *Majestas* trials could be held before the senate, as the senatorial supporters of Avidius Cassius were prosecuted, or before the emperor himself. Marcus Aurelius allowed the senate to try its own but conspirators of other ranks he tried in his own court. The emperor could refer such cases to his Praetorian Prefects but often, when listening to cases himself, would have assessors around him to consult; these would be his *amici* who were often legal experts. *Majestas* was a capital offence, the convicted facing execution or exile and the confiscation of their property leaving their children destitute. This was followed by *damnatio memoriae*, where all records of that person's existence were erased from inscriptions and public documentation, as was the fate of the Quintilii. Often those accused of *majestas*, having lost imperial favour, would commit suicide before conviction allowing their property to be passed onto their children. The *majestas* law also allowed accusations to be made by men of low status against those of privilege, including women. The accused could have 'evidence' elicited under torture or, if this proved unsuccessful, their own slaves could be tortured to provide testimony against their masters.

The charge of *majestas* was often used by the Roman elite as a means of damaging or removing personal enemies and furthering their own interests. The senatorial aristocracy also used this law as a way of gaining the emperor's attention and his *gratia* as prosecution under *majestas* implicitly suggested a concern by the prosecutor for the emperor's safety. If any remotely convincing evidence was presented, the senate as a whole had no choice but to convict in order to prove its own loyalty and concern for the emperor.[1] The more ruthless would often prosecute a man who had lost the imperial favour as a way of winning imperial approval, *gratia* and *beneficia*. It was often men at the start of their careers or those aspiring to senatorial status who initiated these proceedings, the senate itself often being forced to condemn their own for fear of risking imperial disapproval. Commodus had the power to intervene, reduce a capital punishment to exile or even pardon the accused as his father had done. However Commodus wished to promote this climate of fear to undermine his opponents. On a more practical level he would have been unable to evaluate the accuracy of incriminating information. As the Emperor Domitian lamented, 'an emperor's claims to have uncovered a conspiracy are not believed until they have been killed.' A successful *majestas* prosecution also resulted in the accuser keeping half of the condemned's estates and property, the other half being confiscated by the emperor. The sources often simplify the reasons for the plethora of imperial confiscations of senatorial estates under this law as imperial greed or the personal vindictiveness of the emperor, whether he be Tiberius, Domitian, Commodus or Septimius Severus. This is to greatly simplify a complex situation where some accusations are made by the senatorial elite against their peers in the dog-eat-dog atmosphere purposefully unleashed by Commodus in response to the threat he perceived from some of the senatorial aristocracy. Other prosecutions would have been initiated at the request of the emperor himself using loyal adherents in the senatorial and equestrian classes. These men were well known to their peers and were both feared and detested. Another effect of this law was to allow men of lower status to get rich quick by accusing the wealthy elite of *majestas* and on conviction gaining half their property; these individuals were called the *delatores* or denouncers. This was a risky business as failure to prove treason often led to their own execution. Consequently they picked their 'victims' carefully, choosing those whose family were implicated in conspiracies or whose position or favour with the emperor was lost. Even slaves were able to accuse their masters of conspiracy. These would be crucified when Pertinax came to the throne. It was open season on any senator or *equites* who had caused imperial disfavour, hence Marcus Aurelius placing the children of Avidius Cassius under imperial protection: in other words a public announcement that they were off limits.

An example of the workings of the *delatores* were the accusations directed towards Didius Julianus who had responsibility for the *alimenta* in Italy, which provided grants of money to the poor out of imperial funds. As a relative of the condemned Salvius Julianus he was now vulnerable himself so he:

Was accused by one Severus Clarissimus, a soldier, of being an associate of Salvius in his conspiracy against Commodus. But Commodus had already put many senators and many distinguished men to death on the charge of majestas, and so he was afraid of acting too harshly, and therefore pardoned Didius and executed his accuser.

However, despite being pardoned Didius Julianus had still fallen under suspicion and he was exiled to his estates near Milan:

Didius Julianus, at once an insatiate money getter and wanton spendthrift, who was always eager for revolution and hence had been exiled by Commodus to his native city of Mediolanum.

The fact his career, and that of Pertinax, was resurrected after the fall of Perennis, suggests they both fell foul of the Praetorian Prefects' investigations of the Lucilla conspiracy, Perennis encouraged his prosecution without dirtying his own hands. However a significant number of prominent senators had been successfully prosecuted and were executed or exiled leading to a future shortage of men of consular rank. Consequently a number of loyal adherents were nominated as suffect consuls: L Tutilius Pontianus Gentianus; M Herennius Secundus; T Pactumeius Magnus.[2]

The acquittal of Didius Julianus is surprising as the *Historia Augusta* doesn't normally have Commodus worrying about the public's perception of him. Commodus was clearly taking a lead role in the pursuit of the conspirators and hearing the accusation himself, probably with Perennis, he found in favour of the accused based on the evidence and arguments presented and not on his supposed hatred of the senate. His actions show him to be no monster. However he was ruthless in protecting his own person and ensuring the stability of his regime as he gave free reign to the *delatores* throughout his reign. In 189 AD the senator Septimius Severus was indicted by ambitious informers, accused of consulting seers and astrologers concerning the 'imperial dignity' which was also a treasonable offence. Severus was tried before the Praetorian Prefects and acquitted, his accuser being crucified.[3] On Commodus' murder the senate broke out into a mass celebration chanting insults and invectives against the dead emperor, one being: 'to the lions with the delatores ... to the lions with Speratus, that we may be safe cast delatores out of the senate ... the club for delatores ... spies and delatores cast them out of the senate ... suborners of slaves, cast them out of the senate.' It appears Commodus' strategy of sowing division and conflict had been highly successful.

The senator Apollonius fell victim to one of these *delatores* who was described as his servant. He was accused of being a Christian. Apollonius, a man distinguished by his learning and knowledge of philosophy was brought before Perennis and questioned. His informer was also surprisingly punished for his actions, the distinction here being that Apollonius was accused not of *majestas* but adhering to a banned faith. As Apollonius was clearly a senator 'who enjoyed the privileges of birth and wealth', Perennis referred the case to the senate so he could be tried by his peers after the prefect had attempted unsuccessfully to get the senator to renounce his beliefs. The senator defended himself eloquently but he was sentenced to death by decapitation by decree of the senate. On ascending the throne after Commodus' murder Pertinax placated the senate by curbing the activities of the *delatores* and by doing so he hoped to gain the support of the noble aristocracy, as his political position was weak. He lacked the necessary imperial nobility as he was the son of a freedman. Pertinax cancelled *majestas* trials, banished *delatores* from Rome and bound himself by oath not to repeal this measure, whilst prosecuting those who had made false accusations. The varying degrees of punishments reflect the prejudices of the time as some of these *delatores* were senators themselves who escaped with a non-capital sanction, slaves however who had made accusations against their masters were crucified. All those accused in the previous reign were recalled from exile and the bodies of those executed dug up and given a formal funeral by their family with their memory restored and burial in the family mausoleum.[4]

The sources also have Commodus withdrawing from his imperial responsibilities delegating the government to Perennis and focusing instead on the pursuit of pleasure. The *Historia Augusta*, after Lucilla's conspiracy, says Commodus 'never appeared in public readily'.[5] 'Readily' implies that he did in actuality. Herodian says the emperor rarely appeared in public and spent most of his time in the suburbs of the city or on his imperial estates after the attempt by the deserter Maternus to murder him in 186 AD.[6] Herodian being the more reliable source is to be believed as Commodus is seen to attend public festivals after the plot of Lucilla, attending the festivals associated with Capitoline Jupiter[7] and leading a religious procession during the festival of the Hilaria.[8] Close reading of the sources also shows Commodus retaining control of the government: the excuse given for his murder was that he rejected the advice of his own advisors and *amici*! The sources show that the emperor still made appointments to commands and magistracies,[9] meeting delegations, receiving letters and *libelli* and meeting senators in morning salutations in the palace,[10] sending letters and instructions,[11] giving justice;[12] meeting with his *consilium* and listening to the advice of his *amici*;[13] honouring his *amici* with *beneficia*;[14] meeting with the senate. In fact Commodus seems to have dealt with petitions that in the past would have been dealt with by the senate: a request by the city of Aphrodisias in 189 AD was heard by the emperor himself, whilst a similar request by Miletos in 177 AD was brought before the senate by Marcus Aurelius.[15] Many inscriptions throughout the empire show Commodus' name carefully erased as he suffered *damnatio memoriae* on his death but they do demonstrate his involvement with provincial administration. An interesting quote from the *Historia Augusta* throws more light on the truth:

> Commodus himself was so lazy and careless in signing (*libellis*) that he answered many petitions with the same formula (*subscriptio*), while in very many letters (*epistulis*) he merely wrote the word 'Farewell'.[16]

This however was usual practice, the emperors receiving hundreds of such letters, petitions and requests from both imperial officials and subjects every day meaning the emperor's answers to *libelli* as subscriptions were by necessity very brief and were consequently informal, beginning 'name of emperor to petitioner' and devoid of any formal greeting or ending.[17] What the author of the *Historia Augusta* does make clear is that Commodus did receive, read and answer many petitions and 'very many letters'. You would expect that such documentation would have first passed through the hands of imperial officials for prioritizing, that responsibility was given to Perennis as he was sole prefect.[18] This was not unusual practice: the Emperor Trajan directed his governor Pliny to send prisoners from his province to the Praetorian Prefect; the third century legal work *Sententiae Pauli* lays down that officials guilty of extortion were to be sent to the prefects for punishment; in 177 AD we have evidence of an *a rationibus* who delegates an investigation into city officials' interference with imperial flocks to the prefects and prefects regularly heard accusations in the emperor's absence. Commodus continued performing the same governing activities as his predecessors and successors. What was unusual was the fact Perennis was sole prefect and the power and influence he held as he was so highly regarded by the emperor. A situation to be mirrored in the reign of Septimius Severus whose reliance on his Prefect Flavius Plautianus is commented on in the sources.[19] An emperor could not withdraw from his imperial responsibilities and expect to survive. Commodus was to reign for a further decade after the plot of Lucilla and his supposed withdrawal from governance. The limitations of Perennis' power are illustrated by an incident involving another *amicus* of both Marcus Aurelius and Commodus: Aufidius Victorinus. Commodus clearly trusted Victorinus as Prefect of the City which was too powerful a position to grant to a man of dubious loyalty as he commanded the *vigiles*, the police militia. He will also have remained a member of the emperor's *consilium*. Victorinus heard reports, probably from his own *amici* and clients, that Perennis planned to have him killed. Asking for an audience with the Praetorian Prefect, Victorinus asked him why he did not kill him there and then. We do not have Perennis' reply yet Victorinus remained unharmed and in post until he took his own life for unknown reasons. Perennis was unable to remove a rival as Victorinus remained an *amicus* of the emperor, to the extent that he had shared a second consulship with him in 183 AD and on his death the emperor commanded a statue be set to him in his honour. The emperor's *amici* were divided into three categories by this time: firstly, aristocrats who were daily companions of the emperor; secondly, those aristocrats the emperor asked to his formal banquets, *convivia*, in the palace and thirdly, senators and *equites* permitted to attend the imperial *salutatio* every morning in the palace. Victorinus probably remained in the first category having gained unopposed access to the emperor despite the opposition of the Praetorian

Prefect. The fact that Commodus' *salutatio* is hardly mentioned in the sources is not unusual, they are rarely mentioned in the activities of all emperors. If Commodus had discontinued them all the senatorial sources would have made detailed comment, as they did at Commodus' later refusal to invite aristocratic senators to his imperial banquets. The *salutatio* remained for all the elite a symbol of power and influence, the greater the throng awaiting the powerful patron, the greater their reflected glory. The imperial palace was built with this in mind, its atrium capable of holding up to 1,000 persons. However the importance of the morning *salutatio* for those seeking a successful outcome for their requests was greatly reduced in these circumstances as the opportunity for a personal conversation with the emperor in this environment was negligible. The *salutatio* was more an expression of loyalty to the emperor and attendance expected by the elite. This is reflected in Commodus' attitude and demeanour in his interactions with senators which is contrasted to that of his successor Pertinax who conversed 'with all the senators as though he were still prefect of the city'.[20]

Perennis did however successfully use his influence to have a son placed in command of the Illyrian armies. Another man who appears close to the emperor at this time was M Asinius Rufinus who was adlected into the senate with the rank of praetor in 180 AD and then possibly chosen for the suffect consulship of 183/4 AD, a remarkably fast promotion through the *cursus honorum*. His villa has been discovered in Acholla in modern Tunisia and an almost unique mosaic excavated in what was probably his *triclinium*. The labours of Hercules are depicted on large medallions around the room with the unusual placement of Hercules himself in a central motif standing alone. The pose of the demigod is identical to that of an imperial coin of 184 AD carrying the image of Hercules. A nearby inscription dated to before 185 AD as Commodus is referred in it with the epithet Pius and not Felix. The inscription has Rufinus proclaim a close relationship with the emperor which seems to be supported by his lack of posts held apart from the honorary praetorship and priesthood before being given consular status. It has been suggested that the image of Hercules used in the mosaic reflects Commodus' personal interest in the demigod, an association that Commodus was later to develop. The career of his son, Sex Asinius Rufinus Fabianus, has also been preserved on an inscription. He also held posts typical of the *cursus honorum*, many being held under Commodus. One of these was the post of *ab actis senatus* which was held in the office of the consuls. Rufinus' responsibility was to write the official reports of the meetings of the senate, which the emperor could easily control having the son of one of his *amici* holding this post, a post he seems to have performed well in, as he subsequently held the aedileship and then praetorship.[21]

The rising power and influence of new men with military skill and experience was a consequence of the prolonged wars fought by Marcus Aurelius, where military necessity meant men of proven tactical and strategic ability were promoted to important commands. Pertinax, Septimius Severus, Vespronius Candidus, Ulpius Marcellus, Valerius Maximus, Lucius Gratus Julianus, Seius Fuscianus, Paternus and Perennis himself were all of equestrian rank promoted by Marcus Aurelius to important offices of state and all, bar Paternus and Perennis, adlected to the senate by him with most going on to hold consulships. Commodus was merely following his father's policy on promoting men on ability, with all of these continuing to be promoted under Commodus: Pertinax to be Governor of Britain, Proconsul of Africa and then consul with the emperor followed by urban Prefect of Rome; Septimius Severus Governor of Lugdunensis Gaul, a suffect consulship and then Governor of Upper Pannonia with its three legions; Vespronius Candidus Governor of Dacia with two legions; Ulpius Marcellus Governor of Britain with three legions and he continued to hold high equestrian office; Valerius Maximianus was Governor of Numidia by 186 AD fighting Moorish incursions whilst Lucius Gratus Julianus became Prefect of the fleets at Misenum and Ravenna and later Praetorian Prefect and Seius Fuscianus, who had been a close *amicus* of Marcus Aurelius was to be appointed Prefect of Rome after the death of Victorinus and be made consul of 188 AD.[22] In 183 AD Commodus gave the suffect consulship to L Tutilius Pontianus Gentianus who was the alleged lover of his mother having been discovered breakfasting with Faustina by Marcus Aurelius and yet had been rapidly promoted by the emperor to the disgust of the senators.[23]

Where Commodus did diverge from his father was also promoting those who were ex slaves: a step too far for the senatorial elite. Commodus does continue to draw on the advice of senators. Three names appear at the bottom of three letters addressed to the Athenians, dating from before 184 AD when the emperor received the title Britannicus. The same names appearing on three different letters suggests they were not ambassadors to the emperor but advisors called upon by Commodus as they had expertise in the issues being discussed. The first, recorded in order of status, was named Antipater, but presumably of senatorial status as the second man named also was, and was possibly a son or grandson of Tib Claudius Antipater of Ephesus as the issue being discussed was the establishment of the Athenian Gerusia in the same way as the Ephesian Gerusia. The second was plausibly identified as the Senator Gargilius Antiquus who was raised to the patriciate by Commodus; his full name being L Pullaienus Gargilius Antiquus. The third may have been the Athenian sophist Apollonius. This event may explain why in 186 AD Commodus was invited to become an *archon* of the *genos* of Eumolpidae as the Athenian sophist Apollonius was a member of the same *genos*, an invitation the emperor accepted.[24]

The sources do not mention any young senators accompanying the emperor at banquets nor as companions after the plot of Lucilla. Commodus, after his betrayal by the young Pompeianus, Quadratus and the son of Julianus, appears to have been more discerning in whom he invited. Commodus still held banquets in the palace which were famed for their extravagance, not allowing any vegetables to taint his menu which might interrupt the 'succession of dainties'. If the biographer of the *Historia Augusta* is to be believed he liked to perform jokes on his guests displaying two hunchbacks on a silver platter smearing them in mustard. After the joke he then amply rewarded them with advancement and riches. However the *Historia Augusta* frequently repeats malicious gossip, rumour and invective as fact, stating that food was often mixed with human excrement adding the proviso, 'it is claimed' and clearly not substantiated. On Commodus' death much of the imperial property was sold to raise much needed funds and we gain an insight into the opulence of such occasions: auctioned were vessels made of gold, ivory, silver and citrus wood with cups in the shape of a phallus, a symbol of good luck and fertility, but also another example of the emperor's unusual sense of humour.[25] Banquets were used to express imperial wealth and power whilst an invitation to the imperial banquet was both an honour and an opportunity where the emperor, protocols relaxed with the informal setting, was more open to requests and petitions. Also came a raising in status as you were recognized as an *amicus Caesaris*, a mark that the guest had access to the emperor allowing him to extend the number of his own *amici* and clients.[26] There was an expectation that the emperor would invite his *amici*, the leading magistrates present in Rome and members of the senatorial aristocracy to these occassions. Commodus excluded the last two groups causing great resentment. One of Pertinax's first actions on ascending the throne was to reverse this:

> On this same day, also he invited the magistrates and the chief men of the senate to a banquet, a practice which Commodus had discontinued.[27]

The magistrates and the chief men of the senate were one and the same. The Senator Dio, contrasting Pertinax to Commodus, praises Pertinax as he 'conducted himself in a very democratic manner towards us; for he was easy of access, listened readily to everyone's requests, and in answer gave his opinion in a kindly way'.[28] Commodus was the opposite; the senatorial elite found their access to the emperor, restricted and often had to be sought through Perennis. To these men the job of the emperor was the distribution of *beneficia* to the worthy. A letter of Pliny preserves an edict of the Senator Nerva on becoming emperor; Nerva writes that he became emperor 'in order that I might confer new beneficia and preserve those already granted by my predecessors' whilst Aelius Aristides in an oration celebrating the birthday of Julius Apellas in Pergamum, a boy descended from a prominent provincial family with senatorial ancestors writes: 'Preserve his house, granting him such honours from the great emperor as his own ancestors gained from his ancestors.' He was born to a provincial senatorial family. Imagine the expectations of the noble aristocracy tracing their lineage back to generations of prominent consuls and generals, their images lining the walls of their homes.[29]

Epictetus encapsulates the complete reliance of those seeking advancement, honours and status on the emperor and how loyalty was completely dependent upon the *beneficia* granted:

> No one fears Caesar himself, but death, exile, confiscation of property, imprisonment or loss of rights. Nor does anyone love Caesar, unless he is of especial merit, but we love wealth, a tribunate, a praetorship or a consulate.[30]

Even then, when the emperor has showered honours, gifts, privileges, promotions and magistracies, he still failed to gain their loyalty. Seneca writing in the first century writes of senatorial resentments when their expectations were not met by the emperor:

> He (the emperor) has given me the praetorships, but I had hoped for the consulship; he has given me the twelve *fasces* (suffect consulship), but has not made me *consul ordinarius*; he wished the year to be dated by my name, but has failed me with regard to a priesthood; he has co-opted me into a priestly college – but why into only one? He has filled the measure of my *dignitas*, but has contributed nothing to my *patrimonium*. He has given to me what he would have been obliged to give anyone, but has added nothing of his own volition.[31]

There were only about a hundred senatorial and equestrian appointments each year with the emperor's support of a candidacy guaranteeing successful appointment, so many would be left dissatisfied. However the emperor could draw upon other types of *beneficia* such as money, estates, promotion for clients and *amici*, granting of Roman citizenship, equestrian or senatorial status, the *latus clavus*. Dio declares that Commodus was fond of bestowing gifts.[32] However such *beneficia* was reliant upon access to the emperor or his *amici* and this is what the senatorial aristocracy were deprived of.

Commodus had lost his trust in the aristocracy and he did not need, as Herodian claims, Perennis to sow suspicion in the emperor's mind.[33] That had already been done when the aristocratic Claudius Pompeianus Quintianus had tried to murder him declaring the senate had sent him. The problem for any emperor was that the very people who constituted his closest circle, who had greatest access to his person, were the greatest threat to his life, especially if they were high-ranking senatorial nobles or members of the imperial family. The greater the *beneficia* the emperor granted the greater the threat to his own position as the aristocrats' influence and power grew. Increasingly emperors from Augustus onwards had attempted to formalize their friendships with the aristocracy by granting them the symbols of power and influence they craved whilst granting real power and influence to those with the necessary skills, often legal skills, and discriminated in favour of those with more humble origins who posed less of a threat to them. Commodus appears to have returned to a solution that previous emperors had used when they had lost trust in the senatorial elite. They increased their reliance on imperial freedmen whose position and often life depended upon the preservation of the emperor who had promoted them. Yet even this was based on previous precedent. It was Hadrian who promoted men of lower status to his inner circle, scientists and architects. Philosophers were members of Marcus Aurelius' circle and, due to the pressing demands of the 'Northern Wars', men of military ability such as Pertinax. Commodus followed in becoming increasingly reliant on members of his own imperial household, the professional bureaucrats and administrators. Aloys Winterling suggests that it was the second century emperors, Hadrian, Antoninus Pius and Marcus Aurelius who were unusual in including aristocratic senators as their *familiaritas*, their inner circle of advisors. All three had been adopted to the imperial purple and had been brought up as aristocratic senators rather than as future emperors which may account for their increased reliance on men whose status they initially shared. Commodus was born to the purple, and although he was related to many of the aristocratic families in Rome, he was from an early age brought up as future emperor. His promotion of men from his private household, men such as Cleander and Eclectus, men of low social status in the eyes of the senatorial elite, again undermined the distinction between those who should hold positions in the private sphere and those such as the aristocracy, who by right of their *nobilitas* should hold positions of power in the public political sphere. The structures and concepts of the *res publica*, *privatus* and *publicus* had already been subsumed by the concept of *princeps* and Commodus' actions were a natural progression. The *consilium principis*, the emperor's advisory council, had no basis in Roman law and never appears as such in the ancient sources. Traditionally members of the emperor's inner circle of advisors were made up of members of the imperial family, aristocracy and equestrians with legal expertise and the praetorian prefects. Commodus as emperor had the right to choose who were his advisors and study of membership of this elite group shows it was ever-changing, emperors calling on those who were close enough to attend or had a particular expertise or background that could aid the emperor in making his decision. Commodus' overriding concern was his own safety and he would have known his history; Tiberius was rumoured to have been murdered by his Praetorian Prefect,

Caligula, the man whose birthday he shared, and Domitian by his most trusted advisors and members of the Praetorian Guard in Caligula's case and Claudius by his wife and her close associates. For this reason Commodus kept the aristocracy at a distance but the other main threat was the praetorian prefects who were always equestrians and so lacked the social status to aspire to the throne. It was not the whole senate that Commodus and Perennis feared but the aristocratic elite whose expectations of future honours through nobility of birth were far greater than the provincial senators who were often clients of these great families. This elite was described even by Dio himself as 'wealthy and vainglorious'. Their political power had been greatly reduced by the creation of the imperial system and because of this they now attached even greater significance to the symbols of power as a way of maintaining their social position: access to the highest magistracies, priesthoods and other *beneficia* from the emperor. Paradoxically the status of the aristocracy was now reliant on public shows of imperial favour based on the rules governing *amicitia*. This was not a relationship based on equality as the emperor held by far the greater wealth and power, yet it was expected that the recipients displayed public gratitude and loyalty to the emperor. Seneca in the reign of Nero questioned this relationship, condemning the giving of gifts on the understanding of a future return as merely an economic relationship. He urged *amicitia* to be based on mutual respect, the giving of gifts simply an act of goodwill with no greater expectation than wishing the recipient good. On both counts Commodus was disappointed as many of the recipients of his own *beneficia* plotted his murder.[34] When Commodus is murdered the majority of senators turned to this group in the senate house to celebrate their victory in their conflict with the emperor:

> To those senators on whom the fear of Commodus had rested the most heavily, the crowd (of senators) called out: 'Huzza! Huzza! You are saved; you have won.'

Dio would have been present to describe this scene and this group were evidently sat together. The senators who held the consulship were mostly members of the most aristocratic families, and those from the noblest houses sat together on the front seats in the senate house, the place of honour. These aristocrats were given the trappings of power and status they desired by Commodus, the consulship as the *consular fasci* shows throughout his reign. They were, however, denied the substance of power, membership of the *consilium principis* and being an *amicus Caesaris* with access to the emperor and influence over his decisions and actions. One such man was the consul of 185 AD, Triarius Maternus Lascivius, whom the praetorians would attempt to make emperor after the murder of Commodus and against the man's wishes. He is known from an inscription as a *iuridicus* of Asturia and married to a certain Egnatia Procula, the Egnatii being a powerful noble family, an Marcus Egnatius Postumus being made suffect consul in 183 AD. His sister, Pomponia Triaria married C Erucius Clarus, the consul of 170 AD, and their son, C Julius Erucius Clarus was chosen by Commodus as the ordinary consul for 193 AD, as well as being renowned as one of the wealthiest men in Rome. Both Perennis and Commodus needed men of senatorial status as they were the legates of the legions and governors of the provinces so it would have been suicide to declare war on the senatorial class as a whole, nor would such revolutionary thinking even have occurred to them. Romans reacted to situations, and Commodus was reacting to the involvement of a group of aristocratic senators in the conspiracies of Lucilla and Paternus.[35]

To a Roman patronage was based on a reciprocal exchange of *officia* and *beneficia*, an *amicus* in receipt of a favour was in debt with the expectation that the favour would be returned at the appropriate time with a show of gratitude. However the political and social position of emperor meant that this was not a relationship between equals, an illusion that the so-called 'good' emperors perpetuated throughout their reigns. What the emperor expected in return was *gratia* and *fides*. *Gratia* could be expressed through leaving bequests in a will to the emperor, expressions of thanks in the senate but, most importantly, loyalty or *fides*. Seneca explains that 'an emperor protected by his own *beneficium* has no need of guards, he keeps arms for decoration'. The conspirators involved in the Lucilla conspiracy had all been recipients of imperial *beneficia* yet had plotted to murder their patron, the emperor. Nothing was worse than an *ingratus amicus* and was grounds for breaking the bonds of *amicitia*. This is what Commodus had done in response to the disloyalty of the aristocratic senatorial elite. This action however removed the great senatorial nobles as the brokers and mediators of patronage as their lack of access and influence with the emperor removed their ability to arrange *beneficia* for their own *amici* and clients. Past emperors, including Marcus Aurelius, had produced social and political cohesion through these mutual exchange relationships extending from themselves, securing loyalty from the *amici Caesari* through *beneficia* granting them the resources to build their own clientele whose loyalty was indirectly assured through the client's loyalty to their senatorial patron or *amicus*.[36] Commodus saw such a system as broken as *fides* had not been guaranteed and turned increasingly to those whose *fides* was believed guaranteed as they owed their promotions and power to the emperor himself and not on social status, the imperial freedmen and *equites*. Also he felt those bound by close ties of family were allowed access to imperial *amicitia*. He trusted those who he had built a close working relationship since 175 AD, his father's own *amici*, as seen in the careers of Pertinax, Perennis, Aufidius Victorinus, Valerius Maximianus, Lucius Gratus Julianus, Seius Fuscianus and his brothers-in-law. The great patrons were forced to build up their networks of patronage through these *amici Caesari*, but in particular Perennis, hence the senatorial belief that it was the prefect who was now in charge of the government as in their eyes the distribution of imperial *beneficia* was government.

At the start of 183 AD 'Pius' appears on the coinage which might be a reference to his predecessor Antoninus Pius or in response to his devotion to his father, but more likely in response to having survived a murder plot by the favour of the gods who had recognized his own personal and devoted religious fervour as with 'Pius' also went *auctor pietatis*.[37] The attack had a psychological effect on him and, understandably, an increased feeling of vulnerability. In amongst the events, causes and consequences, we lose sight of the human being. His mother had conspired against him, his sister, his *amici* and some of those entrusted with his safety. Some historians place his move to the Vectilian villa at this point, however the *Historia Augusta* refers to the move as a potent of his final death, so it fits chronologically to the year 192 AD and a consequence of the palace on the palatine being extensively damaged in the fire of that year.[38] It is no coincidence that the new palace was near the coliseum and the gladiatorial training school. A tunnel was also dug from his new residence to the amphitheatre to improve his safety of movement, the assassination attempt having taken place as he moved through the dark arches of a building to which the public had access. The assassin had also to be apprehended by the guards themselves and the emperor increased his gladiatorial training in order to defend himself should any future murder attempt take place. As a young man growing up he had fought gladiatorial combats.[39] Clearly Marcus Aurelius had not disapproved of his son's activities and it was recognized that many senators themselves also trained in this manner, the Emperor Septimius Severus reprimanding the senate for the hypocrisy of slandering Commodus in the past for practising as a gladiator when many members of the senate did the same.[40] Severus stood before the senate, many of whose members had recently conspired against him, and ranted at those present:

> You will say that Commodus actually fought as a gladiator. And does none of you actually fight as a gladiator? If not, how and why is it that some of you have bought his shields and those famous golden helmets?

Other items purchased included a gladiator's toga and harness finished with gold and jewels, swords similar to those Hercules was portrayed possessing and necklaces worn by gladiators. The law of 11 AD banned Roman citizens from volunteering to become gladiators or appearing on stage, which was supplemented by a senatorial law of 19 AD which stripped men and women of high status of their class privileges if they appeared as gladiators or on stage. Yet Roman aristocrats were passionate about gladiatorial performances and in private took part in combats themselves. Gladiators were either slaves, criminals condemned to death or prisoners of war and as such were of low social status, so public appearance in the guise of the gladiator was frowned upon by the class and status-conscious Roman elite.[41]

By the second century gladiators had been divided into strict categories: the *equites* or horsemen; the *provocator* or challenger; the *murmillo* named after the Greek term for a kind of fish; the *thrax* or Thracian and the similarly equipped *hoplomachus* or heavily armed fighter; the *retarius* or net fighter and the *secutor* or *contraretarius*. Strict protocols demanded which types were paired together so the *secutor* was always paired with the *retarius*. Commodus in private fought and trained as a *secutor*. He wore a bullet-shaped helmet closed at the front with two eye holes and a low metal crest running front to back on top which would have severely limited his range of vision but protected his head from blows. He had minimal protection on the rest of his body wearing a loin cloth and tubular padding on his sword arm, which unusually was his left, and shield-side leg. He carried an oblong shield called a *scutum* and a short thrusting sword called a *gladius*. His opponent, the *retarius*, wore gaiters on both legs and a padded arm guard that swept up his arm to a metal shoulder guard called a *mancia* and a loin cloth. He carried a wide, round net around 10ft in diameter which he used to ensnare his opponent or trip him, a trident and a *gladius*.[42] In private the emperor fought gladiatorial bouts to submission, sometimes with foils and sometimes with sharpened swords, depending on the skill of his opponent. Ordinarily gladiators fought with dull weapons and most fights were until one gladiator surrendered by taking off his shield and raising the first finger of his fighting hand. Commodus however once actually killed his opponent, by accident it is to be assumed, a mistake that Caligula was also criticized for. He practised with his chamberlains making close passes but on occasion 'he sliced off the noses of some, the ears of others, and sundry features of still others'. One wonders what sundry features these were and whether the chamberlains felt the same way.[43] He practised hunting and shooting animals in his private arena and also trained with his wrestler. He trained as a charioteer driving the chariots in the clothes of a professional charioteer, buying racehorses himself.[44] There were no legal or social restrictions placed on chariot racing. The Emperor Nero trained as a driver, Caligula supervised a race where all the charioteers were of senatorial status. The main distinction between chariot races and gladiatorial combats in the arena were that charioteers and athletes appearing in the games *ludi* were state-sponsored religious festivals whilst gladiatorial bouts were *munera* and technically 'gifts' by rich individuals in their name to the people.[45]

Commodus regularly practised with the gladiators at the school attached to the coliseum, and recent excavations at his villa at Lanuvium have uncovered an amphitheatre measuring 200ft by 130ft with an imperial box and curving walls with yellow, red and purple floors made of mosaics and marble imported from North Africa and the Aegean. There was seating for up to 1,300 people and an underground canal around the theatre indicates that naval battles could be held. A spiral staircase led down 10ft into underground chambers suggesting lifts were used to raise animals and scenery to the floor of the arena. The *Historia Augusta* records that the emperor killed wild beasts at the amphitheatre at Lanuvium in imitation of Hercules.[46] Another imperial villa on the outskirts of Rome along the Via Appia, confiscated from the Quintilii, has been extensively excavated revealing bathing suites, rooms of differing sizes, fountains, pools and masses of statues. Access was marked from the road by a Grand Nymphaeum and monumental fountain intended to impress visitors and passers-by, made of white marble set in a semicircular recess with five niches for statues from which water sprouted. The visitor would then pass along a huge levelled area 120m wide and 340m long surrounded by porticoes which could have been used for racing. At the far end of the complex of buildings was a rectangular and an elliptical court dressed in white marble. It has been suggested that the rectangular court was a grand reception hall like a civil forum with a raised tribunal approached by three steps with a miniature temple beside it and a fountain in an alcove in the corner also made of white marble. The court was entered through a vestibule arranged with a colonnade of four columns paved in the style of a public building with variegated grey marble from Algeria with red limestone chips. The room had one wide central door and two lateral doors leading to an octagonal hall like a mini pantheon with alcoves and underfloor heating. This led to another court with a possible tribunal and a bathhouse. Commodus is said to have bathed seven or eight times a day which is used as an example of his extravagance and proclivity for luxurious living. The elliptical court was an addition made in the late second century when the estate was acquired by Commodus. Around the outside of court were a series of shallow steps, perhaps for seating and an upper gallery for entertaining family and guests whilst watching gladiatorial fights below.[47]

Archaeological evidence supports the view that neither Commodus nor Perennis neglected the needs of the empire. Inscriptions from North Africa record the construction and repair of fortifications along the border, no doubt as a response to the reoccurrence of Moorish incursions and the Moors were defeated in Mauretania.[48] Building inscriptions in Pannonia record extensive work being carried out along the border with the whole defensive system being reorganized. The expression *ripa omnis* on inscriptions can only mean Commodus fortified the border of the whole province along the banks of the Danube. The works at Intercisa are confirmed by three building inscriptions dated to 183–5 AD. A series of building inscriptions on the Eastern Pannonian limes between Aquincum and Intercisa date from 184–5 AD. The inscriptions refer to *latrunculus* which can only refer to Sarmatians beyond the Danube but it does not use the word *hostis* so construction was taking place during a period of peace. *Burgi* and fortlets were built at river crossings as well as watchtowers. Construction took place during the governorship of Plotianus in Lower Pannonia and Vettius Sabianus, Governor of Upper Pannonia between 183–5 AD. Hungarian archaeologists have uncovered new Sarmatian buckle types and burial traditions denoting a new ethnic group appearing on the Hungarian plain which resulted in internal unrest on the borders of the empire. The Romans had treaty obligations to their allies and possibly campaigned beyond the Danube in support of their allies against the invaders. Commodus continued to provide subsidies to his allies in barbarian territory up to his death securing their loyalty and reinforcing the security of the frontier. The *Historia Augusta* states that:

> About this time the victories in Sarmatia won by other generals were attributed by Perennis to his own son.

The successful outcome of the war was celebrated in the coinage of 185 AD with the legend *VO DE SARMATIS*.[49] The position held by Perennis' son is open to debate as the governors of the two Pannonias are known. Herodian describes this younger Perennis' command (referring in error to two as Commodus only recalled one son), as over the 'Illyrian armies … even though they were still young men'. M Sasel Kos suggests that the appointment being referred to was as a legate in command of a legion, possibly Legio II Adiutrix based at Aquincum. This would make more understandable the resentment arosed by the claims of Perennis that his son's actions were the reason for the victories in Sarmatia as the commander of one legion, rather than the strategy of an experienced provincial governor.[50]

In Britain Ulpius Marcellus appears to have restored the situation by 184 AD and pushed the invaders back beyond Hadrian's Wall. The account in Dio is vague and generalized suggesting it was written from memory many years later but, in comparison to all the other conflicts in the reign, he describes the war in Britain as 'the greatest struggle' but Ulpius Marcellus 'ruthlessly put down the barbarians of Britain'.[51] In 184 AD Commodus takes a seventh salutation as Imperator and title 'Britannicus' whilst coins issued celebrate victory. The war had lasted nearly four years with Marcellus even campaigning in lowland Scotland but at this point outpost forts of Birrens, Newstead, Risingham and probably Cappuck and High Rochester beyond Hadrian's Wall were abandoned. An altar stone found at Kirksteads, near Kirkandrews upon Eden records the exploits of L Junius Victorinus Flavius Caelianus as legate of the VI Victrix legion north of Hadrian's Wall and could refer to Marcellus' campaign.[52] A further inscription partly preserving the name of the Prefect of ala Augusta (cavalry regiment) at

Carlisle commemorates the unit's success in slaughtering a band of barbarians dates from 180–92 AD, in which case it would fit with the campaign to restore order to the province.[53] The war had led to an increase in the number of walls built around settlement towns in the province. Permission had to be granted by the emperor. Earth ramparts were built not related to their civic status and at Lincoln the walled area was extended down to the river by an earth rampart. In some cases construction started with fine masonry gates and towers, notably at Verulamium and Cirencester so there was no sign that this was done in haste, but it does reflect increased unrest in the province.[54] A peace treaty was concluded with the Maeatae and Calendonii, tribes beyond Hadrian's Wall, as the first Governor of Septimius Severus, Virius Lupus had to restore order in the province in 197 AD after Albinus had withdrawn soldiers during the civil war. These two tribes are described as being in breach of the previous treaty which must refer to that imposed by Marcellus.[55]

Whilst events went well in Britain and Sarmatia, they took a turn for the worse in Gaul and the Roman provinces in Germany. There had continued to be a problem with deserters and runaway slaves since the reign of Marcus Aurelius in a number of provinces but in Gaul they reached crisis proportions. Herodian describes the leader of this unrest, Maternus as 'an ex soldier of notorious daring', a description to be proved accurate by events. Maternus was probably a legionary from the VIII Augusta legion based in Strasbourg as it was later rewarded with the title *Pia Fidelis Constans Commoda* ('Faithful, loyal, reliable, and useful'). Herodian calls this the Deserters' War so Maternus drew fellow legionaries from this unit and others along the Rhine. However Herodian is clear that Maternus also drew recruits from the marginalized members of society, peasants, slaves, malcontents and criminals. He successfully accumulated large amounts of booty which he shared with his supporters and so attracted further recruits for plundering raids on villages, estates and farms. As his numbers increased he even laid siege to towns and cities. To increase his numbers he broke into prisons and encouraged the condemned to join him.[56] The diverse nature of his supporters is supported by an inscription found at Porta Lirensis on the Rhine dating from the ending of the war, 14 August 186 AD. The fort held detachments from the Eighth legion where an *inquistio saeva* was being held in which those who were prosecuted included both citizens and *peregrini* who were free provincial subjects who had not been awarded citizenship. The *Historia Augusta* also refers to provincials in Dacia, (probably the 12,000 Dacians settled in the province in 181), Britain and Germany rebelling.[57] The area covered by the war according to Herodian covered the whole of the Celtic territory and Spain; Celtic territory covering all of Roman Gaul and the German provinces bordering the Rhine. The existence of the war itself, and its extent, was doubted by historians in the past who pointed to the absence of any reference to it in Dio's account of the reign. However we do not possess Dio's full account but an abridged version edited by the epitomizers so it is probable that the Deserters' War was in the full history written by Dio as Herodian used Dio as one of his main sources for the period. Archaeology has also shown that the war itself covered a vast area to the extent that it was upgraded from a mere policing campaign against bandits and robbers by a declaration of full blown war with a religious, formal declaration in Rome by the emperor of a *iustum bellum*. Maternus would have been declared an enemy of the state, no longer *latrones* but *hostes* which not only defined his status in law but also indicates his strength as leaders of rebellions. Usurpers such as Avidius Cassius, were formally declared *hostes* by the senate.[58] An inscription from Aquae Flavia in Agri Decumates in Germany refers to warfare at this time.[59] A wax tablet also from the Agri Decumentes from 186 AD refers to sentences passed by Iuventius Caesanus, legate of the VIII Augusta legion passed on rebels, the legate being rewarded with the consulship of 190 AD for his loyalty and ability.[60] A military tribune of this legion, C Vesnius Vindex, set up an inscription at Urvinum Mataurense which refers to his unit having been relieved from 'the recent siege (*obsidio*)' whilst the construction of a rampart and ditch in the final stages of the construction of the Upper German lines may have been in response to the threat of Maternus from within the boundaries of the empire. Maternus must have returned with his army to the base of his old legion in the second half of 185 AD hoping to use his influence and contacts with his old comrades to win them over. Their refusal to join the revolt led to a siege which gives the historian the approximate size of Maternus' army as they could confidently surround a legionary base over a period of time containing 4,500 men and be strong enough to not worry about surrounding troops coming to their rescue from the Agri Decumates. No wonder Commodus gave the legion the title 'faithful and constant'. The massive 'Black Gate' at Trier was built at this time, no doubt in response to the massive unrest in the surrounding provinces. Archaeological evidence also shows the war covered much of modern France. Based on analysis of coin hordes the destruction layers at Juliabona (Lillebonne) at the mouth of the Seine can be attributed to Maternus (61),[61] and it is also possible the town near present day Vezelay was destroyed at this time.[62] The area of the Loire was also severely affected by the ravages of the war as excavations show destruction horizons from sites in the area whilst a large number of coin hordes can be attributed to this unrest.[63] Two inscriptions of the career of L Artorius Castus record that he led two British legions together with auxiliaries 'against the Aremoricans' having previously served as Praefectus of VI legion Victrix in Britain. Roman Armorica is north of the Loire encompassing modern Brittany running along the coast to the mouth of the Seine. Some have interpreted this as Castus leading British troops across the empire to Roman Armenia; clearly this is not logical as greater concentrations of troops would be far nearer and the province of Britain was suffering unrest itself.[64] The second inscription refers to his previous post as Primus Pilus (chief centurion) of the legion V Macedonica which was based in Dacia and then he became Praepositus of the Misenum fleet. His promotion to *dux* or leader of two legions is a remarkable jump as he was clearly an equestrian but legionary legates were senators. The title *dux* is not an official title but probably a temporary one allocated to an officer who was acting in a capacity above his rank in command of a non-regular unit of troops, probably a vexillation of legionaries from two British legions. He appears to have successfully carried out his assignment as he was promoted to Procurator Centenarius of Liburnia, a part of Roman Dalmatia on a salary of 100,000 sesterces a year.

The widespread unrest in Gaul and Upper Germany was clearly known to Commodus as he would have been involved in the formal declaration of war, however perhaps he was unaware of the extent of the destruction and the threat to a whole legion in Strasbourg as Herodian describes him flying into a rage at the news despatching letters to his governors accusing them of negligence and 'giving orders for an expedition to be organized against the bandits'. This must be the 'third German expedition' referred to in the *Historia Augusta*. What is remarkable is the fact the senate persuaded him not to lead it in person. An inscription even records an official concerned with preparations for the *expeditio Germanica tertia*.[65] Clearly the relationship between the emperor and the majority of senators remained positive as this was a unique event. There are no other records of an emperor being persuaded by the senate to change a decision he had already made. The last time the senate challenged an emperor was during the reign of Antoninus Pius. The second German expedition was in 178 AD when both Marcus Aurelius and Commodus travelled to the Danube in response to renewed warfare. Although this third German expedition is not mentioned in our other two main sources, this information in the *Historia Augusta* is provided within a list of otherwise factually verifiable commemorative events. The fact Commodus considered returning to the war zone would undermine the picture of the pleasure loving degenerate emperor carefully crafted in Dio and Herodian. The chronological sequence in the *Historia Augusta* places this proposed expedition between Oct 180 and April 188 AD with 184/5 AD fitting best.

A series of crises now appears to have undermined the emperor's confidence in Perennis. The Governors of Gaul and Upper Germany cannot have been the only object of Commodus' rage, especially as further bad news followed, a great military revolt in Britain. A number of factors seem to have bred resentment amongst the victorious legions in Britain. They had won the war and the emperor had celebrated victory on the coinage they were paid with, yet the soldiers were not rewarded with a donative. The fact no donatives were made in these years reflects the financial restraints caused by almost constant warfare in the previous reign and the effects of the plague. Another factor causing unrest was the discipline and personality of Ulpius Marcellus. Dio appears fascinated by his character who he describes as 'frugal', 'incorruptible', yet 'haughty' and 'arrogant', not being of a pleasant or kindly nature. The governor, accustomed to little sleep, would send commands and instructions throughout the night to his officers to role model the volume of work expected for those under his command whilst eating little himself. He even ordered bread from Rome that arrived stale, yet he still ate it.

According to Dio the soldiers rebelled, choosing a certain Priscus, emperor. He declined with the caustic reply, 'I am no more an emperor than you are soldiers.'[66] The *Historia Augusta* suggests that some provincials joined the revolt, perhaps taking inspiration from events in Gaul and Germany.[67] This Priscus can perhaps be identified with Caerellius Priscus, a senator of some standing and perhaps a legate of one of the three legions based in Britain.[68] It is clear from Dio that it was not only the soldiers themselves who revolted but also the lieutenants, who were rebuked for their insubordination. Priscus is himself described as a 'lieutenant'. Perennis' and Commodus' response was to remove the legates of each legion, described as senators in the *Historia Augusta* and replace them with their subordinates who were *equites*. A pragmatic, intelligent and practical response as no *equites* could be raised to the purple due to their lower social status, unlike the legates who were of senatorial status. This would become common practice over the following century and the careers of many *equites* in the reign of Marcus Aurelius followed such paths, the emperor responding creatively to the crises he faced. The coins of 184/5 AD celebrate the loyalty and concord of the soldiers, which usually indicates the opposite.[69] The sources also suggest the decision to remove the senatorial legates for equestrians was Perennis' decision alone but to follow their theme that Commodus had resigned control of the empire to his prefect, they would have to. The anger the soldiers felt was also, according to Dio, directed at Perennis as he was at the helm of government. Criticism of the emperor was a treasonable offence and a person left themselves open to a charge of *majestas* either by the emperor himself or one of the numerous *delatores*. It was much safer to criticize the emperor's main advisor. This decision can perhaps solve the unusual offices held by Q Aurelius Polus Terentianus who is simultaneously described on a commemorative inscription from Mainz as legate of the II Augusta in Britain and legate of XX Primigenia. This is difficult to explain unless he is celebrating a new legionary command in Britain necessitated by a mutiny and the rapid dismissal of the previous legate.[70] The three senatorial legates including Priscus and L Junius Victorinus Flavius Caelianus would have been summoned back to Rome awaiting and facing a very unpromising situation, no doubt fuming at their dismissal having successfully fought the war against the barbarian invaders. Dio records that the lieutenants in Britain chose 1,500 javelin men and sent them to Italy crossing a number of provinces without being apprehended. No mention is made of their purpose or rationale or commander and this group would be met outside of

Rome by the emperor himself.[71] A number of questions spring to mind; how did they cross hundreds of miles of territory without being stopped? Who commanded them? Why javelin men and not legionaries? And, most importantly, why did Commodus grant such a group an audience especially as he was surrounded by thousands of Praetorian Guards? The answer lies in the context of their journey. The three legates, important senators in their own right, would have to cross Gaul which was in the midst of massive unrest with an army of deserters, slaves and criminals on the loose. Such a party would need a large bodyguard to cross the war zone as their number, 1,500, is large for a vexillation but it was known they would be likely to be involved in combat. As the legates had no official position, being dismissed from their posts, they were perhaps unable to draw more regular soldiers, javelin men being their personal bodyguard and being lightly armed could travel fast across the hostile territories. The emperor would not give mere soldiers an audience, especially as they were unlikely to even be Roman citizens, but he would grant an audience to senators, and he was probably eager for their reports on the unrest in Britain. If these soldiers had been sent by rebellious soldiers in Britain then they were deserters. Would Commodus have granted an audience to deserters, especially with the Deserters' War being fought in Gaul and Germany further undermining discipline in the legions? What precedent would this set? Clearly the soldiers must have had an official role escorting the dismissed senatorial legates. What was the purpose of the three legates in meeting the emperor? Recognition for their role in the victory over the barbarian invasion, restitution of their status and *dignitas* and, if possible, revenge on Perennis for their treatment. It is more likely that these 1,500 javelin men were drawn in equal numbers from each of the three British legions and were elite soldiers. It was during this period that legions were creating a specialised unit of lanciarii made up of 500 legionaries armed with 1 metre long javelins who were used for fast mobile attacks and filling in gaps between units in the battle line. In the third century these lanciarii were incorporated into the imperial guard. Inscriptions of lanciarii from the II Parthica dating to 215 AD have been found at Apamea and they fought in the battle of Nisibis in 217 AD. The three legates of each legion drew their guard from the 500 elite lanciarii attached to their commands. The *Historia Augusta* gives some support to this interpretation of events with the javelin men sent with their commanders as the issue of the dismissal of the legates was reported by the actual legates themselves; 'when the matter was reported by the legates in command of the army.'[72] Dio would want to overlook this fact as these senators took an ignominious role in the fall and execution of Perennis, a man he admired. Events seem to have conspired against Perennis with revolts and rebellion across Britain, Gaul, Germany and perhaps parts of Spain as well. Commodus' confidence in his Praetorian Prefect had started to falter, and Perennis' enemies saw their opportunity to have him removed permanently.

An unusual event took place whilst the emperor was visiting the theatre at the festival to Capitoline Jupiter which involved musical, equestrian and athletic events. The emperor was acting as a judge with other members of the priestly colleges, all high-ranking senators. Commodus had taken his seat in the imperial box in readiness to judge the performance of the actors and the seats had been filled by the spectators with the senators sat at the front, the *equites* behind, then members of the *collegia*, and so on ascending to the back where the slaves sat. A man suddenly ran to the front of the stage dressed as a philosopher carrying a rod in one hand and a wallet hanging from his shoulders. Nobody stopped or arrested him as he stood on stage and silenced the crowd with a formal gesture of his hand. He then addressed the emperor:

> Commodus, this is no time for you to be enjoying yourself by spending your time at theatres and festivals. The sword of Perennis hangs poised over your head. Unless you take precautions against this danger, which is not just threatening but already here, you will be destroyed before you realize it. Here in Rome he is collecting forces and money to use against you; in Illyria his sons are bribing the army to support him. If you do not act first against him, you will be finished.

Commodus was left speechless and his entourage refuted the claims, or according to Herodian, pretended to. Perennis understandably gave orders for the man's arrest and he was burned, no doubt after torture. A group of travelling philosophers called Cynics wore the *pallium* and *clava* described in the account and made a virtue of living in poverty and renounced wealth in favour of liberty, their outspokenness a public announcement of this freedom and fearlessness. Herodian suggests his motive was either a desire to win fame through his bravery or money as a reward from the emperor. Clearly Commodus allowed the philosopher to make the approach and did not have him arrested afterwards, yet the man must have known that Perennis would exact revenge, unless he felt he had a powerful protector who could save him from the Praetorian Prefect. It is also strange that he would not have been stopped from interrupting the performance of actors or allowed on stage. This appears to be a prearranged incident whose purpose was to undermine the position of Perennis. Reference to a sword over the emperor's head was clearly intended to encourage Commodus to remember the previous assassination attempt as Claudius Pompeianus Quintianus waved a dagger above him before he intended to strike. After this incident, Perennis' opponents and 'Commodus' companions and self-styled supporters', according to Herodian, judged this an opportune moment to bring a charge against the prefect. Perennis as sole prefect had close control of access to the emperor and, without definitive proof of a plot, any man informing on the prefect would have faced a similar fate to that of the philosopher.[73] The fact that the plot was revealed to him during the religious festivities of Jupitor Capitolinus may have lead him to believe the god was his protector as later proclaimed on his coinage, the coins of 185 AD carrying the title 'Felix', implying divine protection. The sources are clear on who was plotting against Perennis: Cleander and other imperial freedmen. Their motive, according to Dio, was that Perennis was an obstacle to increased power and influence:

And the imperial freedmen, with Cleander at their head, after getting rid of this man, refrained from no form of mischief and … this man (Cleander) had often been prevented by Perennis from doing all that he desired, and consequently he hated him bitterly.[74]

They also had a personal motive, which is supported by Herodian: they 'had previously hated Perennis for his harshness and intolerably supercilious arrogance.'[75] Cleander himself had, along with Perennis, been involved in the murder of Paternus but it appears their alliance was temporary, based on the principle of 'My enemy's enemy is my friend.' The sources provide contradictory assessments of both the character of Perennis and his possible involvement in a plot to remove Commodus. Surprisingly Dio is most complimentary; on his death he laments, 'he deserved a far different fate, both on his own account and in the interests of the entire Roman Empire … For privately he never strove in the least for either fame or wealth, but lived a most incorruptible and temperate life; and as for Commodus and his imperial office, he guarded them in complete security.'[76]

To Dio Perennis was a ruthless, efficient and loyal administrator. Contrast though the views expressed by Herodian and the less reliable, *Historia Augusta*:

Perennis gained complete control and began to aim for the principate itself. First he persuaded Commodus to give the command of the Illyrian armies to his sons, even though they were still young men. Then, while he himself amassed a vast sum of money to win over the allegiance of the army by large donatives, his sons secretly organized their forces in readiness for a coup d'état after Perennis had murdered Commodus.[77]

This hostile view of Perennis is mirrored in the *Historia Augusta*:

He (Perennis) slew whomsoever he wished to slay, plundered a great number, violated every law, and put all the booty in his own pocket.[78]

This contradicts Dio who is insistent that Perennis did not line his own pocket and was moderate in his actions. What the prefect was really like we will never know yet he can be partially judged through his actions.[79] He could certainly be ruthless and had no second thoughts about arranging the murder of anyone he saw as a threat. Yet his motives remain hidden; was he ruthless to protect his own position as Herodian would have us believe or to protect Commodus, the belief of Dio? Dio perhaps benefitted from some *beneficia* arranged by Perennis in his early career or he simply admired him. Perennis held in check the power and aspirations of a number of freedmen in Commodus' court; Herodian seems to have some detailed insights into the workings and machinations of court life and his focus on court personalities suggests he could have been an imperial freedman or imperial scribe. We do not really know. Herodian does explain that he based his history on events 'which I saw and heard in my lifetime. I had a personal share in some of these events during my imperial and public service.'[80] If so he may have had some sympathy with the political restrictions the Praetorian Prefect placed on other freedmen yet he does not portray Cleander in a flattering light.

According to Herodian, Perennis, from the moment he arranged the fall of Saoterus and Paternus, plotted to overthrow Commodus by collecting vast amounts of money to distribute as a donative to the army and arranged for his son to be granted command over armies in Illyria.[81] The logic behind this appears to undermine this evaluation of Perennis. The Praetorian Prefect was a member of the equestrian class, and as such, neither Roman senators nor the populace would at this stage in Roman history be prepared to accept him. Roman emperors had all been senators and would be until the equestrian Macrinus seized the throne in 217 AD, only to be overthrown and executed in 218 AD. It is doubtful that other senatorial commanders of the armies would step aside to allow Perennis or a son to take the throne, feeling their lineage and nobility was far greater. Perennis' son is described as a young man and so, if already a senator, his role in the senate would have been limited having not held a consulship or any other major office apart from a limited army command. According to the *Historia Augusta* this son claimed victories in Sarmatia when true credit should have been given to other unnamed generals, perhaps Vettius Sabinianus. Far from being evidence of the prefects scheming to remove Commodus, it looks more like a parent's pride in a son's achievement, which he may have understandably inflated in his feedback to the emperor on the progress of the campaign beyond Rome's borders. Perennis is also accused of having campaigned to undermine the senate in the eyes of the emperor and planning a revolution based on promoting the power of the *equites*.[82] The only senators that were removed from their posts and replaced by equestrians were in Britain and this was purely in response to an emergency situation as the legions were trying to raise their senatorial legates to the imperial throne, Perennis understood that the legions would not offer the throne to an equestrian. It is therefore difficult to believe some of the ancient sources who claim that he wanted the throne himself.

The sources also appear to contradict one another in explaining the fall of Perennis. Dio and the *Historia Augusta* link his fall to the events in Britain. The 1,500 javelin throwers, according to the *Historia Augusta*, accompanied by the legates themselves, were granted an audience by the emperor outside Rome, probably the Quintilian Villa. The soldiers' hatred of Perennis derived from their perceived insult in being lead by equestrians rather than senators.[83] The emperor, horrified by the actions of his prefect in dismissing senators and replacing them with equestrians, allowed these soldiers to murder Perennis. The emperor then ordered the death of Perennis' wife, sister and sons.[84] Herodian however gives a different unrelated account. It seems highly unlikely that the emperor knew nothing of the dismissal of the senatorial legates as he had kept a close eye on events in Britain, reappointing Ulpius Marcellus as governor of the province with orders to restore order in Britain. He will no doubt have been informed of the attempt by rebellious soldiers to elect a senatorial official, Priscus, to the imperial throne. It defies belief that the emperor had not been aware of, and involved in, the replacement of all senatorial legates in the province in response to this threat to his rule. The legates themselves, not lowly soldiers, would have the status and influence to gain an audience with the emperor. How do we explain the absence of Perennis from this meeting? The prefect clearly had not been informed of this senatorial delegation so whom did they approach to gain access to the imperial presence? The *cubicularius*, Cleander, would have had the influence and power to grant access to these visitors. His control of the freedmen in the palace would allow him to ensure news of the senators' presence was not brought to the attention of Perennis. The senators were clearly aware that Cleander was a potential ally for undermining the prefect. The audience was probably arranged when Perennis was absent in Rome or on his own estates with the senators summoned from Rome, only five Roman miles distant. The delegation then proceeded to describe a plot by Perennis to make his son emperor. Cleander, present as one of the emperor's *amici*, unsurprisingly supported their claim. Dio does not mention any evidence that was used to substantiate the allegations apart from that provided by the *cubicularius*.

Herodian's account of the fall of Perennis differs from that in Dio, but he does refer to evidence used to support allegations of a plot against Commodus. Soldiers from the army of Perennis' son travelled to Rome without the knowledge of their commander carrying coins bearing the portrait of Perennis. They again managed to avoid Perennis even though, in the words of Herodian, 'he was Praetorian Prefect'. The Greek does not make clear whether the portrait on the coins was that of the father or son. The soldiers were granted access to the emperor and showed him the coins for which they were greatly rewarded, Perennis being beheaded that night. Imperial messengers were sent quickly to the headquarters where Perennis' son was based with a letter from the emperor summoning him back to Rome. The son's suspicions were allayed by the friendly tone of the imperial letter which promised him promotion and reassurance from the messengers that his father's orders were given orally as written ones were not required as the imperial letter would suffice. The son set off for Rome and on reaching Italy he was murdered by assassins 'acting on instructions'.[85]

The two accounts are not mutually exclusive and it can be conjectured that both events did take place at this time. However, as Hekster points out, it is highly questionable that Perennis as an equestrian or his son, a low-ranking senator, could have aspirations to the throne or would be accepted as such by the senatorial aristocracy or leading senatorial commanders of the legions and governors of the provinces.[86] However the name of the Governor of Pannonia Inferior of 184–5 AD, Plotianus, has been removed from all inscriptions signifying he suffered *damnatio memoriae* as a result of condemnation under *majestas*. His fall is not recorded in any of the sources but it appears significant that this occurred at the very time of the fall of Perennis. The *Historia Augusta* records that Commodus received the title 'Felix' after he had executed the prefect which can be dated from coins to 185 AD.[87] De Ranieri suggests that it was Plotianus who planned to remove Commodus having the support of a significant number of legions on the Danube and his fall brought about the fall of one of the legates of the legions, the younger Perennis.[88] Did Plotianus have the necessary *dignitas*, patronage and nobility to aspire to the throne? A vastly experienced commander Plotianus and Vettius Sabianus had been tasked with reorganizing the defences along the Danube in the Pannonias and had probably been involved in supporting Rome's allies beyond the Danube in Sarmatia. Sabianus was to survive the fall of Plotianus and he continued to have an illustrious career under Commodus, becoming proconsular Governor of Africa suggesting he was not involved in the plot. However it was probably at this time that Vespronius Candidus Sallustius Sabinianus became legate of the province. He was later nearly killed by troops in Pannonia when he paid a visit to the Pannonian Governor and imperial claimant Septimius Severus. He was hated by the soldiers in the province perhaps as a result of the imposition of harsh disciplinary measures following unrest in the legions after the execution of Plotianus. The *Historia Augusta*, referring to these events states that 'peace was established in the Pannonias, but all by his legates'.[89] One common theme in the accounts of Dio and Herodian is unrest amongst troops who had recently won victories over an external enemy, the troops in Britain against the Caledonians beyond Hadrian's Wall and the Pannonian troops against barbarians in Sarmatia. Normally such victories would be rewarded with the distribution of a monetary donative amongst the successful armies; none were forthcoming. Perennis appears to have been blamed for this by the troops in Britain as to criticize the emperor was tantamount to mutiny. The British armies tried to raise one of their senatorial legates, Priscus, to the imperial throne knowing that if he had accepted a donative would have been distributed to gain their loyalty in the future war against Commodus. Priscus however refused. Perhaps similar unrest in the legions of Pannonia Inferior led to these legions turning to their Governor Plotianus, a senator of greater status and *dignitas* than Priscus. As a legate of one of these legions Perennis' son may have been accused of involvement through mere association with Plotianus and his inability to keep control of his legion.

Cleander must have looked upon these events with thinly disguised pleasure. All the sources agree that the *cubicularius* was the key player in the plot to remove Perennis. He had bided his time whilst Perennis was in the ascendency with the successful uncovering of senatorial conspirators involved with Lucilla and with the initial success in Britain against the barbarian invasion. The increasing numbers of deserters and runaway slaves evident in the previous reign led to a full-scale war under the leadership of Maternus, the governors of provinces in Gaul and Germany losing control of the situation with the insurrection climaxing in the besieging of an entire legion in its own winter quarters. Commodus erupted in rage and no doubt Perennis bore the brunt. The emperor's confidence in his prefect was now starting to waver and even the 'idea' of a threat to him would have been enough grounds for his removal. Events themselves now appeared to conspire against Perennis when the financial constraints caused by almost unremitting war during the reign of Marcus Aurelius and the continuing plague forcing both Commodus and Perennis to refuse the granting of donatives, resulting in mutiny in Britain and possibly Pannonia. Cleander now added fuel to the flames organizing the spectacle at the theatre where a gullible Cynic philosopher was found, eager for fame, and was provided with a script to denounce the prefect. Commodus was bemused, yet another seed of doubt was planted in the emperor's brain. The dismissed and aggrieved British legates who had themselves won victories joined in temporary alliance with the *cubicularius* to conspire against their mutual enemy. The unrest in the legions under the command of Plotianus and his deputy the younger Perennis was too good an opportunity to miss, the sources agree that it was Cleander who provided the supporting evidence 'proving' in Commodus' mind that his prefect was either conspiring against him or managing events to cause massive unrest across the empire and so providing the opportunity for the emperor's removal. Perhaps the finishing touch was the production of coins with the head of the Praetorian Prefect imposed upon them, a relatively simple task. To Dio, Perennis was an innocent victim of Cleander yet Cleander could not have acted successfully against him unless the emperor's confidence in the prefect had already been undermined; that was a consequence of events outside Perennis' control. This is merely supposition but it is supported by the facts in all of the sources and fits with the context and chronology of events. Perennis was himself a political animal as all had to be if they were to rise in the imperial court of any emperor. He was ruthless in his elimination of Paternus and desired to be the most powerful *amicus* of the emperor, blocking the rise of others and leading to the enmity of Cleander. Yet Perennis' actions in efficiently putting down conspirators against Commodus and his removal of any potential threats to the emperor show that Dio's assessment of him was probably nearer the truth. He was loyal to Commodus guarding his safety to the last. Commodus himself does not come out of this well, yet he was a man made by his experiences. He had been surrounded by plots all his life; his mother had probably been unintentionally involved in the revolt of Avidius Cassius and the young Commodus had to be protected in Rome before his rapid transportation to his father on the Danube, his own sister had conspired to murder him as well as some of his young senatorial companions and a number of his father's old *amici*. Fear of sudden death at the hands of an assassin must have constantly played on his mind. Cleander understood the emperor well and played on these fears. As historians we sometimes forget that behind the events, the plotting and scheming, the fiend friendships, the executions, the allegations of conspiracy, lies a human being.[90]

In commemoration of having survived another plot against him Commodus was awarded the name Felix. The name appears on the coins of 185 AD, a cognomen he shared with the Republican dictator Sulla who put many prominent men to death. The comparison is contrived by the sources to link the emperor to the fear generated by the proscriptions instigated by the Republican dictator, yet it is clear 'Felix' or 'the fortunate' implies divine protection after his survival. However Felix could also refer to the celebration of the first ten years of his rule, Commodus taking his commendation before the troops on the Danube on the anniversary of Romulus' ascension into heaven as the commencement of imperial power. A denarius with the legend DPRC dates from this year, *Decannales Primi Romae Constituti*, with an image of Roma with a cornucopia and Victoriola with an ear of corn. Some asses show an oak wreath circled around with the legend *Primi Decenn(ales)*. The message is clear, the rule of Commodus had provided abundance and security to the Roman people. Felix combined with his previously awarded titular, Pius, now prominent on coinage, links Rome's security to the divine favour their emperor was held in.[91]

Chapter Five

Commodus and Cleander:
The Age of Austerity (185–189 AD)

The power and influence of Perennis that had restricted the imperial freedmen was now removed and their influence over the emperor, nurtured by almost daily contact with him in the imperial administration of the empire, enabled them to gain pre-eminence. From the reign of Antoninus Pius the distinction between the public or state related affairs and those of the private, related to the personal property and estate of the emperor, had become increasingly blurred. Antoninus Pius invited the noblest members of the aristocracy to be members of his *consilium* but he also retained a smaller circle of intimate *amici* whom he invited to private banquets (*privata convivia*) as opposed to public, state ones. Even within the imperial household there were distinctions between the emperor's public and private slaves and attendants. In the financial sphere, the public and private *fiscus* were both acknowledged to be at the disposal of the emperor. Marcus Aurelius is noted in Dio as being unusual in asking the senate for permission to use public funds to pay for the wars. Yet it was Marcus Aurelius who blurred the lines between the 'public' advisors of the emperor, the senatorial and equestrian elite, and his personal *amici*, his group of philosophers. Commodus continued to surround himself with his private attendants, the *cubicularii* and other freedmen with whom he had most personal contact.[1] Many of these talented individuals had entered Commodus' household with the death of Verus. One of the most prominent of these individuals, Agaclytus, had been given permission to marry a member of the nobility, Fundania, who was related to Verus. Their son, L Aurelius Agaclytus, would be given permission by Commodus to marry his sister Sabina on the execution of her husband. Another imperial freedman inherited from the household of Verus was Apolaustus Memphius whose *beneficia* is recorded across the cities of Italy signposting his continued power and influence. He appears to have been closely attached to Cleander as his fall resulted in Apolaustus' execution. Another freedman of Verus retained by the imperial household was Pylades who is mentioned in the letters of Fronto. His original magister was P Aelius Pylades, a freedman of Hadrian. Clearly a resilient character, he would survive the fall of Cleander and Commodus to become an influential advisor to the Emperor Didius Julianus.

Others entered the imperial household from the confiscation of the property of Quadratus in 182 AD. Marcia, whose full name indicates she was originally freed by Verus and Eclectus, rose through the imperial household using a range of talents. She had originally been the mistress of Quadratus, would become the mistress of Commodus and later the wife of Eclectus. She is said to have had such influence over the emperor that she persuaded him to grant the return to Italy of all Christians who had been sent to the mines in Sardinia as forced labour.[2] The fact she would exchange her position of influence with the emperor for marriage to a freedman indicates the power Eclectus held at the end of Commodus' reign.

Pre-eminent amongst these was Cleander, brought to Rome as a slave pack carrier, 'a Phrygian by birth, who was one of those normally sold by public auction.' Phrygians were perceived as poor value unskilled slaves and had a low status with many being brought to Rome as young boys. His full name was Marcus Aurelius Cleander suggesting he had been granted his freedom by Marcus Aurelius. He is also described as the *tropheus* of Commodus, his tutor, perhaps taking the place of Pitholaus. He had been involved with Perennis in the plot that led to the murder of Saoterus and his machinations led to the emperor losing confidence in Perennis, his Praetorian Prefect. He was clearly a political animal whose character, skills and personality were well suited to the poisonous intrigues of courtly life. Yet he was also a skilled administrator and was trusted by the emperor, a trust he gradually built up through regular contact with Commodus as his *nutritor* and *cubicularius*. Philo, writing of the intrigues of Helicon, a freedman in the reign of Caligula (Gaius), explains the origins of his influence as he 'played ball with Gaius, exercised with him, bathed with him, had meals with him and was with him when he was going to bed'. Cleander's earlier position of *tropheus* is recorded in a number of inscriptions, however Commodus had a number of tutors and such a position would only grant him limited access to the emperor, unlike the position of *nutritor*. However it was the emperor who decided how much power and influence his *cubicularius* held, a man he knew would be fully dependent on his own survival. The fall of Commodus would mean the fall of Cleander. This, according to De Ranieri, was a conscious decision made by the emperor to continue the centralization of power whilst attempting to retain the existing systems, placating the elite with honours and offices.[3] Roman emperors and the imperial system of governance were essentially reactive in their functions and nature. We have no evidence of Commodus reacting proactively to a situation or anticipating future threats. Emperors made decisions based on petitions, requests, commendations or news of a crisis. Commodus was no different, his decisions were based on the problems and crises he faced in governing the empire; the influence of Cleander and Saoterus before him was in response to their daily contact with him but it was also a reflection of his reduced faith in the loyalty and ability of some of the nobility and equestrian officials. Centralization was mainly a response to the threat of insurrection by powerful commanders of the legions, senators or imperial family members who possessed the necessary nobility, *dignitas*, network of *amici* and clients as demonstrated by the revolt of Avidius Cassius, Lucilla and later Pertinax.

At some point Cleander was given a fictive free birth, like Saoterus, by *restitutio natalium* on the command of Commodus. Cleander was acutely aware that his low social status as a freedman would hinder his ability to build bonds of *amicitiae* with the equestrian and senatorial class. This act would also have allowed Cleander to become a public member of the imperial *consilium* as social and political propriety prevented freedmen from any 'public' recognition of their close working relationship with the emperors, even though it had always been so 'behind the scenes'. Even Juvenal in his parody of Domitian and his *consilium* had no place for freedmen even though this would have enhanced the satirical effect and mirror reality. Commodus was prepared to play to senatorial and equestrian sensibilities but not to the extent that he deprived such talented and driven men from promotion to the highest positions in the state. The emperor would have been aware that permitting a former freedman to publicly hold such a position of influence as an *amicus* of the emperor would be an affront to these classes, yet his previous elevation of Saoterus suggests that such matters were inconsequential to him, forcing Paternus and Perennis to 'remedy' the situation by murdering the freedman. Another freedman in the imperial household was also rewarded in the same fictive free birth, L Marius Doryphorus, as recorded on an inscription, but we know little of his career or influence.[4]

Cleander further strengthened his position by marrying the emperor's concubine Damostratia, presumably after Commodus' affections had turned to Marcia. We do not know whether this was a match made through affection or a calculation on the part of both parties as a way of increasing influence over the decisions of the emperor. What it does indicate is a threat to the position of his wife Crispina who had still failed to produce surviving offspring, and more importantly a male heir. It was probably this nexus of individuals, allied with a group of dissatisfied senators, who worked in undermining Commodus' belief and confidence in Perennis. Cleander was not the first, nor would he be the last, to use his official position as *nutritor* and *cubicularius* to attain wealth, power and influence. In the previous reign of Marcus Aurelius the imperial doctor Galen first came to the notice of the emperor through treating the slave of the *cubicularius* Charilampes. This official is perhaps identified with 'Charilas' to whom Marcus Aurelius' *amicus* Fronto wrote asking to be informed of the best time to visit the emperors in order to ask to be granted imperial *beneficia*. The *nutritor* of Verus, Nicomedes, was raised to the rank of *equites*, continuing to lead a highly successful career culminating in the post of *procurator summarum rationum* with responsibility for the imperial finances.[5] Cleander had taken the post vacated by Saoterus, no doubt the reason for Cleander joining in the plot to remove his predecessor.[6] His rise through the various levels of the bureaucracy to that of *nutritor* is not recorded but by 186 AD a letter sent by Commodus to Athens records his almost unique position as the emperor lists the members of the *consilium*. Cleander is referred to in this correspondence as 'my *nutritor* entrusted with the care of my bedroom and my person'. Furthermore the letter lists the imperial *amici* in order of precedence, Cleander comes second, only preceded by an ex consul and followed by the equestrian posts of *ab epistulis Graecis* and *a rationibus*. Previous to this freedmen had been excluded from 'public' appearances in official documentation or as members of the imperial *consilium*.

The mentioning of an *a rationibus* in the imperial *consilium* is also unique as their financial role often meant they rarely worked closely with the emperor. These posts were often filled by freedmen or equestrians who lacked the necessary patronage to gain a post with greater access to the emperor. The enhanced importance of such a man with financial expertise as an imperial advisor shows how Commodus, despite the allegations of the sources, kept a firm hand on the workings of the government but also indicates increasing concern with the imperial finances. The *a rationibus* Julius Candidus is referred to in the letter as 'my *amicus*', a notable compliment for such a man. The imperial recognition and therefore status of men of such low social standing as the freedman Cleander would have offended the sensibilities of the whole equestrian and senatorial class, but to Commodus, it would have been an advertisement that promotion and imperial access would be based on loyalty and ability, not nobility. Like Caligula before him, Commodus was forced by his suspicions of the senatorial elite, who had in the previous reign carried out administrative tasks, to turn to the members of his imperial household who were after all, the real professional bureaucrats and the nearest the ancient world had to modern civil servants. The Greek orator and historian Dio of Prusa recommends that emperors bind men of talent and ambition to the imperial administration to act as officials or generals. Dio's audience however would have had in mind members of the equestrian and senatorial classes. Commodus extended this to all men of ability working in the imperial household regardless of class.[7] Many of these Pertinax, on ascending the throne, sold or transferred from the imperial household, only to be forced to bring them back into the imperial service when the ex senator realized that the government could not function efficiently without their skills and experience.

Another man who owed his prominence to his legal knowledge and expertise was the equestrian M Aurelius Papirius Dionysius who began his career under Marcus Aurelius. He is the first known individual appointed to a *consilium* on a salary of 60,000 sesterces. It had been assumed that this was the imperial *consilium* but there are no other instances in the historical record of such a promotion without previous widespread legal experience and office. It is more likely the *consilium* being referred to was that of the *consilium* of the praetorian or urban prefects. It is only later in his career that he is referred to as *consiliarus Aug(usti)* when he was granted a salary of 100,000 sesterces. He was promoted to *a libellis*, having held a number of minor posts, and then a *cognitionibus* with responsibility for the imperial law court. These posts involved a close working relationship with the emperor. Commodus was to draw upon this man's vast experience and knowledge to later place him in charge of Rome's grain supply, the *annona*, a prestigious and responsible position that entailed keeping Rome's populace quiescent through the regular supply of free or cheap bread. Interruption in this supply inevitably led to rioting and a potential threat to the position of the emperor.[8]

There can be little doubt that members of the imperial family retained access and therefore influence over Commodus. The aristocratic Marcus Peducaeus Plautius Quintillus had married Commodus' sister Fadilla and held the consulship of 177 AD and later a joint consulship with the emperor. He remained a trusted advisor throughout the reign and would later commit suicide to avoid execution on the charge of *majestas* by the future Emperor Septimius Severus. Fadilla herself had unrestricted access to the emperor and warned him of unrest in the city.[9] Lucius Antistius Burrus was married to the youngest sister Sabina. He was from an African senatorial family from Thibilis, not of ancient lineage, but he clearly resented the elevated position of the freedman Cleander and used his position to try to undermine him. He was distantly related to both Fronto and Aufidius Victorinus but the experienced general and governor Q Antistius Adventus was a close relation, perhaps even his brother.[10] Gn Claudius Severus (an ordinary consul in 167 AD and 173 AD) had married the eldest sister Annia Aurelia Galeria Faustina but his son from his first marriage Ummidius Quadratus, adopted by a nephew of Marcus Aurelius, had been involved in Lucilla's conspiracy. The family continued to prosper with their son Tiberius Claudius Severus Proculus achieving the consulship of 200 AD, requiring him under the *cursus honorum* to have held lesser magistracies such as the praetorship under Commodus. However, like Claudius Pompeianus, his links to members of the Lucilla conspiracy led to his withdrawal from the imperial *consilium*. M Petronius Sura Mammetinus, the consul of 182 AD was married to Cornificia. He was from a wealthy well connected senatorial family of African, perhaps Egyptian, origins. His father had been suffect consul in 150 AD whilst his brother, Marcus Petronius Sura Septimianus, was granted the ordinary consulship of 190 AD. His sister married the illustrious Senator Marcus Antoninus Antius Lupus. Plautius Quintillus, Antistius Burrus and Petronius Sura Mammetinus were influential members of Commodus' *consilium* and had been members of the *consilium* of his father. They would be joined by influential figures in Rome itself who had been the *amici* of Marcus Aurelius.

Marcus Aurelius' general, Aufidius Victorinus was Urban Prefect until his own suicide in 186 AD for reasons unknown, his achievements honoured with the erection of a statue by Commodus. On his death he was replaced by Publius Seius Fuscianus, the lifelong *amicus* of his father who was also awarded a suffect consulship in 188 AD. Fuscianus as Urban Prefect presided in a case brought before him by Jews in the city who had denounced a certain Callistus and his followers as Christians. Fuscianus sentenced them to the mines in Sardinia, only to have his decision overturned by the emperor acting on the advice of Marcia, who if not a Christian herself, had sympathy for this religion.[11] Marcus Aurelius' General, Marcus Valerius Maximianus, on his return to Rome after his governorship of Numidia was awarded a suffect consulship around 186 AD.

The fall of Perennis also led to the resurrection of the fortunes of former *amici* of Marcus Aurelius whose careers had been curtailed by Perennis' suspicions of their loyalty to Commodus. Cleander hoped that these men who had suffered at the hands of Perennis would owe him a debt of *gratia*:

> He loaded with honours men who were recalled from exile; he rescinded decisions of the courts.

Future events were to prove Perennis an impressive judge of character. Pertinax had spent his enforced retirement acquiring vast estates around his father's modest holdings. Commodus sent a letter to the man he had known as a teenager accompanying his father on the tour of the East, 'making amends' for his dismissal from the governorship of Syria and appointing him to the governorship of Britain. He was tasked with replacing Ulpius Marcellus in suppressing the mutiny in the army in that province.[12] This was the second time in his career that Pertinax had been the recipient of what he probably perceived as unjustified removal from official posts, a victim of decisions and intrigues at court. He must have questioned the benefit of loyalty and hard work when it all could be undermined by political manoeuvrings at Rome and the vicissitudes of fortune and fate. Pertinax accepted his new commission in good grace. He no doubt learnt from these experiences, looking to build bonds with prominent figures around the emperor. He had been a victim because of his passive role, now he would take an active role, becoming the master of his own fortune. Others to benefit from the fall of Perennis were Didius Julianus and Septimius Severus. Julianus was allowed to return from his estates and given the province of Bithynia, whilst Septimius Severus became Governor of Lugdunensis. The Deserters' War necessitated the need for experienced commanders, so Severus was given the job of suppressing

Maternus, along with Percennius Niger who was probably the commander of a provincial levy raised in his province of Aquitania. Both, realizing from the fall of Perennis, that Commodus would not tolerate failure, appear to have coordinated their strategies, both militarily and politically, crushing the revolt and also ensuring that the emperor received reports of glowing success, Severus commending Niger as a 'man indispensible to the state'.[13] Severus also seems to have been in ultimate command of these forces as he gained much of the plaudits of the provincials for his rescuing the province from Maternus' army of deserters and robbers:

> And because he was strict, honourable and self restrained, he was beloved by the Gauls as no one else.[14]

He would remain governor of the province until 188/9 AD as his son Caracalla was born at Lyons in 188 AD, and would be granted a suffect consulship at the bequest of Cleander. Both Severus and Niger would later tear the empire apart in a bloody civil war along with the successful commander against the Dacians, Clodius Albinus. Lucius Fabius Cilo, the experienced legate of the XVI Flavia legion from the early 180s AD was made proconsular Governor of Narbonensis whilst Clodius Albinus was transferred to Gaul, probably the province of Germania Inferior or Belgica.[15] Cilo may have served with Septimius Severus as a legionary legate under the governorship of Pertinax until their dismissal by Perennis. His governorship of Narbonensis is attested in a number of inscriptions and Cilo would become a loyal *amicus* and General to Septimius Severus in the civil war that erupted on the murder of Pertinax.[16] The aristocratic Lollianus Gentianus, who was the patron of Pertinax, assumed command of XXII legion Primigentia at Moguntiacum. The revival of these men's careers may have been at the recommendation of Cleander who hoped that his *gratia* would bind them to his position as the senior *amicus* to Commodus. The significant number of old *amici* of Marcus Aurelius retained by Commodus contradicts the sources who try to disassociate the reign of Commodus from that of his father. However Commodus had grown up with these men, travelling the empire with them and listening to their advice in the imperial headquarters on the Danube. These were the men he trusted and he hoped their shared experiences and loyalty to his father would ensure their continued loyalty to him.

The fall of Perennis appears also to have resulted in a renewed positive relationship between the emperor and the senate who were able to persuade him not to personally take charge of the campaign against the deserters. This is reflected in the coinage of 186–7 AD which carries the legend 'Father of the Senate' (*PATER SENATUS*).[17] Cleander would not have benefitted from such a campaign as the emperor would have surrounded himself with men of extensive military experience and Cleander's voice would only be one of many in this *consilium*. Leaving Rome would also have entailed leaving behind a significant proportion of the Praetorians. It is remarkable that these elite soldiers would have stood by to watch a group of deserters tear their prefect, Perennis, apart as reported by Dio and so Herodian is more likely to give the more accurate account in recording that Perennis was beheaded late at night. This reapproachment with the senate was to be undermined by the rise to prominence of the socially inferior Cleander and the desperate need to raise additional tax from those who possessed the greatest wealth: the senatorial elite.[18] The delay in the execution of Perennis probably allowed Commodus to visit the Praetorian fort in Rome from his villa on the outskirts of the city and ensure their loyalty before removing their prefect. As a temporary measure Commodus appointed Niger until long-term appointments could be made once the situation had stabilized. Commodus was to return to the traditional policy of appointing two prefects as one could monitor and check the power of the other. The emperor clearly believed that Perennis, as sole prefect, had abused his position. Niger was therefore joined by another, probably Marcius Quartus. T Longaeus Rufus however was earmarked as the long-term successor to Perennis. He had held the Egyptian Prefecture since replacing Veturius Macrinus in August 183 AD. Rufus is described in inscriptions as *vir emintissimus* and was clearly held in high regard. The natural promotion from this post was to Praetorian Prefecture. An Egyptian papyrus dated to 185 AD records his presence in the province examining the status of a Roman veteran, Valerius Clemens, who had been discharged in 177 AD. The investigation was carried out by Allius Hermolaos, tribune of the Legion II Traiana Fortis who confirmed Clemens' status after he provided discharge papers and other veterans acted as warrantors. Longaeus Rufus is described in the papyrus as the 'former prefect', having received his appointment to the Praetorian Prefecture but awaiting the arrival of his replacement, Faustinianus, who was present in the province by April 186 AD. The delay in his departure from Egypt probably necessitated the appointment of one or more temporary prefects, leading to the accusation in the *Historia Augusta* that prefects were changed almost hourly.[19] Publius Atilius Aebutianus was also chosen as the long-term colleague to Rufus. The guards remained loyal to their emperor, as they would throughout his reign.[20]

Towards the end of the summer of 186 AD the fire of Maternus' revolt was being extinguished by the work of Niger and Severus in Gaul for which Commodus received his eighth and final salutation as 'Imperator'. Clodius Albinus and Helvius Clemens Dextrianus, using legions and auxiliary troops in the provinces bordering the Rhine, restored order in the German provinces. A wax tablet dated to this year from the Agri Decumentes refers to sentences passed by Iuventius Caesianus, legate of the VIII Augusta legion on rebels and bandits.[21] Maternus had also heard news of a force being gathered to oppose him and decided to make one final desperate throw of the dice. His army was not large enough to fight a conventional battle against these forces so he dispersed his remaining men with orders to make their way to Rome using minor little used routes and there, reunited, he planned to murder Commodus 'so covering himself in fame and glory'. Herodian even suggests he had designs on the throne itself, but this must surely be an exaggeration.

Maternus planned to use the festival of the Hilaria to cover his preparations. This prolonged religious celebration reached a high point from 15 to 28 March. On 15 March the brotherhood of the priestly '*Cannophori*' processed through the streets carrying reeds, leading a 6-year-old bull to be sacrificed in honour of Attis. This was followed by nine days of abstinence as the people gave up bread, pomegranates, pork, fish and wine and probably sexual congress. During the night of 22 March a pine tree was cut down in a grove sacred to the Mother Goddess, Cybele, and a ram sacrificed, its blood bathing the roots of the tree. Another procession through Rome was accompanied by songs and music from the *dendrophori* and taken up by bystanders who cried and beat their breasts. Once at the sanctuary the image of Attis was decorated with violets to symbolize blood and death, the people then laying flowers on the tombs around the city. The following day it was the turn of the dancing priests of the Salii who leapt around banging their shields in honour of Mars, the God of War. The 24 March was the Day of Blood. The high priest whipped himself to the sound of clarinets and cymbals to be joined by onlookers who beat themselves with pine cones, cutting their shoulders and smearing their blood over the pine tree and altars. The more committed entered the dance slashing their testicles with sharp stones or flint, whipping themselves in a frenzy. The pine tree was then buried as the Mother Goddess Cybele had done to the body of Attis. This was probably followed by a night's vigil with worshippers reciting prayers until dawn.

On the following day, the 25 March, the resurrection of Attis was celebrated. The Festival of the Hilaria meant rejoicing, which by the time of Commodus, involved a huge carnival. The majority of the guard would be off duty and unarmed, lost in the drunken carousels of the populace. The highlight of this day was a procession by the great and good of the capital. Firstly came the emperor, senators, *equites* and freedmen who carried their most precious possessions through the streets; gold and silver ornaments would have gleamed in the spring sunshine, jewels and statues would be carried behind a statue of Cybele. All wore masks, the owners made up in various costumes, walked along accompanied by musicians. Robert Turcan provides a vivid picture of this scene: 'All the tokens of peoples' wealth and the treasures of the imperial house – things of marvellous material and workmanship – are paraded in honour of the goddess. Free licence is given to all kinds of revels: anyone can disguise himself as any character he wants; there is no position so important or exclusive that someone cannot disguise himself in that dress and play the fool by concealing his true identity, making it difficult to tell the real person from the man in fancy dress.' It was this procession that would allow Maternus and his followers to get close to the emperor, so they hoped, disguised as Praetorians. The fact that Maternus appeared comfortable with disguising himself as a Praetorian has led to speculation that earlier in his career he was a member of the guard but received a dishonourable discharge. Secretly joining the imperial guards escorting the emperor they would strike him down, escaping in the ensuing panic. The irony of the plan in which Maternus' 'played' the emperor in a religious celebration where the boundaries between reality and symbolism were blurred, was not lost on Herodian, nor probably on Maternus himself.[22]

However a plot shared with criminals, runaways and robbers is not going to remain secret for long. According to Herodian a number of the conspirators, not wanting a robber chief as emperor, betrayed the plot before the day of the Hilaria. No doubt a sizable reward was foremost in the minds of these men. Maternus was captured and beheaded, along with many of his followers. Commodus sacrificed on the day of the Hilaria to the goddess in recognition of her role in keeping him safe and announced a public thanksgiving before completing the religious ceremonies. The emperor made a point of joining the procession to wide scale rejoicing and celebration. Commodus was a popular emperor amongst the ordinary people of Rome, and even Maternus recognized that a revolt against him was out of the question due to his support amongst the populace and the Praetorians.[23]

The 26 March was a rest day, undoubtedly needed after the excesses of the previous day and night. At the start of the following day a silver idol with a black stone for its head representing the goddess was transported from the Palatine in a chariot pulled by heifers to the River Almo along the Appian Way. The statue and sacrificial ornamentation was then washed and purified and then the procession returned to Rome. Eight days later the 'Magalensia' began with plays in the theatres presenting religious shows portraying the life of Cybele and the death of Attis. The festivities ended on 10 April with chariot races in the Circus Maximus, the statue of Cybele standing on the central platform that the chariots raced round. The presiding magistrate, which would probably on this occasion have been Commodus, was clad in a toga embroidered with palm leaves. The emperor would want to make a public acknowledgement of his appreciation for the goddess' protection and his deliverance from yet another threat to his life. Coins were issued with the image of the goddess sat inside a saddle on a lion, publicizing his gratitude to the goddess of his salvation. The legends *nobilitas aug(usti)* now appear regularly on coin issues emphasizing his nobility, the scion of an imperial family dating back to Nerva and stressing the fact he was born into the imperial family and not adopted. This belief in his destiny to rule is evident in earlier coinage with the emergence of the Goddess Providentia Deorum in the middle of 184 AD and, for the first time, the mentioning of this goddess on 30 May and 1 November 183 AD in the Arval Acts. The goddess' image gradually disappears on the coinage from late 184 AD as the title 'Pius Felix' supplants this message: the emperor of the Roman people was divinely chosen, destined to rule and his nobility is the only guarantee of continued security and prosperity. This concept was now repeated in coinage in response to the 'conspiracy' of Perennis, the revolts in Britain and Pannonia, Maternus' assassination attempt and malicious rumours spread by his enemies that he was the illegitimate son of Faustina and a gladiator. Coins of 187 AD go a step further carrying the legend *Auctor Pietatis* with the image of sacrificing *Pietas* representing the emperor himself who is presented as the peoples' direct link to divine favour.[24]

In response to the attempted assassination Commodus increased his guard. The Praetorians' power, in these conditions, was magnified. Being responsible for arrests, torture and executions they were in a position to profit from their policing role. After the fall of Commodus, his successor Pertinax attempted to reign in the Praetorians: 'they were prohibited from seizures and damage to property' and they resented 'the end of their unlimited power'. They also were given the right to carry axes within the confines of Rome and their arrogance was greatly resented as they insulted passersby and struck those that displeased them.[25] The guard and the *frumentarii* had always been used as a precursor of the secret police but Commodus had clearly given them almost free reign after the number of plots against him increased.

After the Hilaria, Commodus, according to Herodian, rarely appeared in public, but withdrew to the suburban districts or his imperial estates; by suburban districts Herodian must mean the Quintilian Villa. However the very next paragraph in Herodian's history reveals the true reason for his withdrawal from Rome:

> Just at this time a plague struck Italy, but it was most severe in Rome, which, apart from being normally overcrowded, was still getting immigrants from all over the world. The result was a tremendous toll of life among men and beasts of burden. On the advice of his doctors, Commodus retired for the time to Laurentum, a cooler spot, shaded by huge laurel groves (which gave the place its name). The doctors thought this place was safe because it was reputed to be immune from infectious diseases in the atmosphere by virtue of the redolent fragrance of the laurels and the pleasant shade of the trees.

The population of Laurentum was ordered to follow the prescriptions of Commodus' doctors, filling their ears and noses with sweet-smelling perfume and burning incense and aromatic herbs in their homes. It was believed the polluted air would be forced away by the more pungent scented air; Galen correctly diagnosed that disease can be spread through inhalation. Despite these precautions, the plague spread unabated amongst the population. Herodian notes that animals also died in great numbers at this time which may be no more than coincidence. The plague continued into 188 AD when vows were assumed on the Nones of 'Pius' in an attempt to placate the gods. However the gods continued to be dissatisfied and deaths continued in ever greater numbers.[26]

Note that Commodus only stayed there 'for a time', suggesting he later returned to the environs of Rome when the plague died down. However Rome provided the ideal environment for its continued spread. Dio, recording conditions in the capital around 189 AD describes horrific scenes:

> A pestilence occurred, the greatest of any of which I have knowledge; for two thousand persons often died in Rome in a single day. Then too, many others, not alone in the City, but throughout almost the entire empire, perished.

Dio goes on to describe criminals infecting the population with needles smeared with the poison. In a world without the certainties provided by modern science the causes of disease were ascribed to the wrath of the gods, impure air or the actions of vilified groups in society. What is evident is a climate of fear and terror where rumours are provided with the ideal conditions to multiply and turn into factual events.

The Antonine Plague is estimated to have had a mortality rate of 7–10 per cent which would equate to up to 5,000,000 deaths, magnified by the cramped living conditions in Rome itself, and it was probably at Galen's advice that he move to an area where the purified air that would ensure the emperor's safety. It has been suggested that the plague was an outbreak of smallpox. Galen describes a black rash covering the body with raised blisters accompanied by a high fever, vomiting, bad breath, coughing and diarrhoea. The fact Galen describes the rash as pustular which later blackened suggests haemorrhagic smallpox rather than typhoid and the lack of buboes rules out Bubonic Plague. Survival from infection though confers complete immunity yet the plague returned regularly. These reoccurrences must be due to the disease entering previously unaffected areas of the population with those in Rome who had previously died being replaced, as Herodian states, with new immigrants from areas of the empire that had yet to succumb to an outbreak of the disease.[27] Commodus, remembering the death of Verus and his father from the plague, would not have questioned Galen's advice. His removal from Rome made him far more remote from the senatorial and equestrian elite, many of whom would find it difficult to attend the imperial *salutatios* and request *beneficia* from the emperor. His enemies would accuse the emperor of devoting his time to pleasure rather than the running of the empire, which in their eyes, was the distribution of *beneficia*. Isolated from other influences, the emperor would naturally come to rely to a greater degree on the members of the imperial household that the senate envied and resented, especially Cleander.

A study of documentary evidence from Egypt shows that the plague had a devastating impact on the population size in this vital province, with a significant rise in the wages of unskilled labourers due to a shortage of workers whilst land rents fell. In one well documented village the total amount of land under cultivation fell between 158 AD and 216 AD while land used for fruit and wine production grew as a reduction in the population led to a reduced demand for staple crops. Documentation relating to wheat tax collection for part of the Arsinoite nome in 184/5 AD was significantly smaller than previously whilst the price of wheat remained the same due to demand for feeding Rome's population. However the price of land significantly fell over this period probably due to the difficulties in paying higher wages to cultivate it.[28] If, as is likely, this situation was mirrored across the empire, a large number of Roman landowners would have faced increasing financial difficulty in paying the increased wage costs for cultivating their land, with significant areas of marginal land being left uncultivated with a consequent reduction in the grain supply and rising cost of bread and other staples. The wealthy elite, with their armies of slaves, would not be so badly affected but the majority of smaller landowners who held fewer slaves and relied on seasonal labour during the harvest season or small landholders and tenant farmers would be most severely affected. This is evident in Pertinax's first act on becoming emperor, which was also aimed at gaining the support of the aristocracy:

> The first of his projects (Pertinax) was to make over to private ownership all land in Italy and the provinces which was not being farmed and was lying completely fallow, in lots depending on the recipient's requirements and ability to work it. Even if the land was part of the imperial estates, the man who could farm and cultivate it was to become the legal owner. Farmers were given complete tax immunity for ten years and permanent security of tenure.[29]

The issue was clearly that large areas of land had fallen out of production due to the fact the landowner could not afford the labour to work it. It was only the wealthy aristocracy with their armies of slaves who were unaffected by increased wage demands that would benefit from this law. Tax revenues would have been severely reduced by the reduction in cultivation and also the grain supply to the capital would have been under threat. The reduction of the distribution of the free grain dole to the 200,000 citizens of Rome who were eligible would have led to unrest. An estimated 800,000 were not eligible to the dole and so suffered from the resultant increase in the price of bread, as demand outstripped supply, again causing unrest and disturbances in the capital. It was probably at this time that Commodus ordered Cleander to secure reliable quantities of grain for Rome. Historians had previously believed that the reorganization of the Egyptian grain fleet was from 190 AD when grain shortages were a contributory factor in the fall of Cleander. However Alexandrian coins show the fleet already in existence in 190 AD and coins dated to 186 AD bear the symbol of a grain ship with the words *providentia Aug(usti)*. However, enforced requisitioning of Egyptian grain may account for the avarice and greed Commodus is accused of in the Acta Appiani where an Alexandrian Christian, Appian, in a fictitious confrontation, reprimands the emperor. Cleander would also look to secure the flow of grain from Carthage in the province of Africa as Egyptian grain provided Rome with only 140,000 tonnes, enough to feed it for four months. More roads were also built at this time in the privince of Africa, the limes strengthened and public buildings restored to effect the efficient production and transportation of grain to the ports, especially Carthage.[30] Commodus 'did organize an African fleet, which would have been useful in case the grain fleet from Alexandria were delayed'. It appears the main component of this measure was to organize the Carthaginian grain fleet on the same basis as that of Alexandria, something which had not been done before. There was a concern that grain production was decreasing and there was a need for increased efficiency. The remainder of the capital's food needs were provided by Sicily and Italy itself. The fleet was probably serviced in preparation for transporting the grain and contracts made in advance with owners of the ships who would probably have preferred to transport wine, fine pottery and other luxury goods that provided a higher profit margin, however they avoided harbour taxes, were eligible for Roman citizenship and exempt from compulsory public service. The ships themselves were large three-masted sailing vessels; although smaller vessels existed. They were not built to survive a winter journey but sailed in late spring to arrive in the port of Ostia by June from Egypt but probably earlier from Carthage. The hull of one such ship was discovered near Madrague de Giens in France measuring 40m in length and capable of carrying 400 tonnes.[31]

Reduced tax revenues had been a continuing problem from the previous reign but the new resurgence of the plague with its impact on cultivation and trade must have had a dramatic effect on the finances of the government. The communal state treasury or *aerarium* had reduced importance compared to the imperial *patrimonium* and *fiscus* whose revenues from taxation in the provinces controlled by the emperor eclipsed that of the 'public' treasury. There is a marked decrease in the number of shipwrecks starting in this period. The plague meant less population resulting in less production, smaller food surpluses and less tax income with increased pressure on surviving farmers, especially in hinterland of armed forces, to hand over more of their produce. This resulted in more people moving away from these areas. The army probably constituted about 1 per cent of the population but the majority of government expenditure. Furthermore Maternus and the Deserters' War had also affected food production and ability to raise taxes in Gaul, the German provinces and perhaps Spain whilst the barbarian invasion of Britain and the army mutiny would have reduced tax revenues from that province.

The situation was made worse by climatic changes as studies suggest that the second century was increasingly cold and wet leading to a decrease in agricultural production. Archaeological surveys in the Liris Valley in Campania show a steady decline in rural sites and likewise near Venosa. This may be a result of depopulation caused by the plague or represent change in landownership with landownership becoming concentrated in the hands of a powerful small number of rich landowners who were able to buy the land of smaller farmers who were unable to make a profit from their produce due to increased wage costs. The future Emperor Pertinax was accused of such aggressive purchases greatly enlarging the lands he held around the small estate he inherited from his father. However some areas of the empire prospered at this time; in Africa from the early second century to the late fifth century there is a steady increase in the numbers of agricultural sites which the reorganization of the African grain fleet further helped to stimulate.[32]

Analysis of the weight and purity of the gold *aurei* by G Adams, basing his work on that of Mattingly (*Coins of the Roman Empire in the British Museum*, Volume IV), shows that weights varied considerably in the reign of Commodus, but the average is 111.53g compared to the average weight of the *aurei* of Marcus Aurelius of 111.78g, although the weights of Commodus' reign are more erratic than those in the previous reign. The same outcome is evident in analysis of the weights of the *denarii* and the *sestercii*. In 186 AD the purity and weight of the *denarius* was reduced to 74 per cent and 2.22g which was the largest reduction of purity since the reign of Nero. However there is less variation in the Commodian *sestercii* than the other denominations, probably because the troops were paid in *sestercii* and their loyalty was paramount. A gradual depreciation is evident from 169 AD yet Commodus was clearly financially responsible, contradicting the assertions of the senatorial sources. On the death of Commodus however the treasury was nearly empty with only 1,000,000 sesterces remaining in the vaults. To put this into perspective, by the time of Severus the pay of a legionary was equivalent to 500 *denarii* a year, a praetorian three times that and a centurion five times that of a praetorian to which needs to be added discharge bonuses. Donatives to the soldiers were given on accession and when emperors felt a need usually at five times the annual rate of pay for a praetorian. Marcus Aurelius and Verus had to pay out donatives of 20,000 sesterces, the highest level since the late republic. Furthermore Marcus Aurelius had to distribute 240,000,000 sesterces to troops in Rome alone. If donatives were extended to legionaries at a proportion of 30 per cent as was customary, the total bill was at least another 1,000,000,000 *sesterces*. Furthermore, the empire was no longer expanding so there was no booty from pillaging. Added to this were the monies needed for the corn dole, gifts, *beneficia*, the *annona* and the administrative costs of the government. The empire was broke. However coinage was used to promulgate the imperial propaganda, Commodus understood its importance in promulgating his imperial rule and policies. He centralized control over the mints, closing many outside of the capital. A recurrent theme in his coinage through his reign is an emphasis on *securitas, concordia*, Jupiter, *pax, liberalitas,virtus, fides, fortuna* and his own *nobilitas* and strong support for his rule within the army. However the emperor did introduce significant changes to the normal 'Antonine' propaganda. *Denarii* of 186 AD for the first time carried the title 'Pater Senatus' depicting the emperor carrying a branch in his right hand and an eagle-tipped sceptre in his left, a similar pose to that depicted for Jupiter, associating the emperor with the 'king of the gods'. By 189 AD images of Jupiter would carry the face of Commodus. Other coins from the time show the figure of Tellus Stabilita linking the reign to a time of plenty. The most prominent gods on Commodus' issues are Jupiter, Sol, Hercules and Janus. A medallion issued in 187 AD shows the double-headed Janus on one side, the forward looking head made to resemble Commodus; the message clear, Commodus had provided peace to the empire, the gates of the Temple of Janus being closed, in comparison to the constant warfare of his father's reign. The northern barbarians had been defeated with some tribes becoming allies of the empire, the incursion of Dacia and Britain defeated and rebellion crushed whilst Maternus had been executed and stability restored to Gaul and the German provinces.[33]

The lack of understanding of basic economics and the financial requirements of the state are exemplified by both Pertinax and Dio himself. The empty treasury is blamed by Pertinax on imperial freedmen enriching themselves on tax revenues or on the lavish games, gifts, donatives and banqueting provided by Commodus. All naive in the extreme yet music to the ears of the aristocratic elite who wished to enjoy the benefits of security provided by the army and state yet were not prepared to pay for it out of their wealth. In his history Dio provides a number of solutions to the need to raise revenue. In a speech Dio has Augustus' *amicus* Agrippa deliver on the problems of state finance, he balances the hatred felt towards tax collectors with the necessary revenues required to allow the state to function and army to defend the frontiers. However he continues with the suggestion that all confiscated property from civil wars held as public property should be sold and the money lent to landowners to cultivate the land. Another suggestion is that the gap between income and expenditure should be filled using the profits from imperial mines and estates supplemented by indirect taxes on the sale of produce which people would be willing to pay as long as the emperor was not lavishing money on himself. Dio, and the senatorial order he represented, wanted the state to rely on its own revenues from public and imperial property, reducing reliance on the wealthy elite.[34] Commodus in his need to raise additional revenues introduced indirect taxes on produce transported by rivers, harbours and roads, yet on his death, Pertinax rescinded this measure, playing for support from the senatorial elite but the reduced revenue forced him to reintroduce this and similar taxes, much to the anger of the senate.[35]

Cleander recognized not only the financial peril the empire was in but also the financial constraints that had deprived the victorious armies of Britain and those that fought in Sarmatia of the donatives that they had expected, leading to widespread military unrest. The *pomerium*, or city limits were expanded. This was partly due to the ever increasing population of the capital, but had the added benefit of increasing the taxable regions of the city. Coins of 186 AD were issued with the legend: Concordia Militum; usually indicative of a hoped-for state of affairs rather than achieved. This unrest was partly caused by the failure to distribute donatives to the soldiers after their successful campaigns. Due to the desperate state of the public finances no *congiarium* was distributed to the citizens from Commodus' return to Rome and the fall of Perennis and then only three thereafter, in 186, 190 and 192 AD as was traditional on the emperor's assumption of the consulship. The unrest in the armies led directly to the fall of Perennis, along with some assistance from Cleander himself. Cleander did not want to be in this position himself; the armies would be paid but cuts had to be found elsewhere. The *alimentia* had been suspended in 184 AD whilst coinage of 187 AD celebrates 'The joy of the Emperor' (*LAETITIA AUGUSTI*); distribution of largesse *congriarium* was never distributed. Salaries of imperial officials were held in arrears whilst monies allotted for the repair of roads and public buildings were reduced. The building of public monuments in Rome was greatly reduced, however the *Historia Augusta* is incorrect in stating that there were no public works in existence apart from the baths which Cleander built in his name but according to the late Christian author, Jerome, completed in 183 AD before Cleander's rise to power. The biographer, ignoring the financial constraints that Commodus had to work under, accuses him of deliberately leaving unfinished the public works of his father. The Column of Marcus Aurelius was completed in the reign of his son outdoing the nearby Column celebrating the deification of Antoninus Pius. Nearby, Commodus built a Temple to the Deified Marcus Aurelius and Faustina of which nothing now remains. The Baths of Cleander, later named after the emperor himself on the execution of the *cubicularius*, were built to the south of the later Baths of Caracalla. Herodian describes the dimensions of this building as huge, containing not just a bathing complex but gymnasium. The construction of these monuments would provide jobs for the idle populace in the capital as well as, so Cleander hoped, his increase popularity amongst the masses that used these facilities walking under the inscription with his name on. The emperor did however spend what money he had on beautifying the city with statues and other adornments and was recognized as an aesthetic patron even by his opponents:

> Commodus display in Rome itself many indications of wealth and very many more, even, of a love of the beautiful.

Commodus also provided gardens, the Horti of Commodus decorated with a rounded colonnade with a mosaic of the emperor himself surrounded by his *amici*, including an image of Percennius Niger performing the rites of Isis.[36] Direct taxation was based on a poll tax and a tax on land as recorded in the regular census. A major source of indirect taxation was the *portoria* on exports and imports at the boundary of the empire and occasionally between provinces. This was collected at customs houses and could amount to as much as 25 per cent of the value of the goods. Other taxes were raised on the sale of slaves at auction and a manumission tax, the *vicesima*, paid at 5 per cent of the value of the freed slave. The wealthy paid an inheritance tax of 5 per cent on any properties left to persons who were Roman citizens and the need to raise additional revenues was probably the reason Caracalla granted citizenship to all free males as he raised the tax to 10 per cent at the same time. The costs of the army and veteran's pension funds were supplemented by a tax on auction sales and estates which went towards the *aerarium militare*. Revenues from the imperial provinces went into the imperial *fiscus* whilst those from senatorial provinces went to the *aerarium*, although by the time of Commodus the emperor had access to the revenues of both and no real distinction is made between them in the sources. Individual cities' contributions were calculated on the amount of land they owned, even if it was left fallow. Additional income was generated by the selling of produce from the imperial estates or the rents from imperial land leased by *conductores* as well as estates confiscated from those condemned under the *majestas* law. Commodus caused great offence by requesting funds from the senate from the public treasury for an 'African expedition', probably in response to the unrest that Pertinax effectively dealt with, and when the situation was restored in the province he cancelled his preparations without returning the money to the public treasury but retained it in the imperial *fiscus*. The imperial *fiscus* was used for the benefit of all citizens across the empire and transferred to all new emperors automatically even if they were not related to their predecessor, so all funds were increasingly seen as public funds, but to the aristocratic senators this was a breach of etiquette. The post *ratio privata* is first attested under Commodus with responsibility for confiscated estates in the imperial *fiscus* but the *Historia Augusta* records that Septimius Severus was the first to appoint the *procuatio* of the *res privatae* which appears linked to vast amounts of confiscated property he acquired after the civil war. The *res privata* had been created by Antoninus Pius as a repository of personal property he had held before being adopted as imperial successor by Hadrian. However this private fund quickly acquired a public function as the estates of those prosecuted in public trials were added to it. Its revenues rapidly increased, requiring a public official to manage this treasury. Distinctions between *publicus* and *privatus* grew increasingly blurred. The posts of *a libellis*, *ab epistuli* and *a rationibus* were prominent equestrian posts appointed by the emperor fulfilling a state or public function, yet the same 'public' functions were also carried out by the imperial slaves and freedmen who were part of the imperial household and considered *privatus*. Admittedly Marcus Aurelius had pandered to senatorial sentiments by repeatedly requesting funds from the *aerarium* rather than taking them but the *lex de imperio Vespasiani* made the emperor the ultimate arbiter of what were deemed private and public. The aristocracy clung to the old distinctions from the republic, Dio himself making such a distinction between Commodus' behaviour and actions in private as opposed to those in public, recognizing the imperial palace as a private space. Yet even here morning *salutatio* where the emperor was expected to engage with the public were carried out in the vast audience chamber of the Domitianic building and imperial business was carried out from its rooms and chambers. By this time the very concept of 'emperor' is substituted for *publicus* in a political context and contrasted with *privatus*. The emperor and his court were acting in a distinct role over and above the spheres and definitions of private and public. It was the aristocracy who refused to recognize the changes that had already taken place. Pandering to his narrow senatorial power base Pertinax would later refuse to affix his name to any imperial property as these were in the public sphere and did not belong 'to the private estate of the emperor but to the general public of the Roman empire'. By 'general public' he clearly had in mind his principal backers. Pertinax was trying to reposition the emperor as the servant of the public; the senate, likening the position of emperor to the holder of a magisterial office whose authority was granted on the authority of the senate. A stance rejected by Commodus who saw the imperial throne as his birthright and the favour the gods showed him. Senators were now expected to address him not as an equal but as 'My Lord'.[37]

The finances of the imperial *fiscus* were boosted on the emperor's accession and after significant victories like the successful completion of the 'Northern War' by provincial cities who were expected to send gold crowns to the emperor in celebration of his achievement. Since the reign of Tiberius it was assumed on the death of prominent persons a bequest would be left to the emperor and this had become an established form of income with an imperial freedman appointed who was in charge of inheritances. This gift had long since become an exaction and a test of a person's *gratia* to the emperor, Nero confiscating the estates of those who were ungrateful in not leaving a bequest in their wills. A bequest was a public expression of gratitude by the deceased for past *benficia* and in turn reflected the power and influence of the person remembered. This became enshrined in law with Antoninus Pius ruling that any bequest left to the wife of the emperor who died before the testator became invalid, however a legacy left to an emperor who died in these circumstances was due to his successor and not invalidated by the death of the previous emperor. The shortage of funds and past ingratitude of principal senators led Commodus to enforce this supposed voluntary bequest as a compulsory one. Tacitus reports that Augustus, despite hating the nobility, raised 14 hundred million *sesterces* from these voluntary bequests.[38] All the sources agree that both Cleander and Commodus resorted to raising revenues from every source. An extract from one of the epitomizers of Dio records the lengths he went to:

> neither his other revenues nor the funds provided by Cleander, though incalculable in amount, sufficed him, and he was compelled to bring charges against even women - charges not calling for a capital punishment, yet full of vague terror and threats. In consequence he sold them their lives for a large price and got something from them by force under the guise of a voluntary offering.

A charge of *majestas* would result in the *fiscus* taking the estates of those convicted and would be termed a capital charge yet these charges resulted in those accused making a voluntary offering to the emperor. The *Historia Augusta* provides the context of these charges referring to the actions of Perennis:

> some, against whom there was not even the imputation of a fictitious crime, were accused of having been unwilling to name Commodus as their heir.[39]

Commodus enforced what he felt was his legal right to part of the estates of not only his *amici*, but all the estates of the wealthy Roman elite, including wealthy females who had inherited. The emperor had provided *beneficia* to all the elite classes in the form of gifts, offices and magistracies, granting gifts to patrons that they could pass on to their clients, grants of citizenship, adlections to the equestrian or senatorial class and so on. As the emperor's status, wealth and power meant such gifts could not be returned the reciprocal nature of the bonds of *amicitiae* could only be repaid by loyal service and a bequest in a will recognizing the benevolence of the emperor. This gift was also increasingly seen by emperors as a statement of loyalty to the imperial family. Failure to include an imperial bequest was not a crime in itself but they would inevitably attract accusations of disloyalty and such threats would incur terror, leaving those accused at the mercy of the *delatores* or their enemies in the senate or at court.

Commodus appears to have taken for the imperial *fiscus* the property of those who had left a will that was invalid on the testator's death and had failed to formally complete a new one. It had become common practice that the state acquired the property of those who died without a will or a natural heir. The financial reasoning behind this is clear from Pertinax's law forbidding such actions, declaring before the senate that: 'It is better, O conscript Fathers, to rule a state that is impoverished, than to attain a general mass of wealth by paths of peril and dishonour.'

The problem was clear to all, including Commodus and Cleander: 'the revenues of the Roman empire were insufficient to meet his expenditures.'[40] The sources describe Commodus' and Cleander's revenue raising strategies as greed, declaring that the Romans hated them for it.[41] The sources simplify the reasons for the shortage in funds as the lavish spending Commodus incurred on chariot races, banquets and the Games.[42] Emperors had since Julius Caesar spent lavishly on entertaining the people as a means of gaining their support for their reign. The demonstration of power was demonstrated by all emperors in the wealth exhibited in the imperial palace, the luxurious objects on display and the attire of the emperor himself. Pertinax was able to reduce these costs but stood accused of penny pinching, being mocked by the wealthy nobility. The author of the *Historia Augusta* notes that Pertinax was able to reduce by half the 'usual' costs of the court, indicating that the costs accrued by Commodus were nothing out of the ordinary.[43]

The sources resort to cliché, accusing Commodus and Cleander of making false accusations against the wealthy elite in order to seize their estates. The *Historia Augusta* levels such accusations against Perennis yet it is surprising that if this were factually correct, the senator Dio would have mentioned this in his own history.[44] The provincials that were arrested were probably eminent Syrians linked to the attempt by Condianus to raise a revolt in the province after the arrest of the rest of the Quintilii. Many of those exiled or executed under *majestas* were often tried before their peers in the senate and convicted, many senators not wishing to incur the displeasure of the emperor or wishing to gain his favour even though the members of that august body often felt that the accusations brought before them by *delatores* were false. Commodus was renowned for the gifts and *beneficia* he dispersed to his *amici*, both freedmen of the imperial household and senators which would further encourage men to make such accusations.[45] Commodus would not be in a position to ascertain whether those accused were guilty or innocent, and past experiences would have encouraged him to err on the side of guilt yet on occasion he did pardon men already convicted under *majestas*. The fact that the imperial *fiscus* acquired the confiscated property of the condemned opened the emperor up to accusations of manufacturing such claims to restore the treasury. There was no need for the emperor to interfere directly in these processes as a climate of fear and suspicion amongst the wealthy elite would suit his purposes in undermining opposition. However, unlike his father, who urged the senate to not condemn the senatorial supporters of Avidius Cassius to death but instead exile them on the grounds that the shedding of senatorial blood would tarnish his rule (Marcus Aurelius was not so concerned with shedding the blood of other classes), Commodus allowed relatives and *amici* of the condemned to have a capital sentence reduced to one of exile for monetary recompense, on occasion though he took the money and still executed the condemned.[46]

Cleander appears to have been delegated the task of filling the financial black hole in state finances. The freedmen, unrestrained by the sensibilities of the senatorial or equestrian elite, proceeded to raise funds from the selling of offices, promotions, governorships, military commands, procuratorships, enrolment in the senate or other bodies. Dio refers to one such man, Julius Solon, 'a very obscure man, that he had been stripped of all his property and banished to the senate'. This however does great disservice to Solon, who, in the reign of Septimius Severus, was such a distinguished senator, that the emperor, on entering Rome for the first time, asked him to introduce a *Senatus Consulta* into the senate promising the new emperor would not put any senators to death. Clearly this was a great honour for Solon as he was officially recognized as an *amicus* of the emperor. The emperor himself would have chosen his man carefully, selecting a senator whose prestige and *dignitas* would carry weight within the senate. (Ironically Solon would be executed by Severus not long afterwards for siding with Albinus, one of Severus' opponents in the civil war.)[47]

It would have made no sense to grant such positions of power to potential opponents, nor allow men who lacked the necessary *dignitas* and ability to carry out their tasks which would have impaired the efficient running of the government no matter how much money may have changed hands. Such positions would be filled by men who through loyal service and talent had earned the right to this *beneficia*, and, as in the nature of all reciprocal relationships based on *amicitiae*, would provide a monetary gift in return. This was not a new phenomenon. The Emperor Vespasian granted the post of *dispensator* in the treasury, a post always held by a slave or freedman, to the supposed brother of one of his servants. When the servant asked for the *beneficia* Vespasian decided to interview the man personally and finding that the man was no relation to his servant asked him: 'How much commission would you have paid to my servant?' The man mentioned a sum. 'You may pay it directly to me,' said Vespasian, giving him the post of *dispensator* without delay. When the servant brought the matter up once again, Vespasian's advice was:

'Go and find another brother. The one you mistook for your own turns out to be mine.' The historian Josephus reports in the reign of Nero Syrians bribing the imperial secretary Beryllus to persuade Nero to cancel the privileges of the Jewish citizens of Caesarea.[48]

This incident is striking in two respects. Firstly the sale of official posts was recognized from the early principate and secondly access to the imperial household, even the post of *dispensator*, whose holder would probably never have the opportunity to speak to the emperor, were worth their weight in gold through the influence and opportunities they offered. In the time of Marcus Aurelius, Victorinus, when Governor of Germany tried to persuade an officer not to accept bribes; when persuasion failed he asked the officer to make a public declaration on the tribunal and swear before the gods and assembled troops that he never accepted bribes nor would ever do so. Again the man refused, not on the grounds that such actions would lead to him being publicly condemned and vilified but because he did not want to perjure himself leading to divine punishment. Clearly he felt that acceptance of bribes was widely seen as a reward for gaining high command and the troops and assembled officers would have acknowledged this. Victorinus however had a different perspective and ordered the man to resign his post. As Governor of Africa, Victorinus sent an official back to Rome for the same reasons. The precedent had been set long ago, Cleander extended the principle to some of the lower offices of state. According to Dio he sold senatorships, military commands, procuratorships, governorships before the historian finishes with a flourish, condemning him for selling 'everything'. Most of these appear to be posts that would, in previous circumstances, have been granted on the intervention of a senatorial *amicus* on behalf of a client or fellow *amicus*, in order to extent their patronal network or repay a previous *obligatio*. The posts to imperial provinces appointed in this manner would only be minor provinces away from the frontiers and commanding only a small number of troops, Crete and Cyprus for example. Generally the provinces appear to have been well managed during Commodus' reign and there are no recorded complaints by provincials or charges of *de repetundis*. The modern historian Albino Garzetti, although closely following the ancient sources in painting a dark picture of Commodus' reign, is highly sceptical that the provinces were cursed by corruption and mismanagement. The contemporary Philostratus in his *Lives of the Sophists* shows surprising neutrality to the personality and character of the emperor, in marked contrast to the senatorial sources, but he also praises his actions in promoting philosophers and their works. Senators continued to hold prominent posts, however an unusual appointment was made at this time: P Julius Geminus Marcianus, the first member of his family to enter the senate and consul of 167 AD whilst holding the governorship of Arabia, was recalled from retirement to the office of proconsular Governor of Asia in

185–6 AD, a gap of eighteen years between offices. The province of Asia was highly prestigious and usually granted to recent consuls. His appointment could be an example of money exchanging hands, but why Marcianus would want such a post so long after his previous one is open to debate. The province of Asia contained no legions and only locally raised militia and so held no threat to the regime, but it was a prize many would pay gladly for. There are no accusations that Marcianus' successor purchased the province: Aemilius Frontinus who is recorded putting on trial a prominent Christian named Alexander, whom he acquitted. Frontinus was succeeded by the eminent jurist Arrius Antoninus and then the prominent senator Asellius Aemilianus, who according to Dio 'seemed to surpass all the senators of that day in understanding and experience of affairs, he had been tested in many provinces and as a result had grown conceited'. The allocation of Asia to Marcianus appears to have been unusual and unique. Many of the provincial governors recorded on inscriptions and in the ancient sources had previously served under Marcus Aurelius and would be retained under the Severans indicating that they too had acquired a vast amount of experience that Commodus and his successors were all too willing to draw upon. Tiberius Claudius Candidus' equestrian career showed loyal service to the emperor for which he was adlected to the senate having been responsible as procurator for raising taxes in Gaul and later served as a Severan general in the civil war. Of 111 surviving statue bases dedicated to Commodus, only 4 are from Rome. The remainder from the provinces indicate efficient and popular administration. Surprisingly twenty of these statues were erected after his death, no doubt after the act of *damnatio memoriae* was rescinded by Septimius Severus. That provincials were willing to make dedications to Commodus long after his death suggests a level of popularity across the empire denied in the ancient sources.[49] Commodus' experience in Britain would have ensured all posts were in the hands of men he trusted implicitly.

To our modern perspective, all such appointments are a form of bribery and corruption. However these client/patron relationships were the bedrock of ancient society. However Commodus felt that the aristocracy were not returning the reciprocal bond of *fides* and *gratia* that such *beneficia* demanded as he questioned the loyalty of many members of the aristocracy. The language of *amicitiae* is bound up in the language of debt utilising verbs such as *reddere, pendere, referre* and indicating this relationship was something akin to that between a debtor and creditor. Commodus clearly felt short-changed and demanded his repayment in the form of a monetary return, primarily due to the financial difficulties the administration was in, but also because the nobility were unlikely in his eyes to be loyal, no matter what they may say in the senate and in the morning *salutatio*. From the aristocracy's perspective such *beneficia* should not have to be paid for as they did provide *gratia* in their acclamations in the senate and passing of titles honouring the emperor and furthermore most of these *beneficia* were provided not by an 'equal' such as the emperor, a senatorial *amicus* or even an equestrian prefect, but freedmen, ex slaves, of the lowest social status. Cleander was hated for placing these proud members of the aristocracy in such an invidious position that they became 'the slaves to slaves'. If the *Historia Augusta* is to be trusted, other *beneficia* 'sold' including rights for burial, securing punishments for others, immunity, change of punishments, alleviation of wrongs and selling privileges.[50] Those condemned to death under *majestas* were refused burial in their family mausoleum with all records of their career and honours removed from the public record and a great stigma was attached to those executed as traitors. To the Roman aristocrat and his relatives it was tantamount to their never existing and a cause of great resentment to surviving members of the family. Among Pertinax's first acts was to allow proper burial in their family tombs of those so condemned;

> he removed the stigma attaching to those who had been unjustly put to death … And immediately some bewailed their relatives and others their amici with mingled tears and joy, even these exhibitions of emotion not being permitted formerly. After this they exhumed the bodies, some of which were found intact and some in fragments, according to the manner of death or the lapse of time in each case; and after duly arranging them, they deposited them in their ancestral tombs.[51]

In 189 AD twenty-five senators were granted a suffect consulship for the following year, the number being unheard of. Commodus and his brother-in-law's brother, M Petronius Sura Septimianus, were to start the year as ordinary consuls, with the emperor stepping down and appointing two new suffect consuls at the start of each month. Amongst these numbered proven adherents of Cleander and the regime, Septimius Severus being one. The sources however do not directly state that these men paid for this honour but the information is placed within passages referring to Cleander selling posts. This is one of the tricks the senatorial sources use, using inference to suggest a crime on the part of Commodus and Cleander when no direct evidence existed. The account of Septimius Severus' appointment to the consulship in the *Historia Augusta* makes no mention of the future emperor having had to buy the office:

> He now served his first consulship, having Apuleius Rufinus for his colleague – an office for which Commodus appointed him from among a large number of aspirants.[52]

If Severus had had to buy the consulship, the slander loving *Historia Augusta* would not only have mentioned it but would have revelled in such an act by a great man. We know nothing of Apuleius Rufinus but others who were awarded a suffect consulship around this time included Pescennius Niger, Lollianus Gentianus and perhaps Clodius Albinus. All were members of noble families whilst Lollianus' family were the patrons of Pertinax. All had successfully served Commodus and Cleander in suppressing Maternus in the Deserters' War and would go on to have illustrious careers, Lollianus becoming Governor of Hispania Citerior, Niger Governor of the crucial province of Syria, Albinus appointed to Britain and Severus Pannonia. Another powerful senatorial family prospered under Commodus, the Pollieni. Pollienus Auspex had served Marcus Aurelius as suffect consul in 170 AD and after governing Dalmatia, he was appointed *Iudex ex delegatione Caesarum* between 176 and 180 AD, carrying out the imperial judicial role in Rome in the absence of Commodus and his father on the Danube and in the East. His next appointment was prefect of the *alimentia Appiae et Flaminiae* responsible for distributions of aid to the poor in these regions and then he appears to have been promoted to Proconsular Governor of Africa Proconsularis. His son, of the same name, was awarded a suffect consulship by Commodus at an undetermined date, holding governorships of Hispania Tarraconensis and Dacia. Both were to hold considerable influence in the reigns of Commodus' successors. Other prominent nobles were awarded the ordinary consulship between 185 and 190 AD. The emperor in 186 AD honoured the noble M Acilius Glabrio by sharing the office of consul with him. This Acilius Glabrio has been identified as being the son of the consul of 152 AD, M Acilius Glabrio Cn. Cornelius Severus and Faustina whose name suggests a blood relationship to the imperial family making their son, the suffect consul of 173 and ordinary consul of 186 AD, a member. In 190 AD Commodus shared the consulship with the brother of his sister's husband, M Petronius Sura Septimianus. L Bruttius Quintius Crispinus, his wife's brother, held consular office in 187 AD and Seius Fuscianus held it for a second time in 188 AD, reward for his successful job as Urban Prefect. The prestige and *dignitas* of the consulship was maintained by the emperor and was an honour that the senatorial elite continued to aspire to.[53]

The plague no doubt took a great toll not just on the poor, but the equestrian and senatorial classes as well. Commodus enrolled in the senate freedmen many of whom were extremely rich and qualified through possessing wealth of over a million *sesterces*. The *Historia Augusta* even suggests some were granted patrician status as well although this is to be doubted as the arch conservative Dio would have referred to the offence this caused. Pertinax on his accession ordered a new census, no doubt to rid the senate of those the elite felt unworthy of such status through lack of the required social background or wealth, something quite ironic as Pertinax himself was the son of a freedman. The emperor, reliant upon the imperial household to carry out the functions of government, conferred *beneficia* on those closest to him. An inscription from the imperial villa at Lanuvium records a *pantomimus*, or mime artist and freedman, who was *adlectus iuvenes*.

Commodus raised many senators to the rank of praetor, Pertinax alienating this significant number by introducing a *senatus consulta* reducing the rank and status of these men to less than that of senators who had actually served in office as praetors. These men would in Commodus' eyes remain loyal to him and through natural promotion would become the commanders of the legions and governors of the strategic senatorial provinces. To raise them to praetorian rank would reduce the time before they could be awarded prominant military commands as many of the men whom he inherited from his father were rapidly approaching an age where they would be unable to command or travel to distant areas of the empire, men such as Marcus Valerius Maximus, Acilius Glabrio, Helvidius Pertinax, Vettius Sabinianus. Others had already died, such as Aufidius Victorinus and Claudius Severus or retired to their estates: Claudius Pompeianus. These men, along with the twenty-five suffect consuls of 190 AD, would also form a significant block of support within the senate and, with time and promotions, would sit amongst the noble ex consuls, being called first to give their opinions and pronouncements and so influencing the subsequent debates. At a lower social strata the career of L Annius Fabianus illustrates the new opportunities that existed when men of ability were drawn to the emperor's attention. His father C Annius Fabianus was unremarkable, being a flamen or priest in his home city of Caesarea before being chosen to sit as a judge in Rome on the *quinque decuriae*, he then served as the prefect of a quingenary cohort. His son received the grant of the *equus publicus* from Marcus Aurelius enabling him to commence his equestrian career as commander of the *cohors* IV Raetorum in about 175 AD, and then he served as a tribune in the Third Italica stationed in Raetia where he was decorated in the German War fought by Commodus and Marcus Aurelius. He now appears to have come to the emperor's attention, rapidly completing his third military command in charge of the ala I Flavia Sebastenorum in Caesarea itself before commencing his procurator career as an officer in the imperial fleet at Misenum; then he received the governorship of the small provinces of Atrectine Alps and Tractus Carthaginiensis. His rise in status is reflected in his marriage to the daughter of a senator, Arminia Paulina and their son, Annius Arminius Donatus entered the senate.[54]

The senatorial aristocracy were the holders of the greatest taxable wealth in the empire; the vast majority of the population despised the senate and looked to the emperor for protection from their own land accumulation and exorbitant rents. When the sources refer to 'Romans' it is the elite they are referring to.

Herodian appears for the most part unconcerned by the increased 'taxes' Cleander and Commodus imposed on this group. Commodus remained popular with the army, praetorians and populace of Rome and the empire until his assassination. The senatorial elite were targeted with an additional tax when senators, their wives and children, were obliged to contribute two gold pieces each year on the emperor's birthday, whilst senators in all other cities had to give five *denarii* each. The chronology of events and Dio's use of the word 'finally' suggests this was towards the end of the reign, perhaps 192 AD, after the government had incurred the extraordinary costs caused by the fire that devastated huge areas of Rome with the treasury was almost emptied by expenditures for restorations and repairs to public buildings. These repairs were also necessitated by a fire which struck the capital between 185 AD and 188 AD, probably 186 AD. This event is recorded only by later Christian writers, Dio and Herodian are more focused on the later fire of 192 AD which could be used as evidence of ill omens foretelling the death of the emperor: 'lightning struck the capitol and started a fire, which in its devouring course, burned the library that the fathers had founded in their enthusiasm for learning.' To try to reduce such frequent events Commodus created a new post with responsibility for fire fighting, the *curator aquarum et Minuciae* which would be retained by Septimius Severus.[55]

According to our sources the revenues raised amounted to a 'large sum of money', yet by the end of the reign the treasury was empty with Commodus' successor, Pertinax, also encountering financial difficulties. Cleander was clearly acting under the direct supervision of the emperor as the vast majority of the monies he raised he passed on to Commodus and the imperial *fiscus*, some he retained, making him the wealthiest *cubicularius* the city had ever known. Some of the money was given to Commodus' concubines, no doubt to gain their support and loyalty. Other monies he had himself dispersed as *beneficia* building up his own nexus of clients across Rome and the empire; some he spent on the baths that bore his name, 'and other works of benefit either to individuals or to cities.' Inscriptions bearing his name across Italy and the empire are testament to his acts of personal *liberalitas*, whilst many more bear the chiselled out name of Commodus whose record suffered from the senatorial act of *damnatio* after his murder. Some of this wealth Cleander spent on his houses yet his generosity was necessitated by his low social status, hence the need to build a network based on *amicitiae*.[56]

Cleander first targeted the enemies of his enemy as potential *amici*; resurrecting the careers of those who fell under suspicion in Perennis' investigations following the plot of Lucilla and her senatorial adherents. Pertinax was sent to Britain whilst Septimius Severus was tasked, along with Niger and Albinus, with removing the threat of Maternus. Even Didius Julianus received responsibility for the *alimentia*, not yet trusted with responsibility of appointment to a governorship commanding legions. Pertinax replaced Ulpius Marcellus, whose return to Rome was greedily anticipated by his enemies looking to use his failure to suppress the mutiny in the armies of Britain as the chance to destroy his career and gain half his estates. No doubt he was charged with *majestas*, perhaps being accused of aiding the revolt against the emperor. He appears to have lost his case and, having been condemned to death, no doubt by the senate themselves, he was pardoned by Commodus who did not question his loyalty.[57]

Pertinax received a letter from Commodus making amends for his enforced retirement and loaded him with honours. Perennis was no doubt blamed for his mistreatment, whilst Cleander ensured that his new *amicus* was aware of the debt he owed him in reviving his fortunes. Pertinax had previously served in Britain, probably as a tribune of a legion, but the chaos that greeted him on his arrival in the province would have horrified him. A legion had mutinied and at first it attempted to proclaim Pertinax emperor, much in the same manner that the legionaries had attempted to proclaim Priscus previously. The British army feared the restoration of discipline as well as the inevitable punishments that would be handed out to the main instigators of the unrest. Pertinax refused the dubious honour, and instead attempted to restore order. The result was widespread rebellion, Dio referring to these events as 'the great revolt'. Soldiers from one of the legions set off in search of the governor in order to murder him. The following events are evidenced by one of the rare instances when history and archaeology combine. Archaeologists excavating Lullingstone Villa found a discarded intaglio of winged victory amongst a pile of coins. The intaglio has been identified as the governor's seal, winged victory being his personal emblem and a sign of imperial power. Inside the building excavations revealed two busts carved from Pentelic marble sourced from Greece. One bust has been identified as that of Pertinax, whist the other is probably that of his father, Publius Helvius Successus. The bust of Pertinax had been attacked by weapons, the head being severed from its plinth. It has been suggested that the absence of farming buildings around the villa complex indicate it was the country retreat of the governor. The mutineers had waited until Pertinax was at his country residence knowing his bodyguard would be reduced. They burst into the complex, murdering his guards, advisors and officers, leaving the governor amongst the slain. They then proceeded to loot the property taking gold, silver and precious items, the intaglio being prised from the gold ring which was retained by the looters but the intaglio discarded. There are signs of knife cuts on the gemstone. The statues of Pertinax bore the brunt of the mutineers' fury. Pertinax survived and reeked vengeance upon those that had so nearly killed him, the revolt was crushed and those implicated 'punished very severely'. This phrase suggests he employed decimation. Soldiers selected for punishment would be divided into groups of ten. One man was selected at random by the drawing of lots for stoning to death by his comrades. The remaining soldiers were then given barley rations instead of wheat. The leaders of the rebellion would be executed separately.[58]

Pertinax's miraculous escape and his restoration of order was acclaimed 'on all sides'. Dio preserves a vignette, recording Commodus' attendance of a race at the Circus Maximus whilst his *amicus* was still in Britain. The emperor supported the 'Greens' who had chosen to name one of their horses after the famed general and governor of Britain, an acknowledgement of the favour Pertinax was now held in. The horse, Pertinax, won a race and so the supporters of the Greens shouted out 'It is Pertinax'. Supporters of the other factions replied, 'Would that it be so.' This is not evidence, as Dio would have the reader believe, of dissatisfaction at the rule of Commodus as he remained popular to the end amongst the urban populace and provincials. This was a mischievous attempt to anger the most prominent supporter of their opponents, the Greens. By 187 AD Britain was once more securely held after nearly seven years of invasion and unrest, yet the army of the province seethed with resentment at the severity of Pertinax's actions in securing the province. The governor petitioned his emperor to be relieved of his post citing the legions' hostility towards him. His wish was granted and he returned to Italy. He was given the less pressured post of responsibility for the *alimentia* providing, in theory, aid for the poor but with the financial restrictions, his job was not particularly time consuming or demanding.[59]

Pertinax's return was probably also on the advice of Cleander who looked for allies in his struggle with the emperor's brother-in-law, Antistius Burrus. The court appears to have divided between adherents and *amici* of Cleander and those of Burrus who 'was denouncing to Commodus all that was being done'. There can be little doubt that the emperor was fully aware of what Cleander was doing as the imperial *fiscus* was receiving most of the monies levied by the freedman's extra ordinary financial levies.[60] Burrus was keeping Commodus fully aware of the opinions of the senatorial and equestrian elite. He was born and raised in Thibilis in North Africa, his father was Quintus Antistius Adventus Aquilinus Postumus who had served as governor of a number of provinces under Marcus Aurelius. He had been rewarded for his successful commands in the Parthian War and the war against the Marcomanni with the consulship of 167 AD. His son was married to Sabina before the death of Marcus Aurelius and had also been awarded the consulship of 181 AD by Commodus. Antistius Burrus was supported by a number of powerful and influential figures including Arrius Antoninus who was a highly respected senator, legal expert and former friend of Fronto. Arrius was related to both the noble C Aufidius Victorinus, the consul of 173 AD, who held a distinguished record and the Emperor Antoninus Pius, through his mother Arria Fadilla. In the tumultuous year of 175 AD Antoninus had been given the province of Cappadocia whilst Martius Verus pacified Syria. After the revolt of Avidius Cassius the young

Commodus may have stayed at the governor's residence with his father as he toured the east. Another influential supporter of Burrus was the Praetorian Prefect Atilius Aebutianus who was the patron of the Dalmatian city of Asseria. A statue to him was erected in the forum portico with a plaque describing him as *clarissimus vir*, a title applied only to senators or the most prominent equestrian officials, whilst another inscription describes him as holding the position of Commodus' *tribunus numeri singularium*. He was still Praetorian Prefect in 188/9 AD as he is named in a fragmentary inscription dated to a consul with the cognomen Silane; this could be M Servilius Silanus, the consul of 188 AD; or Q Servilius Silanus, the consul of the following year.[61]

Burrus and Arrius Antoninus were fully aware of Commodus' support for Cleander's methods in raising additional revenues and so by reporting to the emperor what Cleander was doing would not only be futile, it would also be an indirect criticism of the emperor himself; effectively political suicide. Arrius' legal expertise was probably drawn upon as it would have been more politic of them to question the legalities of such financial procurement. It appears it was not Commodus who was annoyed by Burrus' constant interventions but Cleander who must have felt his position was being undermined. Burrus held a position of strength, being married to the emperor's sister and supported by powerful senators but most importantly, by at least one of the Praetorian Prefects. Cleander, however, was a man to make Machiavelli proud. He knew the emperor was fearful of any plots, real or imagined. Any accusation against Burrus originating from himself however would have been treated with scepticism by Commodus, but such an accusation from a trusted and time served *amicus* would be treated differently. One such man existed who owed Cleander repayment on a debt; the reciprocal nature of political and social relationships between the elite now came into play.

Pertinax, his stock in the emperor's eyes riding on the crest of a wave, petitioned a return to Italy as the British legions were now hostile to him after the imposition of severe punishments. He was given the unusual post of *praefectus aliamentorum*. As he was an experienced general he would normally have expected another governorship of one of the more prestigious provinces. However this post allowed Pertinax to remain in or around Rome, especially as there was little or no charity money to distribute due to the financial constraints the government had to function under. It was Pertinax who 'laid before Commodus the charge that Antistius Burrus and Arrius Antoninus were aspiring to the throne'. The biographer of the *Historia Augusta*, in his history of Commodus, makes clear the true mover behind the scenes was Cleander 'because his power was too great that he brought Burrus, the husband of Commodus' sister, who was denouncing and reporting to Commodus all that was being done, and under the suspicion that he was pretending to the throne, and had him put to death'.[62] Pertinax's allegations were convincing, the emperor pronounced judgement. Pertinax's reward would be the Proconsular governorship of Africa, no doubt on the recommendation of Cleander, who needed the services of his *amicus* to solve another crisis. A number of others who defended Burrus were also executed according to the *Historia Augusta* but no names are provided. Perhaps these were *amici* and clients of Burrus and Arrius Antoninus. We can conjecture that these included the Praetorian Prefect Aebutianus who was executed. The sources don't record the fate of the other prefect, T Longaeus Rufus, but if he had been executed alongside his colleague the ancient historians would surely have recorded this. More likely he retired or was adlected into the senate. Arrius Antoninus survived for a short while, serving as proconsular governor of Asia in 188–9 AD.

Sabina, Burrus' wife, was now a potential focus for opposition. She had not been implicated in her husband's fall but the memory of Lucilla's resentments must surely have motivated Commodus to neutralize this potential threat. She was rapidly married to the equestrian Lucius Aurelius Agaclytus, the son of Verus' freedman who had married Fundania, the widow of M Annius Libo, consul of 128 AD. She seems to have spent her remaining years well away from courtly politics in Thibilis in North Africa, her ex husband's birthplace, where numerous inscriptions record her patronage. She was made an honorary citizen of her adopted city. This new union was not blessed with any children.

Two new Praetorian Prefects were appointed: Regillus, of whom little is known, and L Julius Vehilius Gratus Julianus whose career has been preserved on an inscription. He had had a long and distinguished career, decorated for valour in the wars against Parthia by Antoninus Pius and Verus, as well as by Marcus Aurelius and Commodus in the wars on the Danube. It may be here that he came to Commodus' attention. He also was appointed *procurator Augusti* in command of a *vexillation tempore belli (Britannici)* at the time of a 'British war', the word *Britannici* being a restored supposition on the inscription. The chronological sequence suggests this was not referring to the wars in the province at the start of Commodus' reign but earlier, perhaps under Antoninus Pius in 154 AD or Marcus Aurelius in 163 AD. He later served as prefect of the fleet at Ravenna and Misenum before entering the imperial household as a financial secretary; *a rationibus*. The priorities of Commodus and Cleander are evident in this man's career. The financial problems required the appointment of men who could be trusted, and the reduced grain harvests caused primarily by large areas of land falling out of production, led to him being appointed prefect of the *annona* with responsibility for the distribution of grain to the populace. His diligence and skills were recognized by Cleander as he reorganized the grain fleet from Africa with promotion to the Praetorian Prefecture. Commodus appears to have formed a close bond with Julianus; the emperor would publicly embrace his prefect, kissing and addressing

1. Commodus as a youth in the Museum of Cologne, Germany.

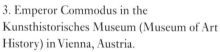

3. Emperor Commodus in the Kunsthistorisches Museum (Museum of Art History) in Vienna, Austria.

2. Bust of Commodus in the National Museum of Rome, c. 180.

4. Bust of Commodus in the Vatican Museum in Rome.

5. Emperor Commodus. *(The Getty Commodus)*

6. Young Hercules wearing a lion skin and carrying a club, now lost. Suggested to be a portrait of the Emperor Commodus.

7. Head of a statue of an emperor (probably Commodus); end of 2nd century AD, shown at the Landesmuseum Württemberg, Stuttgart, Germany.

9. Emperor Commodus. *(Copy in the Pushkin Museum of the original in British Museum)*

8. Statue of Commodus found at Aphrodisias in Turkey. Now in the Museum of Ephesus.

10. Portrait of Emperor Marcus Aurelius discovered at Acqua Traversa, near Rome, 1674.

11. Portrait of Co-emperor Lucius Verus discovered at Acqua Traversa, near Rome, 1674.

12. Faustina the Younger (130–175 AD), wife of the Emperor Marcus Aurelius and mother of Commodus. Marble, c. 161 AD in the Louvre Museum, Paris. Found in the area of Tivoli outside of Rome.

13. Marble bust of the Empress Bruttia Crispina, wife of Commodus, c. 178–180 AD in the Altes Museum, Berlin.

14. Bust of Commodus as Hercules in the Capitoline Museum, Rome, hence the lion skin, the club and the apple of the Hesperides. Part of a statuary group including two tritons to either side of the main figure.

15. Commodus as Caesar on a coin of 175–176. The inscription reads ADCOMMODO CAES AVG FIL GERM SARM. The reverse reads SPES PVBLICA and depicts Spes (Goddess of Hope) walking left, holding a flower and lifting the hem of her skirt. *(Classical Numismatic Group)*

16. Sestertius struck 177 AD on the return from the eastern provinces. The inscription around the laurel-wreathed head reads IMP CAES L AUREL COMMODUS GERM SARM. The reverse shows Marcus Aurelius and Commodus seated left on platform, with an officer beside them. Liberalitas stands before them, holding an abacus and cornucopiae while the citizen on the steps holds out the fold of their toga. Beneath are the words LIBERALITAS AUG. *(Classical Numismatic Group)*

17. A clipeus dated to the early 180s for the lucky return of the victorious Emperor Commodus. From the Museum Carnuntinum, Lower Austria. A clipeus was originally a decorative piece of plating worn on a shield. This commemorative inscription associated the Emperor Commodus with victory in the wars on the Danube and wishes for his safe return to Rome. It would have been hung in a temple or other public place.

18. A sestertius struck under Commodus in 180, commemorating the death of Marcus Aurelius and bearing the inscription DIVVS M ANTONINVS PIVS. Depicted on the reverse is a statue of Marcus Aurelius seated, holding a long sceptre in his right hand and raising his left, within a tristyle aediculum set on ornate car drawn right by four elephants. *(Classical Numismatic Group)*

19. Coin struck in 185 to celebrate the crushing of the revolt in Britain and restoration of the province after the invasions of 180. The laurel-wreathed head is inscribed: M COMMODVS ANTON AVG PIVS BRIT, while the reverse has P M TR P X IMP VII COS IIII P P S-C; VICT BRIT and shows Victory seated on captured shields, inscribing another set on her knee. *(Classical Numismatic Group)*

20. Struck in 186, this coin depicts Commodus, head with the inscription M COMMODVS ANT P FELIX AVG BRIT. On the reverse, Commodus stands on a dais, sceptre in hand, addressing soldiers assembled under three legionary aquila standards. The inscription is P M TR P XI IMP VII COS V P P, FID EXERCIT. Coinage celebrating the loyalty of the army suggests that there had been unrest in the legions. This coinage was produced in response to previous unrest in Britain and in Pannonia. *(Classical Numismatic Group)*

21. A coin struck in Rome in 191 or 192. Commodus is portrayed as Hercules wearing the lion skin within the inscription M AUREL CO-MM AUG P FEL. The reverse shows the club of Hercules with the inscription HERCVL ROMAN AVGV or 'Roman Hercules Augustus'. *(Classical Numismatic Group)*

22. This sesterces of 192 AD shows Commodus wearing laurels with the inscription L AEL AVREL CO MM AVG P FEL. The reverse celebrates the security of the grains supply from Africa and carries the legend PROVID ENTIAE AVG and shows the personification of Africa wearing an elephant skin headdress and with a lion at her feet to right. She is holding a sistrum and passing ears of wheat to Hercules with his club. Hercules has his right foot on the prow of a ship, a reference to the African grain fleet. *(Classical Numismatic Group)*

23. Bronze medallion of Commodus as the god, Janus.

24. Bronze medallion from 192 depicting Commodus as Hercules.

25. A sardonyx of Commodus with attributes of Helios, Apollo and Jupiter in the Hermitage Museum, St Petersburg, Russia.

26. A gold aureus of the Augusta Crispina. The reverse carries the legend VENVS FELIX, showing Venus seated left holding Nike, winged victory, who holds an open wreath in both hands. In her extended left hand Venus holds a sceptre; a dove is sat under her seat. *(Classical Numismatic Group)*

27. A Retiarius armed with trident and dagger fighting against a Secutor, the gladiator mosaic at the Roman villa in Nennig, Germany.

28. Statuette of a Secutor from Andesina, France c. 50 AD.

29. Gladiators fighting animals c. 200 AD from the Zliten mosaic.

30. Gladiators from the Zliten mosaic. From the left a disarmed Retiarius surrenders to a Secutor. In the centre two Murmillos fight each other. To the right a Thracian surrenders to his opponent.

31. Villa of the Quintili showing man–made platform and bathhouse to the right.

32. Villa of the Quintili, Rome.

33. The nymphaeum at the entrance to the Villa of the Quintili complex on the Via Appia.

34. Inscription from 182 AD commemorating building work under Commodus at Castellum Sablonetum (Ellingen) on the Danube in modern Bavaria. The inscription reads: [I]mp(eratori) Caes(ari) [[M(arco) A[u]r(elio) [Co]mmod[o]]]/ Antonino Aug(usto) Ger(manico) Sar(matico) maxim(o)/ trib(unicia) po[t(estate)] co(n)s(uli) III p(atri) p(atriae) kastel(li) (sic) Sablonet(i) mu/rum cum portis lapidi(bus) substitu/tum iussu Q(uinti) Spici Cerialis leg(ati) Aug(usti)/ pro pr(aetore) M[a]mertino et Rufo co(n)s(ulibus) pe/r singulares pedites cura(m) agente/ Aur(elio) Argivo c(enturione) leg(ionis) III Ital(icae). However, the name of Commodus in the top right-hand corner was removed when he suffered damnatio memoriae. (AE 1983, 730).

35. Bust of the Emperor Commodus from the Philippi Museum in Macedonia. The removal of the nose suggests this was a deliberate act following his damnatio memoriae.

36. Coin from 193 of the Emperor Didius Julianus, who swore to avenge Commodus. The inscription reads IMP CAES M DID IVLIAN AVG. *(Classical Numismatic Group Inc (CNG) Munt van CNG coins)*

37. Bust with paludamentum of Roman Emperor Septimius Severus (AD 193–211), said to be have been found in the area of Herculaneum. *(Louvre Museum, Paris)*

him as 'father'. The emperor would normally allow his *amici* to merely kiss his hand, a kiss from the emperor received on the cheeks was a great honour, almost acknowledging an equality in status. Furthermore the father in Rome's patriarchal society was head of the household with responsibility for its safety and prosperity. Commodus appears to provide such *beneficia* on Julianus in the expectation of the prefect feeling obliged to act in a reciprocal way, guarding the emperor's safety at all costs. Julianus appears also to have been on the receiving end of some of the emperor's practical jokes. Whilst attending upon the emperor on official business, clad in his toga and accompanied by all his staff, Commodus pushed him into a swimming pool. We are not told the context of this act, it may have been in a fit of anger on the emperor's part but the preceding sentence in the account in the *Historia Augusta* tells of another practical joke played on dinner guests, who being served an exquisite dish, found that it was in fact 'two misshapen hunchbacks', much to the amusement of the emperor who immediately 'advanced and enriched them'. On another occasion Julianus, by now an elderly man, was ordered 'to dance naked before his concubines, clashing cymbals and making grimaces'. Again the biographer mentions this out of context, but the context can be surmised. The presence of the concubines suggests that Commodus and the Praetorian Prefect will have been in an informal setting, a private imperial banquet. The concubines were themselves powerful and influential individuals, some like Marcia were the emperor's advisor. All had been enriched by Cleander who recognized their important role in courtly politics. After a banquet the entertainment followed, supplemented by an unlimited supply of wine. One of the most influential freedmen in Commodus' court was L Aurelius Apolaustus Memphius who had been returned to Rome with Verus, and after the joint emperor's death, he entered the household of the young Commodus. He is not to be confused with the pantomime artist named L Aelius Apolaustus who is mentioned in a letter to Fronto in 161/2 AD, and who was closely associated with Cleander, sharing his fate in 189 AD. Inscriptions honouring both are found throughout Italy, Memphius being the recipient of such an inscription in 199 AD, ten years after the death of his namesake.

In his earlier life Apolaustus Memphius, originally named Agrippa, was a pantomime or mime artist. Herodian must be referring to Memphius, and others like him such as Pylades, when he says 'clowns and performers of scurrilous acts gained complete control over him'. Both Apolaustus and Cleander, along with other freedmen, were probably attending the imperial banquet as *amici* of the emperor. Apolaustus means 'enjoyable' and 'Memphius' refers either to his origin or, more likely, the Memphian dance which was his speciality. Such dancers move every muscle in their body accompanied to the music of flutes, cymbals and harpists. These dances had to be performed naked to demonstrate the artists' skill and dexterity, hence they are described as 'scurrilous'. The Roman elite paid fortunes to own or employ such performers but it was considered a great loss of *dignitas* to perform oneself. Clearly Commodus, Julianus and other guests, having spent the evening fine dining and drinking, had been watching a performance of mine artists when Julianus was urged to test his own skills, no doubt to the great amusement of the audience.[63]

As well as appointing Julianus and Regillus Praetorian Prefects, Commodus placed Cleander over them with the title *Pugione* or *Bearer of the Dagger*, the dagger being the symbol of the Praetorian Prefects as they were the only officials allowed to be armed in the presence of the emperor. This was a unique position: 'then for the first time there were three prefects of the guard.' Cleander was not granted the office of Praetorian Prefect itself as he was a freedman and to allow a man of such low status such a prestigious office would have offended the equestrian class in particular. The position of *a pugione* is not a name for Praetorian Prefect but implies power similar to that of the prefects whilst being directly responsible for the protection of the emperor. Such a position would naturally limit the power of the remaining two prefects as the *Historia Augusta* claims they were appointed, retained or dismissed at the command of Cleander. Herodian explicitly states Cleander was 'in command of the soldiers' and 'had control of the bodyguard'. The day-to-day running of the guard probably remained in the hands of Regillus and Julianus, but Cleander would hold a supervisory role over them. This unique office also reduced access to the emperor as the two prefects would report not to Commodus but Cleander. This is evident when violence broke out in Rome and Commodus remained in ignorance of these events as Herodian explains: 'the fear of Cleander's power was so such that no one was prepared to tell Commodus what was going on'. This is supported by Dio who records that 'no one had kept him informed of what was going on'. The appointment to *pugione* could not have been made before 186 AD as Cleander is recorded on an inscription dated to before 186 AD without this title but appears as *pugione* on a dedication to the consul T Aius Sanctus which gives him the title *a cubiculo et a pugione*. The appointment best fits into the chronology of events after the execution of Aebutianus.[64] Cleander had gained complete control over access to the emperor as well as neutralizing the position of Praetorian Prefect as a point of opposition to him, as it had under Aebutianus. Yet one is left wondering why Commodus would allow himself to be so isolated from outside events and reliant upon one man. He must have trusted his *cubicularius* implicitly yet feared the potential threat of the Praetorian Prefecture after his experiences with Paternus, Perennis and now Aebutianus. He felt the need for a check on the power and influence of the prefecture, one that Cleander's supervision would provide.

As events and fortune had conspired against Perennis, they did so against Cleander who now faced a crisis in Africa. A rebellion had broken in North Africa which, in conjunction with reduced grain production in Sicily caused by the plague, resulted in a famine in the city of Rome. Pertinax was appointed to suppress this large-scale rebellion, a man whom both Commodus and Cleander had total confidence in after his crushing of the army mutiny in Britain and his disclosure of the 'conspiracy' of Burrus. Cleander no doubt felt that as the son of a freedman, Pertinax would not share the social prejudices of other members of Rome's elite. Neither Dio nor Herodian mention this rebellion, despite the fact that rebellions are mentioned in Britain, Germany and Dacia. The epitomizers of Dio in summarizing his books may have edited out the passages relating to these events, whilst Herodian appears more focused on events in Rome than in the provinces of the empire. He also accuses Cleander of precipitating the famine itself by hoarding grain and so driving up the prices, in order to sell at a large profit. Cleander was already immensely rich so this seems unlikely. Furthermore, there were reasons for the shortage which were entirely out of Cleander's hands, and Cleander was attempting to solve the shortage of grain.[65] It would be political suicide to risk rioting in the city of Rome in order to make a profit from such a practice. A man of such political acumen would never think of taking such a risk.

Careful reading of the sources indicates that Cleander did indeed react to the famine that was gripping the city. As well as appointing his *amicus*, Pertinax, as governor of the grain province of Africa from 188 to 189 AD, he also appointed Septimius Geta to Sicily and then replaced him with his brother, Septimius Severus. The appointment of such prominent senators to the minor province of Sicily illustrates its importance to Cleander at this time. The highly unusual sequence of governors from the same family suggests a need to ensure grain shipments to Rome were in reliable hands. The identity of the governor of the vital grain-producing province of Egypt is unclear for 188 AD but papyri dated to 189–190 AD show that one Tineius Demetrius was governing Egypt but his predecessor was M Papyrius Dionysius. He had already had a distinguished career; he started as an experienced lawyer, gaining promotion into the imperial bureaucracy as *a libellis* and then *a cognitionibus* with responsibility for Commodus' law court. His abilities were clearly recognized by the emperor who advanced him to the imperial *consilium* on a salary of 100,000 *sesterces* and then appointed him Prefect of the Annona with responsibility for the grain supply for Rome. He then appears to have been appointed to the post of Prefect of Egypt, the natural progression for a distinguished equestrian. Strangely this appointment was then rescinded by Cleander, probably before he set out for Egypt and he was reappointed to his previous post. Dionysius' fall from favour had links to the execution of Arrius Antoninus, *amicus* of Burrus and proconsular Governor of Asia. Whilst governor of the province Arrius Antoninus had condemned a certain Attalus. Attalus was a prominent member of the Roman elite who held the necessary influence to successfully approach Cleander seeking revenge upon Antoninus. Cleander saw an opportunity, not only to remove a former adherent of Burrus but the *cubicularius* also hoped to gain the *gratia* of this Attalus. Charges were made against Antoninus relating to Burrus 'plot' to ascend the throne; a charge of *majestas* that would be tried in the imperial court rather than in the senate. Arrius Antoninus was sentenced to death. Both Papyrius Dionysius and Arrius Antoninus were eminent lawyers and their shared occupations would mean they would often have come into contact with each other and become *amici*. Cleander would have become suspicious of all the clients and *amici* of the prominent senator but he would have had no concrete evidence against Dionysius, who remained an *amicus* of the emperor, otherwise he would have shared Antonius' fate as well. The province of Egypt however, was too important to be placed in the hands of someone whose loyalty to Cleander was in doubt and so his order to travel to Egypt was countermanded leaving him in possession of the post he had already held, for which no successor had yet been appointed. A mistake Cleander would regret.[66]

Pertinax, of all the new appointments, had the most difficult task ensuring the grain ships from Carthage left on time. The *Historia Augusta* records that he 'suppressed many rebellions by aid of prophetic verses which issued from the temple of Caelestis'. Caelistis or Tanit was the Goddess of Carthage worshipped in Roman times as Caelestis Afrorum Dea. She was worshipped throughout Northern Africa and Spain; with many soldiers being adherents the cult spread throughout the empire. Originally the goddess was worshipped as the Carthaginian Tanit, but since the Roman conquest of Carthage the goddess had been identified with Juno Caelestis and a huge sanctuary was constructed that dominated the city of Carthage itself. It was described as one of the greatest and most influential sanctuaries in the empire. Sources describe it as being the largest public space in Carthage surrounded by trees in a park-like setting within which stood the temple containing a monumental statue of Caelestis herself. Her priestesses were famous for their oracles who were 'inspired by the goddess, to predict the truth'. The late Christian writer Augustine refers to her priests and choristers who delivered the religious rites to a 'vast assemblage of people'. Ornate Carthaginian stella show Tanit with the crescent moon and sun above her head, her hands holding cornucopia from which pour the fruits of the earth, grapes and pomegranates, all symbols of fertility. Like Tanit, Juno had a warlike aspect, and is often portrayed as armed and wearing a goatskin cloak. Connected to ideas of force and vitality she had a more widespread and complex role, often seen as the protector of the community and deliverer of fertility. In a time of need the people of Africa, like their forefathers before them, turned to the goddess for salvation and an answer to their problems. Augustine, a native of North Africa, being born at Thagaste, gives an indication of one reason why the goddess remained so popular despite his efforts as Bishop of Hippo to convert them to Christianity in the fifth century: 'There are some who dismiss God when they hunger in this world and they ask Mercury or Jupiter to grant a favour which may be granted to them, or they ask the same of her who they call Caelestis, or some other demon.' The *Historia Augusta* refers to many rebellions in the area which were not limited to the city of Carthage but were widespread. The crisis was so grave that Commodus himself contemplated travelling to the province. Provincial unrest would normally not require the presence of the emperor, but the impact of this rebellion in one of the main grain producing areas of the empire, was seen as a direct threat to the stability of the regime itself. Funds were requested from the senate but Pertinax's novel solution to the problem meant the imperial presence was no longer required. The funds however were not returned to the public treasury but retained by the imperial *fiscus*.[67]

It seems more than coincidence that this unrest took place at the same time as Cleander organized a new grain fleet from Carthage. Again the *Historia Augusta* provides an answer: Commodus 'ordered a general reduction of prices, the result of which was even greater scarcity'. With little or no understanding of simple economics, in particular the relationships between prices, supply and demand, both the emperor and Cleander resorted to fixing the price of grain at a price that the financially destitute state could afford. This would have resulted in producers, being unable to cover the costs of production, namely the cost of labour at harvest time, either leaving crops to rot in the fields or attempting to sell privately at a higher price. Unable to deliver on the agreed quota imperial contractors may have requisitioned grain at the lower price to meet their obligations as the political priority for Cleander was feeding the populace of Rome. The result was a shortage of grain in the breadbasket of the empire, resulting in rising prices for the populace of the province and the resentment of the landowners who had been deprived of a greater profit. This would rapidly escalate to widespread unrest with the people turning to Tanit/Caelestis, the goddess of fertility and martial virtues to answer their problems.

It has been claimed that Pertinax himself may have stirred up the rebellion wishing to add to the unrest caused by the execution of the two African senators, Antistius Burrus and Arrius Antoninus to overthrow Cleander. However it was Pertinax himself who implicated both 'conspirators' in the supposed plot and Pertinax's revived fortunes appear to have been due to the patronage of Cleander himself. Such a betrayal of *amicitiae* was viewed in the gravest terms, breaking the very bonds that bound Roman society together. Although Pertinax was a powerful noble who would have been at the centre of a nexus of bonds of *amicitiae* and patronage, it is doubtful that his links in the province of Africa were extensive enough to foster widespread rebellion even amongst the disaffected clients and *amici* of Burrus and Arrius Antoninus.[68]

Pertinax, a consummate politician, rapidly assessed the situation. He probably realized that there were not enough troops in the area to crush the unrest with only one legion in the province based at Lambaesis; the Third Legion Augusta. Military action would also result in further disruption of the grain supply with consequent unrest in Rome. Instead Pertinax utilized the power the goddess held over the people and realized he could use her prophetic powers to promise future abundance and the end of their hunger. This would allow him time to deliver on the promises the goddess made as well as the promises he undoubtedly made to Cleander on his appointment as governor. The leverage he could have used on the priests and priestesses of Caelestis would not only have been political, it would have been reinforced with the threat of military force. No doubt a large financial contribution to the temple would placate the goddess and her officials as well. Augustine again describes the goddess' eunuchs in procession around the city of Carthage: 'They were seen yesterday, their hair moist with perfume, their faces covered in make-up, their limbs flaccid, their walk effeminate, wandering through the squares and streets of Carthage demanding from the people the means to subsidize their shameful life.' Such a procession may have inspired Pertinax to offer financial subsidies from the state in return for favourable pronouncements from the goddess herself. Pertinax as Governor of Africa is also recorded as condemning a prominent Roman for corruption, named 'Fulvius' in an extract from Dio. This 'Fulvius' has been tentatively identified with Septimius Severus' future Praetorian Prefect Fulvius Plautianus, who in *Herodian* is described as being exiled in his early career having been charged with a number of crimes including sedition. At this stage in their careers there appear to be no bonds of *amicitiae* between the Severii and Pertinax, but this was to change.[69]

By the end of 189 AD Pertinax was back in Rome, another crisis solved by this valuable *amicus* of the imperial regime; his reward, the Prefecture of the City of Rome. Both Africa and Sicily were secured by the appointment of other senators who owed a debt of *gratia* to the *cubicularius*, Didius Julianus replacing Pertinax, and Geta with his brother Septimius Severus.[70]

Chapter Six

Nemesis: The Fall of Cleander (190 AD)

The various measures and precautions made by Cleander failed to alleviate the shortage of grain. Unrest in Africa had already effected production in the province, whilst the cost of labour caused by the plague had led to much agricultural land in Italy and Sicily falling out of production as well, resulting in a famine in the capital. Coinage distributed on 1 January 190 AD records the legend 'Everything has turned out well for the dutiful emperor.' The coin shows Commodus sacrificing at an altar before the statue of Neptune, the God of the Sea. A second issue carries the legend *Votis Felicibus* (The vows turned out well), again showing Commodus and another figure sacrificing at a tripod altar in the harbour of Ostia with a slain bull and a lighthouse behind, two grain ships entering the harbour, one piloted by Serapis. Serapis was a Graeco-Egyptian god associated with resurrection and abundance. The obverse legend does not carry the usual *M COMMODUS ANT P FELX AUG BRIT* but *IMP COMMODUS AUG PIUS FELIX*, the change of emphasis in the nomenclature stressing the qualities that got him through the crisis of 189 AD: devotion to duty, in particular, religious duty. *Pius*, good fortune and *Felix*, happiness at the protection shown by the gods towards the emperor. Another issue shows the personification of *Fides* standing to the left holding ears of corn with the legend: 'Loyalty of the Cohorts'. The coins would have been produced in the mints around November and December when the crisis had abated, for distribution at the start of January. The origins of the crisis are clear: Rome was already suffering famine at the start of the summer with reduced yields in the regions close to the capital, but the main supplier of grain to Rome was Egypt. The coinage suggests that poor weather delayed the embarkation of the grain fleet in March/April, hence the emperor's sacrifices to Neptune for calm weather and his location at the main port of Rome, Ostia. As Tacitus has the Emperor Tiberius say: 'the very existence of the people of Rome is daily at the mercy of uncertain waves and storms.'[1]

It is believed up to 200,000 households in the capital were entitled to the distribution of the free grain dole or were entitled to purchase it at a very low price, but the city's population was approaching 1,000,000, of whom 30 per cent were slaves. To provide the dole alone over 300 million tonnes of grain were needed to be transported to Rome each year and held in vast warehouses. It is estimated that by 58 BC this grain dole cost the state up to a fifth of its annual income. The grain was unloaded at Ostia or Portus from the ships, some over 1,000 tonnes, and guilds were employed to use smaller boats to move the cargo along the Tiber and canals connecting the city with its ports. To prevent corruption detailed receipts carried on board the ships recorded the quantity and quality of the grain and kept in sealed pouches along with a sample of the grain loaded in Alexandria and Carthage. This was checked by imperial officials based at the harbour who reported to the Prefect of the Annona. A scarcity of grain would not only cause discontent with those entitled to the free dole but also with the vast majority of the households in the city not entitled to the *annona*. They will have suffered from rapidly increasing prices causing even greater unrest. The mob demanded both bread and circuses. The Prefect of the Annona, Papirius Dionysius, who had responsibility for the transportation, storage and distribution of grain, decided to exacerbate this situation to stir up the mob into demanding the death of Cleander. This was not a new idea, the Roman noble woman Crispinilla had crossed to Africa after the suicide of Nero to persuade the governor of the province to rebel causing a shortage of grain in the capital.[2] Papirius Dionysius, according to Dio, vastly increased the severity of the famine, blaming the shortage on Cleander who stood accused of hoarding in order to gain popularity amongst the populace and soldiers. Allegedly he hoped to increase his popularity by solving the crisis by releasing the grain secretly stored in the warehouses whilst making a hefty profit from selling at the artificially inflated price. This is the propaganda that Herodian chooses to repeat in his account of the crisis. It would in fact have been quite remise of Cleander if he had not tried to buy up grain on the open market to feed the populace. This act was used by the conspirators to accuse him of hoarding, ignoring the fact that there was very little surplus to purchase in the first place.[3] However Papirius Dionysuis had both motive and opportunity. He may have been a close *amicus* of Arrius Antoninus who had been executed after being condemned on a charge of *majestas* emanating from the *cubicularius*, and had his promotion to the post of Egyptian Prefect cancelled on the orders of Cleander. Opportunity was provided by the famine that had already gripped Rome and his post of responsibility for the transportation and storage of the grain enabled him to exploit an already tense and volatile situation. It is highly unlikely that the warehouses in and around Rome would have had the capacity to hold the vast tonnages of grain unloaded in the docks and stockpiled. Nor would it have been possible to keep such hoarding a secret from the starving population. More feasible a plan would be delaying the departure of the grain fleet from Egypt, a delay the emperor would later feel politic to blame on the weather rather than the maladministration of an official he appointed and who was accountable to him. How Cleander delayed the departure of the grain fleet is not recorded in any source but the merchant ships were in the hands of private contractors who were paid by the Prefect of the Annona, so perhaps financial leverage was used. The Prefect of Egypt though would have been fully aware of the delay in departure of the grain fleet and if he valued his life, would have endeavoured to ensure the fleet left on time. However Papirius Dionysius had originally been appointed to replace M Aurelius Verianus whose presence in Egypt is only attested on papyri for August 188 AD. It is possible this man fell to Cleander's desire to place men who were bound by bonds of *gratia* to himself in important posts. The first recorded evidence on papyri for his successor, Tineius Demetrius, is 23 August 189 AD, although it appears he ordered a census of the province in 188/189 AD. The delay in the arrival of a successor to Verianus may have led to a gap in the arrival of the prefect allowing Papirius Dionysius to use this time to order the ships to remain in harbour as there was no Egyptian prefect to countermand such an order. Another possibility is that either Verianus or Tineius Demetrius were working with Papirius Dionysius. Both of their tenures as Prefect of Egypt were very brief, Verianus perhaps feeling resentment at his recall to Rome. He appears to have been removed from his post in 190 AD to be replaced by Claudius Lucilianus or Petronius Quadratus.[4] The rapid and highly unusual turnover of prefects at this time hints at administrative chaos and instability in the province at the very time when a firm hand, like that of Pertinax in Africa, was needed.

The conspiracy to undermine Cleander was clearly well organized and extensive. Papirius Dionysius could not have acted alone. A rumour was spread that it was Cleander who had caused the famine through hoarding, the Romans holding him personally responsible rather than Commodus. The emperor seems in all the sources to have escaped any censure for the crisis, probably as he was seen trying to alleviate the problem by public sacrifices to the gods. From the beginning of 186 AD it was Cleander who was given direct responsibility for securing the steady supply of grain by reorganizing the African fleet and this delegation may have been publicly known. Herodian records that the Romans 'organized themselves in the theatres and shouted insults at him (Cleander) all together'. All the sources agree the famine had been prolonged in its severity which would suggest that such opposition and anger directed towards the *cubicularius* would also have built up over a period of time. The Games, including the gladiatorial combats and the races, were one of the few opportunities for the populace to pressure the emperor for *beneficia* or show disapproval. Whittaker suggests that these demonstrations were organized by the senatorial opposition employing their clients to voice their anger at Cleander. Commodus would have officiated at many of these events and would have been fully aware of the opprobrium his *cubicularius* was now held in. It is doubtful that the clients of the senatorial elite could command such a show of public opposition, their clientele would not filter down to the mass of the people from which they could gain little from acts of *beneficia*. The senatorial clients were mainly limited to the equestrian classes and leaders of the guilds. However the circus factions could hold control over the vast majority of the people and it is significant that the races were at the site where the mob commenced their march on Commodus' Quintillian villa on the outskirts of the city. By the end of the second century the main two factions were the Reds and the Greens; the Whites and Blues were by this time minor factions that were to be subsumed into the larger two. Commodus, like Caligula, was a supporter of the Greens; hence the Blue faction goading him at the races when the horse Pertinax won a race. The charioteers and the leaders had considerable power and influence, Caligula inviting them to imperial banquets, although there is no evidence of Commodus doing the same. The timing of this event was also significant, at the festival linked to the Corn Goddess Ceres. The unrest started after six races had been completed. The Circus Maximus held up to 200,000 people and was used in the Festival of Cerealia, perhaps because one of the two shrines at the southeast turning post was dedicated to Consus, a minor god of the grain store linked to Ceres. The major Festival of the Cerealias was in April, too early for the famine to have bitten into the stomachs of the populace of the city. The festival and games of the Consualia would also have used the Circus Maximus as the ancient shrine was in the stadium itself. There were two dates associated with this festival, 15 December and 21 August with the latter fitting perfectly into the chronological framework of the reduced volume of grain imported from Campania, Sicily and Carthage at the start of the sailing season followed by the delay in the arrival of the Egyptian grain harvest. Consus was the deity of harvest and grain storage, the Temple of Consus being underground as grain was often stored in underground vaults. The shrine was covered by earth all year and was only uncovered on this day when mules, assess and horses were exempt from all work and were led through the streets covered in garlands of flowers. One of the races held in the Circus Maximus included one where the chariots were pulled by mules. According to mythology the Festival of Consulia originated with Romulus who wined and dined his Sabine neighbours and when the men were suitably drunk, Romulus abducted the Sabine women to become the wives of unattached Romans; the 'Rape of the Sabine Women'. The conspirators would have had little problem associating the empty grain stores with Cleander's alleged hoarding. The festival was associated with times of plenty when the harvest had been bountiful and the store full to brimming. To ensure the crowd became aware of the divine anger at the actions of Cleander a creative piece of theatre was stage-managed as the seventh race was about to begin:

> a crowd of children ran into the Circus, led by a tall maiden of grim aspect, who, because of what afterwards happened, was thought to have been a divinity. The children shouted in concert many bitter words which the people

took up and then began to bawl out every conceivable insult; and finally the throng leaped down and set out to find Commodus (who was then in the Quintillian suburb), invoking many blessings on him and many curses upon Cleander.

The 'tall maiden' was probably symbolic of the Goddess Ops or Opis whose festival followed that of Consus on 25 August and again on 19 December, mirroring the festival of the grain storage. Opis was also a goddess of plenty, associated with agricultural produce and wealth, the 'grim aspect' of this goddess signifying the scarcity that the future seemed to hold.[5] The children's cries and lamentations would have reinforced the hunger felt by the children of families across Rome. Carefully choreographed, this was no spontaneous uprising by the people against Cleander but a well managed and planned plot whose breadth and daring was clearly beyond the work of one man, Papirius Dionysius. The mob's anger was not turned against Commodus as you would expect if the conspiracy had been organized by the nobles and aristocrats within the senate as proposed by Whittaker, rather men who hated Cleander. This group hoped to retain Commodus as emperor as they stood to gain by retaining the emperor. Papirius Dionysius' resentment and anger had been exploited by equestrians, concubines and members of the imperial family who resented the *cubicularius'* controlling access to the emperor.

It is at this point that our two main sources, Dio and Herodian, diverge in their accounts. As the mob travelled towards the Quintilian Villa along the Appian Way, they were attacked by soldiers acting under the orders of Cleander who had managed to keep all news of the uprising from the emperor. A significant group of freedmen working with Cleander must have colluded in this censoring of news. Dio records that the 'imperial cavalry' charged the mob, cutting down the fleeing citizens, who turned and ran for the city gates. These troops are recorded as being 'the entire cavalry cohort' who are described as being Cleander's 'warm supporters'. This unit must be the *Equites Singulares Augusti* who were recruited from the finest cavalry soldiers from the *alae*, auxiliary units made up of non-Roman citizens. Hadrian had increased their number from 750 men to 1,000 under the command of a military tribune. These men had a separate base to the Praetorians and a separate command structure, at this time reporting directly to Cleander as *a pugione*. Unlike the Praetorian cohorts who possessed a cavalry arm as well, the *Equites Singulares* consisted of only one cohort, as described in *Herodian*. The arrogant status conscious Praetorians would have been bristling with resentment at having a freedman as their ultimate commander. The two Praetorian Prefects who managed the Praetorians on a day-to-day basis would also resent their limited access to the emperor. They were unable to pass news of the unrest on to the emperor. Herodian records many civilians being cut down by the sword thrusts of the soldiers, others were trampled under the hoofs of the horses and yet more crushed under the feet of the panic-stricken mob. As the cavalry passed through the city gates, the populace who had remained in the city climbed onto the rooftops and hurled tiles upon the heads of the soldiers and horses below who now started to take significant casualties. The horses themselves started to slip on the cobbles of the streets as well as the tiles and stones thrown from above. In fright they threw their riders. At this moment the urban cohorts joined the fight against the *Equites Singulares* adding momentum to the mob's attack and the struggle was now resumed at close quarters. Herodian describes the scene as civil war with soldier attacking soldier and 'destroying each other'.[6]

Dio, in his account, records the attack on the mob by 'some soldiers' sent by Cleander who killed and wounded a few but the crowd, reinforced by 'the strength of the Praetorians' pressed on to Commodus' palace. F Millar questions the accuracy of Herodian's account over that of Dio.[7] Dio had held his quaestorship in 189 AD and had entered the senate and so would have been present to witness these events. Millar recognizes that it is at this point that Dio's account grows in depth, strength and detail. Accordingly, he argues, as an eyewitness Dio's history should take precedence over Herodian's. However we do not have the full account of Dio's history but a summarized version made by the epitomizers. Nor can we discount that Herodian himself was not an eyewitness of these events. Alfody, focusing on Herodian's structure of events, compares this account of popular unrest to other similar passages in his history. He concludes that Herodian edited out events or condensed them for the sake of structural symmetry. However, apart from the differences over which soldiers supported the mob in the fighting, both Herodian and the summarized version in Dio are remarkably similar suggesting the events transpired as Herodian described them.[8] Both describe unrest in public gatherings at games, both agree on Commodus' location on the outskirts of the city; both that the crowd's blood lust was directed at Cleander and not Commodus; both that soldiers at Cleander's behest attacked the crowd who, supported by other soldiers, resisted the attack and continued their advance on Commodus' residence. In fact both accounts may be accurate in their description of these events with both the Urban Cohorts and members of the Praetorians who equally shared no espirit de corps with the *Equites Singulares*, joining together after witnessing the massacre of the unarmed citizens at the hands of these *peregrini*, Roman subjects who were not citizens. This was a unique situation and the unit officers may have been absent, lost control of their units or decided to take a stand of neutrality hoping the removal of Cleander would further their position. Herodian records that after the death of Cleander the soldiers who supported the mob were frightened at the prospect of the emperor's anger 'since they realised that they had been misled into foolhardy actions which he (Commodus) viewed with displeasure'. Some of their officers must have taken a lead in raising their units against the *Equites Singulares*, whether this was due to genuine horror at the massacre taking place on the streets of Rome or because they had already been recruited into the conspiracy, is open to debate.[9] The Urban Prefect who was in command of the Urban cohorts, Publius Seius Fuscianus, was replaced by Pertinax in 189 AD but his condemnation, execution or exile is not recorded in any of the sources. He may have not been directly involved in these events but may have been retired to his estates as he was already an old man, having originally served as consul in 151 AD. Coins issued in the early months of 190 AD proclaim *fides coh(ortium)*, the loyalty of the cohorts. This may refer to the Praetorian cohorts, the Urban cohorts or more likely, both. Such legends infer that at some point their loyalty was questionable; attacking the *Equites Singulares* as they carried out their official orders in the streets of Rome would fall into this category.

In both Herodian's and Dio's accounts Commodus is informed of the approaching mob by members of the imperial household. According to Herodian it was Commodus' eldest sister Fadilla who 'had free access to the emperor'. She suddenly appeared before her startled brother, her hair dishevelled as in the act of mourning, and accused Cleander of raising rebellion amongst the people and the *Equites Singulares* in order to murder the imperial family. Members of the imperial family were hostile to Cleander after his elimination of Burrus. The *cubicularius* had already become suspicious of Fadilla who he suspected of undermining his position. After the execution of Burrus, she knew that her time was short. Fadilla's husband was Marcus Peducaeus Plautius Quintillus, who, as adopted son of Marcus Peducaeus Stloga Priscinus (the consul of 141 AD), belonged to the highest nobility being a nephew of the emperor L Verus through his mother Ceionia Fabia. He had the distinction of being consul in 177 AD, together with the emperor himself and with his wife would survive the overthrow of Commodus by withdrawing to his family estates, only to be executed by Septimius Severus in 205 AD. Other imperial attendants, no doubt already prepped, now added their weight behind Fadilla's denunciations, the freedman Eclectus was probably one of them.[10]

Dio however records that it was the concubine Marcia who reported the news of the advancing crowd to the emperor. Marcia was rumoured to also have been having a relationship with Eclectus, later marrying him after the murder of Commodus. Although this relationship is described as gossip, both in fact shared a long history, having firstly been slaves in the imperial household of Verus and upon his death Marcia was acquired by Quadratus, Marcia becoming his concubine, whilst Eclectus was transferred to the imperial household of the young Commodus. He then also appears to have been acquired by Quadratus who appointed him his *cubicularius*. On the execution of Quadratus after Lucilla's failed conspiracy, Marcia and Eclectus re-entered the imperial household. Marcia, whose full name was Aurelia

Ceionia Demetrias, suggesting she was freed by either Verus or Commodus, would continue to have a great influence upon the emperor with unrestricted access to him as one of his concubines. An honorary inscription from Anagnia, a town southeast of Rome records her patronage. Eclectus was an Egyptian who Herodian describes as 'characteristically given to act upon his impulses and be controlled by his emotions'. Herodian may actually have known Eclectus, but the historian tries to fit individuals' personalities into his belief that the crises of the empire in his lifetime could be put down to the ethnic characteristics of those involved in the key decisions. Eclectus had risen progressively through the imperial bureaucracy and so was a skilled, politically astute and experienced administrator.[11]

As the mob approached the Quitillian Villa Commodus would not have needed to be informed of events, he would have heard the shouts and chanting from even the most secluded room in the villa. As Hekster points out, it is immaterial who informed the emperor as it would have been evident to him that all was not well. The crowd that had started the protest came from the Circus Maximus, which could hold 200,000 spectators. These numbers may have been reduced due to the attack of the *Equites Singulares*, but they had been joined by significant numbers of soldiers from the Urban cohorts. This unit numbered four cohorts of five hundred men and large numbers of Praetorians had probably become involved in the tumult. The Villa of the Quintilii lies on a prominent artificial platform 300m from the Appian Way, commanding unrestricted views in all directions. The entrance is marked by a 'Grand Nymphaeum', a monumental roadside fountain containing five niches which would have held statues, each sprouting water into a large marble basin.[12] Commodus would have known of the approach of the massive crowd long before its arrival. References to Marcia and Fadilla may be stylistic 'invented messengers' but the detailed scene described in *Herodian* suggests otherwise and in fact all were probably involved in the well planned conspiracy, as all stood to gain from the removal of Cleander and none were punished after his fall.

Commodus does however appear to have been caught by complete surprise and, just as he reacted to the news of Maternus' uprising, he exploded in anger. Cleander does not appear to have been present as he had to be summoned to the emperor's presence. An imperial *consilium* may have been rapidly convened made up of Cleander's opponents; Fadilla and her husband Marcus Peducaeus Plautius Quintillus, his other sister Cornificia with her husband M Petronius Sura Mamertinus, his wife's brother Lucius Bruttius Quintius Crispinus (consul of 187 AD), the Praetorian Prefects Julianus and Regillus, and perhaps Eclectus. It perhaps met in the grand elliptical reception hall paved with white marble, the emperor seated on a large tribunal reached by three steps, with a miniature temple beside it. The imperial guard stationed at the villa would have no longer included the *Equites Singulares* who had been dispersed around Rome after failing to prevent the mob's march on the villa. The remaining Praetorians would have been easily crushed by the numbers of the crowd. Furthermore it may have been questionable whether they would have fought against fellow Praetorians if they were in the crowd, although the Urban Cohorts and Praetorians detested one another. Commodus' anger would have been directed at Cleander who had failed to keep him informed of events in the city, events that now placed the emperor and his family in immediate danger. It also appeared that the support of the Roman populace was at a watershed. For the time being they blamed Cleander for their present misfortune but the fickle nature of the mob could mean that at any moment they could turn on the emperor himself. A sea of people would have encamped before the villa calling for the head of the *cubicularius*. Cleander was summoned to the villa, but his fate had already been decided once civil war erupted in the city; according to Herodian he was arrested immediately upon his arrival and beheaded. His head was then stuck on a spear to be handed over to the crowd. According to Dio the body was also handed over to be dragged away and abused. The crowd then returned to the city parading the head through the city streets. Cleander's sons, two according to Herodian, were also executed, and the corpses mutilated before being thrown into the sewers as was the fate of condemned criminals. The sources accuse Commodus of cowardice in bending to the will of the mob. Commodus' gladiatorial combats suggest otherwise. However, he had trusted Cleander to keep him informed of events which all the sources agree he had failed to do, censoring information that was passed on to the emperor, and in doing so, making judgements far beyond his responsibilities. Cleander had lost all confidence and, like Perennis before him, concluded he had clearly become a liability. It was evident that the emperor could not retain the loyalty of the Roman populace and retain Cleander. Balanced against this was the loyal service the *cubicularius* had provided over the years. Commodus made the calculation in the heat of the moment and the axe fell.

The imperial *consilium* continued to meet after the dispersal of the crowd. They advised Commodus to return to Rome that night, fearing the mob, understanding the power it held, might now turn on the emperor himself. No doubt escorted by a strong force of Praetorians the emperor returned from the suburbs 'where he was welcomed with great honour by the people and was escorted in procession back to the palace'. The palace was on the Palatine where the populace felt their emperor should reside. Would the emperor's advisors have recommended such action unless they were sure the crowd would not turn on Commodus? Such confidence seems to suggest they knew from their own manipulations that the emperor remained popular, whilst the mob would be satisfied and glutted with the death of Cleander and his family.

Commodus proceeded to purge any who had links to his former *cubicularius*. A number of concubines at court had had relations with Cleander and these were put to death, including his wife Damostratia who had once been a concubine of the emperor. Several imperial freedmen who held their posts at the *beneficia* of Cleander were also executed, including L Aelius Apolaustus.

> All those who had plundered on every hand, Commodus afterwards put them to death and confiscated their property.

Other imperial freedmen though continued to prosper including Eclectus, L Aurelius Apolaustus Memphius and the shadowy Pylades, who would serve as *cubicularius* to the Emperor Didius Julianus.[13] Many of the *amici* of those deposed were now vulnerable to the *delatores* who were willing to risk their lives to gain instant fortunes from a share of the estates of those successfully condemned. One of these was Septimius Severus who was also linked to the conspiracy of Julius Alexander in Syria through his wife's familiar connections. He was accused in absentia as he was still serving as Governor of Sicily. On his return he was handed over to the Praetorian Prefects for trial having been 'indicted for consulting about the imperial dignity with seers and astrologers'. This was a treasonable offence under *majestas*. However the two prefects acquitted him and crucified his accuser. This has to be dated to 189 AD, or early 190 AD as Julianus was sole prefect by 15 July 190 AD. Severus then served his suffect consulship but the fall of his patron Cleander meant he now spent a year in limbo without being granted appointment to any new office or post.[14] He undoubtedly spent this time attempting to gain the *gratia* of another *amicus* of the emperor in order to further his career. Pertinax, another *amicus* of Cleander, was held in too great esteem by the emperor to be vulnerable to any accusations, whilst Didius Julianus appears to have been protected by Pertinax who 'always spoke of him as his colleague and successor'. Julianus had succeeded Pertinax as proconsular Governor of Africa.[15] There also appears to have been unrest in Egypt at this time, its termination celebrated in a medallion.[16] This unrest may have been the attempt by those linked to the delay in sending the grain fleet to Rome attempting to escape retribution or in some way associated with the revolt of Julius Alexander of Emesa which also occurred in 190 AD. Unfortunately our sources omit any reference to this event.

A number of historians date the fall of Cleander to April 190 AD rather than August 189 AD. They base this mainly on identifying the ceremonies preceding the rising in the Circus Maximus as that of the Cerealia and an inscription dated to 15 July 190 AD naming Julianus as sole prefect.[17] No source records the reasons for the condemnation of Regillus, but the *Historia Augusta* is clear that both Julianus and Regillus survived the fall of Cleander and so were not associated with it, both surviving long enough as joint prefects to acquit Septimius Severus in their court after his return from Sicily.[18] It is also erroneous to identify the ceremony in the

Circus Maximus with that linked to Ceres, as it makes more sense to identify this with Consus, linked to the grain stores that were empty and Opis, the Goddess of Plenty. The conspirators exploited the prevailing conditions of famine in the city to bring the anger and discontent to boiling point. None of the historians who date these events to April 190 AD adequately explain why Pertinax, who had been appointed Urban Prefect by late 190 AD, would betray his benefactor Cleander or survive the consequences of failing to adequately keep control of the urban cohorts. In fact the *Historia Augusta* records that Pertinax rose in the emperor's estimation whilst holding this office:

> he was made prefect of the city, and in this office, as successor to Fuscianus, a very stern man, Pertinax was exceedingly gentle and considerate, and he proved very pleasing to Commodus himself.

The remaining part of the text has unfortunately been corrupted, yet it is difficult to understand such a description of Pertinax's urban prefecture if he had been responsible for order in the city whilst a virtual civil war broke out on the streets. Commodus was so impressed with his *amicus*, that he nominated Pertinax for a second consulship of 192 AD granting the additional honour of sharing it with the emperor himself.[19] If the grain crisis associated with the fall of Cleander is associated to 189 AD it is difficult to understand the coinage issues of 190 AD celebrating *Votis Felicibus* or another carrying the motif showing the personification of *Fides* standing to the left holding ears of corn with the legend: 'Loyalty of the Cohorts'. The emperor would not issue such legends unless the gods had delivered, allowing the grain ships to reach Rome and order had been restored in the capital.

Nemesis was the Greek God of Retribution. Cleander had taken a leading role in the deaths of his predecessors Saoterus and Perennis, as well as removing the threats to his position centred around Burrus and Arrius Antoninus. His own downfall lay in an elaborate conspiracy that he himself would have been proud of. Herodian is almost dismissive of the rise of Cleander, observing 'that some trivial unsuspected quirk of fortune can raise someone from the meanest depths to the loftiest heights and then cast him down again'.[20] The concept of 'fortune', of 'tyche', permeates his whole work but he fails to understand the prejudices this ex slave had to fight against to rise to such a position of power and influence. Ammianus Marcellinus, in summarizing Petronius, the Emperor Valen's father-in-law, compares his cruelty, savagery and lack of compassion to the *cubicularius*, being 'more hated than Cleander'. However the sources reflect the social elitism of the equestrian and senatorial classes, who, in their words, resented being 'the slave of slaves'. Cleander realized he could never throw off their prejudices but tried to win over the people of Rome by constructing magnificent baths and patronizing cities across the empire. All his attempts to build firm foundations for the regime were undermined by the plague leading to reduced financial revenues for the imperial *fiscus* and agricultural production. This resulted in famine and unorthodox attempts to make the wealthy elite pay their fair share of taxes and balance the exchequer.[21] Ruthless, yes, but the attitude of the successful Roman politician in the dog-eat-dog world of courtly politics was attack: destroy your enemy before your enemy destroys you. The Jewish politician Philo, commenting on Caligula's murder of his young imperial rival Gemellus simply comments: 'He (Caligula) being the stronger promptly did to the weaker what the weaker would have done to him. This is defence not murder. Perhaps too it was providential ... that the lad was put out of the way, since some would have been partisans of him and others of Gaius.'[22] This is an objective analysis of the brutal reality of imperial politics, a world in which Cleander grew up from an early age and found himself adept in it. He was however a man of great political and administrative ability who remained loyal to his emperor; something that cannot be said for the conspirators who planned his downfall.

The emperor, awaiting the arrival of the Alexandrian grain fleet, made great show of his pious worship of Isis, Serapis and Anubis. Isis was the ancient Egyptian Goddess of the Earth, Corn and the famous Lighthouse of Alexandria whose attributes were subsumed with Serapis following the Hellenistic occupation of Egypt by the Ptolemies. When Anubis' mother, Nephthys, exposed her unwanted son, Isis found him and then raised him. In return Anubis became an attendant of Isis. The first proposal to build a temple in Rome to Isis and Serapis was made in 43 BC by the triumvirs Mark Antony, Lepidus and Octavian (Augustus) to gain support from devotees of the cult, whilst the aedile M Volusius attempted to escape their proscriptions by wearing the jackal-headed mask of Anubis and the linen clothing of the followers of Isis. The temples of the Iseum and Serapeum on the Campus Martius were built by Caligula and were isolated from the outside world by an enclosing wall. Access to the vast inner courtyard was limited to two monumental gates facing east and west. In the centre of this sacred area stood an obelisk placed there by the Emperor Domitian alongside the massive statues of the Tiber, the Nile and the Ocean signifying the gods' control over the sea and rivers. The two temples, facing each other, could only be entered through a narrow entrance from this inner courtyard. Inside stood statues of the two divinities with side rooms reserved for accommodation for the priests and pilgrims. Within the Iseum would be niches for other gods including Anubis. The ceremony of the 'Navigium' occupied several days commencing on 28 October, the season when the Nile floods receded and the priests wore the black of mourning. Initiates beat themselves with pine cones in their anguish until they were covered in blood symbolizing the death of Osiris and mourning of Isis. The search for the dismembered Osiris was then ritually performed in the temple enclosure before a priest placed the mask of Anubis on their head to mimic the gods' sense of smell that enabled Isis to find the various parts of Osiris to reassemble him. On 3 November a joyous procession left the sanctuary shouting: 'We have found, we rejoice', to accompanying music and dancing to celebrate the reborn Osiris giving life to the seeds of future harvests. Commodus would not waste the opportunity of associating himself with such a religious ceremony at a time of famine and hardship. He shaved his head in the manner of the *pastophori*, a category of priests who helped at religious rites and processions, and carried the idol from the temple through the streets of Rome wearing the doglike mask of Anubis. The *Historia Augusta* adds that he irreverently used the statue of Anubis he was carrying to 'smite the heads of the devotees'. The top-heavy head that the priests wore must have had limited visibility. The emperor accidently hit devotees as they danced around the idol. This is misrepresented as an act of impiety, the exact opposite of the emperor's intention. Members of his *consilium* may also have joined him in procession, Pescennius Niger being displayed on a mosaic in the imperial gardens carrying the sacred objects of the cult. The emperor's participation in this ceremony and the subsequent arrival of the grain fleet made a lasting impression on the people of Rome, to the extent that on his death, it was believed the idol of Anubis moved foretelling the emperor's demise, so closely was he now associated with the Egyptian gods.[23]

Chapter Seven

Commodus: The God (189–191 AD)

C ommodus had been shocked by the fragility of his position and the threat that both the soldiers and the Roman mob possessed to his regime. Both, he had assumed, were completely loyal. Herodian points to this moment as the time where the nature of Commodus' rule changed. He feared a recurrence of mob violence and revolution despite the fact he had been welcomed with popular celebration when he entered the city after the execution of Cleander and his family. Commodus 'cut himself off from his interests in moral studies', whilst Dio reflects this change by commenting that the emperor now 'turned to murder'. Commodus took personal charge of the investigations into the events leading up to the rioting in Rome and gave 'ready hearing to any accusations without admitting creditable witnesses to his presence'. Accusations were no doubt brought by both *delatores* but also senators and equestrians attempting to eliminate political rivals and enemies. Commodus did admit witnesses but these were not according to Herodian 'creditable', suggesting that he listened to evidence provided by slaves and freedmen of the accused rather than limiting his investigations to evidence provided by the equestrian and senatorial classes. On the murder of Commodus the senatorial elite broke out in rhythmic chanting against, not only Commodus, but *delatores*, spies and suborners of slaves, many of these discreditable witnesses being crucified by Pertinax as a deterrent against any further denunciations made by members of the lower classes.[1]

The investigations however soon took a secondary priority with news from Emesa in Syria. A certain Julius Alexander, according to Dio, aroused the jealousy of the emperor in Rome by killing a lion whilst on horseback with his javelin in a hunt. Commodus then ordered his assassination. The *Historia Augusta* however identifies this as a genuine rebellion:

> Yet as a matter of fact there were no rebellions save that of Alexander, who soon killed himself and his near of kin, and that of Commodus' sister Lucilla.

This Julius Alexander has been identified as a member of the Emesene dynasty who were priestly kings of the city with links to the royal families of the ancient kingdoms Sophene and Commagene. The names of this royal house recorded on inscriptions in the surrounding area (Samsigeramus, Sohaemus, Iamblichus, Aziz, Iotape,

Alexio and Alexander) signify their continued prominence after the absorption of the kingdom following the death of Gaius Julius Sohaemus, described as the 'great king', in the reign of Vespasian. Julius Alexander's father may have been C Julius Sohaemus, a consul before 164 AD but appointed King of Armenia by Lucius Verus. Sohaemus is described by the writer Iamblichus as 'the Archaemenid and Arsacid' (the royal family of ancient Persia and Parthia), a man 'descended from ancient dynasts' who reigned 'in succession to his ancestors'. Severus' wife, Julia Domna, was related to this dynasty, as were the future emperors, Elagabalus and Severus Alexander. It seems remarkable that the emperor in Rome would have been sent news of a lion hunt in Syria unless this held some political or religious significance. The Persian and Seleucid kings who had ruled the east before the Roman conquest had built palaces with vast hunting parks well stocked with animals. The hunt was a royal activity symbolizing the ruler's dominance over both man and nature. The lion hunt was possibly a royal activity of the Emesene dynasty which had been prohibited, but re-enacted by Julius Alexander to lay claim to the territories of the old Emesene client kingdom with Parthian support. A coin of 181–2 AD shows Commodus on horseback in combat with a lion. Alternatively Julius Alexander may have hunted and killed a lion as a direct challenge to Commodus' association with the demigod Hercules. The Emperor Domitian had put the noble ex Consul Acilius Glabrio to death for killing a lion in the arena at the Alban amphitheatre. Commodus saw Julius Alexander's activities as a threat and sent assassins to Emesa to murder him. Alexander was the dynastic name of the rulers of Emesa, whilst the name Julius was linked to the priests of the God Elagabal in the city. It seems surprising that he was not arrested by the troops stationed in the province, unless he and his family had control over the priesthood of the deity which could be used to stir up rebellion as suggested in the *Historia Augusta*. Herodian describes the priests of the cult wearing 'barbaric costume', probably of Parthian origin with long sleeves, a gold embroidered purple tunic and trousers with a bejewelled diadem on the head. This description may account for a strange account in the *Historia Augusta* of the emperor murdering 'many others in many places, some because they came into his presence in the costume of barbarians, others because they were noble and handsome'. Commodus would have ordered the execution of the close members of Julius Alexander's family and may have personally interrogated the priests of the Cult of Elagabal in Rome, who appeared before the emperor in full priestly regalia hoping this reminder of his religious role might spare them. Julius Alexander learned of the arrival of the assassins in the city and murdered them at night. This however was only a temporary reprieve and more assassins were sent to kill him. Escaping from Emesa on horseback, accompanied by his teenage male lover described by the *Historia Augusta* as a relative, he headed for Parthia. A skilled horseman, he would easily have made his escape but his young companion slowed his progress and so, on the point of being overtaken by his pursuers, he killed his lover and then himself. The treasonable intentions of the Emesene dynasty would have been covered up by the historians Marius Maximus, Cassius Dio and Herodian who served their relations and descendants as emperors of Rome. One of these, Julia Domna, was married to Septimius Severus whose own position was now weak, having lost his *amicus* Cleander and implicated by his wife's family link to the Emesene dynasty.[2]

By July 190 AD Julianus was sole prefect as he is recorded on an inscription as the only Praetorian Prefect. Regillus was condemned by Commodus, whose fate Julianus was to share before the end of 190 AD suffering *damnatio memoriae*. Many other members of the emperor's *consilium* were accused of conspiracy and removed from court, their ultimate fate uncertain. Papirius Dionysius however is recorded as being executed on the orders of the emperor.[3] The emperor's investigations had shown the conspiracy to remove Cleander had been widespread and penetrating to the closest circles of his *amici*. The emperor's principal advisors would include the surviving members of the imperial family: Marcus Peducaeus Plautius Quintillus and Commodus' sister Fadilla; Marcus Petronius Sura Mamertinus married to Cornificia; Publius Helvius Pertinax recently appointed Urban Prefect; Eclectus who was now promoted to Cleander's post of *cubicularius*. Other prominent freedmen who survived Cleander's fall included L Aurelius Apolaustus Memphius, Pylades and Marcia, the prominent concubine of the emperor. She is described as his 'favourite mistress'.[4] Freedmen of the imperial household gained ever greater influence as Commodus isolated himself from the senatorial and equestrian elite. Pertinax's influence is evident in the selection of Quintus Aemlius Laetus as Praetorian Prefect as he and Eclectus were his *amici*.[5] Laetus came from the province of Africa, originating from Thaenae. He was to rescue the career of Septimius Severus who had not been allocated a command or province since his consulship whilst his brother, Aemilius Prudens, also entered the imperial household as a *comites Augusti*. The remaining prefect was Motilenus whom the *Historia Augusta* states was murdered by the emperor using poisoned figs.[6] The use of poisoned figs as a vehicle to murder rivals was a cliché in the ancient sources, Augustus' wife, Livia supposedly being consummate in its use. If Commodus had wanted to eliminate Motilenus he could quite easily have him condemned for *majestas*. It is more likely that the prefect died suddenly of natural causes but in the poisonous atmosphere of court politics, a darker cause was believed.

Coinage of 190 AD demonstrates that the problem of the famine had been resolved with the arrival of the Egyptian grain fleet. Legends associate Jupiter as the defender of the emperor, whilst Serapis and Cybele are also linked to the preservation of the emperor and successful resolution of the grain shortages: *Mater Deum Conservatrix*

Augusti and *Serapis Conservator Augusti*. Cybele was predominantly an agrarian goddess associated with fertility whilst Serapis was the protector of the African grain fleet. Other issues celebrate Commodus' assumption of his sixth consulship showing the emperor crowned by victory; however of greater significance was the move on the coinage from Commodus merely associating himself with Hercules to the clear statement that he was the new incarnation of the demigod. Antonius Pius, Lucius Verus and Marcus Aurelius had issued coinage and medallions carrying the image of Hercules as the symbol of civic virtue, but this presentation was something different. A Commodian issue dated between 186 AD and 191 AD, but commonly assigned to 186–9 AD, refers to Hercules as the *comes* of Commodus. Trajan and Hadrian had used images of Hercules on their coinage but from 190 AD there was a massive increase in the depiction of Hercules on issues with the legend *Herculi Commodiano* and from December 191 AD *Herculi Romano Augusti*. The gold *aureus*, coinage used by the wealthy elite, carries the divine claims of the emperor with its assertion *HERC COM*. The contemporary Athenaeus writing the Deipnosphistae (Sophists at Dinner) after the death of Commodus wrote that the emperor '… in our own times' sat in his chariot, with Hercules'club beside him and a lion skin spread out below, trying unsuccessfully to imitate the God.' This change can only be the result of the shock Commodus received from the sudden arrival of the mob outside his villa. His depiction of himself as Hercules was bound to alienate the Roman elite, but the emperor made a conscious decision to build the future foundations of his regime on the support of the army and people of Rome and the provinces. A medallion of 191/2 AD makes this explicit showing the emperor in a lion skin, the attire of Hercules, with four children depicting the four seasons with the legend *Temporum Felicitas*. Commodus, in the divine form of Hercules, would bring happiness and prosperity throughout the empire all year, every year. A new golden age was promised with further coins of 190/1 AD declaring *SAECULI TEPORUM FELICITAS*. A medallion of this year shows the sun God Sol with a radiant crown wearing a beard similar to that worn by Commodus, whilst in the bottom right corner of the disc the earth mother Goddess Tellus rests with a horn of plenty: a formal declaration of the golden age. A beardless bust of the emperor dated to 190 AD depicts Commodus as Sol proclaiming the emperor as both divine and super human.[7]

The senate, in order to win the emperor's approval, 'voted that his age should be named the "Golden Age" and that this should be recorded in all the records without exception.' The people were expected to identify the survival of the divine Commodus as essential for the continued *beneficia* of the gods. This depiction of himself was embedded in the Roman and imperial tradition but was at the very limit of what was viewed as permissible. However in the Greek eastern half of the empire this tradition had a much firmer foundation in the presentation and propaganda of Alexander the Great and his Hellenistic successors. Alexander had demanded divine honours for his dead lover, Haephestion, and later for himself, whilst the Seleucid King Antiochus III established a royal cult as an imperial institution with its own priests throughout his vast eastern empire. The Ptolemies of Egypt, following in the tradition of the previous Pharaonic rulers of their territory, demanded divine worship. Worship was voluntary and local dignitaries and city councils bestowed divine honours on their rulers not necessarily believing their kings were the equivalent of the Olympian gods but in acknowledgement of the temporal powers of their rulers whose actions and decisions had a more real, present and immediate effect on their lives than the 'actions' of the immortal gods.[8] During his tour of the eastern provinces and his stay in Egypt as the young Caesar, Commodus would have been viewed and addressed as a demigod, something that he now drew upon in order to secure the loyalty and affection of the majority of his subjects. This was not a sign of his growing madness as the ancient, and some modern, sources would have us believe but a political calculation that would become the established practice of Roman emperors a century after his death. Essentially, like all Roman government, it was not a proactive decision but a reactive one.

Commodus had by these actions rejected the traditional form of imperial rule and the development of political cohesion through the use of reciprocal exchange relationships with the Roman elite through the granting of *beneficia* in exchange for loyalty, *fides*, and *gratia*. An emperor would allow his *amici* to build their own networks of *amicitia* as patrons to their own *amici* and clients. Seneca asserted that 'an emperor protected by his own beneficia has no need of guards'. As a consequence of his own personal experience, from the conspiracy of Lucilla and her senatorial supporters to that of Burrus and the plotting that led to the fall of Cleander, Commodus now felt the need for a radical readjustment of the principles of imperial rule.[9] Like Caligula, whose birthday he shared, he removed senators as the brokers and mediators of patronage and instead he increasingly relied upon the administrative professionals in the imperial household, his freedmen, servants and officials. Commodus now presented himself as the supreme patron making the rest of the empire's population, including the equestrian and senatorial elite, his clients. Imperial government had always been based on inequality; how could an aristocratic senator be the equal of an emperor no matter how proud they were of their lineage and wealth? The rule of the so called 'good emperors' was based on a feigned and illusionary equality with the ruling emperors, men like Marcus Aurelius, who asked the senate for funds that were recognized by all as belonging to the imperial *fiscus*. His son rejected the facade for the brutal reality of the actual political situation. For this he was condemned in the senatorial sources and murdered.

The emperor now carried out measures to reaffirm the loyalty of the populace to his rule. *Congiaria* totalling 140 *denarii* per eligible male citizen was distributed and celebrated on coin issues. The *Historia Augusta* however records that he gave 725 *denarii* which is a huge amount of money that in these times of austerity would have bankrupted the state. This figure must refer to the total amount given in the nine distributions during his reign, two of which were during the joint rule with his father. Seven distributions of 140 *denarii* total 980 *denarii*. Therefore Dio's ascertain that he 'frequently' gave largess of 140 *denarii* is an exaggeration, with some significantly less reflecting the financial constraints Commodus was operating under. Coins proclaim *liberalitas VII*, *Roma Felix*, *Concordia* and *Fides*, stressing the restoration of order and happiness under the direction of Commodus whilst reminding his audience of their reciprocal obligation: loyalty.[10] According to Herodian it was now that the emperor began to train as a charioteer and take part in combats against wild animals. He had in private always trained as a gladiator which Marcus Aurelius knew about and did not condone, and so it appears this activity was also in private. The possible remains of a racetrack have been found at the Quintillian Villa. Dio states that he did not race chariots publicly, adding mischievously that he may have on moonless nights so he was not seen as he was ashamed of his actions, a baseless rumour that was spread by the enemies of the emperor. In private though Dio acknowledges Commodus, wearing the uniform of the Green faction, was constantly practising. The historian indicates the main reason for these actions, to restore the loyalty of the circus factions, especially the Greens. The *Historia Augusta* is more explicit:

> He held many races in the Circus, but rather as the result of a whim than as an act of religion, and also in order to enrich the leaders of the factions.

When attending the races and giving the signal to start, as well as entering the amphitheatre, the emperor wore the Dalmatian tunic which was a long sleeved tunic reaching to the knee. Dio describes this garment as been made of white silk interwoven with gold. Commodus covered this with a robe of imperial purple interwoven with gold spangles and a purple chlamys. These are the women's garments the *Historia Augusta* accuses him of wearing 'time and again' whilst 'drinking quite publicly', actions pronounced to be a breach of Roman propriety. The chlamys was a Greek item of clothing made from a seamless piece of material about the size of a blanket that was worn over the right shoulder and pinned by a fibula. The garment was worn characteristically by Mercury, and he is also described as carrying a wand in imitation of the god. At the end of a gladiatorial fight two slaves, one dressed as Charon and the other Mercury would enter the arena. Charon would ensure the defeated gladiator was dead by hitting the man on the head with a mallet whilst Mercury would burn him with a heated iron wand. Both were associated with transporting the souls of the departed to the underworld, Charon the ferryman carried the souls of the departed over the River Styx and Mercury guided their souls to the underworld. Commodus, as both emperor and Mercury, sat in judgement on life and death, the two becoming subsumed by the other in the person of the emperor. The thousands watching would understand the symbolism; their emperor was more than merely human. The link was made explicit during the races in the Circus Maximus, with the Temple of Mercury standing on the slopes of the Aventine, above and facing the Circus Maximus. Commodus, although a follower of the Greens and known to take part in chariot races in private, even personally inspected chariot horses for his own stable. Yet he never competed publicly in the Circus, although other emperors and Roman aristocrats had. Perhaps this was due to competition for his loyalty with a crowd divided between the circus factions. By appearing as Mercury, he placed himself above such earthly considerations, allowing supporters of all factions to worship both their team and their divine emperor. Commodus also wore the Dalmatian tunic at these public events which, with its associated regalia, was a direct appeal to the soldiery who wore a more basic woollen long sleeved tunic similar to that worn by their emperor. On his head he placed a golden crown covered in precious jewels from India.[11] The revolt against Cleander had significantly started in the Circus and Commodus' investigations had demonstrated the key role the faction leaders had in subsequent events. To execute these powerful men would have exacerbated the delicate situation and invited further unrest. Instead the emperor worked to win the factions over and emphasize his divine superiority. After all the mob's hatred had been directed against his *cubicularius* and not himself, all the sources stressing the populace were still supportive of their emperor even as they marched from the Circus on his suburban villa.[12]

The 31 August 190 AD marked Commodus' thirtieth birthday. This event was marked by a series of coins carrying the legend *COLLANCOM* which has been associated with the emperor's refounding of Rome but usually dated to 192 AD. This problem is rectified by recognizing that in fact there were two foundations in his reign, Rome in 192 AD after the great fire and an earlier one at Lanuvium in 190 AD on his birthday: the inscription on the coin reading in full: *COL(ONIA) L(ANUVINA) AN(TONINIANA) COM(MODIANA)*.

The emperor returned to the place of his birth making the nearby town a colony and so carrying his name. The emperor competed in the guise of Hercules at the subsequent games to celebrate this event, competing in the imperial amphitheatre recently discovered by archaeologists:

He was called the Roman Hercules, on the ground that he had killed wild beasts in the amphitheatre at Lanuvium; and indeed it was his custom to kill wild beasts on his own estates.

Coins were struck in 190 AD to commemorate the refounding of Lanuvium showing Commodus, veiled and wearing a toga ploughing from left to right with two oxen reflecting the religious ceremony associated with such events. The city is one of the few places that is epigraphically proven to have used the titles Commodus later gave to the months of the year and had a flourishing local cult to Hercules. Hercules himself was the mythological founder of many cities including the famous Herculaneum. After 190 AD the images of Hercules on the coinage increase dramatically. Statues of numerous members of the imperial family have been found surrounding the imperial villa at Lanuvium including those depicting Lucius Verus with a cuirass similar in style to those of his coemperor Marcus Aurelius and *paludamentum*, the purple or red military cloak restricted to the emperors. A number have been found of Commodus himself, some depicting him in his youth, beardless with *paludamentum*, and others including ones of Marcus Aurelius, Faustina, Antoninus Pius, who was also born at Lanuvium and Annius Verus. These appear to have been arranged in the bathing complex of the villa. The statues of Commodus must been restored after his deification by Septimius Severus, or never taken down despite his *damnatio memoriae*.[13]

The coins of 190 AD also show a dramatic change in the emperor's hairstyle. Gone are the coiffured and heavy curls of his previous portraiture to be replaced by a very short cut favoured by soldiers, athletes and gladiators. This was an abrupt break from the style that had been promoted by his Antonine predecessors and, up to this point, himself. There may have been a practical reason for this change, having recently shaved all his hair off to act as a priest in the Navigium ceremony of Isis in November of the previous year. Yet the fact he persisted with this haircut suggests a conscious message was being made, advertising his gladiatorial prowess to the world. It was not unusual for emperors or Roman aristocrats to train as gladiators in private or fight in their own arena, as recently discovered at Commodus' villa at Lanuvium. Caligula, Hadrian and Commodus' hero, Lucius Verus, had all trained as gladiators.[14] Commodus may have developed his passion for gladiatorial combats from watching Verus practise as a young child and even in his father's lifetime he had fought 365 bouts out of 735 in total fighting as a *secutor* against *Retiarii* or fighting wild beasts, winning 1,000 gladiatorial crowns. His skill and accuracy with the bow was admired as was his renowned strength. He was able to kill an elephant with a pole and dispatch animals with one blow. His move to the Vectilian villa in Rome was in part due to its location near the Coliseum and the gladiatorial training school which he often attended, even having his own room in the complex to enable him to change and prepare for bouts. When practising he often used foils but during combat he used the same sharpened swords employed by the gladiators themselves. As these acts were carried out in private on the imperial estates or villas he had them publicized in the *Acta Urbis* and *Acta Diurna* which contained the official announcements and news the government wished to make public. In response flatterers, including many senators, granted him titles given normally to victorious gladiators: 'Among other Triumphal titles, he was also given the name "Captain of the Secutores" six hundred and twenty times.'

On a practical level, Commodus' constant practising had ensured that there had been no further attempts on his life by an assassin wielding a dagger, in fact his eventual murderers resorted to poison, fearing even a trained killer would not have been able to overcome him. This may have been his original intention, living as he did in the constant fear of sudden death. Yet as he survived plot after plot he saw himself favoured and protected by the gods, as reflected in his coinage. His thirtieth birthday celebrations coincide with a change in his coinage in which he publicly associates his prowess in the arena to the labours of Hercules, being awarded the title 'Roman Hercules'. At first Hercules was associated with Commodus on coinage as his *comes* or companion and friend. From 190 AD Commodus declares himself explicitly as the new incarnation of Hercules; coinage from December 191 AD declares *Herculi Romano Augusto* and *Herculi Commodiano*. A rare gold *aureus* of 190/191 AD, the coinage used solely by the Roman wealthy elite, carries the legend *HERC COM*: Commodus and Hercules were one and the same. The Roman elite since the formation of the Principate by Augustus had been treated with outward equality and deference by all the 'good' emperors. Commodus had abandoned such a facade for the brutal reality of the political situation which had existed since the formation of the empire. His propaganda now proclaimed his complete superiority to the senatorial aristocracy to the extent that he now presented himself as a demigod, immortal and all powerful. In procession through the streets of Rome he had a lion skin and club on the accompaniments of Hercules, carried before him and during the games these items were placed a golden chair. The *sella curulis* was the symbol of magisterial office since Republican times and was often portrayed on funerary monuments or carried into public assemblies to mark the divine status of members of the imperial family who have been deified by the senate. To have such a symbol associated with living emperors was an overt and public claim to divine status by Commodus. Previous 'bad' emperors had also made this claim, Caligula setting up an empty *sella* or chair in the Temple of Capitoline Jupiter and demanded senators offer *proskynesis* to it, prostrating themselves face down before it. A similar claim was made by Nero. This break with the past is reflected in his change of name dated from coin issues to 191 AD. 'Marcus Aurelius Commodus Antoninus Augustus Pius Felix', the name he had assumed on the death of his father, now became 'Lucius Aelius Aurelius Commodus Augustus Pius Felix', a name Lucius Verus had given up on becoming coemperor with Marcus Aurelius. This was not a rejection of his father or his noble heritage but a return to the name of his birth: Lucius Aurelius Commodus. It was a simple statement that Commodus was not only his own man but a declaration that a new era had begun, a new 'golden age'.[15]

For the senatorial elite a boundary had now been crossed, the consensus destroyed, order replaced by chaos. The *Historia Augusta* provides a list of eminent members of the imperial family and aristocrats who were executed by Commodus at this time;

> he slew the two Silani, Servilius and Dulius, together with their kin, then Antius Lupus and the two Petronii, Mamertinus and Sura, and also Mamertinus' son Antoninus, whose mother was his own sister; after these six former consuls at one time, Allius Fuscus, Caelius Felix, Lucceius Torquatus, Larcius Eurupianus, Valerius Bassianus and Pactumeius Magnus, all with their kin; in Asia Sulpicius Crassus, the proconsul Julius Proculus, together with their kin, and Claudius Lucanus, a man of consular rank; and in Achaia his father's cousin, Annia Faustina, and innumerable others.[16]

This conspiracy is not mentioned in our two main sources but has been confirmed by an inscription on the sepulchre of M Antonius Antius Lupus which still stands on the Via Ostiense. All were charged with *majestas* and on their execution they suffered *damnatio memoriae* with their estates being confiscated and their surviving children left destitute. The inscription was made by the condemned's family and *amici* on the restoration of his name and estates by Commodus' successor, Pertinax. Yet the anguish and anger resonate through the very words carved into the stone:

> To the spirits of the Departed. His amici Marcus Valerius Bradua Mauricus, a priest, Antonia Vitellia, and Quitus Fabius Honoratus Tiberius Annaeus Placidus have completed the second, untouched sepulchre of Marcus Antonius Lupus, pious and faithful augur, patrician, quaestor, associate of Titius, Military Tribune of the 2nd Legion, Prefect, of the highest rank, oppressed by force and whose memory was restored; an undertaking of his wife Claudia Regilla and his daughter Anita Marcellina in order to attest their piety towards him and celebrate his name in perpetuity.

The monument was raised by his surviving relatives including the Pontifex M Valerius Bradua Mauricus and his wife, and two further *amici*, the *praetor urbanus* T Anneaus Placidus and the unknown Q Fabius Honoratus. As heirs to Antius

Lupus' estate they had a vested interest in restitution in order to inherit his wealth, but what is most pronounced is their desire to see his name restored for all eternity. *Damnatio memoriae* removed all trace of a person's existence, it was as though they had never existed. To an aristocratic family who prided themselves of their noble ancestry, tracing their name through the ages, the death masks of their ancestors hanging from the wall of their villa, it was literally a fate worse than death. The righting of such a wrong was also seen as a restoration of the rightful order in both this world and the next.[17] The execution of a senator made enemies of his children, relatives and *amici*, hence the execution of the relatives of the conspirators by Commodus. This is one of the reasons why Marcus Aurelius refused to execute the senatorial conspirators linked to Avidius Cassius despite their guilt being ascertained by the senate. The question arises: where do you stop? Of course Marcus Aurelius had no such compassion for those of equestrian or lesser status, their position to threaten his regime was perceived as minimal.

Amongst the list of those executed, one name stands out: M Petronius Sura Mamertinus, the consul of 182 AD and married to Cornificia, the emperor's sister. His brother, M Petronius Sura Septimianus, had been given the honour of sharing the ordinary consulship of 190 AD with Commodus. Their sister, Petronia, had married Marcus Antoninus Antius Lupus whose sepulchre now granted him earthly immortality. These were powerful figures at the very heart of the imperial family and at the head of a nexus of political connections based on family and the bonds of *amicitiae*. The marriage of Cornificia and Petronius Sura Mamertinus had produced a son, Petronius Antoninus, probably born between 173 AD and 180 AD. This son was executed yet his mother survived, allegedly having an affair with Pertinax before marrying the equestrian Lucius Didius Marinus. In 212 the Emperor Caracalla ordered her death, her last words being recorded by Dio;

'My poor, unhappy soul, trapped in an unworthy body, go forth, be free, show them you are the daughter of Marcus Aurelius!' Then she took off her ornaments, composed herself, opened her veins, and died.

The two Silani should be identified with the consul of 188 AD; M Servilius Silanus and that of 189 AD, Q Servilius Silanus, probably brothers. He shared this magistracy with Dulius Silanus, also condemned. The 'Servilius' identified in the list could be Lucius Verus' brother-in-law, Q Servilius Prudens, the consul of 166 AD and an elderly statesman by this time. A legal case brought before the Emperor Septimius Severus involving the inheritance of a prominent senator whose property was confiscated by the imperial *fiscus* reveals a number of prominent senators in Asia Minor connected to the conspiracy of 191 AD. One of these was Cn Pompeius Hermippus Aelianus, an influential Roman senator and leading figure in Ephesus whose *cursus honorum* survives. He was probably accused of *majestas* by Commodus with his estate being later claimed by a distant relative. An inscription found in Ephesus records a relative of Hermippus who lists amongst his ancestors a Lupus Antoninus, a senator of praetorian rank at the time the inscription was erected. A similar case is recorded in the legal *Digest* with the daughter of Pactumeius Magnus, the suffect consul 183 AD, also claiming her inheritance after the murder of Commodus. Antius Lupus was also from Asia Minor and Sulpicius Crassus, Proconsul of Asia, was also executed at this time. Another conspirator mentioned was Q Larcius Eurupianus who was at the *consilium* of July 177 AD with Marcus Aurelius and Commodus granting citizenship to the family of Julianus from Bansa. Eurupianus was an equestrian at the time and was probably a legal expert whose experience and skills the emperors utilized. He must have been promoted through the *cursus honorum* by Commodus to reach the consulship at an unknown date. The role of such prominent senators clearly demonstrates their rejection of Commodus' divine aspirations and led Commodus to believe that the main foundations of support for his regime lay with the people. In 191 AD it was noted in the official *Actus Urbis* the traditional phraseology of *Senatus Populusque Romanus* was replaced with *Populus Senatusque Romanus*, the reversing of the names granting greater emphasis of the role and importance of the people.[18]

The motives for the involvement of Annia Faustina in the plot are clear: vengeance. Her son and daughter, Titus Fundanius Vitrasius Pollio and Vitrasia Faustina, had been executed by Commodus in 182 AD for involvement in the conspiracy of Lucilla. She had been forced to retire to Achaea after this and it is there that she met her end. The emperor's wife Crispina was also exiled on the charge of adultery and later executed in late 191 AD or early 192 AD.

> His wife, whom he caught in adultery, he drove from his house, then banished her, and later put her to death.

The epitomizers of Dio place this event after their description of the conspiracy of Lucilla but surviving inscriptions refer to her as Augusta until 191 AD.[19] The staggered punishments suggest that after her removal from the palace she later committed another offence leading to her exile and death. The images of Crispina that have survived *damnatio memoriae* are remarkable for the savagery of their vandalism. Often the heads of those who suffered this fate were merely removed from the statues to be stored or buried, their place being taken on the statue by the image of another dignitary who was on the rise. Crispina's heads discovered in Rome and Ostia have been slashed and hacked with heavy blows reminiscent of the treatment of imperial women involved in conspiracies against the emperor, such as Claudius' wife Messalina. Similar attacks using a chisel have been found on a statue of Annia Faustina with its base at Ostia; the eyes, ears, nose and mouth all being removed. The ferocity of the attacks and the similarity in location suggest the local inhabitants expressed their continued loyalty to their emperor through savagely attacking images of those involved in the conspiracy.[20] Crispina, fearing for her life after being caught in the act of adultery, being approached by other members of the imperial family who had access to the palace, no doubt M Petronius Sura Mamertinus, decided to join the conspirators in murdering her husband.

The sources are silent on the details of the plan but the involvement of significant numbers of former consuls suggests Commodus' abandonment of the former principles of government was the main motivation of these aristocrats. Senators of a lower status were drawn in as *amici* or relatives of the main conspirators; the noble and imperially connected Petronii drew in Antius Lupus, who in turn drew in his relatives and *amici* in Asia Minor. The absence of senators commanding legionary armies in the list of those condemned suggests the plot was limited to disenchanted members of the imperial family and the senate. Marcia, Eclectus, Pertinax, the Praetorian Prefects, not only survived the aftermath of the plot but their positions were reinforced, Pertinax being chosen by Commodus to share the consulship of 192 AD with him, Eclectus retaining the post of *cubicularius* and Marcia being given almost the full imperial privileges of an Augusta. The plan probably involved replacing Commodus with Petronius Antoninus, the son of Commodus' sister Cornificia, who would have ruled under the guardianship of his father and relatives. The survival of Cornificia suggests she was either ignorant of the plot or Pertinax intervened on her behalf, both were alleged to have been involved in a later affair.

The gods yet again appeared to have protected the emperor, the coins of 191 AD describing Jupiter as *Defensor Salutius Augusti* and *Jupiter Optimus Maximus Sponsor Securitatis Augusti*. Jupiter was presented as the divine protector of the emperor's welfare, implying divine consent to the emperor's rule. The famous Capitoline bust of Commodus, now in the Palazzo dei Conservatori in Rome, dates from this period. It originally stood in the gardens of the Horti Lamiani, imperial property, and so on show to the emperor himself and his *amici*. The statue retains the coiffured hair of the Antonines and the open gaze of a philosopher emperor. However the most significant development is the synthesis of the emperor with the attributes of Hercules. Commodus holds the demigod's club in his right hand, whilst in the left he cradles the 'Apples of Hesperides', a reference to another of Hercules' successful quests which signified eternal youth and immortality. This is mirrored in the tritons holding a *parapetasma*, a common illusion to immortality. The head is covered by the lion skin worn by Hercules. Unusually the bust reveals the torso of the subject, a reflection of Commodus' pride in his musculature and athletic prowess. Its size, slightly larger than life, extenuates his super human powers. The base is carved with signs of the zodiac, probable references to important events in the lives of Hercules and Commodus, with a globe at the bottom, surrounded with the tritons stressing Commodus' command of both land and sea. The two crossed cornucopias symbolize the peace, wealth and prosperity his rule promised. The statue is the physical embodiment of emperor's claim to be the new Hercules.[21]

The Farnese bust of Commodus represented as the weary Hercules was found near the Baths of Caracalla. He holds the 'Apples of Hesperides' behind his back, but the musculature is again powerful and copied on imperial coinage of this time. This type of portraiture copies the style of Lysippus, the court sculpture of Alexander the Great. Hercules was a prominent theme of Alexander's statues, a link not lost on Commodus' contemporaries. A similar statue was found on the Palatine and would have probably stood in the palace itself.[22]

The cult of Hercules was based in the Forum Boarium (cattle market) in Rome, being linked to Hercules' labours as he killed Cacus on the Aventine Hill for stealing some of his cattle, cattle he had himself stolen from Geryon. He celebrated his victory by sacrificing some of the stolen bulls. The base of the Ara Maxima, which stood in the Forum Boarium, the great altar to the demigod, may be the large 15m square platform found in the crypt of S Maria in Cosmedin. The massive drain cover showing Oceanus with lobster claw horns in his hair and dolphins in his beard probably came from the precinct of the Ara Maxima. The Urban Praetor was tasked with presiding over the annual sacrifice on 12 August, Hercules' birthday. Nine inscriptions recording dedications made by these praetors around the Ara Maxima have survived, three from the reign of Commodus: T Annaeus Placidus, M Cassius Hortensius Paulinus and L Fabius Cilo Septiminus, whose dedication was probably written by his own hand. His personal touch was rewarded by Commodus with a suffect consulship in 193 AD. Late in 191 AD Commodus dropped 'Antoninus' from his nomenclature and adopted as his full style 'Lucius Aelius Aurelius Commodus Augustus Herculeus Romanus Exsuperatorius Amazonius Invictus Felix Pius' (the order of some of these titles varies in the sources). *Exsuperatorius* (The Supreme) was a title given to Jupiter, and *Amazonius* identified him again with Hercules. Two inscriptions from the very end of his reign show Commodus styling himself *omnium virtutem exsuperantissimus* with coins carrying the title *exsuperantissimus* rivalling Jupiter himself. The emperor also created a private cult to 'Rural Hercules' on the imperial estates, appointing one of his freedmen named Onus ('Donkey' after the large size of his genitalia) to the priesthood of this pseudo imperial cult. This was clearly meant to be a prestigious appointment and a position of honour.[23]

At some point in 191 AD, or perhaps earlier, Q Aemilius Laetus, an *amicus* of Eclectus, was made Praetorian Prefect. His brother, Aemilius Prudens, a centurion, was adlected *in comitatu commodi*. Laetus' posts before appointment to the prefecture are unknown, but it is possible he was *Praefectus Vigilum*. The power and influence of Eclectus is demonstrated by the promotion of one of his *amici* to such a powerful position. A new Prefect of Egypt, Mantennius Sabinus, was appointed in 192 AD, replacing Larcius Memor, who had only been appointed two years previously. He may have gained the post on the recommendation of Laetus, Pertinax or Eclectus. Pescennius Niger was awarded the powerful post of *legatus Augusti pro praetore Syriae* which gave him command of large numbers of soldiers, whilst Cornelius Annulius, an *amicus* of Septimius Severus, obtained the province of Africa. A relative of Clodius Albinus, Asellius Aemilianus received Asia having just governed Syria whilst Clodius Albinus was made Governor of Britain. Septimius Severus had found a new patron in Laetus who gained his *gratia* by recommending him for the governorship of Pannonia Superior, with his brother Geta being granted Moesia Inferior. Niger's appointment was, according to the *Historia Augusta*, at the recommendation of Narcissus, Commodus' wrestler who would eventually strangle him. This is surprising considering Niger had already been a faithful and efficient servant to the emperor, serving successfully in Dacia and Gaul helping to defeat Maternus, and he was already recognized as one of Commodus' *amici*, his image being preserved in mosaic along with other *amici* of the emperor, in the Gardens of Commodus. This perhaps is an example of the biographer attempting to sully the emperor's role in government by inferring such appointments were made at the behest of men with no formal role in the government. Syria was one of the most important and volatile provinces in the empire and, as such, it is extremely doubtful Commodus would allocate the province to anyone he did not trust or did not have vast experience. These appointments also demonstrate the restricted pool of suitably qualified, experienced and loyal commanders Commodus felt he could rely on.

Q Aurelius Polus Terentianus was made Governor of Dacia before 192 AD; he had served under Pertinax in crushing the army mutiny in Britain and as a *fetialis*, was a member of the same priestly college as Septimius Severus. Incidentally, Marius Maximus, the main source for the unknown biographer of the *Historia Augusta* was made *legatus* of one of the legions in Lower Moesia under the provincial Governor Septimius Geta. Pertinax remained Prefect of the city of Rome whilst Marcus Peducaeus Plautius Quintillus, the husband of Commodus' sister Fadilla, himself the son of Lucius Verus' sister Ceionis Fabia, must have remained a member of Commodus' *consilium*.[24] It is not surprising that Septimius Severus, Clodius Albinus, Pescennius Niger, Pertinax and Asellius Aemilianus were all placed in key provinces as they had all proven themselves as loyal and efficient in the past. What is surprising is the appointment of Geta as the Severii now controlled five of the ten legions on the Danube. Historians have suggested that even at this stage Laetus, Eclectus, Marcia and Pertinax were plotting the murder of their emperor. What the sources do confirm is that all these appointments were made by Commodus himself, he must surely have been aware of the immense power he had placed in the hands of one family – a family that would appear to be distantly related to the now disgraced Petronii, the executed consul of 190 AD having the cognomen Sura Septimianus.[25] Perhaps he placed too much trust in his old *amicus* Pertinax who had accompanied him to the East with his father in 175 AD, and Marcia, the woman he loved.

Marcia, on the fall of Crispina, was now raised to a position of immense power and influence. Commodus had many concubines, 300 according to the *Historia Augusta*, yet she had always been his favourite. Cleander had enriched her to try and use her influence with Commodus to strengthen his own position, whilst she had retained close ties to Eclectus whose shared progression through the aristocratic and imperial households had brought them closer together. Both were eventually to marry on the successful completion of their conspiracy to murder the emperor. Marcia was now elevated almost to the position of an Augusta having the imperial *vexilla* (flag) carried before her in procession and the *fasces laureati*. However she was not allowed the sacred fire as her status precluded this, being still a concubine. She also had unrestricted access to the emperor, her power reflected in the fact she was able to 'do anything with Commodus'. As Marcia was not his legal wife she could not appear on coin issues yet figures of Amazons may indeed represent her:

> because of his passion for his concubine Marcia, whom he loved to have portrayed as an Amazon.[26]

Commodus' decision not to remarry may have been due to love for Marcia but, by doing so, he had also given up the chance of producing a legitimate successor. Until the exile and execution of Crispina he probably hoped that a male heir would be conceived. However the lack of an heir considerably weakened his position, as the conspiracies of Lucilla, Burrus and the Petronii proved. The highly suspect account of Clodius Albinus in the *Historia Augusta* asserts that Commodus attempted to make Albinus Caesar an appointed successor, an offer that Albinus declined. It seems remarkable that this event is not in Dio's or Herodian's accounts. Although accounts in the *Historia Augusta* on actual emperors are acknowledged to be based on the history of the contemporary Marius Maximus, those of usurpers are based more on fiction than fact. The biographer's volume of actual source material was greatly limited for these more obscure figures and so he appears to have filled in the gaps with his own flights of fancy, especially reflected in letters which he quotes to lend authenticity to his account. On the outbreak of the civil war with Septimius Severus, Albinus would have used such an offer, if it had ever existed, as excellent propaganda in his claim to be the legitimate claimant for the throne above Septimius Severus or Niger.[27]

A remarkable inscription has been discovered suggesting that the son of Lucilla and Ti Claudius Pompeianus, was not always named Ti Claudius Pompeianus, but L or M Aurelius Commodus Pompeianus, these names perhaps being additions to his previous name or he adopted at some point new cognomens.[28] He was to hold the ordinary consulship of 209 AD under Septimius Severus but was murdered by Caracalla. The adoption of the cognomen 'Aurelius Commodus' by this noble under the Severii would have been a certain death sentence. He is named Ti Claudius Pompeianus in *Dio* when recording his death in rioting in Alexandria in 212 AD. It seems likely that such a name must have been given him by his uncle, the Emperor Commodus, on his designation as his chosen successor. Chronologically this best fits with the interlude between the execution of Crispina and the murder of Commodus. It would not have been in the interests of Dio, Marius Maximus or Herodian to advertise this fact as they looked for promotion under the Severii and Dio seems to have been particularly favourable in his presentation of Commodus' successor, Pertinax. It was from this emperor that Dio received his praetorship, then he became an *amicus* of Septimius Severus, Caracalla and Severus Alexander.

Chapter Eight

Commodus: The Gladiator (192 AD)

A t the end of 191 AD or start of 192 AD a devastating catastrophe presented the new Hercules with the greatest challenge to his divine status:

a fire that began at night in some dwelling leaped to the Temple of Peace (Pax/Concordia) and spread to the storehouses of Egyptian and African wares, whence the flames, borne aloft, entered the palace and consumed very extensive parts of it, so that nearly all the state records were destroyed ... vast numbers of both civilians and soldiers carried water, and Commodus himself came in from the suburb and encouraged them. Only when it had destroyed everything on which it took hold did it spend its force and die out.[1]

Marius Maximus, on whom the biographer bases much of his account of the reign of Commodus, was absent on the Danube and so omits detailed references to this disastrous event, apart from repeating as fact the malicious rumour that the emperor had wanted to start a fire to destroy Rome 'as though it was his private colony' but was stopped by Laetus. What the *Historia Augusta* does do is link the two events: the fire and the emperor's decision to refound Rome as a *colonia*.

Herodian's detailed description of the fire suggests he was writing as an eyewitness. The cause he attributes to a flash of lightning in the night or an earthquake. The latter can be discounted but a lightning storm would usually be associated with heavy rainfall which would have dampened the extent of the fire, yet Herodian specifically states there were no rain clouds. He may have attributed the fire to lightning or an earthquake in order to allude to Jupiter's anger at Commodus in direct contradiction to Commodus' claim to be protected by the greatest of the gods. Fires were a continuous problem in Rome throughout its existence and Dio, who was also present in the city, makes clear, it started in a home, perhaps an upturned oil lamp.

The Temple of Peace, standing in the southeast corner of the Forum of Augustus was acknowledged by Pliny to be amongst the most beautiful in the city. It had been built by Vespasian in 75 AD from the spoils of victory in the Jewish War. It housed the treasures from the Jewish Temple at Jerusalem, the numerous works of art collected by Nero and a large library in its annex. Some of the great literary, religious and aesthetic treasures of the ancient world were lost that night. Many of Galen's works were destroyed, a calamity the great man himself regretted. Temples were not only used as places of worship, but also deposit banks for the rich who felt that the presence of both physical and divine guards made them a safer place to store their money and valuables than in their own homes. Monies that were disputed in court cases were also left in temples. The Temple of Peace, being the most prestigious in the city, must have been the 'temple of choice' for most depositors; according to Herodian 'everyone used it as a deposit for his possessions'. That night, he concludes: 'many rich were reduced to penury by the fire. Though everyone joined in deploring the destruction of public property, each person was thinking of their own private loss.' The temple was burnt to the ground, a calamity in itself but the houses surrounding the Forum were the properties of the wealthy elite and these were also engulfed by the flames.

The fire now took hold, travelling across the Forum towards the Temple of Vesta, the temples of Saturn, Divus Julius and Castor, the Basilica Julia, the Porticus of Gaius and Lucius, the Arches of Augustus and Tiberius, the Rostra, and the Domitianic Hall, with its forecourt were all badly damaged. The Temple of Vesta then caught fire, its entrance facing the House of the Vestal Virgins, which housed six priestesses bound by a high walled enclosure. These chaste virgins were appointed by the Pontifex Maximus, who in imperial times was the emperor. They maintained the sacred fire in the Temple of Vesta for a minimum of thirty years when they were then freed from their vows and allowed to marry being provided with a substantial dowry from the emperor. Their duties also involved safeguarding the sacred objects upon whose safety Rome itself depended, such as the Palladium. The Palladium was a cult image believed to have been carried from Troy by the legendary Aeneas and kept from public view. It was believed that this sacred object was a talisman that kept Rome safe and was seen as the cornerstone of Rome's success. The small circular Temple of Vesta was engulfed in flames despite the best efforts of Commodus who was supervising the Praetorians, the Urban Cohorts and other soldiers present in the city. The Palladium was exposed to public sight. The Vestals, the only people allowed to touch the sacred statue, snatched it from the flames and carried it along the Sacred Way up the Palatine Hill to the Palace. The fire seemed to follow, moving across the buildings that lined the side of the hill and into the Palace itself, destroying extensive areas including the library containing the state records. This loss probably accounts for the limited number of legal cases collected by later legal compilers of Commodus' reign. The destruction of the Palatine necessitated Commodus moving to the Vectillian Villa, the site of his eventual murder. The fire continued to rage for several days, destroying large areas of the city before rain and the work of the soldiers and citizens managed to finally stop it.[2]

The fire was a religious, political, financial and social disaster for Commodus. For a demigod whose propaganda regularly announced his piety and divine protection, whilst he claimed to be a divine hero who protected his people. The emperor had associated his rule with the promise of security, safety and plenty despite the famine that had so recently gripped the city. This disaster was seen as an act of divine disapproval, a condemnation of the emperor's claims by the very gods themselves. This is seen in Herodian's account of the alleged causes of the fire. The historian continues:

> Thus the whole incident was regarded as supernatural, since the people on that occasion were convinced that the fire had begun and ended by the force of divine will. Some people forecast from the occasion that the destruction of the Temple of Peace was a portent of war ... As a result of all these tragedies falling on the city one after another, the people of Rome no longer viewed Commodus in such a favourable light.[3]

The destruction of the Temple of Vesta and the exposure of the Palladium to human sight, as well as its near consumption in the flames, and the extinguishing of the sacred fire would also been seen as a sign that the safety of Rome was in imminent danger. The empire could fall. The sacred fire was carried before the emperor in public; the people would not fail to make the connection. Not only was Commodus' status as a demigod being questioned, but also his suitability to rule. That this was probably already felt in private by the nobles was a given, however if questions were now being asked by the ordinary people of the city, the foundations for his rule would rapidly crumble. Many of the poor had lost their homes and were now destitute. A hungry mob had, in his eyes, almost killed him once, he could not allow large sections of the populace to go hungry again or be left without a roof over their heads. The fact many of the wealthy elite had lost fortunes in the fire would probably have not concerned him greatly. However the cost of social relief and the rebuilding of the city would have to be paid for somehow, despite the fact that the finances of the state were stretched by the continuing plague, almost beyond breaking point. Dio records the return of the plague with even greater ferocity after the fall of Cleander and the coinage had been debased again in 190 AD. It was now that Commodus probably introduced his additional tax on the elite of the empire; Dio uses the word 'finally' when describing the imposition of this tax. Senators, their wives and children, were obliged to contribute two gold pieces each year on his birthday in August, whilst senators in all other cities had to give five *denarii* each.[4] The social programme that the emperor must have run is not mentioned directly in any of the sources, focused as they were on the lives and events that affected those in their elite class or reading audience. The repair programme is however hinted at:

he inscribed his name on the works of others: this the senate erased.[5]

It was established practice for the names of those who built or restored buildings to inscribe their names upon them. The Emperor Hadrian brought praise upon himself for restoring and virtually rebuilding the Pantheon built by Marcus Agrippa, Augustus' *amicus*, but refused to place his name upon it and most other buildings he restored. Commodus on his death suffered *damnatio memoriae* and numerous inscriptions across the empire have gaps in their wording where his name has been removed. In Rome though there are few examples of this. Inscriptions record the restoration of the Temple of Peace by Septimius Severus and the Temple of Vesta by his wife, Julia Domna. Some other public buildings appear to have been restored at this time, including the reconstruction of the roof of the Temple of Jupiter Dolichenus, a wooden roof would have been first to ignite in the fire. Inscriptions relating to known reconstruction work on the Temple of Jupiter Heliopolitanus from the reigns of Marcus Aurelius and Commodus and the Thermae Agrippae were according to inscriptions restored by Septimius Severus, although the major part of the work may have been completed in the reign of Commodus, as the baths later carry the title *Commodiane*. The palace on the Palatine also carry inscriptions referring to it as the *Domus Palatina Commodiana* which was probably more than a simple renaming but an extensive reconstruction. It seems probable that Commodus began his restoration programme with rebuilding the numerous *insulae*, the high-rise apartment buildings that the majority of the population lived in. This would make both political and social sense. Our senatorial sources would not be interested in such a programme that focused on the needs of the lower classes. From the passing comment in the *Historia Augusta* it is clear that he did restore some prominent public buildings but the archaeological record has been unable to place these. Dio records:

> Commodus displayed in Rome itself many indications of wealth and very many more, even of a love of the beautiful.[6]

He goes on to record other acts 'of public service' which must be some expression of wealth in a public setting which can only refer to buildings and the 'love of the beautiful' referring to the use of aesthetic statues and designs. The sources repeatedly mention the emperor covering Rome in statues of himself depicted as Hercules. A large bronze statue of Commodus in the guise of Hercules was erected in the two Minucian porticos in the low-lying area near the Theatre of Marcellus. The two porticos were named Vetrus and Frumentaria, and from the latter eligible citizens collected their tickets entitling them to the free grain from the *annona*. Each would have seen the statue of Commodus as they stood in the queue, an unsubtle reminder that it was the emperor to whom they should feel grateful. His *beneficia* of free grain to be reciprocated by their *gratia*, to be expressed as loyalty. This was especially important after the shortages of the previous years. Herodian in a criticizing tone also mentions:

> All over the city he set up statues of himself, and what is more in front of the senate house he put up one of himself as an archer with a bow stretched ready to shoot.

Herodian suggests this was done to induce fear amongst the senate. However it is evident that the statue was a reference to the synthesis of Commodus the emperor with Hercules the demigod, and reminding all of his gladiatorial skill with the bow. Dio, who would pass this statue on an almost daily basis, makes no mention of its supposed threatening message, merely adding:

> Vast numbers of statues were erected representing him in the garb of Hercules.

Interestingly the historian uses the passive in describing this. It was not Commodus but the senate that voted for these to be erected. This is confirmed by the *Historia Augusta*;

> He allowed statues of himself to be erected with the accoutrements of Hercules; and sacrifices were performed to him as a god.

In wishing to gain imperial approval senators introduced proposals that they felt would win the *gratia* of the emperor. Many senators had been adlected into the senate and granted the *latus clavus*, the broad stripe worn proudly on their togas denoting senatorial status. These men had previously been equestrians and some freedmen. Commodus had also raised many senators to the rank of praetor without actual service in the posts. All appointments to the role of consul conferred nobility on the family of the recipient in perpetuity and these appointments were made solely by the emperor. Commodus had only recently appointed twenty-five suffect consuls in one year. An ambitious senator who aspired to high office was virtually guaranteed a post if he was nominated as the candidate of the emperor. There were probably only 100 senatorial and equestrian appointments each year and competition must have been intense. The senate was effectively under the control of the emperor, but only the wealthy aristocrats were resentful as their access to the *beneficia* of the emperor was now limited by the increased influence of the imperial freedmen. Even their place within the senate was being affected by the appointment of so many suffect consuls who, like themselves, would have the right to be called on to speak at the start of debates. Once such a proposal was introduced at the behest of the emperor or if it clearly reflected imperial policy, it would be a brave man to vote against it. Such a move would be a public statement of disloyalty and in the age of the *delatores*, an open invitation for a charge of *majestas*. By appointing so many men to high office Commodus could draw upon their services in appointments to provinces that commanded significant numbers of troops. As time went on the pool of experienced men that he could trust had become increasingly shallow. These new appointments would expand his options, as these men owed him loyalty through their appointments to praetorships and consulships. Commodus was not trying to circumvent the traditional structures of rank and social structure, merely to use and adapt it to his own needs. The traditional Roman approach to the problems of government was evolution not revolution. Ironically, despite the perceived affront to the dignity of the office of consul, it was the statues of Commodus as Hercules that seem to have raised the aristocrats' anger to almost hysterical proportions, shouting out in rhythmic waves on news of the death of Commodus a few months later:

> On all sides are statues of the foe, on all sides are statues of the murderer, on all sides are statues of the gladiator. Let them be cast down ... Let the statues of the gladiator be overthrown.[7]

The greatest of all statues, the enormous Colossus outside the Coliseum, also received a makeover. Originally constructed by Nero to represent himself, it stood over 120 Roman feet high. Vespasian then adapted the statue to represent Sol. Commodus added a club and placed a bronze lion at its feet to represent Hercules. According to Dio, the *Historia Augusta* and Herodian, the head of Sol was removed and replaced by one of Commodus. Hekster doubts that Commodus did substitute the face of Sol with his own, basing this on earlier confusion in the sources as to the identity of the face on the statue. However all our sources are in complete agreement that Commodus placed his own image on the Colossus wanting to associate himself with Hercules. On the base Dio recollects what the emperor had inscribed:

> Champion of the secutores; only left handed fighter to conquer twelve times (as I recall the number) one thousand men.

Clearly Dio is attempting to remember the actual wording when writing his history many years after the events he is describing. Herodian adds that Commodus included also his usual family names, but omitted the title 'Germanicus' for 'Victor of a Thousand Gladiators'. Perhaps a lack of room on the base to fully inscribe his name led to the omission of 'Germanicus'. Commodus felt it was important to emphasize his gladiatorial skills in comparison to the war like Hercules. A later epitomizer of Dio, Peter the Patriarch, records a different form of the inscription which is reflected in the *Historia Augusta*. This can be combined to form the following suggested inscription:

L Commodus Hercules, palus primus, secutorum qui (primus et?) solus scaeva vicit sescenties vicies.

The *primus palus* is referring to the first and most important centurion of a legion; the *primus pilus*, whilst the *palus* was a wooden pike used as a training weapon by gladiators. Another later source summarizing Dio records that the inscription 'was written by Lucius Commodus Hercules and upon it written a well known couplet':

Jove's son, victorious Hercules am I
Not Lucius, even though forced that name to bear.

This is so different from other recorded inscriptions it can easily be discounted. The position of the Colossus is important, standing outside the most famous gladiatorial arena of them all, and also next to the gladiatorial training school. The Vectilian Villa, Commodus' new palace in Rome whilst the Palatine palace was repaired, was close by. As the emperor went to officiate over the Games or train with the gladiators he would have passed his own image in Olympian form, confirming his own super human stature, skills and abilities. The people of Rome would also pass it as they attended the gladiatorial combats in the Coliseum or wandered around the shops and booths of the prostitutes outside, their confidence in their emperor reaffirmed. The links between his gladiatorial abilities were advertised in the city bulletins and confirmed on the inscription below the shinning gilded bronze statue of the emperor. Coins of 192 AD publicized this new Hercules across the empire; on one side they show the head of Commodus covered with a lion skin whist the reverse has a standing Hercules resting his right hand on a club with its left dragging a lion by its back paws, perhaps a copy of the rearrangement made to the Colossus itself. At the same time the emperor demanded to be addressed as 'Hercules, son of Zeus', and in procession often carried a club whilst wearing a lion skin covering his head. He also wore garments 'that gave the impression of feminine extravagance and heroic strength at the same time' which is a Roman interpretation of the priestly sacred robes worn in the Greek east for the Cult of Hercules. By the summer of 192 AD he was officially identifying himself with Hercules. Speidel argues for this date because a papyrus from Fayum in Egypt records Hercules in Commodus' title on 11 October 192 AD. Also in 192 AD he adopted the formal style of *Invictus Romanus Hercules*. A relief found in the imperial villa has Hercules dressed in 'female' robes depicting *Hercules Venator*. Hercules was often described using the title *Effeminatus*, which Commodus also adopted, leading to the claims in the *Historia Augusta* that he was bisexual. Members of the imperial household were appointed to priesthoods in a private cult to the Roman Hercules on his private estates, paid for by the *fiscus*, and in this capacity sacrifices were made to him. This freedman appears to have been purchased as a slave and gained employment in the imperial household based on the size of his male member. A novel way to break the ice at the imperial banquets and yet another indication of the emperor's rather unusual sense of humour. In another example he placed a bird on the head of a man who had a few remaining white hairs which the bird supposedly pecked thinking they were worms.[8]

The cult of the imperial Roman Hercules was not just limited to Rome. Statues of Commodus in the guise of Hercules have been found throughout the empire. A statue found in the headquarters building at the Roman fortress at Kongen in Germany possibly depicts Commodus with the attributes of Hercules. In Africa a centurion dedicated an altar to the Roman Hercules in Volubilis in modern day Morocco. Close by are the remains of a mosaic dating from approximately the same time depicting the labours of Hercules. Another mosaic found at Oudina (Uthina), also in North Africa, is dated to the late second century in which Hercules and Victoria face frontally, Hercules is naked but for a lion skin and 'Victoria' to his right holds a wreath over the demigod's head. This is almost identical to a mosaic in the theatre of Ostia which is Commodian in date and reflects the impact of imperial propaganda. A paved mosaic from the Villa of Acholla in modern day Tunisia built by the native senator Asinius Rufinus, who was awarded the consulship by Commodus in 184 AD, shows Hercules and his labours. Even in the distant provinces the emperor was commemorated as the divine hero. On Hadrian's Wall, a bronze figurine of Hercules was made wearing the attire of a gladiator with a short tunic, broad belt and helmet, whilst at Ajka in Pannonia a statue of Hercules was found bearing the similar facial features of Commodus in the villa of a Roman veteran. On the very borders of the Roman Empire facing Parthia, an altar was dedicated by a decurion, dedicated to the safety of Commodus:

> emperor, Pacifier of the World, Invincible, the Roman Hercules. Aelius Tittianus, decurion of the cavalry cohort II Ulpia Commodiana, paid this vow to the Genius of Dura, on the sixteenth day before the Kalends of the month Pius, under the consuls Flaccus and Clarus.

The date of this inscription is 17 March 193 AD, three months after the murder of the emperor whose safety the gods were asked to protect. From this inscription it appears Commodus was granted additional titles by the senate; that of *Pacator Orbis*, Pacifier of the World, and *Dominus Noster*, Our Lord. Commodus was the first to use this title which would be conventionally used by later emperors. Close by archaeologists found a bust depicting the Roman Hercules. The association of Commodus with the demigod Hercules resonated with the army. Evidence for the impact of imperial propaganda on the provincials is nowhere near as extensive. The coin issues of provincial cities understandably make play on their emperor's divine aspirations but then they would do so, hoping for imperial *beneficia* through sincere expressions of their loyalty. One of the first cities to do so was Ephesus, recently rebuilt after the devastating earthquake thanks to the financial *beneficia* of Marcus Aurelius and Commodus. A medallion dated to shortly before August 191 AD makes reference to Commodus as Hercules, whilst other cities rushed to catch up. On an individual level, beyond the confines of the military, there is mounting evidence of an initial impact of the Roman Hercules on the daily life of the majority of the population. Archaeological finds in Britain suggest the cult of Commodus as identified as Hercules was common and this also reflects the zeal of provincials, especially the inhabitants of Britain, who made a political choice to show special devotion to Commodus as a demigod rather than substitute their own gods or others from the Romano Greek pantheon.[9] There had existed for many generations the opportunity to make sacrifices to the emperor through the imperial cult which may have satisfied the needs of the provincials. The short time span, from mid 191 AD to his death on the last day of 192 AD was too little for a major impact to be made on the minds of the majority of the population of the empire.

Returning to Rome itself, the extensive nature of Commodus' rebuilding programme is reflected in his assertion that he had virtually rebuilt the whole city. Hercules is remembered in mythology as helping mankind through his labours which were so superhuman in their arduous nature that the man became a god. Like Hercules himself, who founded cities in his name (Herculaneum being an example), Commodus, the new Hercules would refound Rome. On a political level Commodus needed to rebuild the confidence of the populace in his status as a demigod under divine approval who was ushering in a new 'golden age'. After the devastation of the fire he could not abandon the propaganda campaign he had started, this would have led to ridicule and political suicide. Instead he threw himself into this propaganda with renewed zeal. In fact, according to the *Historia Augusta*, it was Marcia who suggested the refounding of Rome. Coins carry the legend *COL(onia) AN(toniniana) COM(modiana)*, his rebuilding of Rome had made the city the 'immortal, fortunate colony of the whole earth'. This was more an expression of fact than a symbolic pseudo political message espoused by Hekster who suggests Commodus was addressing the populace of the

Roman Empire inviting them to take symbolic possession of their capital. Walking through the streets of Rome itself in 192 AD, a recent arrival would have heard Latin, Aramaic, Greek, Hebrew, Egyptian, Gaelic, as well as languages of those people who lived beyond the boundaries of the empire. Rome's population was ever-changing, it was a physical representation of the people of the whole empire. This is what Commodus recognized in the title he applied to the capital itself. He was attempting to solidify his claim to be the founder of new Rome in the manner of Hercules.[10] Commodus had been raised to be joint emperor with his father in 175 AD before the assembled legions on the Danube on the anniversary of Rome's original founder, Romulus' ascent into heaven. This may have held a particular resonance for him and now he could claim also to be the new Romulus. His refounding of Lanuvium as part of the celebrations of his thirtieth birthday where he acquired the title of the 'Roman Hercules' suggests this was an evolutionary idea in his mind, not revolutionary. To the senatorial elite, this is exactly what it was.

The senators however continued to shower honours and titles upon the emperor. They awarded him a *conditor* or founder's statue in his honour made of solid gold with Commodus standing beside a bull and a cow.

> In his honour a gold statue was erected of a thousand pounds weight, representing him together with a bull and a cow.

Such images are associated throughout the Greek and Roman world on coins and other images with the refounding or founding of cities, actions associated with the tradition of the *aratrum* ritual. The founding ritual for a Roman colony involved the pulling of a plough by oxen over the land planned for the gates of the town. This image is again repeated on the imperial coinage bearing the legend *Hercules Romanus Conditor*. The senate also voted that the reign of Commodus be known universally as the 'golden age' and this be recorded on all public documents.[11]

Commodus portrayed himself as the *patronus* of all. The senate was ordered to rename Rome 'Commodiana', the legions 'Commodian', and the day the senate passed these measures was also to be known as 'Commodiana'. The emperor appears to have placed the proposal to the senate in person ensuring its successful passage. The senate then not only passed the resolution with feigned enthusiasm, but went on to vote for itself to be renamed 'Commodian' as well as granting the emperor the title 'Hercules'. The months were also renamed: Amazonius, Invictus, Felix, Pius, Lucius, Aelius, Aurelius, Commodus, Augustus, Herculeus, Romanus, Exsuperatorius, whilst the emperor assumed the titles 'Amazonius' and 'Exsuperatorius' as well as various others. The *Historia Augusta* provides a different order but epigraphical evidence supports the dates given in Dio. August, the month of the emperor's birth was named 'Commodiana' and December, perhaps the month of Marcia's birth, being named 'Amazonius'. The new dating system appears to have had minimal impact, mainly due to the time between its introduction and cancellation being so limited. Again it is the army that appears to have shown most enthusiasm for it, inscriptions record the dating system being used by the 22nd Primigenia Legion in Mainz, Germany and the 3rd Augusta in Lambaesis in North Africa. The inscription from Dura Europas also records that army units rapidly accepted the title 'Commodiana'. These titles strengthened the bond between the army and its emperor. Lanuvium is the only other place that appears to have used the new titles, but as a recently refounded colony of the emperor, failure to do so would have been a sign of disloyalty.[12]

Provincial cities attempted to strengthen their connections with the emperor by requesting the renaming of existing games or creating new ones in order to celebrate his new status. Ephesus renamed the 'Artemisis' and 'Hadrianeia' after Commodus and worshipped him in the form of Dionysius; Athens had already in 188/9 AD asked Commodus to be their archon which he gladly accepted, and now celebrated the 'Kommodeia' in his honour, as did Miletus, Caesarea Mauretania, Thebes and Tyros. Tarsus, a city according to mythology founded by Hercules, built a second temple for the imperial cult dedicated solely to Commodus as did Corinth. Provincial coins show many cities naming themselves Commodian. Many of these cities were to retain the games they initiated in Commodus' honour even after his death and *damnatio memoriae*, Antioch until 237 AD, Athens to at least 212 AD, Miletus to 240 AD and Caesarea Mauretania until the mid-third century. This was no superficial adherence to Commodus but a genuine expression of loyalty.

The Hellenistic Greek cities had traditionally expressed their loyalty to their ruler in this way, but the retention of these celebratory games after Commodus' murder suggests that the cult of the Roman Hercules took real hold in a short space of time. Since Hellenistic times in the Greek east cults had been founded for individual kings and Roman emperors and their families by cities where they were worshipped as gods. Alexander the Great and various Hellenistic kings often appeared symbolically attired as various deities. Romans had traditionally elevated deceased emperors and members of the imperial family to the status of a divinity. Vespasian on his deathbed ironically exclaimed that he felt he was becoming a god. Both Commodus' father and mother were deified by the senate and from that moment Commodus styled himself the 'son of a god'. Furthermore living emperors and their families had their own temples and were worshipped and sacrificed to as part of the imperial cult. Caligula was the first living emperor to permit his worship as divine with his own temple in Rome in which he constructed a life-size statue of himself in gold to which sacrifices were made. He also appeared in public portrayed as a range of gods including Hercules. Commodus had drawn upon his reading of Caligula's life in the works of Suetonius. His own experiences in the east as he toured with his father after the failed revolt of Avidius Cassius would have introduced him to this concept. The *Historia Augusta* suggests the next logical step, also followed by Caligula, the deification of the reigning emperor, was in fact introduced by the senate itself:

And in truth, on the occasion when he laid before the senate his proposal to call Rome Commodiana, not only did the senate gleefully pass this resolution, out of mockery, as far as we know, but also took the name 'Commodian' to itself, at the same time giving Commodus the name Hercules, and calling him a god.

This is reflected in the account in Dio with the senatorial historian asserting that Commodus bestowed upon himself the name Hercules 'in addition to a great many other names'. Dio tries to ignore the ignominy of the senate deifying the emperor as ambitious senators seized the opportunity to gain imperial favour by introducing such a resolution that no one dared to oppose. Commodus, of course, did not have to accept the deification, yet it appears he did.[13]

The Roman imperial system had originally been based on a concept of equality between the emperor and the senatorial aristocracy, when in reality, no equality ever existed. For most of the population of the empire Commodus' assertion of certain divine qualities would not be revolutionary and were clearly readily accepted. Yet one group would never accept this, the group that had most to lose, the senatorial aristocracy. However, after the death of Commodus which precipitated nearly 100 years of civil wars and barbarian invasions, such perceptions of the imperial status would be accepted by all, even by what remained of the aristocracy. The Emperor Aurelian's (270–5 AD) coins declare himself 'born to be god and lord' and declare him to be 'deus'.

A demigod could not treat his subjects as equals and Commodus introduced a new formal greeting to the senate to reflect this and so to stress his superiority to all:

The Emperor Caesar Lucius Aelius Aurelius Commodus Augustus Pius Felix Sarmaticus Germanicus Maximus Britannicus, Pacifier of the Whole Earth, Invincible, the Roman Hercules, Pontifex Maximus, Holder of the Tribunician Authority for the eighteenth time, Imperator for the eighth time, consul for the seventh time, Father of his country, to the consuls, praetors, tribunes, and to the fortunate Commodian senate, Greeting.[14]

The wording is virtually identical to how the emperor was addressed in the dedicatory altar from Dura Europas.

Commodus, in the manner of the demigod Hercules, promoted his good deeds for the benefit of mankind by ensuring the grain supply was secure. In Ostia, one of the harbours for the African and Egyptian fleets, there is evidence of a rebuilding programme. A mosaic that decorated the ceiling to the theatre shows Hercules being crowned by 'Victoria'. Brick stamps from the theatre show that extensive rebuilding and enlargement was begun by Commodus but a large inscription dated to 196 AD claims the rebuilding was the work of Septimius Severus and his son Caracalla. This was the fate of other building work initiated by Commodus. Floor mosaics outside a row of sixty rooms have been also dated to the reign of Commodus. They show ships and grain measures, the rooms probably being the offices of shippers and merchants. A large number of Hadrianic grain warehouses (*horrea*) were also added to with the building of the large *Horrea Antoniani* on the banks of the Tiber. Two temples built by the shipwright guild (*fabri navales*) and carpenters were unfinished at the time of the death of Commodus and so were dedicated to his successor, Pertinax. A Commodian brick stamp was found at the headquarters of the *annona* in the city indicating substantial building work was initiated at this time. Such work is probably to be associated with the refounding of the city as 'Colonia Felix Commodiana.' The African grain fleets were also renamed as the 'Commodiana Herculea' and Carthage 'Alexandria Commodiana Togata'. The people of Rome were to be in no doubt where their next meal was coming from. The Baths of Cleander were renamed the 'Thermae Commodiae', Hercules was the patron god of hot springs and their associate healing properties. The baths were said to be built by Cleander but Jerome places the construction in 183 AD. Perhaps this is when construction started and continued until 187 AD, being named after the *cubicularius* who supervised the final stages.[15]

The popularity of the emperor after the effects of the fire had been restored. He had secured the grain supply and started an extensive rebuilding programme which in itself would create jobs for many whose homes had been destroyed. There were also two distributions of *congiaria* in 192 AD, those eligible collecting their tokens from under the gaze of the Roman Hercules. According to Dio these were at higher than normal rates and were meant to alleviate the suffering and hardships caused by the fire. Commodus also appears to have organized a series of races at short notice in the Circus Maximus, rushing in from the Quintillian Villa. This would have kept the people and the faction leaders happy. The emperor also appeared in the arena in a series of exhibitions in order to demonstrate his gladiatorial skills. These were not actual combats but practice sessions, the combatants armed with wooden or blunt weapons:

He himself would enter the arena in the garb of Mercury, and casting aside all his other garments, would begin his exhibition wearing only a tunic and unshod.

This probably took place before the actual combats took place. Before the assembled populace Commodus was again reinforcing the link between himself and Hercules. However simulated combat was not the same as actual combat. The refounding of Rome would require celebratory games and Commodus decided to use this as an opportunity to present himself as the Roman Hercules by actually fighting in the arena.[16]

The gladiatorial games were much more than a bloody battle to the death to gratify an adrenaline fuelled mob. They were steeped in religious symbolism. On one level they reminded and reassured the audience of Roman power, combat in the arena symbolizing Rome's superiority in war and the triumph of Roman order over barbarian chaos. On a deeper level they represented the daily struggle with life and death faced by all, especially with thousands in the city dying daily from the plague with many also dying in the flames of the devastating fire. The heroic death of the gladiators modelled how the people themselves should face death: heroically. The emperors had also used the games to maintain political and social control, this being one of the few occasions where the people and emperor met. These were opportunities for the emperor to be seen by his people and for the people to make demands of their emperor. The sheer numbers involved allowed the crowd to risk the emperor's anger by demonstrating or expressing dissatisfaction with current affairs, as was successfully manipulated by Papirius Dionysius and his associates in the fall of Cleander. The games acted like a safety valve allowing discontent to be voiced before reaching the point where the emperor became threatened. Therefore no emperor seriously considered putting an end to such spectacles, even when they disapproved of them, as Marcus Aurelius is said to have done.

On a yet deeper religious level, the games also signified the defeat of death through bravery, *virtus*, and fighting skill; the very qualities embodied by Hercules. Cicero, discussing how to deal with physical pain, concludes that Romans who wish to possess *virtus*, one of the most important qualities in a human, must not fear pain or death. He cites examples of famous soldiers and gladiators to illustrate his point, considering such individuals as the embodiment of courage, power and strength. If Commodus wished to be Hercules reborn, in his eyes, he would have to fight in the arena. By entering the arena Commodus would re-enact the demigods' triumph over death, he would challenge death itself and his survival would reinforce his superhuman nature. Also the emperor, through his deeds and labours in the arena could symbolically project himself as their protector and saviour; they would become 'the People of Commodus':

He entitled the Roman people the 'People of Commodus,' since he had very often fought as a gladiator in their presence … the people regularly applauded him as though he were a god.[17]

The problem for Commodus was the status of gladiators; they were both admired and despised at the same time. A law of 11 AD banned Roman citizens from volunteering to become gladiators or appearing on stage. This was reinforced by a law in 19 AD that banned senators and equestrians and their descendants or relatives from appearing in the arena, a crime punishable with loss of their rank, status and privileges. Yet many Roman aristocrats remained passionate about gladiatorial combat and the stage, Commodus' armour, helmet and weapons being avidly sort after when auctioned by Pertinax. Many wealthy Romans trained and fought in private much as Commodus did, but never in public as the emperor now considered. This brought on *infamia*, disgrace and association with the lowest social order; that of slaves, prisoners of war and criminals, the fertile recruiting ground of the gladiatorial training schools. The fame and heroic status of gladiators did attract some volunteers, the so called *auctorati*, who had to swear the oath that was incompatible with Roman citizenship; from that moment on they agreed to be on the receiving end of 'burning, imprisonment, or death by the sword' and, most importantly of all, a rejection of their freedom. The price of these men had been limited by Commodus and Marcus Aurelius to 120,000 *sesterces* as many had been conscripted in the Northern War. Effectively these men were voluntarily agreeing to become slaves. On winning a duel, the successful gladiator would win a palm branch as the symbol for victory, but also money and other gifts from the official in charge of the games. Whilst he lived the successful gladiator could win both wealth and fame, but rarely for long.[18]

There were however no legal penalties for men of status appearing in chariot races. Nero was a driver and Caligula officiated a race where all the competitors were senators. This is probably because these games or *ludi* involving chariot races were based on religious celebrations whilst gladiatorial combats were *munera* and technically 'gifts' by rich individuals in their name to the people, historically to commemorate a deceased member of their family. So why didn't Commodus use the Circus Maximus to publicize his status as the new Roman Hercules? Firstly the 'Labours of Hercules' were best symbolized in the hunts and physical combats of the arena rather than the chariot races of the circus. Secondly the spectators in the circus were divided into factions, of whom Commodus was well known to be a supporter of the Greens. A performance in these circumstances would divide his audience rather than unite them behind the imperial embodiment of Hercules. In the arena there were no factions, all could support Commodus as their divine champion and patron.[19]

Although despised on a social level, successful gladiators won acclaim and almost godlike heroic standing. Even a defeated gladiator, if he had fought well, could receive the gift of life from the crowd. Usually games were fought using blunt weapons with most duels ending with the defeated man surrendering by taking off his helmet and raising the first finger of his fighting hand to the crowd. Games provided by the emperor were different as he could hold games *sine missione* which entailed sharpened weapons, the combatants fighting to the death. These were by far the most popular, the crowd screaming, according to Seneca, 'Kill him! Lash him! Burn him!' and the defeated earning a final 'He has it!' The winner would stand on the blood soaked floor of the arena, absorbing the ovation of the thousands present, awaiting their decision on the fate of the man who lay under his boot. Death for this man, if not certain, was likely. However several inscriptions record the careers of gladiators who died outside of the arena, not all having won all their fights. One records a man who died at 30, winning 21 fights, drawing 9 and losing 4, but being allowed to survive. The thrill for the crowd was not just witnessing the combat, but deciding on life and death in the manner of the gods themselves.[20]

Gladiators were also incredibly attractive to women, even their sweat was greatly sort after as an aphrodisiac. On the eruption of Vesuvius, one wealthy woman, adorned with jewels, was found next to the bodies of a number of men at the Pompeian gladiatorial school, some still chained to the wall. Juvenal tells the story of Eppia, the wife of a senator, who ran off with Sergius, a gladiator:

> Was it good looks and youthfulness that set Eppia on fire? What did she see in him to endure being classed with gladiators? After all, her Sergius had already begun to smooth his throat, an injured arm presaged retirement; and his face was seriously disfigured, a furrow chafed by his helmet, a huge lump on the bridge of his nose, and a nasty condition provoking a forever weeping eye. He was a gladiator though. That makes them Hyacinthus; that's why she preferred him to her children and country, husband and sister. They love the steel.[21]

Commodus had always trained and fought as a *secutor* who were always paired with a *retarius*. He appears to have had the first room in the gladiatorial barracks, the *Ludus Magnus*, where he rested after bouts and changed. A *cryptoporticus* leads from the *Ludi Magnus* into the Coliseum, its superb stucco reliefs decorating its walls strongly resembling other such reliefs dated to Commodus' reign. This passage allowed the emperor to train and practice in the great arena itself, away from the public gaze. The advantage of the *secutor* was a helmet that covered the whole of the face which also extended down to protect the back of the neck. A high metal ridge ran from the crest of the head down the back of the helmet which would have affected its balance. This 'fin' combined with the smooth bullet shape of the rest of the casing was designed to resemble a fish's head. The *secutor's* opponent, the *retarius*, was armed with a net in the guise of a fisherman. Vision however was limited to two small eye holes and so was extremely restricted. His opponent was armed with a trident whose prongs could not penetrate a narrow grating on the helmet. The helmet was also extremely heavy, those being found at Pompeii being nearly twice the weight of a legionary's helmet. However the gladiator wore less armour than a legionary, the combined weight totalling 20kg with an additional 4–7kg for the helmet. As fights tended not to last longer than ten to fifteen minutes the weight was manageable for a trained fighter.

The *secutor* was also protected by a large rectangular legionary shield, the *scutum*, and a padded linen sleeve on his sword arm. On one leg he wore a leather gaiter, however a loin cloth provided no bodily protection. He was armed with a *gladius*, the short thrusting sword of the legionary. His matched opponent, the *retarius*, had even less protective armour. He wore no helmet or greaves, nor did he carry a shield. He did have a *galerus*, an outwardly curving tall metal guard worn on his left shoulder, gaiters on his legs and a padded linen armguard as worn by the *secutor*. His weapons were based on those of the sea, a weighted net, long dagger (*pugio*) and a trident with three prongs. The *retarius* would lead with his left shoulder, ducking down below the shoulder guard when necessary. The outward curve ensured that he did not hit his face against the metal edge as he avoided the blows from the *secutor*. The *retarius* would launch his net using an underarm cast either aimed at the feet of his opponent to trip him, or try to entangle his sword arm leaving him defenceless. If successful he would move in with his trident, or if already lost, the long dagger. If the *secutor* avoided the throw of the net, the *retarius* would attempt to recover it, manoeuvring round this opponent using the *secutor's* restricted vision to his advantage. Movement was the *retarius'* best form of attack and defence and his limited armour would facilitate this.

If the *retarius* was unable to retrieve his net, he would hold the trident in two hands, thrusting at the exposed flesh of his opponent below the shield or either side, parrying blows with the prongs or shaft of the trident. The length of the trident would keep his enemy at bay. The *secutor*, movement limited by his heavier armour, would duck behind his shield, further restricting his vision. This would be the opportunity the *retarius* had been manoeuvring for, rapidly moving into his blindside to make a thrust around the curved edges of the *scutum*. If his trident was lost, the *retarius* had his long dagger, but now the advantage would be firmly with the better armed *secutor* and his end was probably not long in coming.

The *secutor's* main tactic would be to try and get as close to the *retarius* as possible, entering within the circle created by the length of his opponent's trident.

This would also make it impossible to throw the net. In such instances the *retarius* would swing the net around his opponent's feet in order to bring him down. The *retarius* would retreat if his attempted trip failed. Time was on the side of the lightly armed *retarius* as his opponent's strength was weakened by his heavy armour with the heat of the sun and the reduced air supply in his enclosed helmet. The *secutor's* attacks would also have to be carefully timed and rapid as his vision was greatly reduced. The armour and weapons of the *secutor* and *retarius* were designed to make them equally matched, the advantages and disadvantages of their equipment providing each with an equal chance of victory.[22]

According to the unreliable account in the *Historia Augusta*, Clodius Albinus, as praetor, was tasked with organizing Commodus' games:

> Next he served his praetorship under Commodus, and a very famous one it was. For at these games Commodus, it is said, gave gladiatorial combats in both the Forum and the theatre.[23]

The Forum was used for gladiatorial displays and by theatre, we perhaps should assume the biographer meant the amphitheatre, the Coliseum, as confirmed by Dio and Herodian. Albinus though had probably been made suffect consul in 185 AD or 186 AD after which he served as Governor of Germania Inferior where he helped to crush the unrest during the Deserters War and then he served in Britain in 192 AD. The only time Commodus is recorded as actually fighting in the arena was at the end of his reign in 192 AD. Albinus probably held his praetorship under Commodus, and as praetor he was responsible for organizing games on behalf of the emperor, however they were not the ones that the emperor fought in.

The games themselves are recorded as lasting for fourteen days and have been linked to the *Ludi Romani* from 5 to 19 September, but this is fifteen days in length. Another suggestion for the games was the *Ludi Plebeii* from 4 to 17 November, a duration of fourteen days, but chariot racing was held for the last three days. No such races are mentioned in connection with the games the emperor participated in, however the very fact the emperor did appear in the arena in combat may have meant the races that followed were of little importance in comparison to what had occurred in the Coliseum and so were passed over without comment. The *Ludi Capitolini* lasted for sixteen days whilst the *Ludi Saeculares* were celebrated approximately every hundred years leading to games in 88 AD and 204 AD but these only lasted three days and nights. *Ludi Capitolini* were also held in 47 AD to commemorate 800 years since Rome's founding leading to games in 148 AD. These games were announced by heralds who invited the people to 'a spectacle, such as they had never witnessed and never would again'. This reflects the view held at the time that a lifetime was approximately equivalent to a hundred years and so no person would ever see two such games in their lives. This wording is perhaps reflected in Herodian's description of Commodus' advertising of his games:

> As news spread, people flocked to Rome from all over Italy and the neighbouring provinces to be spectators at something they had never seen or heard of before.

Commodus seems to have used this formula for the *Ludi Plebeii* of 192 AD as nobody had ever seen an emperor performing as a gladiator in their lifetime nor would they ever again. Clearly Commodus meant his appearance in the arena to be a one-off. However his choice of wording for the heralds was also meant to evoke similarities to the *Ludi Saeculares* as he had declared the refounding of Rome and he wished to celebrate this event, as well as publicize his confidence in the future of Rome. This was made more immediate by the destruction of the temples of Peace and Vesta, and exposure of the Palladium to public view. The original *Ludi Saeculares*, said to have been inaugurated on the overthrow of the last king of Rome and the establishment of the Republic, was also a time when the city was afflicted by a terrible plague. The officials then had sought to placate the offended gods who had sent the illness by carrying out sacrifices to Pluto and Proserpine, deities of the underworld. The plague reportedly stopped. The sacrifices of gladiators in the arena of death at Commodus' games would placate the gods again and hopefully the present pestilence that was ravaging both Rome and the empire would also stop. Commodus would appear as Mercury, the god who conveyed the souls of the dead to the underworld and also as Hercules: to not only officiate at the games but demonstrate his manifestation as the demigod through unrivalled prowess and skill. The *Ludi Plebeii* were dedicated to Jupiter and it cannot be coincidence that Herodian, before describing the publicizing of the games states that Commodus demanded 'to be called Hercules, the son of Zeus', Jupiter being the Roman equivalent of the Greek Zeus. In Herodian's mind the games and Commodus' title were linked. Heralds crossed Italy and bordering provinces spreading Commodus' promise that 'he would kill the wild animals with his own hand and engage in gladiatorial combat with the stoutest of young men'.[24]

Both Dio and Herodian were present at these games, Dio probably only for the days the emperor competed. Their purpose in writing their accounts was to provide a record for posterity of the unique events they experienced but also to ridicule the emperor. Marius Maximus was on the Danube and so the account in the *Historia Augusta* must also be taken with a degree of questioning. Before each day of the games Commodus appeared before the senators in the normal morning *salutatio* as the incarnation of Hercules:

Before entering the amphitheatre he would put on a long sleeved tunic of silk, white interwoven with gold and thus arrayed he would receive our greetings.

This was probably the priestly trappings of the devotees of the cult of Hercules. To introduce the concept of his reincarnation as the new Hercules to the people he staged a theatrical recreation of Hercules' sixth labour of the Stymphalian birds. Hercules had to drive away an enormous flock of man-eating birds which had roosted at a lake near the town of Stymphalia. Having no idea how to scare the birds away, Athena provided Hercules with a massive pair of *krotala*, bronze clappers made by Hephaistos, the God of the Forge. Hercules climbed a nearby mountain, clashed the *krotala*, and shot the startled birds with his bow as they took flight. Commodus ordered all the men in the city to be rounded up who were lame and dressed these up in imitation of the story, supposedly killing them with arrows and blows from his club. The account appears in both *Dio* and the *Historia Augusta* with only minor differences, but significantly the account in *Dio* appears as a theatrical staging of the event, sponges being used as stones and Commodus 'pretending' they were giants. Later the same historian states unequivocally that the emperor 'in public ... refrained from ... shedding human blood'. The event seems to have been twisted from a harmless theatrical performance to introduce the idea of Commodus appearing in the games as the Roman Hercules to something far more sinister. Dio records that the people did not want to enter the Coliseum as a rumour was spread that the emperor was to use spectators themselves as the symbolic representation of the birds and shoot them too. However the historian describes that the whole equestrian and senatorial orders attended, their presence a testament to their acquiescence to the emperor's presentation of himself as the new Hercules. Herodian, also present, describes the amphitheatre as being 'packed'. The only absence was Claudius Pompeianus, claiming old age and infirmity. However his sons did attend. The senatorial elite sat in the front rows close to the action and near the imperial box. With the theme and religious symbolism now set for the populace, the games began.[25]

The event opened in the amphitheatre with Commodus in the guise of Hercules Venator, Hercules the hunter. A hunting exhibition usually started the day's events, followed after lunch with gladiatorial contests in the heat of the afternoon. The emperor had spent many months practising with highly skilled Parthian archers and spearmen from Mauretania. Animals had been sourced from across the empire and beyond; bears, a tiger, a hippopotamus, elephants, ostriches, deer, gazelles, a range of horned animals but not bulls (in acknowledgement that Hercules captured the Cretan bull and later released it), over 100 lions and leopards. This huge administrative burden was born by the creation of new administrative posts. Of the ten new procurator posts created by Commodus, one was for a *subcurator ludi magni* and five more for *procuratores familiae gladiatoriae*. Most Roman, Herodian included, had only seen many of these creatures in pictures before, but all were now to be slaughtered in the arena. The arena had been divided into four sections, so reducing the manoeuvrability of the animals. A specially erected raised platform allowed the emperor to move across the top of the four partitions above the animals below. Animal hunts, the *venatio*, took on many different forms including hunts, watching performance animals or the execution of condemned criminals who were thrown to the wild beasts. *Venatores*, like gladiators were slaves, condemned criminals, prisoners of war or volunteers. Commodus initially demonstrated his skills with both the spear and bow, killing an elephant and a tiger. From the top of the partition he then pursued deer and gazelles as they ran, killing or wounding all with one shot each. Spears were used to kill the lions and leopards. The crowd, including Herodian, were astonished by his accuracy:

> One never saw him take a second shot and it was always a fatal wound ... his marksmanship was generally agreed to be astonishing.

Ostriches were decapitated using crescent shaped arrow heads and a leopard was killed by the emperor's spear as it was about to pounce on its human victim. The symbolism would not be lost on his adoring crowd: Commodus was the saviour of mankind. These *venatores* preceded the main gladiatorial contests for each of the fourteen days. On some days he descended from the platform to the floor of the arena to dispatch the less dangerous animal, some being captured by *bestiarii*, assistants in the animals fights, and then killed by the emperor. On one occasion 100 lions were released at once from trap doors in the floor of the arena. Commodus made a great show of only having 100 spears, each of which found its target. The creatures were then lined up for the assembled crowd to count and marvel at his Herculean labour. The first Labour of Hercules had been the slaying of the Nemean lion which lured warriors to their death by posing as an injured woman before transforming itself into a lion and killing its startled victim. Differing versions exist as to how Hercules eventually dispatched the beast; one is that he slay it with arrows piercing its mouth as its fur was impenetrable. Using one of its paws, Hercules skinned the lion which he then wore over his head. Commodus proved himself superior to the demigod by killing not one lion, but a hundred. The Labours of Hercules involved him killing birds, lions, a hind, a boar and sacrificing cattle as well as the more difficult to source Hydra and three headed dog, Cerberus. These are many of the animals Commodus is recorded as killing. The Cretan bull Hercules had to capture, then later release, suggesting that a bull was used in the games and captured by the emperor in the arena, but released and not killed like the other animals. Another of Hercules' labours involved stealing the belt of Hippolyta, the Queen of the Amazons. An account of Commodus re-enacting this labour is perhaps partly preserved in the *Historia Augusta*:

> He had been called 'Amazonius' moreover, because of his passion for his concubine Marcia, whom he loved to have portrayed as an Amazon.[26]

The senators were ordered to celebrate the emperor's performance by addressing him as 'Amazonius', again a reference to the Labour of Hippolyta's Belt. Coins celebrating these events depict Commodus as Hercules and Marcia as an Amazon. Perhaps the two re-enacted the ninth Labour of Heracles who, with a band of friends, sailed to the island of Paros. There they were met by two of King Minos' sons who killed two of Hercules' companions. The avenging Hercules exacted retribution, killing the two sons and demanding the population of the island provide two warriors to replace the two he had lost. He then journeyed to the land of Themiscyra where the Amazon queen lived. She was suitably impressed by Hercules and his companions and agreed to become his consort until the Goddess Hera intervened, persuading the Amazons that their queen was being abducted against her will. Hercules, thinking the attack was a carefully crafted plot, killed Hippolyta and took her belt.

After each bout Commodus took a drink of sweet wine from a cup shaped in the form of a club which he theatrically drank in one. This was in imitation of Hercules Bibens or Hercules the Drinker, the senators responding with the traditional salute: ' Long life to you.' After appearing as a *venatores* in the morning Commodus rested for lunch before reappearing in the afternoon as a gladiator. A fee of a million *sesterces* was charged for each appearance to emphasize the uniqueness of having the Roman Hercules appearing in the games with the inflated cost being an attempt to disassociate himself from the low status of the slaves, criminals, and prisoners of war he now fought as gladiators. The emperor entered the arena 'stripped and carrying his weapons'. Commodus fought left-handed, something he was particularly proud of. Dio is clear that the emperor did not fight using the sharpened blades but the wooden training swords, he held 'the wooden sword in his left' and 'in public he refrained from using steel and shedding human blood'. Herodian however refers to him 'wounding' his opponents, but not killing them. The wounds were probably inflicted by the hardened wood or lead tipped points of the practice swords, something referred to in Aurelius Victor. The emperor's bouts are described in Dio as 'sparring matches'. To avoid the cynics' response that his opponents were already primed to let him win, the emperor at times allowed the crowd to select his opponent but he also chose some probably from a line of men displayed before him. The cynicism of the sources leads to their belittling the gladiatorial skills of the emperor who had no difficulty winning every bout as 'they let him win', his bouts being demeaned as mere 'child's play'. After each victory Commodus publicly kissed his Praetorian Prefect Laetus and Eclectus, 'through his helmet'. This must have been difficult as the helmet encompassed the whole of his face and more likely he embraced them, a great honour, showing the assembled thousands, including the senators, that these were the emperor's *amici* and almost equals. This action suggests he himself did not believe he was divine as such a gesture infers near equality, normally the hand of the emperor was offered to be kissed. Here the emperor is the one embracing his *amici*, which he did on more than one occasion. Clearly both men were standing close to him on the floor of the arena as he fought. The assembled senators were given cues to chant their support of the emperor and his display:

> we would shout out whatever we were commanded, and especially these words continually: 'Thou art lord and thou art first, of all men most fortunate. Victor thou art, and victor thou shalt be; from everlasting, Amazonian, thou art victor.'[27]

All pretence at equality between senators and emperor was cast aside. Previously imperial office had been treated as magistracy bestowed by the senate and people of Rome. Commodus viewed his imperial status at first as his by right through nobility of birth, later adapting this concept to one of divine will, being the son of gods and blessed with divine favour as exemplified through his survival of countless plots and conspiracies. Dio records what was perceived to be a thinly veiled threat aimed at these senators:

> And here is another thing that he did to us senators which gave us every reason to look for our death. Having killed an ostrich and cut off its head, he came up to where we were sitting, holding the head in his left hand and in his right hand raising aloft his bloody sword; and though he spoke not a word, yet he wagged his head with a grin, indicating he would treat us in the same way.[28]

The account is not in *Herodian*. Perhaps he was not present on that day, or not being a senator, was unsighted being seated in a different section of the crowd. What is certain is that the assembled senators felt this was a threat directed against them. The nobles and aristocrats would be sat on the front row, the seating being allocated in order of status, so perhaps this gesture was aimed at them rather than the whole body of senators, many of whom owed their position in the senate to imperial *beneficia*. Commodus was left-handed and so his sword hand would be his left, yet Dio deliberately draws the reader's attention to the fact he held his sword in his right and the severed head in his left. Holding the sword in his right would have felt unnatural to the emperor so he clearly made a conscious decision to do this. The Latin word for left is *sinister* from which the modern English word sinister or evil is derived. The left was also seen in religious terms as unlucky, augurs studying the movements of birds believed an approach from the left was an unfavourable omen, unlike one from the right. However many scholars believe the Latin '*sinister*' was derived from *sinus* meaning pocket, a traditional Roman toga having only one pocket being located on the left. The Latin for right is *dexter* meaning also skill from which the modern word dexterity is derived. Commodus appears to be symbolically signalling to those noble senators he now considered his opponents by holding the bloody sword in his right hand signifying his skill as a gladiator and warrior whilst his enemies need to remain in his pocket, under his direction, if they wished to avoid the fate of the ostrich. Holding the severed head in his left also suggested that further opposition would literally be very unlucky for them. The threat was clearly understood.

After the sparring bouts involving Commodus, the gladiatorial competition proper began with sharpened, steel weapons. Commodus sat at first on a gilded platform, dressed as Mercury with his wand, built for him in the arena itself and then later he would take his place in the imperial box. As Mercury on the first day he personally paired the contestants in the arena and as Mercury he supervised the proceedings. The whole fourteen-day event dripped with blood and religious symbolism. When a group of gladiators had defeated their opponents and showed great reluctance to kill their comrades 'Mercury' ordered them to be chained together in groups and then fight each other. There was to be no quarter, some gladiators not only killing those in their own group, but also then attacking other groups as well. The slaughter over the days was immense, Dio records that 'great numbers of men were killed'.

Deep religious symbolism was associated with these events. As Mercury, a god traditionally linked to gladiatorial contests, the emperor presented himself as the arbiter of life and death. Appearing as a gladiator Commodus faced death itself and finished the victor. To symbolize this he ordered the spectators to watch his performances dressed in mourning clothes:

> For when he was intending to fight once more as a gladiator, he bade us enter the amphitheatre in the equestrian garb and in our woollen cloaks, a thing that we never do when going to the amphitheatre except when one of the emperors has passed away.

The woollen cloaks were black and the same worn by the majority of the people of Rome at funerals. The emperor's helmet was also carried in and out of the amphitheatre on the last day of the games using the Gate of Libitina, the same gate used to carry the dead gladiators out of the arena, whilst he had presided over the events of this day dressed in the clothes of a mourner. Commodus also descended to the floor and plunged his hands in to the gaping wound of a slain gladiator, wiping the blood over his head. Blood was perceived to have magical properties and would be seen as adding to his superhuman abilities. The emperor was fighting for his subjects, risking his life for them, the people of Commodus. He had, like Hercules, faced death and survived, and was now reborn as the Roman Hercules just as Rome had been reborn after the fire. Thanks to the *beneficia* of their new god the people could look forward to a 'golden age'.[29]

The reaction of the senatorial elite to these games is reflected in the disdain of Dio, Marius Maximus and Herodian. However the general populace appears to have revelled in the appearance of their emperor as a gladiator in the guise of Hercules, protecting them from the vicissitudes of life. Herodian grudgingly recognizes this in his line: 'So far Commodus was still quite popular with the mob.'[30] And then the historian continues to express the 'shame' of the emperor appearing as a gladiator, putting him in the eyes of the elite, on a par with slaves, criminals and prisoners of war. The crowd however lauded him like a god:

the people regularly applauded him in his frequent combats as though he were a god.[31]

Commodus had restored the situation after the setback of the fire, to the extent that the people now associated their emperor as not only having divine support and consent to his rule but also he had become their divine guardian. Hercules dedicated his life to helping mankind and so achieved immorality.[32] The Roman Hercules, imitating the demigod, also presented himself as the protector of mankind, securing the grain supply, rebuilding Rome after the disastrous fire and also providing jobs. Commodus had sought divine protection from the plague through sacrifices and active participation in religious rites, hosted elaborate and expensive games to win divine approval for the new golden age and ushered in an age of peace after ending the near continuous wars of his father. This image that Commodus sought to portray as the protector of mankind is reflected in a late Christian source, Dracontius, who at the end of the fifth century describes Commodus as a poet and a good man through his *pietas* which he likened to Julius Caesar, Augustus and Titus, an emperor who 'set to verse the expectation that he would become a god, and urged other leaders to follow his example of goodness'. Other Christian sources describe him as an 'avid builder and religious man' and for Christians themselves the reign of Commodus was a time of 'peace' for the church, perhaps due to Marcia's influence over the emperor.[33] The provincials appear to have enthusiastically embraced the concept of their emperor being both gladiator and the new Hercules. The famous mosaic dated to the reign of Commodus at the substantial villa excavated at Nennig, south of Trier in Germany, shows in sumptuous detail a *venationes* and gladiatorial contest with a *retarius* fighting a *secutor* whose back is turned away from us. Numerous artefacts from across the empire depict gladiatorial figures associated with Commodus. The Roman army eagerly adopted images and dedications linked to the Roman Hercules. Only a small group of elite senators resented the undermining of their position as powerful patrons restricting their ability to distribute lavish *beneficia* through limited access to the emperor. The nobility resented the need to gain *amicitiae* from men like Cleander and Eclectus who they felt were beneath them, becoming in their words 'slaves to slaves'. These nobles put their own interests before the needs of the state, mainly because they saw themselves as the embodiment of the state, the same thinking they abhorred Commodus for. The emperor's murder would lead to nearly 100 years of civil wars, unrest, barbarian invasion and the death of the vast majority of the Antonine aristocracy.

Chapter Nine

The Death of a God (December 192 AD)

T he problem with discovering the truth behind conspiracies is that by their very nature they are secretive affairs. If a conspiracy fails the survivors who are not caught wish to avoid any connection with it to evade punishment, but also association with a failed plot brings with it the ignominy of failure. Conversely with a successful plot all want to be associated with it even when they were not involved to bring rewards from the succeeding regime. History is written by the winners and this is certainly the case with the murderers of the legitimate Antonine emperor. The successful conspirators however would need convincing reasons to justify murdering their emperor. Dio's account suffers from the bias he shows towards Commodus' successor Pertinax, from whom the historian received his praetorship. Both Herodian's and Dio's accounts differ in the detail but agree that the emperor was planning some form of ceremony for the Saturnalia that again involved the gladiators.

According to Dio, the Praetorian Prefect Laetus and Eclectus, were angered by the emperor's gladiatorial display in the arena, so when Commodus proposed to murder the two consuls Erucius Clarus and Sosius Falco and appear on New Year's Day from the gladiatorial barracks as both *secutor* and consul, they decided the emperor had gone too far. Commodus already possessed the first cell in the barracks in order to change after his practice bouts. As both men had opposed Commodus' plan, they now feared for their lives as the emperor, in a fit of anger, threatened them with death. However there are a number of problems with this account. Both consuls still remained very much alive despite the fact Commodus was supposedly planning their removal. Furthermore both Laetus and Eclectus had stood with the 'Roman Hercules' a few weeks previously on the floor of the arena before the applauding thousands and were repeatedly embraced affectionately by their emperor. Why would the emperor have done this if they disapproved of his appearing as a gladiator? What had changed to convince them that the emperor making a second appearance with gladiators was suddenly unacceptable? Yet according to Dio they were 'displeased at the things' Commodus was doing. It is understandable that the equestrian Laetus might have had serious misgivings over the *infamia* the emperor brought down upon himself by appearing in public as a gladiator, but why would the ex slave and imperial freedman Eclectus, who was discriminated against by his 'social superiors' for once being of the same social status as that of the 'gladiator' Commodus, be affronted by his emperor's association with the lowest strata of society? At a later date these two close *amici* of the emperor brought Marcia into the conspiracy. Eclectus and Marcia had a shared journey through various posts in the imperial household. According to the *Historia Augusta* it was Marcia's idea to refound Rome as a colony of Commodus and she was seen by the senate as implicitly involved in all the 'crimes' of the emperor. Dio completely omits Pertinax's role in the plot, the conspirators approaching him and informing the surprised Prefect of the City 'what had been done' after the murder had taken place. It is highly unlikely the conspirators would plan to murder the emperor without having a successor in mind who had already agreed to the post. The only way the plotters could survive after the murder, especially two low status imperial attendants, Marcia and Eclectus, was to ensure the successor was fully in their debt so that their later removal would bring down *ingratia* upon the new emperor's head. The *Historia Augusta* is in no doubt that Pertinax was fully involved in the plot: 'Pertinax did not avoid complicity when a share in this plot was offered him by the other conspirators.' The fourth century emperor Julian also knew of Pertinax's prominent role in the conspiracy. It is Herodian who reveals the link between the main conspirators, both Eclectus and Laetus were *amici* of Pertinax.[1]

It is also difficult to understand why Commodus would murder the two new consuls, men who would have been personally appointed by the emperor himself. C Julius Erucius Clarus Vibianus, the son of the consul of 170 AD, was probably married to the sister of the ex Consul Triarius Maternus, the consul of 185 AD. His consular colleague was Sosius Falco, one of the wealthiest men in Rome and according to a study of nomenclature by E Champlin, related to the imperial family through L Verus' sister, Ceionia Fabia through a second marriage to a Sosius Falco. Champlin suggests she had a son by another marriage to a Plautius Quintillus, M Peducaeus Plautius Quintillus being identified as offspring of this union. He was the consul of 177 AD who was married to Commodus' sister Fadilla. Sosius Falco however appears not very grateful for Pertinax, Laetus and Marcia saving his life for when Pertinax addresses the senate the day after the assassination to thank Laetus for his role in elevating him to the throne, Sosius Falco replies: 'We may know what sort of emperor you will be from this, that we see behind you Laetus and Marcia, the instruments of Commodus' crimes.' Evidently Sosius Falco had no association with Laetus in the conspiracy and appears totally unaware that his life was in any danger even after being supposedly saved by the actions of the conspirators. It is more likely that the propaganda spread by Pertinax and the conspirators after the murder had been incorporated into Dio's account. The historian himself complains of the difficulties of imperial history in general and in particular on the added difficulties of discovering the truth of real or alleged conspiracies. Predominantly his sources would have been based on interviews with his senatorial *amici* or reports sent to him by them. There is no objectivity in his history and he claims none.[2] Perhaps in this case his information is based on a private conversation between the Emperor Pertinax. What Dio's account does confirm was that the plot was essentially limited to a few key figures in the emperor's entourage and that it had been carefully planned over considerable time.

Herodian's account of the motivation of the conspirators suggests it was carried out with little preparation or time. The impression he gives is of a desperate act planned in panic in response to the revelation of plans for execution of the emperor's loyal *amici*. Herodian describes an argument which had developed between Commodus and Marcia over the emperor's plan to emerge from the gladiatorial barracks during the Saturnalia. Dressed in his gladiatorial armour, escorted by a bodyguard of gladiators, he supposedly intended to order the execution of many leading senators in order to share out their property to the soldiers and gladiators. Eclectus and then Laetus tried to dissuade him but they too were angrily dismissed. Commodus then wrote a list of those to be executed on a writing tablet before falling asleep in a drunken stupor. Marcia, Eclectus and Laetus headed the list. The emperor's child slave, who had unlimited access to the private apartments, found the tablet and started to play with it, running out of the imperial bed chamber only to be stopped by Marcia. Reading the list of names the horrified concubine ran to the *cubicularius* and Praetorian Prefect. Through fear and pure survival instincts they hurriedly organized the death of the emperor before he woke to put his planned execution list into action. Many historians have noted the similarity between this account and the death of Domitian and questioned the accuracy of Herodian's account purely on these grounds. Furthermore it seems remarkable that Herodian feels no need to explain the contradictions in the behaviour of Eclectus and Marcia who had previously advocated these or similar policies yet now were fervent opponents of them. It has also been questioned as to who would have carried out the execution of Laetus as he was sole prefect.[3]

There are however significant similarities in both Dio's and Herodian's accounts. This may reflect the common origin of the story: Pertinax's imperial propaganda. The conspirators had to justify their actions and lend credibility to Pertinax's regime through acting as the 'saviour' of the senate. Pertinax's greatest weakness was his humble origins as he was the son of a freedman and there were numerous senators whose nobility, in their eyes, was far greater than the new emperor's. The two main sources agree that Commodus planned to continue the theme of the 'Roman Hercules' during the Saturnalia. Two aspects of this festival would have appealed to the theatrical and religious aspirations of the emperor. The Saturnalia was felt to be one of the oldest ceremonies in Rome, dating to the mythological reign of Romulus, Rome's original founder. Secondly Saturn was a god associated with agriculture who reigned over a world that had entered its 'golden age.' These were religious associations that the emperor would wish to associate himself with. The 'Roman Hercules', dressed as a *secutor* to remind the 'people of Commodus' of his exploits in the arena, would emerge again as the new Hercules, the son of Jupiter, ushering in Rome's new golden age. The fifth century writer Macrobius in his poem *Saturnalis* describes Saturn as a charioteer, his left hand holding a thunder bolt and his right an ear of corn, the attributes of Jupiter and the Sun, Sol Invictus. These festivities began on 17 December and involved a range of activities from the exchanging of gifts and dining with the gods whose statues were laid out on couches to the reversal of social position with slaves being waited on by their masters. Gambling and dice playing were permitted and it was rare to find a sober Roman in the city. The conspirators chose their time wisely as New Year's Eve would be the last opportunity to take part in the merry-making, the people and the Praetorian Guards would be busy in their cups, as would the emperor. Equally important, most of the soldiers would be unarmed during the festival in order to reduce drunken fights leading to fatalities. The murder was not planned on the spur of the moment.[4]

It is hard to understand the motivation of the conspirators. The two key men were Laetus and Eclectus who later brought Marcia into the plot. Laetus was sole prefect and so was at the pinnacle of the equestrian career structure. There appears to have been no political rivalry between them as they were to work closely together to remove Commodus. The lowly born Eclectus would have no real issues with an emperor posing in the arena as a gladiator in the guise of Hercules. Eclectus and Laetus appeared at the emperor's side in the Coliseum and were embraced by him, a very public imperial recognition of their power, influence and standing. It is difficult to see these figures arguing with Commodus over his planned reintroduction of the 'Roman Hercules' six weeks later. Why would the Praetorian Prefect and *cubicularius* risk their power and position in removing one emperor for another who may in the future remove them from their positions? Marcia, who had a close bond with Eclectus, had even encouraged the emperor in his Herculean propaganda and was closely associated by the senate with Commodus' policies. The reception of Pertinax in the senate demonstrates the hatred many senators felt towards Eclectus, Laetus and Marcia. The antipathy of the nobility towards them ruled out any senatorial involvement in the plot to remove the emperor. Marcia herself was treated almost as a wife by the emperor, having virtually all the symbols of an Augusta apart from the imperial fire being carried before her. Her power and influence over Commodus must have been immense, all the sources agree that he loved her dearly, the Amazon queen to his Hercules. Yet she was prepared to relinquish all this as she supposedly opposed the emperor's appearance as a gladiator and execution of the consuls on New Year's Eve.

We come now to Pertinax. His star could have been no higher in the emperor's eyes. The *Historia Augusta* records that 'he proved very pleasing to Commodus himself' and in recognition of this held the ordinary consulship with the emperor for a second time.[5] It was Pertinax's influence that probably engineered the promotion of Laetus and Eclectus to their posts. Pertinax was by now an old man, but still held the strategic post of City Prefect with command over the city, its law courts and the Urban cohorts. Pertinax may have resented the emperor appearing as a gladiator but his low-born status meant he would always be perceived as a social inferior by the senatorial nobility. Commodus' preference for promoting on ability rather than status suggests he had more in common with the emperor he murdered than the senatorial aristocracy. Finally it was Pertinax, who, as one of Marcus Aurelius' *consilium* and *amici*, was commended by the dying emperor to look after his son, who as a young boy, he accompanied round the eastern provinces after the failed revolt of Avidius Cassius. It was Commodus who had resurrected his career after the fall of Perennis, appointing him to the province of Britain in order to crush the army mutiny. These powerful politicians had nothing to fear from Commodus and owed him an immense debt of gratitude which they were to repay by shedding his blood; hence the elaborate propaganda and misinformation after the emperor's murder.

Marcia's role in the conspiracy is the key to understanding the true motivations behind the plot. It appears the emperor's love for his 'wife' blinded him to an adulterous liaison. Herodian records that it was rumoured that Eclectus and Marcia were having an affair:

Eclectus, who normally visited her (Marcia) in his capacity as the official chamberlain, quite apart from the gossip that said he was having an affair with her.[6]

There seems some substance to the allegation that they were having an affair as both were, after the death of Commodus, to marry.[7] The exile and execution of Crispina will have focused their minds. If the rumour was widespread, as Herodian suggests, it could only be a matter of time before it was brought to the emperor's attention. Commodus viewed Marcia as his wife in all but name and probably would have married her if her status had been high enough. Her full name; Marcia Aurelia Ceionia Demetriade suggests she was the daughter of Euhodes Aurelius Sabinianus, himself a freedman in the service of L Verus. With the death of Verus she reappears as the mistress of Quadratus, who probably acquired her through inheriting his mother's household, Annia Cornificia, the sister of Marcus Aurelius. Being the daughter of a freedman and a concubine would prohibit even the egalitarian Commodus from making her his wife.[8] It was fear of discovery and the desire to be officially united in marriage that drove Marcia and Eclectus to plot the emperor's murder.

Pertinax's motivation was simply the allure of the imperial throne. He was a wily politician, being all things to all men. Dio portrays his benefactor in glowing terms, but perhaps the *Historia Augusta*, drawing on Marius Maximus' personal acquaintance with Pertinax, provides a more accurate character evaluation: Pertinax 'was not greatly beloved; certainly, all who talked freely together spoke ill of Pertinax, calling him the smooth tongued, that is, a man who talks affably and acts meanly'. The *Historia Augusta* pointedly remarks that he acted towards the senators in the same manner as when he was Urban Prefect, treating them with 'reverence'.[9] This was a man the nobles in the senate felt they could do business with. Over time they undermined his loyalty to Commodus with the offer of support for his rule in return for his promise to govern in close association with the leading senators. E Champlin is probably correct in identifying a deal between these men and Pertinax although he errs in the detail of this agreement. On the night of the murder of Commodus we surprisingly find both Acilius Glabrio and Claudius Pompeianus in Rome to meet the new emperor on his accession to the throne. Claudius Pompeianus had long since retired to his rural estates having been humiliated by the conspiracy of his wife Lucilla and his son Claudius Pompeianus Quintianus, the offspring from a previous marriage.[10]

Dio, an eyewitness to these events, mentions this was the only time he saw Claudius Pompeianus in the senate, as after the murder of Pertinax, he again retired to his estates at Terracina. The fact that he was present on the night of the murder presupposes that he knew of the plan to assassinate Commodus and wished to lend his support to Pertinax, his old client. Pompeianus would never have forgiven Commodus for executing his first son. His second son through Lucilla, Commodus' executed sister, was heir presumptive. E Champlin points to this meeting and Pertinax's refusal to name his own son Caesar as evidence of a deal, whereby Pertinax was to be a caretaker emperor for Pompeianus' surviving son Aurelius Commodus Pompeianus. Yet Pertinax never adopted this man as his heir. The fact Pertinax did not name his own son as heir was more a recognition of his own weak position. The young Pertinax was sent with his sister to the country estates of their grandfather and Pertinax on attaining the throne legally bestowed his private estates upon his children, separating their fate from his own. Dio is correct when he explicitly explains the reason for this, 'because he had not yet firmly rooted his own power'. This is supported by Herodian who describes the new emperor being beset by 'serious misgivings' once he had been taken to the palace. Dio is however incorrect in his belief that his wife Titiana was refused the honour of Augusta by her husband as inscriptions and coins record her as being titled Augusta. When Pertinax sat in the senate, Claudius Pompeianus and Acilius Glabrio were given the honour of sitting next to the emperor on the imperial bench. This was a public statement of joint rule. Although both these nobles were to publicly refuse the throne offered to them by Pertinax, this was merely a propaganda tool to reaffirm their loyalty to Pertinax as sole emperor on the understanding that his rule was based on the advice and influence of the noblest men in the senate. Claudius Pompeianus decided to take the most prudent route on behalf of his young son by waiting upon events and also looking after his son's interests by being a key member of the new emperor's *consilium*.

Acilius Glabrio is tenuously linked by Champlin to the imperial family via a mysterious Faustina, a dynastic name of the imperial family, whom he identifies as either the mother or the daughter of M Annius Libo, the consul of 128 AD and so the cousin of Marcus Aurelius. This mysterious Faustina Champlin also suggests could be a daughter of Marcus Aurelius' younger sister, Annia Cornificia Faustina. He bases his argument on an analysis of the nomenclature of Acilius Glabrio's family members and their offspring. Although well argued the links are tenuous. Even if Acilius Glabrio was the great nephew of Marcus Aurelius, his claim to the throne was no greater than that of other prominent nobles, for example Marcus Peducaeus Plautius Quintillus, the son of Ceionia Fabia who was the sister of L Verus, and married to Commodus' sister Fadilla. Furthermore Claudius Pompeianus' son had a greater claim to the throne than all of them. Glabrio and Pertinax met the morning after his accession simply because he was 'the most nobly born of all the patricians' and a man of his status would add *gravitas* to Pertinax's new regime.[11]

The involvement of the sole Praetorian Prefect in the conspiracy is more difficult to fathom. An *amicus* of Pertinax, he was now in such a powerful position as sole prefect that he was effectively his own man. As Praetorian Prefect he was also a powerful *amicus* of Commodus, being able to use his influence with the emperor to appoint Septimius Severus and his brother to key commands on the Danube with control over five legions. Even Laetus' own brother, who had merely been a centurion in the army, was promoted through his influence to the emperor's guard. Yet mere weeks after the successful plot to remove Commodus, Laetus would conspire against Pertinax. From this it would appear it was Pertinax who was the fulcrum around which the conspiracy revolved and Pertinax would not have been Laetus' choice of emperor but at the time he went along with the plan for his own short-term gain. He then planned to improve his situation further by fair means or foul. Laetus appears to have become disenchanted with Commodus as the emperor refused to take his advice. Dio and Herodian mention Laetus trying to dissuade Commodus from appearing as a gladiator, something which, as a high-ranking equestrian he may have disapproved of. Yet he does appear to condone this act by appearing with the emperor on the arena floor and furthermore he is described by Sosius Falco, the consul of 193 AD, as the 'instrument' of Commodus' crimes. This unflattering evaluation of Laetus' character is supported by Dio who describes him as being completely untrustworthy:

> Laetus, however, did not remain permanently loyal to Pertinax, or I might better say, he was never faithful even for a moment; for when he did not get what he wanted he proceeded to incite the soldiers against him (Pertinax).

Unfortunately Dio does not specify what the Praetorian Prefect wanted. The *Historia Augusta* claims Laetus was displeased by Pertinax's integrity and regretted he made him emperor whilst Pertinax rebuked Laetus for revealing various secrets. Just as Laetus had felt Commodus failed to heed his advice so did Pertinax. Laetus desired a non-entity on the throne so he could be a proxy emperor. He had been building up a network of *amici* who had received his *beneficia* in one form or another. Septimius Severus and his brother Geta had received their commands at the recommendation of the Praetorian Prefect and Didius Julianus, probably implicated in the plot of the Petronii, escaped through his intervention.[12]

The conspirators faced a number of problems. Firstly the sheer physical strength of the emperor and his ability with the sword made a physical assault upon him, as in 182 AD, an extremely risky undertaking. A group of armed men might be successful in cutting him down but the Praetorians remained loyal to their emperor. The loyalty of the Praetorians to any successor would be problematic as they would likely want to exact revenge on the assassins. Even the involvement of Laetus in the plot did not guarantee the obedience of these cohorts who had sworn an oath to protect Commodus. The emperor remained popular with the people of Rome who viewed him as their patron, guaranteeing their safety, sustenance and divine favour. The soldiers across the empire appear to have viewed an emperor who fought as a gladiator with admiration; he was a demigod who like them regularly faced death and fought to secure the safety of the empire. Their commanders had remained loyal to Commodus with many being awarded consulships and other honours, Clodius Albinus and Pescennius Niger, the Governors of Britain and Syria amongst them. The murder of the emperor would inevitably present the successful conspirators with further threats to their position.

The timing of the murder was the key. Most of the senate would be present in Rome to escort the new consuls from their homes to the senate house as 1 January was the inauguration for all new magistrates. The senate would collectively swear its oath to obey the acts of the Caesars. Around the empire the soldiers would parade before the images and standards of their emperor and swear their oath of loyalty to a man who would by this time be lying dead in his own palace. More importantly most of the imperial guards in the palace would be the worse for drink having taken full advantage of the final day of the Saturnalia festivities. Discipline had been relaxed by Commodus to further ingratiate himself with the Praetorians. The Praetorians around Rome would be engaging in various revelries and be completely unarmed. Commodus himself would be drinking in his private apartment and would in his relaxed state happily accept cups from the hand of his lover, Marcia. His food would be poisoned so removing the physical threat of the emperor's unrivalled skills with the sword. The body would be removed inside rolled up bed clothes by imperial slaves, bribed beforehand to carry out the task. The half drunk guards would be lax in their duties and not examine the removal of items from the emperor's rooms, the threat to the imperial person being from those entering the rooms. The movement of the numerous slaves around the palace at all times of day and night would be so common that it would not draw any suspicion or interest from the guards. The body would be transported out of the city to avoid detection. For the future integrity of the new regime it was important for Pertinax to be completely disassociated from the events in the palace and the death of the emperor. Pertinax could claim that he was innocent of any involvement in the demise of their emperor in order to retain the loyalty of the Praetorians. He would be holding a public banquet with his *amici* and only be 'informed' of the death of the emperor through a visit from the Praetorian Prefect who would naturally inform the City Prefect of the death of the emperor as a matter of urgency. Pertinax, accompanied by Laetus, was to address the Praetorian Guard blaming Commodus' death on natural causes, attributing his sudden demise to his licentious lifestyle. The Guards' loyalty was then to be assured by the promise of a donative. The leading senators had already been summoned to Rome and were to meet Pertinax and elect him emperor. The military prestige of the new emperor would appeal to the soldiers and their commanders who could do little once Commodus was dead. As an insurance against any military intervention, five legions on the Danube were commanded by the Severii who had been appointed to their posts through the *beneficia* of Laetus. Such planning would have taken a considerable amount of time to facilitate and make the necessary arrangements. The plot was not hatched on the spur of the moment as suggested in Herodian's account.

The sources agree on the death of Commodus. On the evening of the final day of the year Marcia added some poison to the emperor's beef according to Dio, wine according to Herodian. The *cubicularius* ordered the personal servants to go to their quarters. Something they probably appreciated in the holiday season. Trusting his 'wife' the emperor accepted these dainties and became violently ill. The plan immediately started to go wrong. Commodus' immense strength and physical health, combined with the fact he vomited up some of the contents of his stomach, meant that death was not instantaneous. Herodian suggests he may have taken an antidote to the poison which he asserts that emperors did before each meal. The emperor, now in considerable pain, went to the bathhouse in the Vectilian Villa. A later source says it was his doctor, who was also involved in the plot, who persuaded the emperor to go to the palaestra or wrestling arena attached to the baths. There he vomited up more and Marcia and Eclectus became increasingly concerned that he might survive. The two found one of the palace freedmen, Narcissus, who was Commodus' personal wrestling partner. With rising panic and in desperation the two offered the athlete a substantial bribe to end the life of the emperor. Narcissus entered the bathhouse and strangled the emperor who, due to his already weakened state, was unable to defend himself. Two slaves wrapped the body up and took it past the guards who were either asleep or half drunk. No real attempt was made to investigate the slaves' load as it was none of their business to check this. The body was carried through the palace from the private quarters to the main entrance hall. It was then loaded onto a cart and transported to the suburbs. One manuscript of Herodian records that it was taken to a place called Aristeum, which could possibly be Proasteion as this was the word used to describe the Quintillian Villa earlier in Herodian's work. Such a location would ensure the body was not discovered but far enough away to be viewed as and when necessary. The body had to be removed from the Praetorians if Pertinax and Laetus' story that the emperor had died of natural causes was to be believed. The sight of the body may also have caused the guards to riot. The body was held by P Livius Larensis, the *procurator patrimonii* who had responsibility for the private estate of the emperor. He would later hand it over to the consul elect L Fabius Cilo who was a member of the priestly *sodalis Hadrianalis* for burial in the Mausoleum of Hadrian. As Pontifex Minor, Larensis would have been aware of Commodus' religious aspirations. According to late second century Greek rhetorician Athenaeus, he had been placed in charge of temples and sacrifices by Marcus Aurelius and he was 'well versed in religious ceremonies ... and learned in political institutions'. Commodus would have drawn upon his knowledge yet he appears to have disagreed with his policies, appearing to willingly cooperate with the conspirators in the removal and safe keeping of the body, only handing it over to the consul on the direct orders of Pertinax.[13]

It was by now the middle of the night. Laetus and Eclectus 'together with a few men who were in the plot, came to Pertinax's house'. One of the main reasons for the success of the plot was the limited numbers who knew of its existence. The watchman was raised and they entered. Propaganda was later spread by the new emperor that he expected at that moment to be arrested on the orders of Commodus and be taken away for execution. The *Historia Augusta* however records how pleased Commodus was with his City Prefect, something which must have been made well known as it was recorded in this history. Pertinax then had to be 'reassured' that Commodus was indeed dead and he sent one of his trusted companions to view the body. At this late hour Pertinax is described as still being on his couch and had not retired to bed; no doubt waiting anxiously on news of the assassination. Supporters of Laetus and Pertinax were then ordered to act as messengers, informing the leading senators of the death of the emperor. Herodian records the excitement of the senators:

> Everyone rushed to and fro paying their visits to their patrons and telling them the news, especially if they were people of importance or wealth since they were the ones whom it was known Commodus was also making plans to destroy.

Herodian continues by describing dancing at the altars and temples, many thanking the gods as well as directing shouts of abuse at the dead emperor. There can be little doubt that it was the aristocrats and their *amici* and clients who would be taking part in these celebrations and who would gather in the senate to acclaim their new emperor. The people of Rome itself would have little to celebrate and Commodus' supporters in the senate would have done well to keep a low profile and stay away.

The party then travelled through the now crowded streets to the Praetorian Camp collecting adherents, armed clients and slaves as they went to make a more imposing sight. Much of the populace rushed to the camp as well to be witness to these events and see what the reaction of the Guards would be. The gates of the camp were opened by some of the conspirators allowing the baying crowd in. The Praetorians remaining in the camp were assembled and surrounded by the partisans of the wealth nobility and the conspirators. Both Laetus and Pertinax then addressed the assembled troops, Laetus having previously promised Pertinax that he could win them over as he was their commanding officer. The death of their emperor was blamed on 'apoplexy' after choking through overeating. Clearly it was agreed to try and keep as close to the truth as possible. Pertinax was then introduced to the assembled men and greeted with a resounding silence. Dio records that whilst giving his speech the Praetorians 'remained perfectly quiet' and concealed their anger. Herodian describes their reaction as 'cautious and hesitant', an understatement. As large crowds had now gathered around the camp the guard 'felt compelled to join in and salute Pertinax as Augustus'. At first this was only by a few of the soldiers but gradually the pressure told and more joined in. Strictly speaking the senate bestowed the title 'Augustus' whilst soldiers gave that of 'Imperator', but Herodian may be in error here. Due to the festival they were unarmed, suggesting the mob outside the camp was well armed. These would be the supporters, clients, freedmen and slaves of the leading senators who had been gathered as the Praetorians were addressed. Also many of the Praetorians were not in the camp but had been cavorting in the streets joining in the festive holiday activities. Outnumber and 'outgunned' the soldiers seethed with resentment at the murder of their emperor. Many also feared that the privileges Commodus had granted them, including the right to carry an axe, would now be rescinded and military discipline restored by the new emperor. When Pertinax promised them 12,000 *sesterces* a man there appears to have been some acclamation, but muted and restrained.[14]

Pertinax was now escorted to the senate house by leading senators, Laetus and Eclectus and a mob of senatorial clients and servants, all proclaiming him 'Augustus'. Senators tried to approach their new emperor to offer their greetings and support but were unable to do so because of the large crowd of adherents that surrounded him. It was just before dawn when they approached the Curia or Senate House, but the attendant had fled so the doors remained locked. Instead Pertinax waited in the Temple of Concord which must have been restored by Commodus after the fire which had destroyed large areas of the Forum. There the *Historia Augusta* records a meeting between Pertinax and Claudius Pompeianus who, forewarned of the plot, had returned to the city from his estates to strike a deal with the new emperor. The agreement probably enabled Claudius Pompeianus to retain a restraining hand upon Pertinax as his *amicus* in the interests of his own young son. The *Historia Augusta* records that the two were joined by all the magistrates. The assembled senators then broke into rhythmic chanting associated with the orchestrated chanting that had been used recently to acclaim Commodus in the arena. The hatred and resentment the assembled senators exhibited was remarkable, witnessed by both Dio and Marius Maximus. Dio's summary closely supports that in the *Historia Augusta*. The keys to the locked doors were found and Pertinax entered the Senate House accompanied by the consuls. Here he was greeted as emperor by those present. Those senators who had supported Commodus would have been minded to stay away at this point whilst others would have been keen to gain the new emperor's gratitude by publicly expressing their loyalty to the new regime. The senators then broke out into chanting which Dio describes as descending into unpalatable abuse of the murdered Commodus as they 'wished to indulge in wanton insolence'. The *Historia Augusta* records the scene in more detail:[15]

From him who was a foe to his fatherland let his honours be taken away; let the honours of the murderer be taken away; let the murderer be dragged in the dust. The foe of his fatherland, the murderer, the gladiator, in the charnel house let him be mangled. He is foe to the gods, slayer of the senate, foe of the gods, foe of the senate. Cast the gladiator into the charnel house. He who slew the senate let him be dragged with the hook; he who slew the guiltless, let him be dragged with the hook – a foe, a murder, verily, verily. He who spared not his own blood, let him be dragged with the hook; he who would have slain you (Pertinax), let him be dragged with the hook. You were in terror along with us, you were endangered along with us. That we may be safe, O Jupiter Best and Greatest, save for us Pertinax. Long life to the guardian care of the Praetorians! Long life to the Praetorian cohorts! Long life to the armies of Rome! Long life to the loyalty of the senate!

Let the murderer be dragged in the dust. We beseech you, O Sire, let the murderer be dragged in the dust, Hearken Caesar: to the lions with informers! Hearken Caesar, to the lions with Speratus (a leading senatorial informer)! Long life to the victory of the Roman people! long life to the soldiers' guardian care! Long life to the guardian care of the Praetorians! Long life to the Praetorian cohorts!

On all sides are statues of the foe, on all sides are statues of the murderer, on all sides are statues of the gladiator. The statues of the murderer and gladiator, let them be cast down … While you (Pertinax) are safe, we too are safe and untroubled, verily verily, if in very truth, then with honour, if in very truth, then with freedom.

Now at last we are secure; let informers tremble. That we may be secure let informers tremble. That we may be safe cast informers out of the senate, the club for informers! While you are ruler, the club for informers!

Let the memory of the murderer and gladiator be utterly wiped away. Let the statues of the murderer and gladiator be overthrown. Let the memory of the foul gladiator be utterly wiped away. Cast the gladiator into the charnel house … More savage than Domitian, more foul than Nero. As he did unto others let it be done unto him. Let remembrance of the guiltless be preserved. Restore the honours of the guiltless, we beseech you. Let the body of the murderer be dragged by the hook … Call for our vote, call for our vote, with one accord we reply, let him be dragged with the hook … He who plundered temples, let him be dragged by the hook. He who plundered the living, let him be dragged by the hook. He who set aside testaments of the dead, let him be dragged with the hook. We have been slaves to slaves. He who demanded the price for a man, let him be dragged by the hook. He who demanded a price for a life and kept not his promise, let him be dragged with the hook. He who sold the senate, let him be dragged with the hook. He who took from sons their patrimony, let him be dragged with the hook.

Spies and informers, cast them out of the senate. Suborners of slaves, cast them out of the senate. You, too, were in terror along with us; you know all, you know both the good and the evil. You know all that we were forced to purchase; all we have feared for you sake. Happy are we now that you are emperor, in truth. Put it to the vote concerning the murderer, put it to the vote, put the question. We ask your presence. The guiltless are yet unburied, let the body of the murderer be dragged in the dust. The murderer dug up the buried; let the body of the murderer be dragged in the dust.'

Dio adds other insults, referring to Commodus as 'an accursed wretch', a 'tyrant' and 'the charioteer, the left handed, the ruptured.

The chanting was deliberate, mirroring the chants and rhythms these same senators had so recently felt obliged to acclaim the 'Roman Hercules' with in the Coliseum. Their humiliation was replaced now by a divine sense of vengeance. The crowd of senators then turned to 'those senators on whom the fear of Commodus had rested most heavily' and called out to them, 'You are saved, you have won.'

This group were obviously sat together and must have constituted the aristocracy, many of whom were the former consuls who sat on the front benches. On these benches would sit the great dynasts, members of the Annii and Ceionii, the Ulpii, Aelii, Aurelii with familial connections to the imperial family. With them sat the Pedanii Fusci, Aelii Lamiae, Vettuleni Civicae, Plautii Quintilli, Servilii Pudentes, Domitii Lucani, Ummidii Quadrati, Vitrasii Polliones, Claudii Severi, Petronii Mamertini, Antistii Burii, Junii Rufini, Bruttii Crispini, Pompeii Falcones and Erucii Crispini. Many of these were members of the Antonine aristocracy who had been ennobled by being granted the consulship by Commodus' recent predecessors. Some, a small minority, could trace their ancestors back to the days of the Republic: the Calpurnii Pisones, Cornelii Scipiones Orfiti and Acilii Glabriones. Acilius Glabrio, the former *amicus* of Marcus Aurelius, had recently and surprisingly returned from his self-imposed exile on his country estates. He was foremost amongst the 'best men' having suddenly had a remarkable improvement in his sight and hearing. This list of the 'best men' is similar to the lists of those executed for conspiracy under Commodus. A similar list was produced by the *Historia Augusta* for those executed by Septimius Severus after the civil wars that their actions helped to precipitate. These families, in their eyes, were the elite and so felt they should have unrivalled access to the imperial *beneficia*, backing any candidate who seemed to offer the best chances of retaining such power and influence. Each dynastic family had their own *amici* and clients to provide for and their reduction in influence led to these clients searching for other patrons who could provide what they wanted. Pertinax, an emperor whose father had been a freedman, must have been to many of them a short-term solution to the 'problem' that was Commodus.[16]

The nobles saw Commodus as a criminal, refusing even to use his name. After execution the bodies of criminals were dragged through the streets of Rome

by a hook and then thrown into the River Tiber. However Pertinax refused to
have Commodus' body desecrated and informed the senate that he had already
ordered Livius Laurensis to hand it over to the consul elect Fabius Cilo for it
to be buried in the Mausoleum of Hadrian. Perhaps he did this in memory of
the emperor who had trusted and promoted him, or in respect to the memory of
his father Marcus Aurelius. More likely he realized such a move would incite the
already angry and resentful Praetorians into open revolt and so endangering his
own life and that of the senate. Praetorians had escorted Pertinax to the senatorial
meeting and stood guard outside, no doubt listening and burning with fury at the
insolent and degrading manner in which their dead master Commodus was being
abused. It would not be long before they were plotting to exact revenge. Yet it is
the anger and resentment of the senate that resounds through these passages of
the senatorial historians. However their list of grievances is focused only on the
perceived injustices to their class. They refer to themselves as the 'people of Rome'
and declare their 'loyalty'. This loyalty was not to their emperor. The aristocrats
and nobility understood loyalty in terms of the traditions of the Republic that
had long since ceased to exist. It was the 'good' emperors who pandered to these
customs and treated the nobles with feigned equality. Not so Domitian, Nero,
Caligula and Commodus. All murdered.

What is also remarkable from this passage is the revelation of the wily Pertinax
who won over the trust of the leading senators by expressing his own 'fears' for
his life, despite the fact Commodus had openly shown his trust in him by sharing
the consulship and commended him in public as well as promoting men whom
Pertinax recommended; Laetus being one of them. Pertinax had been plotting
for a considerable time as he knew some of the senators 'have feared for your
sake'; those who knew of the plot and risked their lives by not revealing it to the
emperor. There was also a significant group within the senate that had supported
Commodus. The assembled senators were aware also of the threat the Praetorians
and army posed to their 'restoration' of order. Events were to show that their
fears were well founded. Their own naivety was believing that ratification of the
new emperor by the 'august' body of the senate would be accepted by the real
arbiters of power; the army commanders, all of whom owed their posts to the
beneficia of Commodus. As messengers were sent across the empire to inform the
army of the change in emperor, many were immediately thrown into prison. The
governors of the provinces, being the consummate politicians that their position
demanded, wished to wait upon events.[17] Firstly they needed to ascertain the truth
behind the message and avoid becoming implicated in an unsuccessful plot against
Commodus. Secondly they needed time to build up support and draw upon the
bonds of *amicitia* with other prominent *amici* in positions of power and influence.

The Severii on the Danube owed their position to Laetus but Niger in Syria and Albinus in Britain were not so tied.

The news that Pertinax refused to have Commodus' body thrown into the Tiber was met with anger and dismay in the Curia:

> At this the senate cried out: "With whose authority have you buried him? The buried murderer, let him be dug up, let him be dragged in the dust."

The Pontifex Maximus, Cincius Severus, was called to make a speech. He denounced the burial and formally called for the statues of Commodus to be destroyed and the months renamed. Cincius Severus would later be accused by Septimius Severus of attempting to poison him and executed. Pertinax allowed the senate to vent its anger. A *senatus consultum* was passed which allowed those condemned for *majestas* to be reburied in the family graves or mausoleums and their memory restored on inscriptions and in the family homes.[18] The family of Antius Lupus were to benefit from this. Commodus suffered *damnatio memoriae* and his name was chiselled from inscriptions across the empire and all state and legal documents. The numerous statues around the city bearing his image were either destroyed or their heads removed to be stored and replaced later by heads of those emperors and politicians who were in the ascendant.

The people of Rome had nothing to gain from the restoration of senatorial influence. Pertinax could not pander to them as this would undermine whatever support he had amongst the noble families. Oaths and sacrifices were then made in the name of Pertinax who was then escorted to the palace on the Palatine which must have been repaired by Commodus, rather than the Vectilian Villa, to try to escape public association with his murder as well dissociate himself from the previous reign. The crowd of supporters waved branches of laurel as dawn broke over the city. Pertinax chose as the watchword, 'Let us be soldiers' which he issued to a Praetorian tribune. This was the same watchword he had used whilst commanding on the Danube many years before. Unfortunately, the tribune and the rest of the Praetorian cohorts, not having fought on the Danube, took the password as a direct insult, suggesting they had previously not been good soldiers. Immediately they responded by looking for an alternative to the senate's choice of emperor.[19]

The new emperor probably had a few hours' rest before he again descended to the Senate House, refusing to be preceded by the sacred fire or any imperial regalia including torches. He paid deference to the nobles whose support he badly needed by awaiting formal confirmation of his powers by the senate. As he entered the entire house rose to join in his acclamation as 'Augustus'. At first Pertinax made a show of refusing the offer saying men of greater nobility should be chosen in his stead and pleaded old age. He approached Acilius Glabrio and taking him by the hand offered him the imperial bench. The senate then broke into entreaties and concerted pleading and urging Pertinax to accept the throne. Pertinax protested that there were many senators standing around him who were better suited to the position, ironically probably the very same thought was going through many heads present. This was a clever piece of theatre as these nobles were forced to publicly deny any desire for the throne. The scene had probably been carefully managed and planned during the few hours he had after dawn, along with Glabrio and Pompeianus. With feigned reluctance, Pertinax accepted. His wife was probably also given the title Augusta, but he declined the title of Caesar for his son, so disassociating him from imperial rule and, if his father should be overthrown, providing his son with a chance of survival. Pertinax gave a speech of thanks, but the authenticity of that recorded in *Herodian* has been doubted.

The consuls then stood to praise the new emperor and condemn Commodus. As Commodus and Pertinax were the ordinary consuls of 192 AD, these men must have been the suffect consul. Quintus Tineius Sacerdos being one, the son of Quintus Tineius Sacerdos Clemens, the ordinary consul of 158 AD and Pontifex. He and his brother, Quintus Tineius Clemens, the consul of 195 AD, would continue to have illustrious careers, becoming Proconsul of Asia and sharing a second consulship in 219 AD with the Emperor Elagabalus, whose own extreme actions and religious policies would end in his own assassination. The eccentricities and erratic behaviour of Elagabalus do not appear to have stretched the loyalty of Tineius Sacerdos. The other suffect consuls would also be called to speak: L Julius Messala Rutianus, P Julius Scapula Priscus, and C Aemilus Severus Cantabrinus. All were complimentary towards Pertinax, as was to be expected. The new emperor then returned his thanks and praised Laetus who he said was instrumental in the murder of Commodus. This was too much for the consul elect, Q Pompeius Sosius Falco, a patrician whose consular ancestors stretched all the way back to the reign of Trajan. He now rose to attack Pertinax:

We may know what sort of emperor you will be from this, that we see behind you Laetus and Marcia, the instruments of Commodus' crimes.

Pertinax stood to reply. 'You are young, consul, and do not know the necessity of obedience. They obeyed Commodus but against their will, and as soon as they had an opportunity, they showed what had always been their desire.'

Pertinax was caught between a rock and a hard place. His reply would have convinced no one, yet he had to defend Laetus as he was the only person who could control the Praetorians and Marcia who was the lover of Eclectus, reappointed as *cubicularius*, and in charge of the imperial household. However the retention of these three, so closely associated with Commodus, would undermine his legitimacy in many of the nobles' eyes. Furthermore Pertinax was of low birth, unlike the man he had murdered, and many of those standing before him in the senate. These nobles would resent such a man as their emperor and consider themselves as legitimate alternatives. Dio refers to them as the 'wealthy and vain glorious' who looked down upon the socially inferior emperor. Herodian acknowledges that Pertinax was fearful as 'there were some members of noble birth in the senate'. They would most probably be dissatisfied with the succession passing from an emperor of the highest nobility to an upstart whose family lacked status and *dignitas*. Pertinax must by now have felt the plans so carefully laid were rapidly unravelling. The loyalty of the Praetorians was extremely doubtful despite the support of Laetus and the promise of a large donative and much to his surprise, he now faced hostility from nobles within the senate.

After this minor confrontation further titles and honours flowed from the senate. Pertinax was granted the usual titles but also asked to also be known as 'Chief of the Senate' or *Princeps Senatus*, in order to publicize his intention to listen and act upon the views of the prominent senators. Claudius Pompeianus and Acilius Glabrio were given the unique distinction of sitting on the imperial bench in the house signifying their joint rule with the emperor. Flavius Sulpicianus, the emperor's father-in-law, was made City Prefect and so controlled the important Urban Cohorts. He had previously served as Proconsul of Asia under Commodus. Pertinax then took a formal oath that he would never condemn a senator to death. Shortly after he probably rescinded the *majestas* law. The senate's support was being bought, especially with the restoration of the property and memory of those previously sanctioned under *majestas* charges and immediately friends and family of those so condemned broke into tears and cries of joy. The emperor then invited 'the magistrates and chief men of the senate' to an imperial banquet that night in the palace, something which Commodus had long since ceased to do. This was a public statement announcing that access to imperial *beneficia* was now opened again to the senatorial elite. The emperor was then escorted to the Temple of Jupiter to make the necessary sacrifices, and then other temples, to gain the support of the gods. The Praetorians however watched in horror and disgust as the statues of Commodus were thrown down, vandalized and removed all over the city. To make matters worse that night Pertinax again used the same watchword and issued orders that discipline would be restored in the guard cohorts whose soldiers were now forbidden from carrying an axe. The emperor's support base was extremely narrow and his actions would narrow it further still.[20]

Chapter Ten

Restored to the Heavens

It took a mere three days from Pertinax's accession for the first conspiracy to emerge. The Praetorians seized Triarius Maternus Lascivius and brought him to the Praetorian camp in order to declare him Augustus. He appears to have been a very reluctant usurper. Probably being left in a room to change into the imperial regalia, the naked senator escaped and came to the palace seeking the emperor's protection. Not all the guards were informed of the plot as they did not detain him but brought him before Pertinax. The terrified man was allowed to leave Rome to a rural retreat away from the political intrigues of the capital.[1]

This incident is only recorded in the *Historia Augusta* which describes him as 'a senator of distinction'. Why did a section of the guard choose this man, seemingly without him being sounded out before hand? There were senators who had a closer familial link to Commodus. This attempt appears to have been an almost immediate and spontaneous response to the anger the Praetorians felt at the murder of Commodus and the threat to their unrestricted licence to seize property. They dreaded the restoration of constraints on their behaviour and actions.[2] There appears to have been little planning or preparation. However Triarius was not merely a senator in the wrong place at the wrong time, he was chosen as an eligible candidate because of his *nobilitas* and family connections.

Triarius Maternus Lascivius was the ordinary consul of 185 AD. Edward Champlin has convincingly reconstructed his family connections based on inscriptions and analysis of his family names. He was an *iuridicus* or legal expert from Asturia and married to Egnatia Procula. She was a member of the powerful senatorial family of the Egnatii and a relative of Egnatius Capito, probable suffect consul of 182 AD and M Egnatius Postumus, the consul of 183 AD. Their son, A Triarius Rufinus became ordinary consul in 210 AD. Triarius Maternus Lascivius' sister was Pomonia Triaria who was married to C Julius Erucius Clarus Vibianus, the ordinary consul of 193 AD and the leader of the great Antonine family of the Erucii Clari. It was this man, along with his colleague, that it was alleged Commodus planned to kill on the eve of the New Year. Other relatives probably included L Junius Rufinus, the proconsul of Macedonia in 194 AD and L Junius Rufinus Proculianus, legate of Dalmatia in 184 AD.[3] The Praetorians appear to have selected him as an appealing well connected alternative to Pertinax, who lacked their illustrious forbearers. The plan came to nothing due to the understandable reluctance of their stooge to play the pawn to the machinations of others. If the Praetorians had wanted to continue Commodus' dynasty their choice should have fallen upon Claudius Pompeianus' son or Marcus Peducaeus Plautius Quintillus who was married to Fadilla, Commodus' sister. Claudius Pompeianus was too closely associated with Pertinax who was deeply implicated in the murder of Commodus and so unworthy for their consideration. His son was probably out of reach on the family's country estates, away from the turmoil in the capital. Marcus Peducaeus Plautius Quintillus disappears from the historical records after the assassination, only to re-emerge with the murder of Pertinax and the accession of Didius Julianus who promised to avenge the death of Commodus. Marcus Peducaeus Plautius Quintillus, if he had any sense, and his survival in the court of Commodus suggests he did, would have made a hasty retreat to his country estates on the death of his brother-in-law. Consequently the Praetorians would have been unable to bring him to their camp. What the plot also shows is the lack of control Laetus now had over the Praetorian cohorts who resented his role in the death of Commodus and his public support of Pertinax. Laetus' power lay in his control of the guard and Pertinax must have now questioned whether it was politic to retain him in his post. Removing him would appeal to the nobles in the senate, Pertinax's only real power base.

Pertinax now appears to have backtracked on the restrictions he had promised to the power of the Praetorians. He also promised the populace that he would provide a hundred *denarii* per man as Commodus had promised before his death, so alleviating unrest in the guards and the people of Rome, induced, according to the *Historia Augusta*, by fear. The new emperor now came face to face with the financial problems faced by Commodus throughout his reign. There was only 1,000,000 *sesterces* left in the treasury and Pertinax had already promised a donative of 3,000 *sesterces* a man to the Praetorians in addition to monies promised to the populace of the capital. Pertinax brought this state of affairs before the senate, blaming the 'wonderful freedmen' in the imperial household, pandering to the senatorial prejudices. The grim reality of the imbalance between state income and expenditure Pertinax either failed to grasp or decided to turn a blind eye to for short-term gain. Faced with the same financial crisis as that of his predecessor Pertinax decided to make matters worse by rescinding many of the taxes that Commodus had placed on those who owned most wealth, the senators. Pertinax made a political decision not to risk the support of this key group and by doing so jeopardized the finances of the state. He allowed both state and private uncultivated land to be claimed by any landowner who could farm it. He was primarily concerned by the reduction in the grain supply and need to increase yields. Many small and medium sized landowners had been unable to find the required labour at a price they could afford due to the plague and their land had been left fallow. Such a law allowed large areas of land to be seized by the great senatorial landowners with their armies of slaves at the expense of the small and medium freeholder. Yet to the politically astute Pertinax he would have killed two birds with one stone; increasing agricultural production and increasing the support of the senatorial elite. In addition to the security of legal tenure, this land was immune from taxation for ten years.[4]

Pertinax remitted all customs duties that Commodus had imposed on river traffic, harbours and roads within the empire, probably collected on the borders of provinces. This must have greatly reduced state revenues, but the main beneficiaries would have been the senatorial class who had the capital to transport goods across the empire and the Mediterranean. Furthermore the tax that Commodus imposed on the senatorial class which was raised on his birthday would have also been rescinded with his death. Pertinax is not recorded as introducing a similar tax. He also refused to pay sums of money Commodus had paid to Rome's allies beyond the Danube and Rhine. An entirely risky policy which would increase resentment and the prospect of war which would have cost the empire far more in both financial and human terms than the sums required in paying the tribute. Pertinax also reduced state income from wills, declaring that old wills were legally valid until a new one was drawn up and refused legacies left as a result of flattery or legal complications which had deprived heirs and relatives a part of their inheritance. Confiscated estates which had become part of the imperial *fiscus* were also restored to the families of those condemned under *majestas* and they were provided with compensation as well. A fixed sum was put aside for public buildings. This has been interpreted as the new emperor creating a fund to ensure monies were spent on restorations. However it is more likely that Pertinax was creating a limit to such spending as the restoration projects that Commodus was committed to after the fire were probably vast. Many of these projects were therefore put on hold and were completed by Septimius Severus after building work was reduced by a lack of funding. Such measures are recorded by Dio, a senator himself, as demonstrating 'the most economical management and most careful consideration of public welfare'. Pertinax stood before the senate declaring: 'It is better, O Conscript Fathers, to rule a state that is impoverished than to attain a great mass of wealth by paths of peril and dishonour.'[5]

The *alimentia* that provided support for the poor had been suspended by Commodus nine years previously and many equestrians had not been paid salaries due to them. Pertinax restored both, hoping by these measures to gain the support of the equestrian class and his move to provide for the poor of Italy probably derived from his frustration at having no funds to provide for them when he held the post of *Praefectus Alimentorum* under Commodus. Faced with the need to pay the Praetorians and the populace the promised cash distribution, and with income greatly reduced and expenditure increased, Pertinax resorted to a fire sale of imperial furnishings and property. His sale of Commodus' property also had a political motive as well, inflaming senatorial disdain and prejudices against the previous emperor as well as linking himself to the rule of Marcus Aurelius, who organized a similar sale to pay for the German war rather than ask the senate for an increase in taxes or a request for public funds. Senators who had so recently condemned Commodus, and plotted against him, now fell over themselves in bidding for his personal belongings. Slaves and concubines were sold; many though were skilled imperial administrators. Some of these had been given humorous nick names by Commodus but were now publicly humiliated. Silk robes with gold embroidery, tunics, mantles and cloaks including those made in the manner of the Dalmatians, purple cloaks in the Greek fashion and those made for military campaigns were auctioned off. The sources don't explicitly comment on the link these clothes had with Hercules, yet this regalia clearly was worn by Commodus in his role as the 'Roman Hercules'. The wealthy senators competed in their bids for possession of the very items they so despised their former emperor for wearing. Gladiatorial togas were sold, chariot harnesses fashioned with gold and jewels, swords carrying the image of Hercules, necklaces worn by gladiators and the former emperor's famous golden helmet. The funds raised are described as 'immense'. Pertinax officiated at the auction, making careful note of the buyers. Some would have been sympathizers of the dead emperor and would need to be watched. Others hoped to add to their prestige by revealing such items at their dinner parties. The monies raised were not used to reduce the financial black hole but pay the people and Praetorians their promised money. However, despite the vast amounts raised, Pertinax was unable to pay the Praetorians all that had been promised and when he later claimed in the senate he had, the freedmen and Praetorians present 'became highly indignant and muttered ominously'.[6]

As the financial situation grew steadily worse Pertinax looked to the imperial freedmen to pay back monies they had acquired under Commodus. This would further alienate many of the officials he had to rely on for the efficient running of the imperial bureaucracy, as they were 'kept within bounds with a strong hand, and so in this way brought upon himself a bitter hatred'.[7] He made public the monies they had received in order to further discredit Commodus and blackmail them into returning these funds. Commodus' shadow continued to cast itself over Pertinax who felt the need to undermine his predecessor's reputation at every opportunity. The new emperor was also playing to the nobles but he was also desperately in need of further funds. Many of those slaves and imperial freedmen he had sold or removed from the imperial bureaucracy he was later forced to re-employ; such was the loss of skilled and experienced officials that the administration of the empire had started to suffer. He reduced court expenditure by half through the reduction of the number of freedmen and made imperial banquets a more austere affair. However it became increasingly clear to all that Commodus' games and courtly expenses were not the reason for the imbalance in state finances. Income did not meet expenditure as tax revenues were not enough to support the state. Pertinax was compelled to make a humiliating admission of such before the senate when:

> he was forced in violation of a previous promise, to exact certain revenues which Commodus had remitted.

To add further humiliation the nobles arranged for the son of his father's former patron, Q Hedius Rufus Lollianus Gentianus, himself a consul, to stand up and admonish the emperor for breaking his former promise. Pertinax excused his actions 'on the grounds that it was a case of necessity'. The sources however did not give Commodus such latitude, Commodus' revenue measures were a consequence of either greed on his or Cleander's part or the 'numerous' games that were provided for the populace.[8]

Pertinax treated the senatorial class with the outward displays of equality. The imperial banquets had been used by emperors to emphasize their superiority over their aristocratic peers. These were reduced in opulence from the 'absolutely unlimited to a fixed standard'. He also sent dishes from his banquets to senators as a mark of *beneficia*, for which the nobles made fun of him in private. In marked contrast to his predecessor he allowed senators to make frequent requests at the *salutatio*, giving his opinion 'in a kindly way', he regularly attended senatorial meetings and made frequent proposals in person. This was in deliberate contrast to Commodus who towards the end of his reign had held legal inquiries and investigations in private, relying on his Praetorian Prefect and imperial officials for advice. Pertinax held his sessions openly with his *consilium* made up of the most prominent nobles. This group would have included Acilius Glabrio and Claudius Pompeianus. However even within the senate, Pertinax created enmity and division. The senate was purged of spies and informers with slaves who had provided testimony against their owners being crucified. Those senators who had made allegations against their peers were tried before their peers and if convicted, suffered severe punishment but were excused execution. Many of these would have used the courts as part of the normal political manoeuvrings which dated back to the Republic. With senatorial control firmly in the hands of the nobles who had opposed Commodus, the law would give rise to many acts of vengeance. A new census was ordered to further weed out those partisans of Commodus who remained. The emperor in person proposed a *senatus consultum* that those senators who had been adlected to the status of praetor by Commodus were to be ranked as inferior in status to those who had actually been appointed by Commodus and served in the post. Commodus had made 'countless' such appointments and this unsubtle demotion created bitter hatred of Pertinax amongst 'many men'. Commodus had a large body of support in the senate who were now being purged by the noble families with the connivance of the emperor who was totally reliant on the support of this small power-hungry elite.[9]

The weakness of Pertinax's position is exemplified by his inability to replace Commodus' magisterial appointments both in Rome and the provinces. To do so would have sparked a revolt by governors who had command of significant bodies of troops. The only governors he might rely on were the Severii on the Danube who had secured their appointment through Laetus' commendation to Commodus. Even the removal of Laetus might induce these men to revolt. To try and secure the loyalty of the Severii to himself, rather than the Praetorian Prefect, Pertinax appointed C Fulvius Plautianus, a relative of Septimius Severus who would become his Praetorian Prefect, to an important post, probably that of Prefect of the Vigils. Even this hints at desperation as Plautianus is likely to be the Fulvius prosecuted by Pertinax for corruption whilst Proconsul of Africa, and ejected from the province.[10]

Laetus realized his position was extremely precarious. As commander of the guards he was indispensable to the emperor as long as he could control them and they accepted his orders. However many Praetorians resented their new emperor as the murderer of Commodus and the man who had deprived them of many of the privileges they had enjoyed under the previous regime. In public the Praetorian Prefect 'kept speaking well of Pertinax and abusing Commodus'. Yet the guard cohorts were becoming increasingly mutinous: 'For a time after the beginning of the reign they behaved obstructively and disobediently when orders were given to them.'[11] Laetus realized he was losing control of the Praetorian cohorts and so changed tack. He was probably aware that leading officers in these units planned once more to overthrow Pertinax. They selected the Consul Sosius Falco as a potential successor to Pertinax as he came from a noble family and was one of the wealthiest men in Rome. The Praetorians would only back a man who had the capacity to deliver a significant donative as reward for their support, something Pertinax had failed to do. Sosius Falco had come to the attention of the emperor's enemies by firstly objecting to Pertinax's association with Marcia and Laetus himself on the very day he was given imperial power. Then he had complained to the senate about Pertinax's integrity. The *Historia Augusta*, in a garbled and corrupted account, refers at this point to a slave who appears to be from the household of Sosius Falco who makes a claim before the senate that he was the legitimate successor to Commodus being the son of a 'Fabia'. It is difficult to believe a slave would ever claim to be the legitimate emperor or be granted an audience before the assembled senate. Unfortunately the manuscript does not preserve the name of this man's father; however it appears he was from the household of Ceionius Commodus. It is highly unlikely that a slave would make such a claim, especially in an era where slaves making false accusations were routinely crucified. Champlin reconstructs an alternative reading of the corrupted manuscript which has the slave making the claim on behalf of his master, the Consul Sosius Falco. The 'Fabia' in the text is conjectured to be Ceionia Fabia, sister of Lucius Verus. Her son M Peducaeus Plautius Quintillus would therefore be Sosius Falco's half-brother, Ceionia Fabia marrying twice, once to a Sosius Falco. Falco's known father, Quintus Pompeius Sosius Falco, was the ordinary of consul 169 AD but his wife is unknown from inscriptions or the historical sources. Champlin sees this and the previous attempted coup of Triarius Materrnus Lascivius as linked as the potential usurpers appear to be related to the Consul Erucius Clarus, Triarius being his uncle and Falco his brother-in-law. Clarus' son is recorded on an inscription from Diana Veteranorum in Numidia; his full name being C Julius Rufinus Laberius Fabianus Pomponius Triarius Erucius Clarus Sosius Priscus. From his name his ancestry can be reconstructed and known relatives eliminated leaving his unknown mother's ancestry as Laberius Fabianus Sosius Priscus. Champlin speculates that she was the daughter of the consul of 169 AD, Q Pompeius Senecio Sosius Priscus, and so the sister of Falco. Champlin sees from this a senatorial plot involving the families of Erucius Clarus and Sosius Falco who planned to replace Pertinax with firstly Triarius Maternus and then Sosius Falco himself, who was perhaps related to the imperial family of Commodus. The slave was used to confirm Falco's better claim to the throne. Laetus appears to have been aware of the plot and stood back to see how events progressed, allowing the conspirators and officers in the guard to communicate unhindered.[12]

The conspirators waited until Pertinax was at the coast reviewing arrangements for the corn supply, probably at Ostia or Portus. Sosius Falco was to be escorted to the Praetorian Camp and be invested with the purple. However before the plan could reach fruition, Pertinax was informed of its existence. Rapidly returning to Rome the emperor summoned the senate to denounce the Praetorians who resented him despite the fact, so Pertinax claimed, their promised donative had been paid in full. Dio admits that all those present knew full well that this was not in fact true, and he only inflamed the anger of the guards and freedmen present at the meeting even further. The senate then declared Sosius Falco a public enemy. The consul vehemently denied any knowledge or involvement in the plot but he was still condemned and, on the point of being sentenced to death, Pertinax stood up voicing his opposition, exclaiming; 'Heaven forbid that any senator should be put to death while I am ruler, even for a just cause.' Sosius Falco instead was banished to his country estates.[13]

Laetus was not implicated in the plot, probably because he led the investigation into the conspiracy as Praetorian Prefect. He did however continue to play a double game. Many of the Praetorian officers resented their commander's involvement in the overthrow of Commodus and his subsequent role in the new government. Laetus had them executed, pretending that he was doing so on Pertinax's orders as they had been accused of involvement in the plot of Sosius Falco. A slave from the household of Sosius Falco supposedly provided the evidence the prefect needed to implicate large numbers of Praetorians.[14] Dio describes 'many of the soldiers' as being 'put out of the way'. Laetus removed opposition to his prefecture within the guard but also stirred up hatred of Pertinax whose death he now welcomed. Many Praetorians now feared that they too would suffer a similar fate and were probably encouraged to do so by Laetus in the hope that unrest in the guard cohorts would alleviate him of the need to assassinate Pertinax himself.

On 28 March unrest in the Praetorian camp was reported to the emperor who sent his father-in-law and City Prefect, Sulpicianus, to calm the situation. Pertinax had been planning to visit the Athenaeum, an auditorium built by Hadrian, to hear a recital by a renowned poet but changed his mind with both an unfavourable sacrifice and disconcerting news. He cancelled his day's planned entertainment and sent his Praetorian escort back to their camp.[15] The situation was growing more unstable by the hour and at midday between two and three hundred Praetorians left the camp fully armed and headed towards the palace. Sulpicianus was either unaware of their departure or unable to stop them. What is clear is that Pertinax was not notified of their approach until they burst into the palace itself. These 250 men were probably all that remained from the group who had been involved in the attempt to place Sosius Falco on the throne. The hatred the emperor was held in was now evident in the actions of both the day guard in the palace and the freedmen. Large numbers of Praetorians remained in the palace and the *equites singulares* were within a short ride away, yet no attempt was made to halt the advance of this small group. The Praetorians on guard at the outer door of the palace deserted their posts, followed by those guarding the interior corridors. The 250 had formed a wedge formation expecting some form of attack, their spears and swords drawn. None came. The doors of the palace were in fact opened by the slaves, freedmen and attendants who urged the band on as they passed from room to room, through the porticos and towards the vast banqueting Hall of Jupiter. It had been left to the emperor's wife to inform her husband of their approach. Pertinax ordered Laetus to use his influence to facing down the potential assassins. Laetus accepted the order and then crept out of the palace using an alternative route covering his face. The prefect was either ashamed of his actions or feared he would share his emperor's death if he was recognized by the assassins. He reached the palace portico without any trouble, most servants and guards having fled, and then made his way home leaving the emperor to his fate. Pertinax was now urged to flee by 'a few' who remained loyal. Among these were his wife and Eclectus, whose own fate was bound to that of Pertinax's. No mercy would be shown by the Praetorians. The ex-members of Commodus' household continued to cheer the advance of the soldiers through the palace. Marcia does not appear to have been present and had no doubt fled the palace at the urgings of her husband, Eclectus. Some advised Pertinax to flee to the 'people'. Yet the people of Rome had no reason to harbour the murderer of Commodus, so the people Herodian refers to are no doubt the senatorial aristocracy who had the most to lose by his death. Others urged him to hide in the palace, however Pertinax was many things but never a coward, and he decided to use his status as emperor and successful general to meet the threat head on as they entered the private imperial chambers.[16]

Pertinax left his rooms and met the angry guards face to face. Fool hardy, noble, brave? All of these. The emperor addressed them as they stood before him; their eyes lowered in shame and muted hatred. All but one sheathed their swords. Pertinax, according to Herodian, blamed Commodus' death on natural causes rather than a plot instigated by himself. The emperor knew the unpaid donative was clearly not the main motivating factor in the minds of his potential murderers. Tausius, a Tungrian from northern Gaul, still refused to lower his eyes or sheath his sword. As Praetorians were drawn from Italy, Tausius may have been a member of the *equites singulares* who joined the group as they marched from the Praetorian camp to the Palatine. Members of this Germanic bodyguard saw loyalty in personal terms, to the dead emperor he had sworn to protect, rather than to an abstract concept of Rome itself. To him exacting vengeance would have been a matter of honour. The emperor though had won over some of the party who withdrew. Tausius turned in anger to his retreating comrades before addressing Pertinax himself: 'The soldiers have sent you this sword.' He struck the emperor down. Pertinax covered his head with his toga, with his dying words he uttered a prayer to Jupiter the Avenger. The spell had been broken and the soldiers fell upon the prone figure. Eclectus now attempted to defend his master, wounding several of the assailants before he too was cut down. The soldiers then cut of the head of Pertinax and stuck it on a spear before returning to their camp, securing its gates and manning the walls, there awaiting upon events.[17]

This had clearly not been a planned usurpation but one carried out in the heat of the moment. No plans had been laid for a potential successor nor was one even searched for. This was about vengeance. The passions of the guard had been whipped up into a frenzy by the actions of Laetus. Already angered by the murder of Commodus and the withdrawal of privileges they had been granted by him. Embittered by the reduced donative, they had witnessed their comrades being arrested and executed on the accusations of a mere slave whilst senators crucifying any slaves who had provided evidence against them under Commodus. Their own prefect, who had clearly been involved in the murder of their beloved Commodus, now seemed powerless to restrain the actions of Pertinax. Those most under threat decided to seize the moment. The actions of the whole of the guard and the palace freedmen demonstrate the hatred they felt towards Pertinax.

Confusion now reigned. Dio records some fleeing to their homes, perhaps fearing their denunciations of Commodus would result in the guard hunting them down. Others appear to have fled to the soldiers, no doubt the Praetorian camp. These feared the prominent members of the senate exacting vengeance on them for their support for Commodus during his reign, the restraining hand of Pertinax now being removed. Sulpicianus, Pertinax's son-in-law, remained in the camp, not as a prisoner but as a man who sensed an opportunity. He hoped to profit from the situation by gaining the support of the Praetorian cohorts for his own acclamation.

There now occurred one of the most infamous events in Roman history. M Didius Severus Julianus, a man who under Commodus had been exiled for association in the plot of Lucilla, and then recalled to become one of the richest men in Rome, now made his way to the gates of the Praetorian camp. News had spread that the empire was for sale, the throne going to the highest bidder. Didius Julianus was the son of the eminent jurist Salvius Julianus and had been brought up in the household of Marcus Aurelius' mother, Domitia Lucilla. According to Herodian it was his wife Manlia Scantilla and daughter, Didia Clara, along with a number of clients, who during a drunken dinner party persuaded him to use his fortune to win over the Praetorians. The *Historia Augusta*, based on the history of Marius Maximus, who was not present in Rome at the time, records two Praetorian tribunes persuading him to make counter bids for the empire. Didius Julianus now offered the guards inside a larger donative than that offered by Sulpicianus. The guards standing on the ramparts now took on the role of auctioneers, with the alarmed Sulpicianus now not only facing a rival but the real possibility that the loser would be executed by their opponent. The bids rose and rose again with some of the Praetorians acting as messengers, Didius Julianus being asked, 'Sulpicianus offers so much; how much do you raise him?' To which the same question was then made to Sulpicianus. Sulpicianus held the advantage being both in the camp itself and holding the post of City Prefect so having greater *auctoritas*. He suddenly raised his offer to 20,000, Julianus had been meekly raising by bids of smaller amounts. In desperation Julianus now reminded the Praetorians that as Pertinax's son-in-law he would seek revenge on the Praetorians who had murdered him and he promised to restore the memory of Commodus as well as restoring the honours, statues of the 'Roman Hercules' and their privileges that the senate had removed. With one final flourish Julianus held up his fingers to the men on the rampart indicating that he would increase his bid by another 5,000 as well as promising to pay the money immediately. The Praetorians immediately acclaimed him emperor and voted him the name 'Commodus'. The gates of the camp were thrown open and he made the traditional sacrifices surrounded by thousands of guardsmen whose loyalty would last until they had received their money. The Praetorian cohorts in full armour and in closed battle formation with all their standards restored with the image of Commodus marched to the senate house, escorting their new Commodus, the Emperor Didius Julianus. The guards recognized that the way in which the new emperor had been chosen would have raised great hostility and anger and so were prepared for it. However the crowds stood off, neither opposing the events they witnessed, nor supporting them. Hoping to intimidate the assembled senate house the guard then proceeded to surround the Curia. The senatorial aristocracy were now gripped by fear, especially those that had fervently supported Pertinax or crossed Julianus. Dio was one of these as he had received the praetorship and other honours from Pertinax and successfully prosecuted Julianus in a number of trials. Non attendance at the acclamation of a new emperor was tantamount to open opposition and certain failure to gain future imperial *beneficia* and inevitable charges of *majestas*. Many decided to resort to safety in numbers; staying isolated in one's home invited a lonely death. Like many of his senatorial peers, Dio bathed and had dinner, perhaps fearing it would be his last. The senators then gathered and attempted to push their way through the masses of guards surrounding the senate house to acclaim the new emperor and hear his acceptance speech. Didius Julianus told his guard to remain outside, yet their very numbers would focus the minds of the senators inside. The emperor urged those assembled to remember the kind of man he was. This message was clear to all present; loyalty would be rewarded but opposition would not be tolerated. Many, Dio states, both feared and hated him, their emotions coming full circle from the murder of their nemesis Commodus. The nobles faced an uncertain present; a situation they had helped to bring about.[18]

Didius Julianus then retired to the palace and, supposedly finding the meagre banquet laid out for Pertinax, sent slaves out to procure more extravagant luxuries including oysters and fattened birds, which he then dined upon as the body of the previous emperor still lay within the precincts. Ironically it is the *Historia Augusta* that dismisses this as a lie spread by Julianus' enemies in order to undermine his popularity and draw parallels to the supposed extravagance of Commodus. In fact he gave no banquets until Pertinax had been buried. The presence of Pylades in Julianus' inner circle, one of Commodus' most prominent freedmen, suggests that the new emperor recognized the importance of this group in the efficient running of the imperial government. He hoped to gain the support of those freedmen who had felt victimized and ostracized by Pertinax. The *Historia Augusta* reports that the palace servants of Commodus had even been plotting to murder Pertinax in the baths. Although doubted by some modern historians this does have a ring of truth to it. How apt for Commodus' palace freedmen to plan to murder of Pertinax in the very place Commodus had been strangled. Revenge is a dish best served cold. Many of the imperial freedmen and bureaucrats looked to the reign of Commodus with pride and longing. The sarcophagus of Marcus Aurelius Prosenes, which lists various posts held during his career including *procurator munera* with responsibility for the games before gaining promotion to *procurator patrimonii*, stresses the importance of Commodus to his career and takes evident pride in his association with this emperor. Clearly Commodus was loved, not hated by a large proportion of the population, as those reading this inscription were meant to see Prosenes' association with Commodus in a positive light.[19]

At the urging of the Praetorians, Laetus was dismissed that night from his post as sole prefect and replaced by Flavius Genialis and Tullius Crispinus. The Praetorians had clearly despised their former prefect for his involvement in the murder of Commodus and then supervising the execution of large numbers of their comrades after being 'implicated' in the plot of Sosius Falco. However bonds of *amicitiae* existed between the new emperor and the ex prefect as Laetus appears to have previously protected Julianus from the 'clutches of Commodus', so Laetus escaped with his life. His ultimate fate however was not long delayed. Suspected of support for Septimius Severus on the Danube after Septimius had risen in revolt against Julianus, he was executed along with Marcia. Didius Julianus appealed to the Praetorians by positioning himself as the avenger of Commodus. Marcia's death would have been seen as delayed justice by the Praetorians just as Severan forces advanced on Rome. Their loyalty was again questionable as Julianus had been unable to provide the full amount of the monies promised to the guard on his election to the throne. Both Marcia and Laetus were hated by the senate being associated with Commodus' presentation of himself as the new Hercules and the refounder of Rome. Significant numbers of the senate looked to Septimius Severus, or the other usurpers, Clodius Albinus and Pescennius Niger, as their new saviours. Julianus' position rapidly became untenable. The increasingly desperate Julianus even appointed a known associate of Septimius Severus, D Venturius Macrinus, as a third Praetorian Prefect, a post Septimius had already appointed him to. Macrinus had been Commodus' Prefect of Egypt from 181 AD until 183 AD and seems to have been dismissed by Perennis, a fate shared by Pertinax, Septimius Severus and Didius Julianus. Septimius Severus had risen in revolt on 9 April, twelve days after the murder of Pertinax and succession of Julianus. He presented himself as the avenger of Pertinax, one of the legions under his command as Governor of Upper Pannonia, the I Aduitrix, had been led by Pertinax twenty years before. Detachments from the three Pannonian legions had been summoned to declare him emperor whilst the six legions in Dacia and Moesia declared for him at the same time. His two sons were also summoned from Rome, away from the clutches of Julianus. Severus would not have acted without testing out support amongst the soldiers, legates and governors along the Danube and Rhine with the legions in Raetia, Noricum and the Germanies also supporting him. So it appears that twelve days between the murder of Pertinax and his declaration of vengeance would not be long enough for messengers to be sent to these officials, delicate negotiations to be held and replies returned.[20] More likely Septimius Severus had been planning this move against Pertinax and decided to utilize his murder by acting as a loyal avenger of Pertinax rather than Commodus who was despised by many prominent senators whose support Severus now needed. Yet by 195 AD Septimius Severus was presenting himself in these very terms, as *divi Commodi frater*, the brother of the divine Commodus. Herodian has Septimius Severus give a speech to the assembled troops blaming the 'mistakes' of Commodus' reign on his advisors and inexperience. Although fictitious in its details, the speech fits the historical context. Commodus had been immensely popular with the soldiers and many of the legionary commanders owed their positions to him. These experienced military men who owed a debt of *beneficia* to their now dead benefactor would join Septimius Severus; their numbers included Claudius Candidus, and Flavius Secundus Philippianus. Another of Commodus' experienced generals, Clodius Albinus, had been proclaimed emperor by the legions of Britain but at first he allied himself with Septimius Severus having been offered the office of Caesar.[21]

Pescennius Niger, Commodus' Governor of Syria, had been proclaimed emperor by the eastern legions and had been plotting his move for a considerable time. The day after the murder of Pertinax, Julianus had greeted the senators in the palace at the morning salutation and then proceeded from the palace, through the forum to the senate house. As he was about to make a sacrifice to Janus before the entrance, the crowd started shouting at him, calling him 'stealer of the empire' and *parricide*. Julianus, in an attempt to mollify the crowd, promised them a distribution of money to which they declared, 'We don't want it! We won't take it.' The yells and shouts echoed across the enclosed forum amplifying the noise and commotion. Fighting broke out as the Praetorian escort tried to disperse the crowd resulting in running battles across the city. Gradually worn down, the mob retreated to the Circus Maximus, where they barricaded themselves in entreating for Pescennius Niger to come to their aid. Niger had not risen in revolt at this time but the crowd's repeated and continuous demands for him to become emperor is cited by Herodian as the reason why he rose in revolt, expecting Rome to turn to him without little effort on his part.[22] However news of these events could not have been passed to him across the Mediterranean by the time he declared himself emperor and, more likely, he had already begun using agents in the city to prepare for his planned revolt at the end of the month. The mob's retreat to the circus suggests the faction leaders were closely involved in managing the rising in support of Niger and brought forward their plans after the unexpected murder of Pertinax. The circus was besieged by the Praetorian cohorts. The mob was only able to hold out for a day, but being unable to persuade the Praetorians to join them, they surrendered. The circus factions and the populace had long been cultivated by Commodus and it is probable that both coups led by Niger and Severus were originally prepared against Pertinax, their battle cry based on avenging the death of Commodus.

The murder of Pertinax allowed Commodus' brother-in-law to return to Rome. M Peducaeus Plautius Quintillus held considerable influence as an augur, a former consul, a nephew of Verus and married to Commodus' sister Fadilla. His political acumen, which had served him so well in prospering in the feral atmosphere of court politics during the reign of Commodus, enabled him to quickly assess the political situation. He realized Didius Julianus' situation was hopeless and, along with a vast majority of the senate, attached himself to Septimius Severus whose army was rapidly approaching the capital. The two probably knew each other well as *amici* of Commodus. The increasingly desperate Julianus summoned Tiberius Claudius Pompeianus from his rural estates to where he had retired yet again after the death of Pertinax hoping to offer him the throne, but he refused on the grounds of old age and poor eyesight, an ailment from which had temporarily recovered after the murder of Commodus. To have accepted such an offer would have meant the death of his own son as he lacked the necessary military support in the face of the advancing Severans. His son would meet his end in Alexandria on the orders of Septimius' son Caracalla. Julianus, realizing his end was now near, entered the senate to propose that the senate, Vestal Virgins and priests, with the emperor at their head, meet Septimius Severus as he marched on Rome in the guise of supplicants holding fillets in outstretched hands. Plautius Quintillus, as the most senior former consul present was called upon to speak by Didius Julianus. The old man rose to oppose this action declaring that if Julianus could not withstand an opponent by force of arms he had no right to rule. The presiding emperor was publicly humiliated and his weak position publicly exposed. Other senators rose to follow Plautius Quintillus' lead. The frustrated and humiliated Julianus retired to the palace to contemplate the mass murder of the senate. The Praetorians' loyalty had run its course and they refused to force the senate to comply with their impotent emperor's demands. The emperor recalled the senate and proposed that Septimius Severus be made joint emperor. This was put to the vote and approved, the senators no doubt hoping to avoid slaughter and looting on the streets of the capital. However Septimius' agents had already been at work. The guard had been suborned with the promise that if they handed over the murderers of Pertinax to Septimius Severus and refused to fight, they would 'suffer no harm'. The Praetorians obeyed with the obliging senate rapidly sentencing Julianus to death in a meeting called by the consuls. Septimius Severus was declared sole emperor. A tribune was despatched to the palace, now deserted of Praetorians. Coming across Didius Julianus he slew him, the emperor's last words being, 'But what evil have I done? Whom have I killed?'[23]

M Peducaeus Plautius Quintillus' support of Septimius Severus had probably bought him his life. He and his wife retired to their rural estates. However in 205 AD *delatores* used the unstable atmosphere created by the discovery of a plot to kill Septimius Severus by his Praetorian Prefect, Plautianus, to accuse Plautius Quintillus under the *majestas* law despite the fact he was 'interfering in no one's business and doing aught amiss'. Deciding to commit suicide to avoid his estates being taken by the imperial *fiscus* he 'called for his shroud, which he had made ready long before'; and on perceiving that it had fallen to pieces through the lapse of time, he said: 'What does this mean? We are late.' Then as he burnt incense, he remarked: 'I make the same prayer as Servianus made for Hadrian.' Servianus had at one time been the Emperor Hadrian's nominated successor along with his grandson. However Hadrian changed his mind, instead opting for Antonius Pius, and close to death Hadrian ordered the death of Servianus and his grandson. Perhaps Plautius Quintillus had hoped to succeed the childless Commodus at some point or following his murder gain the necessary support to attain the throne. He was probably a more able, loyal and deserving claimant than either Pertinax or Didius Julianus but fate and circumstance conspired against him. It appears that despite his close association with Commodus he was widely admired, being described as 'a man of the noblest birth and long counted among the foremost men of the senate'.[24] We are left ignorant of Fadilla's fate, nor do we know if she was still alive in 205 AD to witness the death of her noble husband.

On entering Rome Septimius Severus kept his promise to the Praetorians, they were to suffer no harm, but they were also deprived of their posts. Secret messages were sent to the Praetorian tribunes and centurions promising rich rewards if they accepted his orders. The rank and file however were ordered to leave their weapons and armour in the Praetorian camp and assemble in ceremonial dress outside Septimius Severus' camp in order to swear their oath of loyalty. Following the orders of their tribunes they marched out wearing wreaths of laurels and assembled on the parade ground whilst a detachment of Severan legionaries proceeded by a more circular route to take the unoccupied Praetorian camp. As the new emperor stood on the tribunal his legionaries surrounded the guard with weapons drawn. They were then harangued for murdering Pertinax and selling the empire. They were then stripped of their ceremonial belts which denoted military service, the *cingulum*, and forbidden from approaching within 100 miles of Rome on pain of death. The surrounding legionaries then rushed forward and removed not only their belts but daggers inlaid with silver and gold, as well as their ceremonial uniforms and insignia. The humiliated guards were then dismissed, an ignominious end for such an elite unit of the Roman army that had served both Marcus Aurelius and Commodus loyally. As the cashiered soldiers departed one man was followed by his loyal horse that refused to leave him despite his attempts to urge the animal to go. The man, increasingly overcome by grief, slew his horse and then himself.[25] The guard that replaced them was to be made up of legionaries who had distinguished themselves in service to Septimius Severus and would be drawn from legionaries across the empire rather than being limited to Italians. One of Septimius Severus' first acts was to hunt down all the conspirators involved in the murders of Pertinax and Commodus. The message had to be clear: even a successful assassination attempt would ultimately lead to retribution for all conspirators. Narcissus, Commodus' wrestler who had ended the life of the poisoned and the prone emperor, was hunted down and given to the wild beasts in the arena. Before this execution the announcer proclaimed the reason for the fate of this criminal, the message was made explicit to the audience, many of whom would be the same senators who had celebrated Commodus' death.[26]

The civil war that now erupted across the empire divided the Roman elite with some supporting Septimius Severus, others Clodius Albinus and yet more Niger. The senate however remained as duplicitous as ever. Septimius Severus, on his defeat of Clodius Albinus in 197 AD, found amongst his dead rival's private papers letters from prominent senators expressing support for Albinus or providing him with sizable gifts. During his absence from Rome the senate had also passed a resolution in praise of Clodius Celsinus, a relative of Albinus. He had the head of Albinus sent ahead of him to Rome and in a fury Septimius Severus returned to the city. He summoned the senate on his arrival and rising from the emperor's chair when all had been assembled, he bitterly denounced not only individual senators but the senate as a whole. Reading from a prepared speech the emperor praised the severity of Sulla, Marius and Augustus in dealing with their enemies whilst denouncing the lenient manner in which men such as Caesar and Pompey had dealt their opponents, only to be rewarded with their own assassination and murder. Dio, who was present at the meeting, describes how Septimius Severus then proceeded to defend Commodus and attacked the senate for 'dishonouring the emperor unjustly, in view of the fact that the majority of its members led worse lives'. Dio then quotes from the emperor's speech directly:

> For if it was disgraceful for him with his own hands to slay wild beasts, yet at Ostia only the other day one of your number, an old man, who had been consul, was publicly sporting with a prostitute who imitated a leopard. But, you will say, Commodus actually fought as a gladiator. And does none of you

fight as a gladiator? If not, how and why is it that some of you have bought his shields and those famous golden helmets?

Thirty-five senators who had openly sided with Albinus, Septimius then released and treated with utmost respect. The distinction being that these were men of honour who had demonstrated loyal service to their *amicus* Clodius Albinus. Their actions could be understood and respected. However twenty-nine other senators, those we can assume who had secretly conspired against Septimius, he had arrested and condemned to death, Pertinax's father-in-law, Sulpicianus, being one of them. Those that had sent the secret letters to Albinus were also arrested immediately but others he suspected of disloyalty but had no concrete evidence against them. Consequently the emperor attempted to persuade Erucius Clarus to implicate other supporters of Albinus by promising him his life and a pardon. Erucius Clarus chose death. The Senator Julianus however was far more compliant and on his testimony many prominent senators stood accused of *majestas* and were executed. Many of the Antonine aristocracy that had conspired against Commodus met their end in this way, being accused by Septimius Severus of supporting either Albinus or Niger. The *Historia Augusta* provides a detailed list of the condemned, among whom are members of the Cerelii, Aelii, Antonii, Severii, Sergii, Fabii, Ceionii, Valerii and a Petronius junior; forty-one in total. Dio records the atmosphere in the senate: 'all pretended to be loyal, but sudden news would catch men offguard, their faces revealing their true inner most feelings.'[27] Ironically Julius Solon, a senator denounced in the sources for spending his fortune under Commodus to gain the broad stripe on his toga denoting senatorial status, was one of those executed at this time. This purge was reminiscent of those instigated by Commodus at the end of his reign and its origins were the same; the duplicity and insatiable plotting of the aristocratic elite to gain greater influence and access to imperial favours by supporting a rival who would be placed in their debt. The treasury, which had been seriously depleted by the financial giveaways Pertinax had instigated to buy the support of the aristocracy, was now temporarily replenished with the confiscated funds taken from the large numbers sentenced under *majestas*. The offices of the *res privata* were now set up across the regions of Italy to manage these newly acquired estates whilst one of Commodus' prominent informers, Aquilius Felix, was given the task of revising the lists of *equites*, no doubt ejecting those whose loyalty Septimius questioned. These included sixty or more officers and officials who had served Albinus. Felix probably settled a few of his own scores as well.[28]

Septimius Severus' speech marked a continuation of Commodian policy towards the senate. The emperor understood that this body could not be trusted and saw his predecessor's actions as being born from the realities of power politics in ancient

Rome. In his summation the emperor demanded the deification of Commodus and the restoration of his name and as well as the creation of a new priest, the *flamen Herculanius Commodianus*, to officiate at religious ceremonies. Septimius had already been referring to Commodus as his 'brother' as well as calling himself the 'son of Marcus'. This repositioning of his 'official' view of Commodus began as early as 195 AD where a Severan inscription records the emperor's new title of *divi Commodi frater*, brother of the divine Commodus.[29] The senate, many of whose number now feared for their lives, passed the necessary resolution. Commodus was now officially recognized as a god, a gift bestowed by the very men who had denounced him for aspiring to such status. If Septimius Severus was merely trying to secure the position of his dynasty by linking himself to a previous emperor he could have chosen Pertinax in whose name he rose in revolt. He had already avenged Pertinax's death at the hands of renegade members of the Praetorian Guard and restored the honour of Rome after the shameful auctioning of the empire. However Pertinax was incredibly unpopular amongst the imperial household, significant numbers of the lesser members of the senate and his name brought no bonds of loyalty with the army. The only group that remained loyal to the name of Pertinax was the noble aristocracy who had shown no more loyalty to Septimius Severus than they had to Commodus. The massive purge of their ranks had also instilled as greater hatred of himself as they had held for Commodus. Pertinax also had a surviving son who would have as great a claim to the throne as the adopted son 'Septimius' and the removal of his 'brother' by fair means or foul would dishonour the memory of his 'adopted father'. Furthermore Pertinax's father-in-law, Sulpicianus, was one of the aristocrats executed.

Septimius Severus had received the imperial *beneficia* of Commodus on several occasions, notably after his successful campaigns in the Deserters' War, receiving the honour of a consulship and the appointment to posts in Sicily and on the Danube. He now found himself in a similar position to his murdered benefactor having become aware of the conspiracies and plots by the aristocratic members of the senate. His rage mirrored the frustrations and betrayals felt by Commodus as he at first sought to work with the nobility but conspiracy followed conspiracy, some real, some perhaps manufactured by powerful equestrians and freedmen close to the throne, yet all in Commodus' eyes a threat to his life. Commodus, unlike Pertinax, also had no children which would have complicated the situation. Importantly he remained popular with the imperial freedmen who surrounded the new emperor, and especially with the army. On the return of the Severan army from its campaign against Albinus in Gaul, three members of the *equites singulares Augusti* made a dedication on the safe return of their emperor and his Praetorian Prefect, C Fulvius Plautianus, to 'Unconquered Hercules'. The association of this demigod to Commodus would have been fresh in their minds and their choice perhaps significant. Many of Septimius Severus' prominent generals owed their position to Commodus and probably still felt a degree of loyalty to his name. The loyalty of the army was paramount to Septimius and he massively increased their pay from 300 *denarii* to 450, a financial outlay Commodus never considered, constrained as he was by the financial crisis he inherited from his father and the continued ravages of the plague. This was partly paid for by the vast amounts of property confiscated in the Severan purges and another debasement of the coinage. Funds were also found for lavish games in Rome and a large distribution of largesse.[30] The final touches to the rebuilding programme in Rome that were instigated after the great fire were completed with dedications made in the name of Septimius Severus or his wife, rather than the emperor who had lavished most of the money and energy. A study of the rule of Septimius Severus bore remarkable similarity to the methods used by Commodus, the difference being that our main sources – Cassius Dio, Herodian and Marius Maximus, upon whom the *Historia Augusta* relied upon – pursued their careers under the shadow of the Severans. To fall foul of the reigning emperor was at best the end of your career or in the worst case, a charge of *majestas* resulting in exile or death. History, after all, is written by the winners.

Epilogue

A 'Kingdom of Gold' or of 'Iron and Rust'?

Famously Dio, commenting on the transition from the reign of Marcus Aurelius to that of Commodus laments that 'our history now descends from a kingdom of gold to one of iron and rust.'[1] Perhaps he was parodying Commodus' declaration of his reign as the birth of a new golden age and his reference to himself as the 'Golden One'. This theme, expanded upon in the rest of his history and that of Herodian and the *Historia Augusta*, was seized upon by the eighteenth century English historian Edward Gibbon in his seminal history of the empire, creating a picture of Commodus as a mad megalomaniac whose grasp of reality was limited at first but negligible by the time of his murder. Such an image was essentially senatorial propaganda as the conspirators had to justify the assassination of a legitimate emperor whose nobility stretched back to the Emperor Nerva. Many of those that conspired against him owed their position either to his father or to Commodus himself. Deprived of access to imperial *beneficia* by the emperor's promotion and increasing reliance on men of low birth but outstanding ability, they had to find a 'legitimate' motive for his removal rather than that of unadulterated self-interest. They had to present their actions as 'honourable'. When the sources refer to the 'people' celebrating the emperor's death, it was to the senatorial elite that they make reference. Ironically the involvement of these aristocrats in the conspiracies increasingly drove Commodus to become even more reliant on the imperial freedmen whose own power and life rested on the emperor's survival. The murder of Commodus would lead to a series of civil wars that would decimate the nobility that had plotted against him and bring the empire close to destruction.

The description of Commodus' long reign as that of 'rust and iron' is to be balanced against his own proclamation of a new golden age. The empire that Commodus inherited was not one of gold. Apart from the senatorial nobility the empire was suffering from the financial costs of almost constant war exacerbated by the plague that Verus' victorious army had brought back from the East. That financial cost had been paid for by the gradual debasement of the coinage yet Marcus Aurelius refused to increase the taxes on the wealthy elite to pay for the increased expenditures, creating a structural weakness in the financial security of the state.[2] With reducing revenues Marcus Aurelius was reduced to fire sales of imperial property to pay for the campaigns on the Danube. Although politically stable, plotting within the imperial family was not dealt with effectively by Marcus Aurelius. His wife was clearly behind the fall of Herodes Atticus at Sirmium, encouraging her young daughter to petition the emperor on behalf of Atticus' enemies, amongst who were numbered the Quintilii. This powerful senatorial family were amongst the first to conspire against her son. The sources all agree that Faustina was involved in some way in the revolt of Avidius Cassius against her husband; she must have known full well that the victory of the usurper would be a death sentence for her son. Her daughter Lucilla, brought up as an Augusta, acquired her mother's traits and was angered at her lost status on the death of her husband, the Emperor Verus, and subsequent marriage to the provincial Claudius Pompeianus. Adding fuel to the flames precedence was then given to Commodus' wife Crispina. Driven by these insults she conspired with members of the nobility to plot the murder of her own brother. All the sources are in agreement that this was a major turning point in the reign of Commodus. He had ruled up to this point in the manner of his father, apart from the increased prominence given to the imperial freedman Saoterus. His problem was: who to trust? This was a problem for all emperors due to the paradoxical nature of their position; a patrimonial monarchy that existed alongside a republican aristocracy. The honours and powers granted to the emperor demonstrated the social and political superiority of his position and at the same time the inferiority of the senate who totally relied upon access to imperial *beneficia* to bolster their own status as great patrons and the need to reward their own *amici* and clients.[3] The conspiracy of Lucilla was to Commodus the shock that made him question the principles his father had ruled the empire, the principles he had attempted to follow. An *amicus* who received *beneficia* was expected to demonstrate loyalty and *gratia*. Yet those prominent Romans who had become involved in the plot had broken the bonds of *amicitia*, becoming *ingratus amici*[4] Commodus now started to reject the veneer of equality so artfully practised by his father for the harsh political reality of imperial rule. An understandable response following in the footsteps of previous emperors, including Caligula whose birthday he shared and whose life he probably studied. Commodus, Caligula, Nero and Domitian, men who followed a parallel course, all shared the same fate. In his position as emperor, Commodus held control over all posts, promotions, appointments, monetary grants, privileges and symbols of status. He was in effect the supreme patron of all, the senatorial aristocracy included. Married to this was his struggle merely to preserve his own life. Power lay in personal contact with the emperor, primarily these were members of the imperial family, then the *amici Caesaris*, the friends of the emperor, and then imperial officials. Yet the greatest threat to his life came from the very men whom he relied most heavily on to carry out the governance of his realm. Commodus' response was simple: if significant members of the senatorial aristocracy could not be trusted, they would have only limited access to the imperial person. Consequently the *amici Caesaris* increasingly became the men he came into contact with the most, the professional bureaucrats so despised by those now deprived of power. This was not a conscious or deliberate policy by the emperor, Roman government was entirely reactive in its nature. Patronage still formed the basis of social and political society, but now it was the *equites* and freedmen who were the brokers of imperial *beneficia*. The great and the good became in their words 'the slaves to slaves'. To an aristocratic senator this was an unnatural inversion of normal social roles as senators were forced to accept the humiliation of approaching and even bribing a social inferior for patronal favours for themselves, their *amici* and clients. Favours which they believed were theirs by right. Commodus' solution to the threat to his life was far from new; the Emperor Vespasian is said to have received his first legateship through the *gratia* of the imperial freedman Narcissus and even the senatorial philosopher Seneca attempted to secure his restoration to favour through the interventions of the freedman Polybius. Under the Emperor Domitian the poets Martial and Statius felt the need to dedicate their works to the *ab epistulis* Abascantus, the *a libellis* Entellus and the *cubicularius* Parthenius.[5] What was different was the reduced access of the nobility to the emperor. It was the equestrians Perennis and Laetus, and the freedmen Cleander and Eclectus who became the gatekeepers. Commodus however felt far more secure; he unwisely felt that the power and indeed life of such men rested on the preservation of his own life. An *equites* nor a freedman could ever dream of ascending to the imperial throne. Unfortunately for Commodus this arrangement did not stop such men conspiring with prominent nobles who had the *dignitas* and *nobilitas* to aspire to such heights. So Lucilla, Ummidius Quadratus and Claudius Pompeianus Quintianus felt they held the required prestige to take the throne, as did the Petronii and perhaps Burrus. Opposition gravitated to such men as viable alternatives to Commodus and so became if not actual, then potential conspirators.

Commodus appears entirely human in his increasingly desperate hunt for a group of advisors and officials in whom he could place unquestioning trust. His own mother had been implicated in a conspiracy against his father and effectively threatened his own life. Then his loyal *amicus* Saoterus was murdered, a deed in which the Machiavellian Perennis managed to implicate another of Commodus' close *amici*, Paternus. This event followed shortly after his own sister had tried to murder him along with Claudius Pompeianus Quintianus with whom he shared youthful adventures and other leading members of the senate, some of them *amici* he had inherited from his father. He had placed his trust in his sole Praetorian Prefect, Perennis, and together with the emperor, they managed the empire efficiently and effectively. Perennis' position was undermined by the whisperings of Cleander and events in the provinces. There was a legionary revolt in Britain, combined with increasing unrest in Gaul and the German provinces caused by widespread brigandage and desertion led by Maternus. Perennis appears to have hidden the extent of this until the scale of the war became too large to hide any further, with whole legions being besieged in their own fortifications and cities plundered. Commodus is described as flying into a rage at having not been kept fully informed of these events. Unrest in the legions in Pannonia followed with the senatorial Governor Plotianus implicated. Cleander seized the opportunity to remove his rival; Perennis' son was linked to the risings on the Danube and associated with the treachery of Plotianus. Against this background of treachery senatorial legates, recently dismissed from their British commands, sought an audience with the emperor to air their grievances, an audience no doubt arranged through Cleander. Commodus' trust in his Praetorian Prefect was now damaged beyond repair as it was made to appear that his lack of full disclosure of events in Gaul and Germany was only the tip of the iceberg, as the legions of Britain and Pannonia appeared to be no longer loyal. Cleander successfully implicated the Praetorian Prefect's son in the chaos. Commodus now placed his trust in his new saviour, just as Perennis had presented himself as the shield of Commodus in hunting down the conspirators involved in Lucilla's plot, Cleander posed as the emperor's protector. Yet the *cubicularius* was to fall in the same way as his predecessor. Eclectus and other prominent freedmen felt their power limited by the influence of the *cubicularius* and sought to undermine his position. They were joined by surviving members of the imperial family wanting vengeance on Cleander for his manoeuvrings that led to the execution of Burrus. Cleander, like Perennis, was eager to retain the confidence of the emperor in his abilities and so failed to keep Commodus fully informed of the grain shortages, partly caused by the plague but made worse by the actions of Papirius Dionysius. The emperor was however made fully aware of the situation when a mob thousands strong appeared at his country villa and Cleander's enemies made him aware of the virtual civil war that had broken out in his capital. To Commodus, Cleander's actions in censoring the business of empire that was presented to the emperor was tantamount to treason and he paid for this with his life, as did others who had helped to ensure the emperor had been kept ignorant of facts.

Eclectus, like Perennis and Cleander, now presented himself as the emperor's saviour in removing the freedmen linked to Cleander as well as some of those implicated in the tampering of the grain supply. The powerful Petronii became the family around which aristocratic opposition to Commodus and the influence of imperial freedmen now coalesced. The son of Commodus' sister Cornificia and M Petronius Sura Mamertinus could carry on the imperial line whilst his father would ensure the nobles would be granted full access to the emperor, a promise

Pertinax would later make. Yet the conspirators lacked the unrestricted access to the imperial person that the Praetorian Prefect Laetus, the *cubicularius* Eclectus and his secret lover Marcia had, thus ensuring the success of their plot. After ruling and surviving for thirteen years it is perhaps ironic that his murder was caused by love. He was blinded by his love for his concubine, the Amazon queen to his Hercules. Marcia herself had acquired the skills and attributes that ensured her own survival through the vicissitudes of courtly life with her own lover, Eclectus. The fate of Crispina, caught in an adulterous relationship, focused their minds. Rumours were already spread about their relationship and they calculated it would be only a matter of time before their liaison came to the ear of the emperor. Laetus, perhaps fearing his influence was on the wane, and remembering the fate of previous holders of his post, looked for a more malleable emperor on the throne who owed his position to him and whose *gratia* would ensure continued access as broker of imperial *beneficia*. There were no conflicts or grievances on the conspirators' parts towards imperial policy in the presentation of Commodus as the new Hercules; in fact some sources have Marcia encouraging the emperor in his idea of refounding Rome in the manner of Hercules. All three would appear in the arena at the emperor's side, being kissed and embraced by him, so clearly and publicly associated with imperial policy, Marcia herself dressed in the garb of the Amazon queen. Survival was the primary motivation for Eclectus and Marcia, yet Laetus and Pertinax eyed supreme power. All four, along with thousands of others, would over the following months and years pay with their lives for their actions. Commodus placed trust in his family and close *amici*, but in his eyes he was repaid with treachery; his mother, his sister, his wife, Paternus, Perennis, Cleander, Petronius Sura Mamertinus, Antistius Burrus and Pertinax. Perhaps his mistake lay in where he placed his trust, but to survive in the poisonous atmosphere of court intrigues, even in the reign of Marcus Aurelius, one had to have developed certain 'qualities' that made aggressive political manoeuvring, duplicitous friendships and temporary alliances the norm. Marcus Aurelius was clearly respected and loved by his *amici* and this is the main difference between his success and his son's failure to survive courtly intrigues. Commodus was respected, he reigned for thirteen years and so had the necessary qualities and attributes, but he was not loved by his *amici*, he was feared.

As Commodus stood immobile waiting for the sword being waved above his head to fall, the assassin Claudius Pompeianus Quintianus' words rang in his ears: 'See! This is what the senate has sent you.' He must have felt impotent, paralyzed by the suddenness of his end, and yet later despised himself for not reacting as a trained gladiator and defending himself. It was members of his guard who apprehended Quintianus before the fatal blow could be given; in response Commodus appears to have increased his training as a gladiator, spending hours every day with his sparring partners. This was not an example of his self-indulgence but a reaction to that moment when he had stared death in the face. Perhaps later in the arena he revisited the attempted assassination, starring at death once more, but this time reacting decisively, overcoming his opponents. Even his eventual murderers never doubted that a physical confrontation with the emperor would end in their own deaths. Poison was used to negate his physical threat, the pain of its progress through his body so incapacitated him that his wrestler was able to strangle him to death. Sudden death must have been a continual, nagging ever-present fear. That he remained sane and rational throughout his reign has been doubted by both ancient and modern historians. However his governance and actions were entirely rational and logical.

The ending of the Northern War is blamed in the sources on Commodus' desire to return to the pleasures of Rome. Commodus had long been fighting on the Danube alongside his father and on Marcus Aurelius' death Commodus continued campaigning beyond the Danube. When he did eventually return to Rome at the end of the campaigning season he left capable commanders with orders to continue the war until the barbarians had been fought to complete submission. His father had fought the war to annihilate the tribes on the northern bank, hoping to create new provinces in the area, an area made waste by the scorch and burn tactics used. There was little valuable farm land or resources, no roads, towns or cities. The proposed provinces would have created a vast salient requiring even greater Roman forces to police. The over-extended frontiers would have been vulnerable to attack on three sides. At the same time the war had been draining the empire dry, the treasury was empty and the army and people of the empire tired of continual warfare. Britain had been invaded by tribes from beyond the wall and Commodus had not been to Rome since he left with his father in August 178 AD. Whether or not historians agree with Commodus' decision to end the war, the thinking process behind it was both logical and reasonable. However the outcome of his decision cannot be denied; generations of peace in the Danubian provinces. New defences were built and forces reorganized bringing stability and prosperity to the region.

The ending of the war had alleviated but not solved the financial crisis. The plague continued to affect agricultural production, trade and tax revenues. Marcus Aurelius had failed to introduce any adequate measures to deal with this as the only viable solution was to increase taxes for those who commanded the greatest wealth, the senatorial elite. Marcus Aurelius did not want to undermine his close relationship with this class and resorted to short-term emergency measures such as the sale of imperial property and debasement of the coinage. Commodus, liberated by the actions of some members of the elite in attempting to murder him, decided to remedy the structural deficit by increasing the taxes on the revenues and land of the landowners, resulting in the stock accusations of greed and avarice being levelled against him. The confiscations of the estates of those sentenced under *majestas* were credited not to actual conspiracies in the sources but also the greed of the emperor and his freedmen. Despite these measures revenues continued to fail to meet imperial expenditure. This was not due to the expenditure on games that all emperors used to retain the loyalty of the people of Rome, but the effects of the plague which appears to have become more devastating as his reign progressed. As many of the recipients of *beneficia* had not demonstrated loyalty and *gratia*, Commodus and Cleander required a financial contribution for imperial favours, honours and some minor posts which were granted in return for bribes. However the context of this policy is understandable and should be judged from the perspective of an ancient society where such financial transactions were widely prevalent. Yet the Roman elite considered themselves a class apart from those of lower status who considered this an everyday fact of life. To the Roman aristocrat this was another indignity forced upon them in order to humiliate and degrade their *nobilitas*. Pertinax, pressured by his aristocratic backers, rescinded Commodus' financial measures, only to find within weeks that they were a necessity as the state faced bankruptcy. He faced the public humiliation of having to reintroduce many of them. Commodus, unlike his predecessor and successors, did not bury his head in the sand when faced with the structural deficit in state finances, but the situation would not be solved until Caracalla extended Roman citizenship to all provincials, thereby vastly increasing the numbers liable to the taxes associated with citizenship.

As a young man touring the eastern provinces with his father, Commodus must have been struck by the Hellenistic worship of the imperial person as a god. Temples and sacrifices were made to the Greek pharaohs of Egypt and the Seleucids who had ruled much of the near east. Commodus was already the son of the deified Marcus Aurelius and Faustina and his prowess in the arena drew comparison to the martial qualities of Hercules. Commodus, like Hercules, saw himself as the defender of mankind whose actions would usher in a new golden age. Like Hercules he confronted death both in the arena and in his escape from almost incessant threats to his life. Hercules achieved immortality through his deeds, his own good deeds would assure his own immortality. His presentation of himself in the arena was essentially a religious and political propaganda; the future prosperity of Rome, the empire and its people was dependent on the life of Commodus, reborn as the 'Roman Hercules'. The message was proclaimed on coinage and medallions, dedications on altars, the renaming of the grain fleets, the months of the year, the renaming of military units and Rome itself, refounded after its destruction and devastation in the great fire. Hercules himself had founded cities; the Roman Hercules had refounded Rome for the benefit not just of its own populace but the peoples of the whole empire. In his role as emperor Commodus was the supreme patron and protector of mankind. Grain was provided to the population of the capital, collected under the shadow of a vast statue to Hercules and sacrifices were made to win the support of the gods by the God Emperor Commodus, whose very survival demonstrated Jupiter's divine favour. The empire was protected by an army led by Commodus and financed by him, worshipped by soldiers who associated their emperor with Hercules the hunter and warrior. Statues across the empire demonstrated the popularity and resonance of this association. In the Greek east cities asked for permission to rename themselves or their games in his honour or build temples to celebrate the new Hercules. Although these official demonstrations of loyalty may be motivated by the desire for future honours and privileges from the emperor, personal dedications suggest that imperial propaganda took a firm hold amongst the population as a whole. Mosaics have been uncovered imitating official imperial motifs of Commodus depicted as Hercules, as well as statues of the Roman Hercules and dedications on altar stones.

We are presented with two extremes; the senatorial sources present the reign of Commodus as one of iron and rust, whilst imperial propaganda heralds the birth of a new golden age. For the senatorial aristocracy this was indeed a period of ever reducing power and influence. Personal access to the emperor was now filtered by his Praetorian Prefect or *cubicularius*. Although the morning *salutatio* continued, this was not the ideal situation to have requests considered by the emperor or favours granted. Commodus had ceased to invite the senatorial elite to his official banquets where the aristocrat could draw the emperor aside to petition on behalf of himself or a client or sit close enough to the imperial couch to engage in conversation. Increasing court hearings were held in private with the emperor seeking the advice of the equestrian Praetorian Prefects or other equestrians and freedmen. Yet not all senatorial careers suffered under Commodus' reign. Of his father's old *amici* some like Claudius Severus retired due to old age but his family continued to prosper, as did that of Gaius Bruttius Praesens, his son attaining the consulship of 187 AD. His father's close *amicus*, Victorinus, was City Prefect until his suicide, only to be replaced by another of Marcus Aurelius' *amici*, Fuscianus and then Pertinax. Other prominent generals of Marcus Aurelius continued to have illustrious careers, Clodius Albinus and Pescennius Niger amongst them. The ordinary consulship remained the preserve of the elite but Commodus was merely granting them the trappings and symbols of power. Acilius Glabrio shared the ordinary consulship of 186 AD with the emperor himself, but soon retired to his estates, excusing his absence on old age and failing health. There remained a direct interconnection between office and honour. This Augustan settlement had created a fundamental contradiction in the political and social structure of imperial rule.

The emperor was still required to communicate and interact with the aristocracy as if the old republic still existed, yet on another level it had to be made implicit that all power, wealth, honour and influence derived from the exalted position of the emperor. This made the political situation structurally unstable.[6] As long as the emperors continued to employ the traditional forms of political and social interaction using the traditional forms of *amicitia* to retain their own position the necessary changes would always be blocked. Through force of circumstance previous emperors had attempted to change this system through the rejection of these structures from the *res publica* for the creation of an absolute, autocratic monarchy which the Principate of Augustus had always been. Our senatorial sources however negate the actions of these emperors as the actions of mad men: Caligula, Nero, Domitian and Commodus. Winterling in his analysis of Caligula's alleged madness finds that this emperor's actions were based on clear logical thought processes laced with a cynical sense of humour. The ancient medical writer, A Cornelius Celsus, defined the symptoms of *insania* as irrational behaviour, unfounded fears and foolish talk. The fears of both Caligula and Commodus were not unfounded; their very murders suggested they each had to deal with a real and significant threat to their own existence. Both emperors' behaviour was clearly rational but to the aristocracy their very status was threatened by imperial policies. To the elite the very social fabric and cohesion was being undermined as the aristocracies' ability to maintain their *amici* and clients depended upon access to imperial *beneficia*.[7]

As Commodus found the reservoir of trusted senators increasingly reduced, no doubt made worse with deaths from the plague, he adlected many men who he could trust to the rank of praetor. He also appointed large numbers of suffect consuls who could be relied upon to take command of the provinces containing large numbers of troops, Septimius Severus amongst them. Although such appointments were made out of political and military necessity such actions angered the senatorial elite who felt their status was being undermined. These men, most with an interest in the preservation of Commodus' regime, were angered when their status was reduced by Pertinax under pressure from the nobility. These prominent individuals made up a significant proportion of the senatorial officers in the armies of Septimius Severus, Clodius Albinus and Pescennius Niger during the civil wars. The senate was a body divided against itself, many owing *gratia* to Commodus for their promotions and elevated status whilst significant numbers of the old aristocratic families schemed and plotted to remove the emperor for a candidate who would restore their privileged access to the imperial person. It was the latter group that the *delatores* targeted and it was this group who massed in the senate house on Commodus' murder, who were acclaimed as having been saved as if they had won a 'war'. Dio describes them as 'the senators on whom the fear of

Commodus had rested most heavily'.[8] In other words there was another group of senators who had little or nothing to fear from the emperor. For the senatorial elite this was indeed a period of iron and rust, yet their ranks were to be decimated in the purges following the civil war and the survivors would live in just as much fear of Septimius Severus and his son Caracalla.

The equestrian class appears to have gained additional influence under Commodus. Increasing numbers of this order were granted senatorial status, the *latus clavus*, by the emperor, and for the first time one of their number, an *a rationibus*, is described in a letter sent to Athens in 186 AD as a member of the imperial *consilium*. Furthermore Perennis, suspecting the loyalty of the senatorial legates in command of the British legions after the soldiers attempted to acclaim Priscus emperor, recalled them and placed the legions under the temporary command of their equestrian officers. Commodus was more concerned with ability rather than nobility and recognized the professionalism of these imperial officials, including the low-born freedmen. During the nearly incessant civil wars following his murder, Commodus' position would become the norm with equestrians attaining ever greater power and influence until one, Macrinus, was acclaimed emperor in 217 AD on the murder of Caracalla, without previously holding senatorial status.

Like all emperors Commodus used 'bread and circuses' to retain the loyalty of the populace of Rome whose adversaries were the senatorial elite, making them Commodus' natural ally. The plague must have ravaged their numbers yet, despite a grain shortage caused partly by the plague and made worse by the treasonable actions of some imperial officials, the emperor retained their affection. When fire destroyed many residential areas of the city, the emperor was on hand directing his soldiers in the creation of fire breaks. His rebuilding of the city was interrupted by his untimely death and it was left to others to claim the recognition for the rebuilding projects he had started.

The security of the empire was never seriously threatened by external invasions. The Danube remained secure and an invasion of Dacia and Moorish incursions were effectively dealt with. The most serious threat came from the invasion of Britain at the start of his reign and the destruction of 'the wall', identified by most historians as Hadrian's Wall. Another of Marcus Aurelius' generals, Ulpius Marcellus, was restored to his former post as governor and threw the barbarians back, campaigning even beyond the wall itself. However the strict discipline he enforced and the lack of a donative caused by the financial restraints Commodus and Perennis were operating under caused a revolt amongst these legions, which was crushed with some difficulty by Pertinax. Legionary unrest in Pannonia was probably associated with the activities of Plotianus, and was easily dealt with. The greatest disturbances to the provinces in both extent and threat were the Deserters' War, caused partly by the continued northern wars of Marcus Aurelius drawing troops away from the interior towards the borders of the empire and enforced conscription. Once effective military action was taken by Commodus, Maternus was forced into the desperate measure of attempting the assassination of the emperor himself. Unrest in Africa was similarly dealt with without the need for expensive military intervention. From 180 AD until 192 AD the majority of the empire experienced widespread peace and security. Even a potential rebellion in Syria being organized by Julius Alexander was dealt with efficiency and speed before it broke out. Archaeological surveys show prosperity being restored to the provinces to the south of the Danube but the plague continued to ravage large areas.

The history of the Roman Empire under Commodus was not an era of ' iron and rust', except for some of the leading aristocratic families, just as Roman history under Marcus Aurelius was not a golden age, except for the same aristocratic elite who had unhindered access to imperial *beneficia*. Commodus reacted to the threats to his person with the same policies and actions as other emperors who faced a similar situation. It would have been expected that Commodus would have studied the reign of Caligula as they shared the same birthday and faced the same threats from members of the imperial family and the aristocratic elite. At first Caligula had ruled, according to the senatorial sources, in a praiseworthy manner, but in 39 AD he discovered a plot against his life led by many of the aristocratic ex consuls. In a rage he entered the senate chamber to praise his predecessor Tiberius who had executed many senators on the charge of *majestas*. He publicly examined every case demonstrating that it was the senators themselves who were responsible for their sentences 'some by accusing them, others by testifying against them, and all by their votes of condemnation'. And he added: 'If Tiberius really did do wrong, you ought not by Jupiter, to have honoured him while he lived, and then, after repeatedly saying and voting what you did, turn about now.' Later in his speech he theatrically takes the role of the dead Tiberius who addresses his successor Caligula:

In all this you have spoken well and truly. Therefore show no affection for any of them and spare none of them. For they all hate you and they all pray for your death; and they will murder you if they can. Do not stop to consider then, what acts of yours will please them nor mind it if they talk, but look solely for your own pleasure and safety, since that has the most just claim. In this way you will suffer no harm ... you will also be honoured by them, whether they wish it or not. If however you pursue the opposite course it will profit you naught in reality; for in name you will win an empty reputation, you will gain no advantage, but will the victim of plots and will perish ingloriously.

If Commodus read this speech, as he surely would have, he might have paused at this point, reflecting on his own experiences. His father had taken the opposite course advocated by Caligula in the guise of Tiberius, and faced the revolt of the aristocratic Avidius Cassius whom he had repeatedly honoured and counted as his *amicus*. He would have considered the role of his own mother in this plot and later his own sister, both drawing heavily on aristocratic support within the senate. Commodus had followed his father's advice in working with the senatorial elite left to him as his guardians but the conspiracy of Lucilla had led him to question this course, the 'conspiracy of Perennis' had led him to reject it outright. Commodus, returning to the words on the scroll in front of him, continued to read Caligula's advice: 'For no man living is ruled by his own free will; on the contrary, only so long as a person is afraid, does he pay court to the man who is stronger, but when he gains courage, he avenges himself on the man who is weaker.' The speech is remarkable in its resonance through the ages, the Emperor Septimius Severus over 150 years later would stand in the same spot and rage against the senatorial elite, drawing attention to their hypocrisy, their fickle praise of Commodus whilst he lived, their vitriolic condemnation of him in death, but most of all he came to the same conclusion praising the cruelty of Sulla, Marius and Augustus whilst those who chose the 'milder' course were murdered. Then, like Commodus, Domitian, Nero and Caligula, he ruled with a fist of iron keeping the survivors of his purge of the aristocracy at arm's length.[9]

What was this other course that Commodus chose? It appears very similar to that of Caligula; indeed the ancient sources draw our attention to the similarities between their reigns. According to the *Historia Augusta* Commodus put to death a man for merely reading Suetonius' account of the life of Caligula. The real reason for this man's fate has been placed out of context by our source yet it shows that even contemporaries were aware of the similarities in their rule.[10] Winterling suggests that Caligula wished to create an autocratic monarchy on Hellenistic models, disavowing the Augustan settlement and establishing his imperial household as the government, his freedmen were given power and functions which elevated them above the position of the aristocracy; for Caligula's Helicon and Callistus read Commodus' Cleander and Eclectus. Caligula, like Commodus, raised himself above the aristocracy by acquiring from the senate divine honours, extending the palace down towards the Forum so the entrance was guarded by the Temples of Castor and Pollux. A golden statue was erected with a temple to the emperor and its own college of priests whilst Caligula himself appeared in public wearing attire associated with the gods. So Commodus had statues of himself wearing the adornments of Hercules erected around Rome including the giant colossus outside the coliseum. Commodus did not go as far as Caligula who ordered aristocrats to prostrate themselves before him and offering his feet to be kissed, but he did use pseudo religious ceremonial to distinguish his person and role far above that of the aristocracy. He carried the lion skin and club of Hercules before him in procession whilst wearing imperial purple trimmed with gold. The imperial extravagance displayed in the palace and at elaborate banquets were an ostentatious statement of wealth and power which not even the wealthiest aristocrat could ever hope to compete with. The creation of an imperial autocracy was a natural progression from the compromise that Augustus created 200 years previously, a political structure that was unstable. The Roman system of government did evolve into this autocratic monarchy. By the time of Diocletian at the end of the following century the senatorial aristocracy in Rome had been completely separated from the real fountain of power, the emperor. Court pseudo religious ceremonial raised the emperor, surrounded by officials of the imperial household and personal attendants, far above mere mortals. The emperor was venerated as the embodiment of Rome itself, appointed by the gods to rule and closer to the divine than the rest of humanity.[11]

The death of Commodus brought about nearly 100 years of instability, barbarian invasion and civil war, competing generals raised to the imperial purple by armies whose loyalty no longer rested on a dynasty that was traced back through imperial adoption to the first century Emperor Nerva. With the death of Commodus the Roman Empire did indeed enter an era of 'iron and rust'. Had he lived he may have managed the transition from the Principate to the absolute monarchy of the later Roman Empire with less bloodshed and upheaval. The army, imperial household and the vast majority of the population remained loyal to his name even after his death. For many, despite the plague and rising costs of food, this was a golden age. However even if Commodus had lived, it is doubtful that political unrest would have been averted. Even if he died a natural death, he had no children. Any children he had with Marcia would be considered illegitimate and her low status precluded official marriage. His nearest relative was the son of prominent aristocrat Claudius Pompeianus who would appear to have acquired the name Commodus in recognition of his claim to be Commodus' successor. Another alternative would have been Marcus Peducaeus Plautius Quintillus, married to his sister Fadilla and himself related to Marcus Aurelius' coemperor Lucius Verus. Yet both were scions of senatorial aristocratic houses and were more likely to chose the 'milder' course and perpetuate the existing political system despite its inherent instability and paradoxes.

Commodus appears as a totally rational yet imperfect human being, capable of making mistakes, feeling pain, suffering and desiring love. He lived most of his life under the shadow of sudden death yet attempted to rise above this. His elaborate ceremonial and presentation of himself as the 'Roman Hercules' in the arena for which he is mostly remembered was ultimately in order to symbolize his deeds and labours as the 'helper of mankind'. In 197 AD the Emperor Septimius Severus elevated his 'brother' Commodus to the realm of the gods which he commemorated on coins. 'Herculanius' Commodus was granted his own priests and religious observance of his birthday. The new god seated on high would have laughed at the irony of it all; the senate, at the wishes of an emperor their own actions helped to place on the throne, was forced to pass a decree granting divine honours to a man whom they had considered 'debased'.[12]

Notes and References

Introduction

1. *Historia Augusta* (HA), *Verus*, 8.1 (Loeb Classical Library, Harvard University Press).
2. HA, *Verus*, 2.4.
3. HA, *Verus*, 8.8–9.3.
4. Seneca, *De Beneficii* 1.5.5 (Loeb Classical Library, Harvard University Press); R P Saller, *Personal Patronage under the Early Empire* (Cambridge University Press, 2002) pp. 12–15.
5. R P Saller, *Personal Patronage under the Early Empire*, pp. 59–62.
6. A Birley, *Marcus Aurelius: A Biography* (Routledge, 2001) pp. 152–7; HA, *Marcus Aurelius*, 14.5.
7. *Dio, Roman History* 72.22.1 (Loeb Classical Library, Harvard University Press).
8. *Dio*, 72.10.1–4.
9. A Birley, *Marcus Aurelius: A Biography*, p. 174.
10. *Dio*, 72.7.1–5.
11. A Birley, *Marcus Aurelius: A Biography* p 176.
12. Brian Campbell, *The Roman Army; A Sourcebook* (Routledge, 1994) pp. 64–65.
13. *Dio*, 72.36.4

Chapter 1

1. *Herodian*, Book 1. 5 in Loeb edition; HA, *Marcus Aurelius* 19.1–9; Geoff W Adams, *The Emperor Commodus; Gladiator, Hercules or Tyrant?* (BrownWalker Press, 2013) pp. 76–77.
2. HA, *Commodus*, 1. 8 in Loeb edition.
3. *Herodian*, 1.2.1.
4. HA, *Commodus*, 1.5–6.
5. *Galen*, 16.650.
6. Grosso, *Lotta politica*, pp. 122–3.
7. A R Birley, *Marcus Aurelius*, pp. 197–8; *Dio*, 73.1.1; HA, *Commodus*, 1.7; Fergus Millar, *The Emperor in the Roman World* p. 92, 105 and 497; A R Birley, *Marcus Aurelius*, p. 206; Philostratus, *Life of the Sophists* 2. 12; Marcus Aurelius, *Meditations*, 1.17.4 and 1.17.7; *Herodian*, 1.13.7–8; G Adams, *The Emperor Commodus* (BrownWalker Press, 2013) pp. 85–87.
8. HA, *Commodus*, 1.5–6; O Hekster, *Commodus, An Emperor at the Cross Roads* (Amsterdam, 2002) p. 90 citing BMCRE 3 nos 136–140, 936–941 and pp. 118–119; Geoff Adams, *The Emperor Commodus* p. 74 and 77; Fronto, *Correspondence* (Ad Antoninum Imp i.3).
9. *Herodian*, 1.13.1 in Loeb; O Hekster, *Commodus* p. 90; HA, *Commodus*, 10.3.
10. Marcus Aurelius, *Meditations*, X, 27.

11. HA, *Verus* 1.1 and 4.2; E Champlin *Fronto and Antonine Rome* (Harvard University Press, 1980) p. 140. Full name Lucius Ceionius Aelius Commodus Verus Antoninus but he did not bear all these names at the same time.
12. HA, *Verus*, 2.5–7.
13. HA, *Verus*, 4,7–9; HA, *Marcus Aurelius*, 12.8.
14. Tertullian, *Apologeticus*, Chapter 33,4.
15. HA, *Marcus Aurelius*, 12,7–12; HA, *Verus*, 3.6; HA, *Marcus Aurelius*, 15.1.
16. Augustine, *Confessions*, 6.8.13; HA, *Marcus Aurelius*, 12.12; Cohen, 3, p. 169.
17. HA, *Marcus Aurelius*, 13, 5.
18. HA, *Verus*, 8.8 and notes in Loeb.
19. HA, *Verus*, 8.11 and notes in Loeb; HA, Verus, 1.9.
20. HA, *Verus*, 8.9.
21. *Dio*, 71.3.1a and A R Birley, *Marcus Aurelius*, p. 149.
22. A R Birley, *Marcus Aurelius*, pp. 150–151; HA, *Marcus Aurelius*, 13. 2–5.
23. Frag. Vat 195 and A R Birley, *Marcus Aurelius*, p. 155.
24. HA, *Verus*, 9.3–6; HA, *Marcus Aurelius*, 14.1.
25. *Dio*, 73.1.2 and 73.16.2; *Herodian*, 1,6.1; HA, *Verus*, 9.7.
26. HA, *Verus*, 9.3.
27. See stemma in A R Birley, *Marcus Aurelius*, p. 238.
28. HA, *Verus* 7.11 and notes.
29. D Potter, *The Roman Empire at Bay* p. 92; ILS 406; ILS 1909
30. *Herodian*, 1.13.8 see notes. Another freedman at court was Pylades, referred to as *temris sui primus* (ILS 5186) who would survive the fall of Commodus to have influence under Emperor Didius Julianus: A R Birley, *Marcus Aurelius*, p. 159.
31. Frank McLynn, *Marcus Aurelius, Warrior, Philosopher, Emperor* p. 445; HA, *Marcus Aurelius*, 20.6–7 and 21.9; *Dio*, 73.4.5; HA, *Verus*, 10.3–4; A R Birley, *Marcus Aurelius*, p. 161; *Herodian*, 1.8.4; Eutropius, *Breviarum*, 8.13; A R Birley, *Marcus Aurelius*, p. 160.
32. *Dio*, 71.32.1; Corpus Medicorum Graecorum 5.8.1; 130.11–132; *Galen*, pp. 661–4 and Frank McLynn, *Marcus Aurelius, Warrior, Philosopher, Emperor* p. 349.
33. *Galen, On Prognosis* 10.22,12.1–12.
34. See stemma in A R Birley, *Marcus Aurelius*, p. 236 and 238.
35. HA, *Marcus Aurelius*, 21.4–5.
36. Frank McLynn, *Marcus Aurelius, Warrior, Philosopher, Emperor* p. 355.
37. HA, *Didius Julianus*, 1. 6–7.
38. HA, *Marcus Aurelius*, 21.10 and notes in Loeb.
39. HA, *Pertinax*, 2.4.
40. HA, *Pertinax*, 1.5– 2.5 and notes in Loeb edition.
41. HA, *Pertinax*, 7.7.
42. Cambridge Ancient History, 2nd Edition Vol XI (2000) p. 171.
43. Lilybaeum, AE 1964, 181 and A R Birley, *Marcus Aurelius*, p. 174.
44. Carnuntum, AE 1982, 778 and Oliver Hekster, *Commodus: An Emperor at the Crossroads* (Amsterdam, 2007) p. 32.
45. RIC III. 296 no 1046 (dated 171/2 AD).
46. *Herodian*, 1. 3 –5; HA, *Commodus*, 11. 13–14.
47. Philostratus, *Lives of the Sophists* II,1; HA, *Commodus*, 1.11 and 12.2; Cohen iii, p311 no 599.

48. Frank McLynn, *Marcus Aurelius, Warrior, Philosopher, Emperor* p. 359; Richard P Saller, *Personal Patronage under the Roman Empire* p. 56 cit Philostarus, *Lives of the Sophists.*
49. HA, *Commodus*, 1.9.
50. *Dio*, 73.1.1.
51. HA, *Commodus*, 8.5.
52. A R Birley, *Marcus Aurelius*, p. 186.
53. *Dio*, 72.22.2.
54. *Dio*, 72.28.2.
55. *Dio*, 72.22.3.
56. *Dio*, 72.22.2.
57. *Dio*, 72.10.5.
58. HA, *Marcus Aurelius*, 24.6–7.
59. HA, *Marcus Aurelius*, 24.7 and HA, *Avidius Cassius*, 7.2–3 (*Dio*, 72.23.1–2 however states Avidius Cassius seized upon a rumour of the emperor's death to the make his bid for the throne).
60. Philostratus, *Lives of the Sophists* 2.1.13.
61. *Dio*, 72. 23.3 -27.1.1; Fronto, *Epistula Faustinae ad Marcum* 10.1.
62. L' Annee epigraphique (Paris 1888 ff) or AE 1920. 45 (Sabinianus).
63. HA, *Commodus* 2.1.
64. Cohen iii p266 f., nos 291–294.
65. A R Birley, *Marcus Aurelius* p. 187; G Adams, *The Emperor Commodus* pp. 90–91.
66. Amanda Claridge, *Rome, an Oxford Archaeological Guide* (Oxford University Press) pp. 185–6.
67. *Dio*, 72. 27. 3–28.1; O Hekster, *Commodus* pp. 91–2.
68. *Dio*, 72. 28.2.
69. HA, *Avidius Cassius*, 9. 4–5 and A R Birley, *Marcus Aurelius* p. 192.
70. HA, *Marcus Aurelius*, 25. 5–12.
71. HA, *Marcus Aurelius*, 26. 10–12.
72. Frank McLynn, *Marcus Aurelius, Warrior, Philosopher, Emperor* p. 381 and CIL xiii 1680, 6768.
73. *Dio*, 72. 29.1–2.
74. *Dio*, 72. 27.3.
75. A R Birley, *Marcus Aurelius*, p. 189.
76. Frank McLynn, *Marcus Aurelius, Warrior, Philosopher, Emperor* p. 382.
77. HA, *Pertinax*, 2.10.
78. *Dio*, 72. 29.2.
79. A R Birley, *Marcus Aurelius*, p. 190–1 and Frank McLynn, *Marcus Aurelius, Warrior, Philosopher, Emperor* p. 383.
80. *Dio*, 72.29.1.
81. *Dio*, 73.7.4.
82. HA, *Marcus Aurelius*, 19.1–2; 27. 11–12; 29.1 and *Herodian*, 1.3.1.
83. Inge Mennen, *Power and Status in the Roman Empire, AD 193–284* p. 151.
84. ILS 1344 (Ephesus).
85. Fergus Millar, *The Emperor in the Roman World* (Duckworth, 1977).
86. HA, *Marcus Aurelius*, 26. 5 and *Dio*, 72.29.1.
87. A R Birley, *Marcus Aurelius*, p. 191.

88. HA, *Marcus Aurelius*, 26. 4–10; *Dio*, 72.29.1, 72.30.1.
89. A R Birley, *Marcus Aurelius*, p. 191 and Frank McLynn, *Marcus Aurelius, Warrior, Philosopher, Emperor* p. 387.
90. Philostatus, *Lives of the Sophists*, 2.1.12.
91. Philostatus, *Lives of the Sophists*, 2.7.
92. *Dio*, 27. 31.1.
93. HA, *Marcus Aurelius*, 25. 7–12.
94. *Ammianus Marcellinus*, 22.5.5.
95. HA, *Marcus Aurelius*, 26.1.1.
96. HA, *Pertinax*, 2.10; HA, *Marcus Aurelius*, 26.13; O Hekster, *Commodus* p. 175.
97. O Hekster, *Commodus* pp. 175–7; Philostratus, *Lives of the Sophists*, 2.9.2.
98. HA, *Marcus Aurelius*, 27.1.
99. A R Birley, *Marcus Aurelius* p. 194.
100. A R Birley, *Marcus Aurelius* p. 194.
101. *Dio*, 27. 31.3.
102. *Dio*, 27. 32.1–2.
103. See Cohen iii p228 nos 1–2 as cited in HA, *Commodus*, 2.3 Loeb edition; Q Hekster, *Commodus* p. 91 citing RIC 3, nos 510,517–9,1391; G Adams, *The Emperor Commodus* p. 93–7; Szaivert 'Munzpragung'no1072.
104. 103 HA, *Commodus*, 2.4 and HA, *Marcus Aurelius*, 22.12.
105. HA, *Marcus Aurelius*, 16.2.
106. HA, *Marcus Aurelius*, 27. 5.
107. Martin Beckman, *Column of Marcus Aurelius: the Genesis and Meaning of a Roman Imperial Monument* (University of North Carolina Press, 2011) Chapter one, The Date and Purpose of the Column; G Adams, *The Emperor Commodus* p. 119. Adams (p. 39) assumes the Column of Marcus Aurelius was completed in 193 AD but fails to explain why Commodus fails to appear in it if by his calculations it was completed in his reign.
108. Marcus Aurelius, *Meditations*, 9.11, 10.4 and see 11.18.
109. Oliver Hekster, *Commodus: an Emperor at the Crossroads* (Amsterdam, 2007) pp. 23–5; G Adams, *The Emperor Commodus* pp. 49–50.
110. A Birley, *Hadrian: The Restless Emperor* (London, New York, 1997) pp. 289–90).
111. *Herodian*, 1.5.5.
112. Michael Grant, *The Antonines: the Roman Empire in Transition* (Routledge, 1996) p. 62.
113. ILS 398.
114. Dio, 73.22.6.

Chapter 2

1. Fergus Millar, *The Emperor in the Roman World* (Duckworth, 1977) pp. 15–17 and 241.
2. Pliny, *Pan.*, 79.7.
3. Philostratus, *Lives of the Sophists*, VS 2,1; Codex Justinianus CJ IX 51,1.
4. Richard P Saller, *Personal Patronage under the Early Empire* (Cambridge University Press, 1982) p. 61–2 citing Seneca.
5. Suetonius, *Vespasian*, 2.3.
6. Richard P Saller, *Personal Patronage under the Early Empire* pp. 62–69.

7. Epictetus, *Discourses*, 4.1.47f.
8. Epictetus, *Discourses*, 2.14.18.
9. Pliny, *Letters*, 1.18.3.
10. Suetonius, *Vespasian*, 21.
11. *Dio*, LXXVI. 17,1–3.
12. *Dio*, LXXI.6.1.
13. Digest 1,18,14 as quoted in Fergus Millar, *The Emperor in the Roman World* (Duckworth, 1977) and A Birley, *Marcus Aurelius: A Biography* p. 199.
14. Digest 44.2.1 and cited in A Birley, *Marcus Aurelius: A Biography* p. 200.
15. Digest 36.1.23 and cited in Frank McLynn, *Marcus Aurelius: Warrior, Philosopher, Emperor* p. 407.
16. Digest 48.5.53 (32) and cited in A Birley, *Marcus Aurelius: A Biography* p. 199.
17. Digest 48. 5.39 (38) and cited in A Birley, *Marcus Aurelius: A Biography* p. 199; A Garzetti, *From Tiberius to the Antonines* p. 544.
18. *Dio*, 72.33.1.
19. A Birley, *Marcus Aurelius: A Biography* p. 198 and notes p. 287; Frank McLynn, *Marcus Aurelius: Warrior, Philosopher, Emperor* p. 645; HA, *Didius Julianus*, 1.9.
20. HA, *Pertinax*, 2.11.
21. Digest II. 4.1 and cited in A Birley, *Marcus Aurelius: A Biography* p. 201.
22. Digest 29.5.2 and cited in A Birley, *Marcus Aurelius: A Biography* p. 201.
23. Frank McLynn, *Marcus Aurelius: Warrior, Philosopher, Emperor* p. 409 and notes p. 645; A Birley, *Marcus Aurelius: A Biography* p. 204; O Hekster, *Commodus* p. 153 citing CIL 6.632=EAOR I 55–6 no 46; Micheal Jarrett, *A study of Municipal Aristocracies of the Roman Empire* p. 163.
24. Eusebius, *The History of the Church* 5. 1.4–51. See also A Birley, *Marcus Aurelius: A Biography* p. 202–3.
25. Richard J A Talbert, *The Senate of Imperial Rome* (Princeton, 1984) p. 291 and Frank McLynn, *Marcus Aurelius: Warrior, Philosopher, Emperor* p. 409.
26. Fergus Millar, *The Emperor in the Roman World* (Duckworth, 1977) p. 342.
27. Richard J A Talbert, *The Senate of Imperial Rome* (Princeton, 1984) p. 240–252.
28. HA, *Marcus Aurelius*, 27.6.
29. Richard J A Talbert, *The Senate of Imperial Rome* (Princeton, 1984) p. 291–2.
30. A Birley, *Marcus Aurelius: A Biography* p. 201.
31. CIL VIII. 10570.
32. Fergus Millar, *The Emperor in the Roman World* (Duckworth, 1977) p. 2445–7.
33. HA, *Commodus*, 13.7.
34. A Birley, *Marcus Aurelius: A Biography* p.205.
35. Tony Honore, *Ulpian: Pioneer of Human Rights* (Oxford University Press, 2002) p. 154 citing Digest 12.3.10; 22.3.26; 40.10.3; 25.3.6.1; O Hekster, *Commodus* p. 75 note 195 (citing Digest: 12.3.10; 22.3.26; 25.3.6; 27.1.6.8;35.3.6;40.10.3; 49.14.31); G Adams *The emperor Commodus* p. 120; HA, Commodus 13.3; Eusebius, *History of the Church* 21.5.
36. Philostratus, *Lives of the Sophists* 2.9.
37. Dio, 72. 32.3.
38. A Birley, *Marcus Aurelius:A Biography* p. 204.
39. Herodian, 2.3.3.
40. Fergus Millar, *The Emperor in the Roman World* (Duckworth, 1977) p. 95.

41. HA, *Commodus*, 4.8.

42. Fergus Millar, *The Emperor in the Roman World* (Duckworth, 1977) p. 124.

43. *Dio*, 73.10.1 and *Herodian*, 1.8.1.

44. Philip Barker, *The Empire stops Here* (Pimlico) p. 191 and 195.

45. HA, *Marcus Aurelius*, 27.8.

46. Philostratus, *Lives of the Sophists* 2.12.

47. Fergus Millar, *The Emperor in the Roman World* (Duckworth, 1977) pp. 190–201.

48. *Dio*, 72.33.2–3.

49. R Syme, *The Roman Revolution* (Oxford University Press) pp. 73 and 386.

50. Seneca, *De Benificia* 1.5.5.

51. R P Saller, *Personal Patronage under the Early Empire* (Cambridge University Press, 1982) pp. 41–57.

52. *Dio*, 72.33.3.

53. Birley, *Marcus Aurelius: A Biography* p. 187.

54. Birley, *Marcus Aurelius: A Biography* p. 142 and Frank McLynn, *Marcus Aurelius: Warrior, Philosopher, Emperor* p. 413.

55. HA, *Pertinax*, 2.11.

56. Birley, *Marcus Aurelius: A Biography* p. 205 citing Digest 38.17.

57. Fergus Millar, *The Emperor in the Roman World* (Duckworth, 1977) p105 citing ILS 1344 (Ephesus).

58. *RIB* 594: The inscription was dedicated by a *singularius consularis*, an officer nominally appointed to the staff of the consular governor, who had specific and widely varying duties. Julius Maximus was perhaps sent to watch over the Ribchester garrison, because the quarrelsome and truculent natures of these auxiliary soldiers could only be dealt with by someone possessing a bit more 'clout' than an ordinary *praefectus*.

59. Peter Salway, *History of Roman Britain* (Oxford University Press, 1997) p. 160. Caerellius Priscus : His rule as governor is recorded on an altar at Mainz, and he probably governed Britain between 178 AD and 180 AD. He also served in Thracia, Moesia, Raetia and Germania. See also Birley, *Marcus Aurelius: A Biography* p. 251.

60. A Birley, *Marcus Aurelius: A Biography* p. 207.

61. *Dio*, 72.33.3.

62. *Dio*, 72.33.4.

63. *Aurelius Victor*, 16. 12.

64. *Dio*, 72. 18.1.

65. *Dio*, 72. 21.

66. *Dio*, 72.18–19.

67. HA, *Marcus Aurelius*, 24.5 and 27. 9–11.

68. *Dio*, 72. 20.2 and 72.33.4.

69. A Birley, *Marcus Aurelius: A Biography* p. 254 and Oliver Hekster, *Commodus: an emperor at the Crossroads* (Amsterdam, 2007) p. 42.

70. *Herodian*, 1.6.7; *Dio*, 73.2 and HA, *Commodus*, 3.5.

71. Frank McLynn, *Marcus Aurelius: Warrior, Philosopher, Emperor* p. 414.

72. *Dio*, 72.20.1–2.

73. Jessica Vahl, *Imperial Representations of Clementia: from Augustus to Marcus Aurelius* (2007) MA dissertations DigitalCommons@Master: McMaster University p. 52.

74. *Dio*, 72.20.1–2.
75. *Dio*, 72.20.1 states Marcus Aurelius' campaigns against the Marcomanni and Quadi were not for conquest of land but to inflict vengeance for attacks on the empire. Also *Gladiator* edited by Martin Winker (Blackwell Publishing, 2005) Arthur Eckstein, *Commodus and the limits of the Roman Empire* p. 56 onwards.
76. *Herodian*, 1.3. 5.
77. *Dio*, 72.36.2.
78. *Herodian*, 1.3. 5.
79. HA, *Marcus Aurelius* 28. 1–3 and Aurelius Victor *Epitome de Caesaribus*, 17.
80. *Dio*, 33.4.
81. *Herodian*, 1.4.1–6.
82. *Dio*, 72.34.1
83. G Adams, *The Emperor Commodus* pp. 129–137; F Grosso, *La Lotta Politica al Tempo di Commodo* (Academia delle Scienza) (Turin, 1964); *Herodian*, 1.4.7; HA, *Marcus Aurelius* 18.1–3 and 19.1–5; *Dio*, 72.33 and 34.1.

Chapter 3
1. *Dio*, 73.12.
2. *Herodian*, 2.3.3.
3. HA, *Marcus Aurelius*, 20.6.
4. *Herodian*, 1.6.6.
5. *Herodian*, 1.2.2.
6. A Birley, *The African Emperor, Septimius Severus* p. 79.
7. A Birley, *Marcus Aurelius, A Biography* p. 244 and 247.
8. *Herodian*, 1.5.1.
9. *Dio*, 72.34.110 and HA, *Marcus Aurelius*, 18.2–4.
10. F Millar, *Emperor in the Roman World* pp. 355–360.
11. *Herodian*, 1.5.1–8; G Adams, *The Emperor Commodus* p. 135.
12. *Herodian*, 1.6.1–8; HA, *Commodus*, 3.5; *Dio*, 73.2.
13. *Dio*, 73.2.
14. HA, *Marcus Aurelius*, 27.11.
15. *Herodian*, 1.3.5. See Oliver Hekster, *Commodus: an emperor at the Crossroads* (Amsterdam, 2007) pp. 40–41 for discussion of attitudes of modern historians to Commodus' peace settlement.
16. Eutopius, *Breviarium*, 8.15; Orosius, *Christian History*, 7.16.1; O Hekster, *Commodus* p. 169; Michael Jarrett, *A Study of the Municipal aristocracies of the Roman Empire in the West, with special reference to North Africa* (Durham University, 1958) e theses pp. 231–2 citing VIII 619 =11780 = ILS 2747.
17. *Dio*, 73.2.1–4 and 3.1–2 and note 1p75.
18. *Dio*, 73.8.2.
19. JC Mann (Hermes 91 iv 1963 487 to 8) shows that RIB 2148 an altar from Castlecary RIB2148 records a vexillation from 2nd Legion Itallica reinforcing 6th Legion after its losses in the invasion; M Brassington 'Ulpius Marcellus' Britannia Vol 11/November 180 pp. 314–15.
20. D Mattingly, *An Imperial Possession; Britain in the Roman Empire* (Penguin, 2007) and David Breeze, *The Northern Frontiers of Roman Britain* (Book Club Association, 1982) p. 126.

21. Guy de la Bédoyère, *Roman Britain: a New History* (Thames and Hudson 2010) Ulpius Marcellus is testified as governor on a diploma of 178 AD, and leading the Roman army in a British war of about 184 AD under Commodus by Dio. He also appears on an inscription from Chesters recording *aqua adducta*, 'the bringing of water' by *ala II Asturum* during his governorship. He thus served under Marcus Aurelius (161–80 AD), and Commodus (180–92 AD), and during their period of joint rule (177–80 AD) explaining an inscription from Benwell where he is named as serving under unspecified joint emperors.

22. *Herodian*, 1.6.1–8.

23. Herodian mentions without criticism the importance of a new emperor returning to Rome e.g. *Herodian*, 3.15.6 on the death of Severus, Caracalla rushes back to Rome and *Herodian*, 5.2.3 criticizes Macrinus who also was involved in military matters at the time, for not making for Rome himself on his accession where 'he was wanted and the people were continually calling for him in noisy demonstrations' i.e. Roman plebs expect return with increasing unrest. *Elagabalus*, 5.5.1 hurries to Rome after the death of Macrinus without negative comment.

24. *Dio*, 72.36.4 and Oliver Hekster, *Commodus: an emperor at the Crossroads* (Amsterdam, 2007) p. 43 citing D Rathbone, *Villages, land and population in Graeco-Egypt* PCPhS n.s. 36 (1990) 103–42;114.

25. *Dio*, 73.1.2.

26. *Dio*, 73.2.1–4.

27. *Herodian*, 1.6.8–9.

28. *Herodian*, 1.7.1.

29. *Dio*, 73.2.2–3.

30. F Millar, *The Roman Empire and its Neighbours* (Duckworth, 1981) p. 230 and Corpus Inscriptionum Latinarum 3.3385, CIL 3.14370 (=ILS 5338); G Adams, *The Emperor Commodus* p. 263 citing CIL II.6057.

31. Philip Parker, *The Empire Stops Here* (Pimlico, 2009) Aalen pp. 144–5, Ellingen pp. 147–8, Oescus pp. 220–2, Apulum pp. 268–9 and Napoca p. 270; M Grant, *The Antonines* p. 184; C Ruger, *Roman Germany* Cambridge Ancient History XI pp. 635–63; A Garzetti, *From Tiberius to the Antonines: A History of the Roman Empire AD 14–192* (Methuen and Co Limited, translated by J R foster) p. 531. R J A Wilson, *What's New in Roman Baden-Württemberg?* JRS Vol 96 November 2006 p198-212

32. See *Commodus and the limits of the Roman Empire* by Arthur Eckstein, p. 56 onwards in *Gladiator: Film and History* (Blackwell, 2005); F Millar, *The Roman Empire and its Neighbours* p. 230.

33. F McLynn, *Marus Aurelius: Warrior, Philosopher, Emperor* p. 424.

34. *Herodian*, 1.6.1.

35. Statius, *Silv*, III.3 and PIR c860.

36. Pliny, *Panegyric*, 88, 1–2.

37. Cambridge Ancient History: *The High Empire* p. 209. It is reported of Vespasian that one of his most trusted *ministri* had requested for someone whom he claimed to be his brother the post of *dispensator* in the treasury, which was responsible for receiving and paying out money. Since the *dispensator* always had to be a slave, the supposed brother must also have been a slave or freedman. The request was completely successful, although in this case Vespasian himself collected the

sum which had been agreed for the appointment, since he had seen through his minister's intention.7575 Suet. *Vesp.*, 23.2. 76; *Dio*, LXVI. 14.1 ff.

38. HA, *Commodus*, 3.6.
39. F Millar, *Emperor in the Roman World* p. 81.
40. *Herodian*, 1.6.4.
41. HA, *Marcus Aurelius*, 14.5–6.
42. *Herodian*, 1.7.2–4.
43. F Millar, *Emperor in the Roman World* pp. 31–2 citing Mamertinus' account of the journey of the Emperors Diocletian and Maximian in 290/1 in Panegyric III (II) 10.5.
44. *Herodian*, 1.17.12; HA, *Commodus*, 17.3.
45. HA, *Commodus*, 13.1–2 the writer citing the Senator Marius Maximus and his biography of Commodus as his source. *Dio*, 74.2.3.
46. Eleonora Cavallini, 'Was Commodus that bad?' in *The Fall of the Roman Empire: Film and History* edited by Martin Winkler (Wiley Blackwell, 2009) pp. 102 –116. Restoration of peace must have been welcome by large sectors of Roman population exhausted by war. Eusebius in his Ecclesiastical History (History of the church) quoting an anti Monatanist treatise which probably arose in 172 AD says: 'Surely it is now obvious that this … is a lie?' (Referring to the prophesies of the Montanist Maximilla which foretold long wars and anarchy) 'today it is more than 13 years since that woman's death, and there has neither been general nor local war in the world, but rather – even for Christians – continuous peace, by mercy of God', Eusebius, *Ecclesiastical History*, 5.16.19. The 13 years must coincide with Commodus as the Marcomannic Wars preceded his reign and those wars of Severus waged after it. Otherwise dating would extend to 232 which would have been too late for the treatise as it refers to Montanism as a recent movement. Composition probably around 192. Commodus also left Christians undisturbed as reflected in *Dio*.
47. Fergus Millar, *A Study of Cassius Dio* (Oxford, 1964) p. 14.
48. *Dio*, 73.4.3.
49. *Herodian*, 1.7.6.
50. Oliver Hekster, *Commodus: An Emperor at the Crossroads* (Amsterdam, 2007) p. 47 citing AER 1953.79.
51. Fergus Millar, *A Study of Cassius Dio* (Oxford, 1964) p. 120; G Adams, *The Emperor Commodus* p. 268 citing CIL 14.2922. F Millar, *The Roman Empire and its Neighbours* p. 180; A Garzetti, *From Tiberius to the Antonines* p. 535.
52. *Dio*, 73.1.2 and *Herodian*, 1.8.3.
53. *Herodian*, 1.8.1.
54. Oliver Hekster, *Commodus: An Emperor at the Crossroads* (Amsterdam, 2007) p. 38.
55. Oliver Hekster, *Commodus: An Emperor at the Crossroads* (Amsterdam, 2007) pp. 44–45 citing Duncan Jones, 'The Impact of the Antonine Plague' figs 2–11, 13, 16–8.
56. A Birley, *Marcus Aurelius, A Biography* p. 159; *Cambridge Ancient History: The High Empire* p. 169; R P Duncan Jones, 'Impact of the Antonine Plague', *Journal of Roman Archaeology* 9 (1996) pp. 108–136.
57. *Dio*, 73. 3.2–3.

58. *Dio*, 73.8.1; HA, *Niger*, 1.5.
59. Commodus was acclaimed Imperator for the fifth time (see Cohen III2 p. 337, nos. 840–847) as cited in Loeb edition of HA, *Commodus*, 13.5 note 2; Zsuzsanna Varhelyi, *The Religion of Senators in the Roman Empire: Power and Beyond* (Cambridge University Press, 2010) p. 103.
60. F Millar, *A Study of Dio* by Millar p. 128; Gauis Vettius Sabinianus had a distinguished military record having served as Governor of Pannonia Superior and for loyal service during the revolt of Avidius Cassius had been appointed suffect consul in approximately 176 AD and then he served as imperial legate in Dalmatia dealing with bandits. In 179 AD the emperors appointed him Governor of Dacia, a post he was to hold until 182 AD when he was again appointed by Commodus to Pannonia. His illustrious career was to end with appointment to governorship of Africa in 191 AD; HA, *Didius Julianus* 1.9 and 7.5; J E H Spaul, *Governors of Tingitana* in Antiquites Africaines 1994 vol 30 pp. 246–7; Malalas, *Chronicle* 12.2.3 which O Hekster, *Commodus* p. 84 believes was based on local sources.
61. O Hekster, *Commodus* p. 84 citing CIL 2.1405; AE 1912.136 (=ILS 9467); CIL 2.4114 (=ILS 1140); For imperial banquets see *Dio*, 73.4.5 and proposed links to Pompeainaus, *Dio*, 73.4.3–4.
62. P A Brunt, 'Administration of Roman Egypt', p. 141 *Journal of Roman Studies 65*, (1975).
63. Oliver Hekster, *Commodus: An Emperor at the Crossroads* (Amsterdam, 2007) p. 50 note 61 citing CIL 6.2010a; R P C Weaver, *Familia Caesaris, A Social Study of the Emperor's Freemen and Slaves* (Cambridge, 1972) p. 43, 282–3; G Adams, *The Emperor Commodus* p. 168.
64. *Dio*, 73.12.2.
65. Richard J A Talbert, *The Senate of Imperial Rome* (Princeton University Press, 1984) p. 422.
66. Richard P Saller, *Personal Patronage under the Early Empire* pp. 61–9.
67. Pliny, *Paneg* 23.3.
68. Seneca, *De Ben* 1.5.45.
69. Richard P Saller, *Personal Patronage under the Early Empire* pp. 9–10.
70. Martial, *Epigrams* XII, 29.
71. Richard P Saller, *Personal Patronage under the Early Empire* p. 66; Epictectus Discourses 41.148.
72. Oliver Hekster, *Commodus: An Emperor at the Crossroads* (Amsterdam, 2007) p. 52; Aloys Winterling, *Caligula* (University of California Press, 2011) pp. 16–19.
73. Oliver Hekster, *Commodus: An Emperor at the Crossroads* (Amsterdam, 2007) p. 52 note 72 points to Diana Lucifera and Iuno Lucina on coinage indicating hope of a birth, and Fecundiatas could mean actual birth: RIC 3, nos 666–7, 680. Cf. BMCRE 4, clxxix. Theory first developed by J Aymard, *La conjuration de Lucilla*, REA 57 (1955), pp. 85–91; 88–91. For Lucilla's complaints see Herodian, 1.8.3–4.
74. *Dio*, 73.4.5.
75. *Dio*, 1.8.4; A Birley, *Septimius Severus: The African Emperor* (Batsford, 1988) p. 61; Oliver Hekster, *Commodus: An Emperor at the Crossroads* (Amsterdam, 2007) p. 52; F McLynn, *Marus Aurelius: Warrior, Philosopher, Emperor* pp. 427–8.

76. *Dio*, 73.4.4.
77. *Herodian*, 1.8.5. However verb used could be future tense: note 2.
78. *Dio*, 73.5.3–4.
79. CIL VI 2099.12 note 3 in Loeb translation of *Dio* Book 1 p. 47. For alternative dates and further discussion of date of conspiracy see Oliver Hekster, *Commodus: An Emperor at the Crossroads* (Amsterdam, 2007) p. 52 note 70.
80. *Dio*, 73.4.4. The late historian Ammianus Marcellinus 29.1.17 says Commodus suffered an almost fatal dagger wound to the hand from the Senator Quintianus, 'a man of lawless ambition'.
81. Oliver Hekster, *Commodus: An Emperor at the Crossroads* (Amsterdam, 2007) p. 53 and John Charles Traupman, 'The Life and Reign of Commodus', *Ph.D thesis* (Princeton, 1956) p. 49; A Garzetti *From Tiberius to the Antonines* p. 532.
82. HA, *Commodus*, 4.4 and 6–7; *Herodian*, 1.8.8.
83. HA, *Commodus*, 4.2 and 4.7.
84. David Potter, *The Roman Empire at Bay* AD *180–385* (Routledge, 2004) p. 68; Note in Loeb edition of Herodian Book 1 p. 49 note 4 citing Grosso, *Lotta politica* 34 and 39.
85. S Bingham, *The Praetorian Guard: A History of Rome's Special Forces* (I B Tauris and Co Ltd, 2013) p. 91.
86. HA, *Commodus*, 4. 5–7.
87. *Dio*, 73. 10.1
88. CIL VI 41273; Cleander involved in plot: *Dio*, 73.12.2. Adlection of Paternus, see F Millar, *Emperor in the Roman World* p. 295.
89. *Dio*, 73.5.1–2.
90. HA, *Commodus*, 3.1.
91. *Dio*, 73.5.3.
92. F Millar, *A Study of Cassius Dio* (Oxford University Press, 1964) pp. 124–5.
93. HA, *Commodus*, 4.9–10. On Aquilius Felix: HA, *Didius Julianus* 5.8; HA, *Niger* 2.6; HA, *Septimius Severus* 5.8; CIL 10.6657=ILS1387; AE1945.80 on rise to a *censibus equitum Romanorum* and Oliver Hekster, *Commodus: An Emperor at the Crossroads* (Amsterdam, 2007) p. 58 note 104.
94. HA, *Pertinax*, 3.1–2; 9.7; 3.3.
95. Severus' Fourth Legion: HA, *Severus*, 3.6; HA, *Commodus*, 4.9; A Birley, *Septimius Severus: The African Emperor* p. 73; HA, *Commodus*, 5.13.
96. Richard P Saller, *Personal Patronage under the Early Empire* pp. 71–2 citing *Dio*, 58.4.5.
97. F Millar, *A Study of Cassius Dio* (Oxford University Press, 1964) pp. 124–5 and CIL 3.12487/CIL816530, CIL 22689; D Potter, *From Tiberius to the Antonines* pp. 532–3.
98. *Herodian*, 1.6.6 and *Dio*, 73.20.1.
99. *Cambridge Ancient history: The High Empire* p. 184.
100. *Herodian*, 1.8.7.
101. Richard P Saller, *Personal Patronage under the Early Empire* p. 73. citing R Syme, *The Roman Revolution*.
102. O Hekster, *Commodus* pp. 92–3.
103. HA, *Commodus* 9.6; O Hekster, *Commodus* p. 132; Robert Turcan, *The Cults of the Roman Empire* p. 244 citing CIL XIV, 66.

Chapter 4

1. F Millar, *Emperor in the Roman World* pp. 521–22; Aloys Winterling, *Caligula* pp. 26–28; Aloys Winterling, *Politics and Society in Imperial Rome* (Wiley-Blackwell, 2009) p. 112; *Dio*, 59.16.2–4.
2. Oliver Hekster, *Commodus, An Emperor at the Crossroads* p. 68; HA, *Pertinax*, 9.10; HA, *Didius Julianus*, 2.2; *Dio*, 74.11.2.
3. HA, *Severus*, 4.3–4.
4. Eusebius, *The History of the Church*, 5.21; HA, *Commodus*, 18.1–19–9 on the senate's reaction to Commodus' death. For Pertinax's measures see HA, *Pertinax*, 6.8;7.1; *Herodian*, 2.4.8.
5. HA, *Commodus*, 5.1.
6. *Herodian*, 1.11.5.
7. *Herodian*, 1.9.2.
8. On rejection of advice of Laetus and Eclectus, *Herodian*, 2.2.6. Appointments see *Herodian*, 1.10.5.
9. *Herodian*, 1.9.1; HA, *Severus*, 4.4; HA, *Commodus*, 3.5, 8.1 and 9.10.
10. *Dio*, 73.8.3 and 73.17.3; HA, *Commodus*, 5.1 and 13.6; HA, *Niger*, 3.5; James H Oliver, 'The Sacred Gerusia and the Emperor's Consilium', *The American* www.ascsa.edu.gr/pdf/uploads/hesperia/147433.pdf; HA, *Pertinax* 3.9–10.
11. *Herodian*, 1.9.9; 1.10.2; *Dio*, 73.16.3; HA, *Pertinax*, 3.5; CCLXXVII.3 (1972),11, no2.
12. *Herodian*, 1.13.7; *Dio*, 74.11.2; HA, *Pertinax*, 3.7.
13. *Herodian*, 1.13.7; HA, *Severus*, 4.5.
14. *Dio*, 73, 11, 1–2; Philostratus, *Life of the Sophists* 2. 12; PIR2, G 80.
15. HA, *Commodus*, 9.1 and J Reynolds, *Aphrodisias and Rome* (London, 1982) pp. 118–24 no 16 and p. 448 no 125, chapter 15 section 5.
16. HA, *Commodus*, 13.6–8.
17. F Millar, *Emperor in the Roman World* p. 242 as evidenced on papyri and inscriptions.
18. *Dio*, 73.9.2; *Herodian*, 9.1; HA, *Commodus*, 5.2.
19. F Millar, *Emperor in the Roman World* pp. 122–131.
20. Hekster, *Commodus: the Empire at the Crossroads* pp. 55–6; Aloys Winterling, *Politics and Society in Imperial Rome* p. 48 and 91; HA, *Pertinax*, 13.3.
21. O Hekster, *Commodus*, pp. 179–80; *Dio*, 73.11.11–2. Perennis' son *Herodian*, 1.9.1. Herodian mentions two sons but later only mentions one and only one is mentioned in *Dio*. It may be that he had two sons of whom only one was old enough to be appointed to such a post. There is no epigraphical record of this appointment and governors of the Pannonias at this time are conjectural. In Pannonia Superior: C Vettius Sabinianus whilst in Pannonia Inferior L Septimius Flaccus attested for 180/2 and L Cornelius Felix Plotianus in 184/5; Michael Jarrett, *A Study of the Municipal Aristocracies of the Roman Empire*, pp. 135–8 based on ILA 297 cf PIR A 1247, AE 1954, 58.
22. Loeb, HA, *Didius Julianus* p. 360 note 1 citing CIL iii. 1092; Hekster, *Commodus: the Empire at the Crossroads* p. 62; Karol Klodzinski, *Equestrian cursus honorum* based on the careers of two prominent officers of the Emperor Marcus Aurelius in www.academia.edu/1872904/Equestrian_cu; Seius Fuscianus in HA, *Marcus Aurelius*, 3.8; HA, *Commodus*, 12.10.

23. HA, *Marcus Aurelius*, 29.1 and HA, *Commodus*, 8.1.
24. James H Oliver, 'The Sacred Gerusia and the Emperor's Consilium' in *The American* pp. 329–34 www.ascsa.edu.gr/pdf/uploads/hesperia/147433.pdf.
25. HA, *Commodus*, 5.4;11.1–5; HA, *Pertinax*, 8.5.
26. Richard P Saller, *Personal Patronage in the Early Empire* p. 62.
27. HA, *Pertinax*, 6.2.
28. *Dio*, 74.3 4.
29. Pliny, *Epistles* (Letters), 10.58.7–8; Aelius Aristides Or. XXX Keil 28 and Richard P Saller, *Personal Patronage in the Early Empire* p. 41.
30. Epictetus, *Mor.*, 470c.
31. Seneca, *De ira*, III,31,2 as quoted in F Millar, *Emperor in the Roman World*.
32. *Dio*, 73.16.2; Richard P Saller, *Personal Patronage in the Early Empire* pp. 50–51.
33. *Herodian*, 1.8.2.
34. *Dio*, 74.3.4; Seneca, *De Beneficiis*, 1.1.1 and 2.1.1; Aloys Winterling, *Caligula* p. 121; Aloys Winterling, *Politics and Society in Ancient Rome* p. 41, 53–55, 80 and 92–93; John Crook, *Consilium Principis: Imperial Councils and Councillors from Augustus to Diocletian* (Cambridge, 1955) p. 104.
35. Edward Champlin, *The Heirs of Commodus* p. 297–9; *Dio*, 74.2.3.
36. Richard P Saller, *Personal Patronage in the Early Empire* pp. 12–15,35–45, 69–78; Seneca, *De Ben*, 1.5.5 and *De Clem*, 1.13.5, Pliny, *Ep*, 10.5 and 10.6.
37. Michael Grant, *The Antonines; The Roman Empire in Transition* (Routledge, 1996) p. 76.
38. HA, *Commodus*, 16.3.
39. HA, *Commodus*, 12.11.
40. HA, *Commodus*, 12.11.
41. HA, *Pertinax*, 8.4; *Dio* 76.8.3 and David Potter, 'Gladiator: Gladiators and Blood Sport' in *Gladiator: Film and History* (Blackwell, 2008) pp. 73–86.
42. Allen Ward, 'Gladiator in the Historical Perspective' in *Gladiator: Film and History* Ed by Martin Winkler pp. 39–40.
43. *Dio*, 73.17.2–3; HA, *Commodus*, 5.5 and 11.10; Suetonius, *Caligula*, 32.2.
44. *Herodian*, 1.13.8; 1.17.11, HA, *Commodus*, 2.9; *Dio*, 73.10.2 and 73.17.1.
45. Suetonius, *Caligula*, 18.3. David Potter, 'Gladiator: Gladiators and Blood Sport' in *Gladiator: Film and History* (Blackwell, 2008) pp. 73–86.
46. Deborah Chatr Aryamontri: Montclair University http://www.montclair.edu/chss/center-heritage-archaeological-studies; HA, *Commodus*, 8.5.
47. Amanda Claridge, *Rome: an Oxford Archaeological Guide* (Oxford, 2010) pp. 434–7; G Adams, *The Emperor Commodus* pp. 195–8; HA, *Commodus*, 11.5.
48. Notes from Loeb: HA, *Life of Commodus* p. 296 citing Dessau, *Inscriptiones Selectae* p. 396; HA, *Commodus*, 13.8; Successes in Mauretania: (L'Annee Epigraphique Paris (AE) 1888–) 1953, 79, AE 1957, 203 and Dessau *Inscriptiones Latinae Selectae* p. 386; F McLynn, *Marcus Aurelius*, p. 430 ff.
49. Sarmatian war dated to obverse of coin from 185 AD *VO DE SARMATIS* (BMC IV (1940) 166) (cf Grosso, *La lotta politica* … cit p. 489 n4.
50. P Kovacs, 'Burgus building instructions of Commodus from Pannonia', taken from *Sylloge Epigraphica Barcinonensis (SEBarc)* VI, (2008), pp. 125–138 (ISSN 2013–41180) citing M Sasel Kos, *A historical outline of the region between Aquileia, the Adriatic and Sirmium in Cassius Dio and Herodian* (Ljubljana, 1986) pp. 342–352

esp p. 347/8. (www.raco.cat/index.php?SEBarc/article/download/208217400); Also *Dio*, 74.6.1; HA, *Commodus*, 6.1; *Herodian*, 1.9.1.

51. F Miller, *A Study of Cassius Dio* (Oxford, 1964) p. 128 and *Dio*, 73.8.1; 73.8.

52. L. Junius Victorinus Flavius Caelianus: This man was legate of VI Victrix and recorded his exploits north of Hadrian's Wall on an altar found at Kirksteads, near Kirkandrews upon Eden. He can be inferred to have gone on to be legate of Germania Superior from a dedication at Stockstadt to Jupiter Optimus Maximus and his personal Genius by a member of the governor's staff, the *beneficiarius consularis* G. Secionius Senilis. Date is uncertain, but should precede the division of Britain, therefore c. 122–212.Source: *RIB* 2034 (Kirksteads); *RIB95*, 794, note to 2034; *CIL* xiii.6638 (Stockstadt). From *People of Roman Britain* by Guy de la Bédoyère.

53. P Sextianus [...]: Prefect of *ala Augusta* at Carlisle. The stone, a decorative window or niche, seems to date to about 180–92. Source: *RIB* 946 (Carlisle). From *People of Roman Britain* by Guy de la Bédoyère.

54. Peter Salway, *A History of Roman Britain* (Oxford University Press, 1997) pp. 162–3; M Grant, *The Antonines* p. 66 suggests Marcellus may have temporarily reoccupied the Antonine Wall at this point.

55. D Mattingly, *An Imperial Possession; Britain in the Roman Empire* (Penguin, 2007).

56. *Herodian*, 1.10.1–2. Some historians, including G Adams, *The Emperor Commodus* (2013) pp. 295–6 believe that as the account of Maternus and the Deserters' War only occurs in *Herodian*, it is purely a fictitious event. However they provide no substantial motive for Herodian to make up such an account when all other aspects of his work on the Emperor Commodus are supported by either Cassius Dio or the *Historia Augusta*. Indeed the growing body of both archaeological and epigraphical evidence confirms and supports the account of Maternus in *Herodian*.

57. Notes from Loeb, *Herodian*, pp. 61 and HA, *Commodus*, 13.5.

58. Thomas Grunewald, *Bandits in the Roman Empire: Myth and Reality* (Routledge, 2008) pp. 110–137; *Herodian*, 1.10.1.

59. Inscription from Aquae Flavia in Agri Decumates AE (1956) 90 cf Egger, Germania 36 (1958) 373–85.

60. Wax writing tablet from Agri Decumentes in Rottweil (AE 59 141); Inscription set up in the Italian district of Urvinum Mataurense in honour of its patron C Vesnius Vindex, military tribune of VIII Augusta during whose service the legion had been relived from 'the recent siege', the legion was given the titles 'faithful, constant, the emperor Commodus' own'. A Alfoldy in *Bellum Desertum* (1989) convincingly argues this was Maternus; all cited in Thomas Grunewald, *Bandits in the Roman Empire: Myth and Reality* (Routledge, 2008) pp. 110–137; *Cambridge Ancient History, The High Empire* p. 188; 'The Crisis of the Third Century AD in the Roman Empire: A Modern Myth?' Lukas De Blois found at *www.phil-fak. uni-duesseldorf.de/.../Blois.*

61. Michael Grant, *The Antonines* p. 149; (1956) S Szadeczky-Kardoss on basis of coin hordes pointed to destruction at Juliobona at mouth of Siene as in indication of Deserters War, S Szadeczky-Kardoss, *Juliobona es Maternus felkelese* ArchErt 83, (1956), pp. 18–23; K Hekster, *Commodus* p. 65.

62. Notes from Loeb, *Herodian*, p. 61 citing Loius, Rev Arch 11 (1938) 253.

63. G Mangard, *L'inscription dedicatoire du theatre du Blois l'Abbe a eu (siene-maritime)* *Gallia* 40 (1982) pp. 35–51 published his reconstruction of a building inscription of a temple in Blois l'Abbe probably from the Severan period by L Cerialis Rectus who cites one of his titles as an 'officer in charge of controlling banditry'. Also a remarkable number of coin hordes dating to the reign of Commodus (Mangard as above) in Haute Normande. G Ch. Picard, *La republique des Pictones* n105 555f Dem, *La revolte de Maternus* n 105 pp. 77–840 was able to show extensive unrest in the area south of the Loire in modern Poitou in territory of the Pictones showing destruction horizons from reign of Marcus Aurelius from the Marcomannic Wars to Commodus (Picard as above) including the civitas capital Limonum, modern Poitiers.

64. Inscription of L Artorius Castus, H G Pflaum, *Les carriers procuratoriennes equestres sous le Haut - Empire Romain*, vol 1 Paris (1960) 535ff no196). The inscription recounts his military career including that he led two British legions together with auxiliaries 'against the Aremoricans'. (CIL III 1919 with 14224 = ILS 2770 adversus Arm(oricano)s). On the basis of chronological indicators in the inscription this was around 181. Previous to this the memorial states he was commander of VI legion Victrix in Britain. Went on to have a successful career after serving in Armorica as centenary procurator. Taken from Thomas Grunewald, *Bandits in the Roman Empire: Myth and Reality* (Routledge, 2008) pp. 110–137. A second later inscription translation, Lucius Artorius Castus, Primus Pilus of the legion V Macedonica, Prefect of the Legion VI Victrix [...] Breeze, David John, Dobson, Brian, Roman Officers and Frontiers, Franz Steiner Verlag, (1993) p. 180.

65. *Herodian*, 1.10.3; HA, *Commodus*, 12.10. Also CIL 5.2155(=ILS 1574 also refers to the *expeditio III Germanica* whilst a revolt by Saturninus in the same area is also referred as Bellum Germanicum; CIL 6.1347 (=ILS 1006) See K Hekster, *Commodus*, p. 66; ILS 1574 quoted in *Cambridge Ancient History* Vol XI (Cambridge University Press, 2007) pp. 189–90; Jerzy Linderski, *Roman Questions II Habes)* (Franz Steiner Verlag Stuttgart, 2007) p. 242, 244–6, 256–8, 260–1: doubts link between a 'third German expedition' and the revolt of Maternus. However he does suggest that the besieged VIII legion was relieved by local levies commanded by Niger. This appears doubtful considering a whole legion had been unable to break the siege and yet locally raised part-time soldiers were able to do so.

66. *Dio*, 73.9.2 and HA, *Commodus*, 8.4.

67. HA, *Commodus*, 13.5.

68. Inscription recorded on an altar at Mainz in Germany refers to a Caerellius Marcianus ... with the last name missing but postulated as Priscus: his post in Britain is open to discussion with a governorship before 178 a possible suggestion but it makes more sense that he was a legate of one of the three British legions. The fate of Caerellius Priscus is unknown. He had a wife, Modestiana, a daughter Germanilla and a son Marcianus. Marcianus is identified with Caerellius Macrinus, in 197 AD on the orders of Emperor Septimius Severus he was executed, probably because he had supported his rival Clodius Albinus. *THRAC MOES SVP RAET GERM SVP ET BRITT ET MODESTIANA EIVS ET CAERELLII MARCIANVS ... ET GERMANILLA FILII*. 'Conqueror in *Thracia, Moesia, Raetia, Germania* and *Britannia*, Caerellius Marcianus

[Priscus?] and his family, Modestiana [his wife?] and his daughter Germanilla.' (*CIL* XIII.6806; *Ager Nerviorvm*).

69. HA, *Commodus*, 6.2 and 13.5; M Grant, *The Antonines* p. 66.
70. *People of Roman Britain* by Guy de la Bédoyère citing: *AE* (1965) p. 240 (Mainz); Birley (1971), p. 338.
71. *Dio*, 73.9.2.
72. HA, *Commodus*, 6.3. E J Brill, 'Leaders and Mass Movements in Late Antiquity: Studies in Honour of Zvi Ya'vets', edited by Irad Malkin and Z W Rubinsohn (1995) pp. 132–4; Paul Elliot 'The Legions in Crisis: Transformation of the Roman Soldier AD 192-284' Fonthill 2014 pp. 96–7.
73. *Herodian*, 1.93–6; Whittaker, *Historia*, 13 (1964) p. 365.
74. *Dio*, 73.9.4 and 12.2.
75. *Herodian*, 1.9.6.
76. *Dio*, 73. 10.1.
77. *Herodian*, 1.9.1.
78. HA, *Commodus*, 5.7.
79. F Millar, *A Study of Dio* p. 128.
80. *Herodian*, 1.2.5 and discussion of his status and occupation in introduction of Loeb edition pxix and following based on arguments put forward by Stein, *Dexippus et Herodianus* 72ff; Grosso, *Lotta politica* pp. 33–5; Cassola, *NRS* 41 (1957) p. 221.
81. *Herodian*, 1.9.1.
82. *Herodian*, 1 8.8 and F McLynn, *Marcus Aurelius*, pp. 430–2.
83. P A Brunt in Classical Quarterly 23 (1973) pp. 172–5 based on a differing translation of *Dio*, 72.9.2. HA, *Commodus*, 6.1 refers to 'deputies of the armies' which has been argued by Blunt to mean deputies of the 1,500 delegation of javelin men. However the wording in HA, *Commodus* is clear: *legati execitus*; legates of the army. The biographer of the Historia Augustus used the work of the contemporary senator Marius Maximus (*Commodus*, 15.5) and although clearly embellished the biographer would have no reason to change the wording of this earlier work; *legati*. To a senator such as Maximus with military experience *legatus* was a senior commander of senatorial rank whose *dignitas* would have been insulted if he were placed in command of javelin men.
84. *Dio*, 73.9.4; HA, *Commodus*, 6.2–4.
85. *Herodian*, 1.9.9–10.
86. Hekster, *Commodus*, p. 63.
87. HA, *Commodus*, 8.1 and note 1 to Loeb edition of *Herodian*, 1.9.10 p. 58.
88. De Ranieri, *La gestione politica* p. 412 as cited in Hekster, *Commodus*, p. 64.
89. Peter Kovacs, 'Burgus building inscriptions of Commodus from Pannonia' in *Sylloge Epigraphica Barcinonensis* (2008) p. 137 citing CIL VIII, 823.
90. Loeb edition of HA, *Commodus*, 8.2–4 note 3 citing Cohen iii p. 233 no 49.
91. O Hekster, *Commodus*, p. 94.

Chapter 5

1. Aloys Winterling, *Politics and Society in Imperial Rome* (Wiley Blackwell, 2009) p. 97.
2. See Chapter 1 p. 7; *Dio*, 73.4.6–7; ILS 5186; On Apolaustus; HA, *Verus*, 8.10. Verus maintained an actor called Agrippus, surnamed Memphius, whom he had

brought with him from Syria and he acquired the name Lucius Aurelius from his patrons. His status was almost equivalent to a trophy of war. His skills are reflected in his given name 'Apolaustus' meaning 'enjoyable'. He was a famous dancer and pantomime artist and a favourite of Lucius Verus. After his manumission he took the name L Aelius Aurelius Apolaustus Memphius suggesting he was manumitted by Commodus. He is commemorated in numerous inscriptions and received many honours in the cities of Italy; *Cambridge Ancient History* p. 210.

3. Philo, Legatio, 30; C De Ranieri, *Retoscena politici e lotte dinastiche sullo della vicenda di Aurelio Cleandro* RSA 27 (1997) p. 146 and 407.

4. O Hekster, *Commodus, An Emperor at the Crossroads* p. 68; *Cambridge Ancient History* p. 209 citing Oliver (1989) no. 209; on Cleander, cf. also Dio LXXII. 12.3 ff. and *AE* (1961) no. 280; *Dio*, 73.12.1–2; *Herodian*, 1.12.2 and note 3 page 75 of Loeb edition; Philo, *V A*, 8.7.12; Lucian, *Dialogues of the Dead*, 2; CIL 6.1847; *Cambridge Ancient History: The High Empire* p. 209.

5. F Millar, *Emperor in the Roman world* p. 81 citing ILS 1740, HA, *Verus*, 2.8 and Pflaum, *Carrieres*, no. 163.

6. *Dio*, 73.12.2.

7. F Millar, *Emperor in the Roman world* p. 81 citing AE (1952) 6; *Dio*, of Prusa *Third Discourse on Kingship* p. 132, 110, 120.

8. HA, *Pertinax*, 7.8–10; F Millar, *Emperor in the Roman world* p. 94.

9. *Herodian*, 1.13.1; Aloys Winterling, *Caligula* p. 123.

10. See PIR 2 A1088.

11. From Hyppolitus' *Philosophoumena*: 'Now, pretending that he (Callistus) was repairing as it were to his creditors, he hurried on their Sabbath-day to the synagogue of the Jews, who were congregated, and took his stand, and created a disturbance among them. They, however, being disturbed by him, offered him insult, and inflicted blows upon him, and dragged him before Fuscianus, who was prefect of the city. And (on being asked the cause of such treatment), they replied in the following terms: "Romans have conceded to us the privilege of publicly reading those laws of ours that have been handed down from our fathers. This person, however, by coming into (our place of worship), prevented (us so doing), by creating a disturbance among us, alleging that he is a Christian." And Fuscianus happens at the time to be on the judgment-seat; and on intimating his indignation against Callistus, on account of the statements made by the Jews, there was not wanting one to go and acquaint Carpophorus concerning these transactions. And he, hastening to the judgment-seat of the prefect, exclaimed, "I implore of you, my lord Fuscianus, believe not thou this fellow; for he is not a Christian, but seeks occasion of death, having made away with a quantity of my money, as I shall prove." The Jews, however, supposing that this was a stratagem, as if Carpophorus were seeking under this pretext to liberate Callistus, with the greater enmity clamoured against him in presence of the prefect. Fuscianus, however, was swayed by these Jews, and having scourged Callistus, he gave him to be sent to a mine in Sardinia.' Fuscianus was probably more concerned with the need to keep order in the city and Christians entering a synagogue to convert Jews could easily escalate to rioting in the volatile streets of the capital.

12. HA, *Commodus*, 6.10–11; HA, *Pertinax*, 3.4–5.

13. HA, *Didius Julianus*, 2.2; HA, *Septimius Severus*, 3.8; HA, *Pescennius Niger*, 3.3–5.

14. HA, *Severus*, 4.1.
15. Frank McLynn, *Marcus Aurelius* pp. 433–5; HA, *Clodius Albinus*, 6.4 and note 2 p. 472 in Loeb; *Herodian*, 1.10.3 note 2 p. 63 in Loeb edition.
16. See CIL 6.1408 (= ILS1141); 6.1409 (= ILS 1142); AE 1926.79. For his career, see PIR 2 F27; Alfoldy Senat, App.II, pp.141–142; Barbieri Albo, no.213, Barnes; A Birley, *Septimius Severus* p. 76.
17. HA, *Commodus*, 6.4 and 12.8; M Grant, *The Antonines* p. 184 citing RIC III p. 424 no 502.
18. *Dio*, 73.9.4; *Herodian*, 1.9.8.
19. HA, *Commodus*, 6.7; *Herodian*, 1.9.10 note 2 p. 59 in Loeb edition; *Women and Society in Greek and Roman Egypt: A Sourcebook* edited by Jane Rowlandson, Roger S. Bagnall (Cambridge University Press) p. 185; P A Brunt, 'The Fall of Perennis' in *Classical Quarterly 23* (1973) pp. 172–177; CIL III 14137=ILS 8998; A S Hunt and CC Edgar, *Select Papyri 2*, 315, 1963 as recorded in columbia.edu/cu/libraries/ins...nput/MiU_apis_20050623.txt; P. Oxy. II 237.
20. *Herodian*, 1.10.4.
21. O Hekster, *Commodus, An Emperor at the Crossroads* p. 66; Rottweil (AE 59 141) as cited in *Bandits in the Roman Empire: Myth and Reality* by Thomas Grunewald (Routledge); A Garzetti, *From Tiberius to the Antonines* p. 538.
22. *Herodian*, 1.10.5–7; Robert Turcan, *The Cults of the Roman Empire* (Blackwell, 2008) pp. 44–6; Thomas Grunewald, *Bandits in the Roman Empire: Myth and Reality* (Routledge).
23. *Herodian*, 1.10.4 and 1.10.7.
24. O Hekster, *Commodus* pp. 92–94; Robert Turcan, *The Cults of the Roman Empire* (Blackwell, 2008) pp. 46–49; HA *Commodus*, 8.1; HA, *Marcus Aurelius*, 19.7.
25. *Herodian*, 2.4.4; *Herodian*, 2.4.1.
26. *Herodian*, 1.12.2–3; HA, *Commodus*, 12.11.
27. *Dio*, 73.14.4; RJ and M L Littman, 'Galen and the Antonine Plague', *The American Journal of Philology* 94 no 3 pp. 243–255 (The John Hopkins University Press); Cheston B Cunha and Burke A Cunha, 'Great Plagues of the Past and Remaining Questions' pp. 12–14 in *Paleomicrobiology: Past Human Infections* edited by D Raoult and M Drancourt (Springer-Verlag Berlin Heidelberg, 2008).
28. Walter Scheidel, *Roman Well being and the economic consequences of the Antonine Plague* (Princeton/Stanford University Press, 2010) pp. 15– 21.
29. *Herodian*, 2.4.6.
30. O Hekster, *Commodus* p. 84; In the *Acta Appiani* (a scrap of which is in Yale University Library), Appian, a gymnasiarch of Alexandria, is portrayed as boldly resisting the Emperor Commodus to his face. He contrasts Commodus' avarice and dishonesty with the philosophic kindness of his father Marcus Aurelius. Appian is urged by his fellow-prisoner Heliodorus to go forth calmly to his death: it will be his glory to lay down his life for his native city, Alexandria (P. *Oxy.*, 33, ii, 7ff). *Herodian* Loeb edition p. 87 note 1 citing RIC III 422; HA, *Commodus*, 17.7; Paul Erdkamp, *The Grain Market in the Roman Empire* (Cambridge University Press) p. 230.
31. Michael Charles and Neal Ryan, *The Roman Empire and the Grain Fleets; Contracting out public services in Antiquity* (Queensland University of Technology) pp. 4–22.

32. Hekster, *Rome and its Empire* (Edinburgh) pp. 33–34; HA, *Pertinax*, 3.4; R P Duncan Jones, 'Effects of the Antonine Plague' in *Journal of Roman Archaeology* 9 (1996) pp. 108–136.

33. Frank McLynn, *Marcus Aurelius: Warrior, Philosopher, Emperor;* G Adams, *The Emperor Commodus* p. 39, 63; HA, *Pertinax*, 7.6; *Dio*, 74.5.4; O Hekster, *Commodus* pp. 98–102; G Adams, *The Emperor Commodus* pp. 209–216.

34. *Dio*, 73.16, 1–3; 74.6,2; 74,8,4; F Millar, *A Study of Cassius Dio* pp. 110–111.

35. *Herodian*, 2.4.7.

36. Statues: HA, *Commodus*, 9.2 and *Dio*, 73.15.6. Alimentia: HA, *Pertinax*, 9.3; Quote from *Dio*, 73.7.4. Buildings: HA, *Commodus*, 17.5–7; Amanda Claridge, *Rome: an Oxford Archaeological Guide* (Oxford University Press, 2010) p. 203 and 221; L Richardson, *A New Topographical Dictionary of Ancient Rome* (Hopkins University Press, Baltimore, 1992) p. 244; G Adams, *The Emperor Commodus* pp. 208–218; *Herodian*, 1.12.4–5; M Grant, *The Antonines: Roman Empire in Transition* (Routledge, 2005) pp. 73–4; HA, *Pertinax*, 9.3; HA, *Niger*, 6.8–9; on the distribution of congriarium in the reign see A Gazetti, *From Tiberius to the Antonines* p. 536 to 540.

37. O Hekster, *Rome and its Empire* (Edinburgh) pp. 33–34; Philip Parker, *The Empire Stops Here* (Pimlico, 2009) pp. 324–49; F Millar, *Emperor in the Roman World* p. 155, 171; Aloys Winterling, *Politics and Society in Ancient Rome* (Wiley-Blackwell, 2009) p. 59 and 70 -73; HA, *Severus*, 12.4. See *Dio*, 78.9.1–6 on revenues raised by Caracalla and 73.10.3 and 17.1 for distinction between Commodus' public and private actions; *Herodian*, 2.4.7; CIL VI 930=ILS 244.

38. Suetonius, *Nero*, 32; Tacitus *Annals*, 1.8.1; F Millar, *Emperor in the Roman World* p. 15; Aloys Winterling, *Politics and Society in Ancient Rome* p. 51.

39. *Dio*, 73 .16.2 Cf Exc Val as quoted in Loeb edition page 105; HA, *Commodus*, 5.14.

40. HA, *Pertinax*, 7.4–5; HA, *Commodus*, 7.8.

41. *Herodian*, 1.12.5.

42. *Dio*, 73.16.2; HA, *Commodus*, 9.1 and 16.7.

43. Nobles mocking Pertinax's austerity measures: *Dio*, 74.1.4; HA, *Pertinax*, 9.2.

44. HA, *Commodus*, 5.14.

45. HA, *Pertinax*, 7.2; *Dio*, 73. 16.2.

46. HA *Commodus*, 19.6.

47. *Dio*, 73.12.3 and 75.2.2.

48. Suetonius, *Vespasian*, 23.2; Aloys Winterling, *Politics and Society in Imperial Rome* p. 89.

49. *Dio*, 73.11.4 and 756.2; Eusebius, *A History of the Church*, 18.5; O Hekster, *Commodus* pp. 79–80 citing CIL 2.1405.AE 1912.136 (=ILS 9476), CIL 2.4114 (=ILS 1140); Michael Jarrett, *A Study of the Municipal Aristocracies of the Roman Empire,* pp. 208–9; G Adams, *The Emperor Commodus* p. 257; J M Hojte, *Roman Imperial Statue Bases: from Augustus to Commodus* (Aarhus University Press, Aarhus 2005) pp. 571–89; A Garzetti, *From Tiberius to the Antonines* p. 543; D Potter, *The Roman Empire at Bay* p. 94.

50. Richard Saller, *Personal Patronage under the Early Empire* pp. 10–17; *Dio*, 73.12.3; *Ammianus Marcellinus*, 26, 6, 9; HA, *Commodus*, 14.4 and 19.6; *Dio*, 73.10.2.

51. *Dio* 74.5.3.

52. O Hekster, *Commodus, An Emperor at the Crossroads* p. 68; Dio 7312.4; HA, *Commodus*, 6.9–10; HA, *Severus*, 4.4.
53. HA, *Clodius Albinus*, 1.3; HA, *Niger*, 1.3; Inge Mennon, *Power and Status in the Roman Empire*, AD 193–284 pp. 107–118; Edward Champlin, 'The Heirs of Commodus' in *The American Journal of Philology* Vol 100, no2 (The John Hopkins University Press, Summer, 1979) pp. 288–306.
54. J M Reynolds - J B Ward Perkins, *The Inscriptions of Roman Tripolitania* (London, 1952); C De Ranieri, *Retoscena politici e lotte dinastiche sullo della vicenda di Aurelio Cleandro* RSA 27 (1997) pp. 155–6; Richard Talbert, *The Senate of Imperial Rome* pp. 240–48; Michael Grierson, *A Study of the Municipal Aristocracies in the Roman Empire in the West, with special reference to North Africa* (1958) (Durham e-theses-Durham University found at http://etheses.dur.ac.uk/1980/) pp. 129–30 based on VIII 9374, VIII 17900=ILS1436, VIII 17899, AE 1901,195 and 1949, 38 p. 159, no. 606 = AE, 1953, 188. See also CIL, XIV, 2121 = ILS, 5193, HA, *Commodus*, 6.9; HA, *Pertinax*, 7.1 and 6.10–11.
55. *Dio*, 73.16.3; Orosius, *Christian History*, 7.16.2; Eusebius, *Chron. Rom*, 15.9; O Hekster, *Commodus* p. 79.
56. *Dio*, 73.12.5.
57. *Dio*, 73.8.6.
58. HA, *Pertinax*, 3.7–10, *Dio*, 74.41–3; M Henig, 'The Victory Gem from Lullingstone Roman Villa' in *Journal of the British Archaeological Association* 160 (2007), pp. 1–7.
59. HA, *Pertinax*, 4.1–3; HA, *Commodus*, 6.11; *Dio*, 74.4.2–4.
60. HA, *Commodus*, 6.11 and 7.1; HA *Pertinax*, 3.7.
61. PIR 2 A1088; Frank McLynn, *Marcus Aurelius* p. 434; A Birley, *Marcus Aurelius* p. 134, 157, 191; Anamarija Kurilic, *Ruling Class of Asseria: Magistrates and Benefactors and their familiae and families* nrcak.srce.hr/file/59664; Charles Klodzinski, *Praetorian Prefects of the Emperor Commodus* KLIO PL ISSN 1643–8191, Vol 20 (1) 2012 pp. 3–44; CIL 6,31154; CIL VI 3682= CIL VI 31158; A Birley, *Septmius Severus* p. 77; M Grant, *The Antonines* p. 10.
62. HA, *Pertinax*, 3.7–8; HA, *Commodus*, 6.11.
63. CIL VI.798; ILS 1327 (CIL VI. 31,856); *Dio*, 73.14.1; HA, *Verus*, 8.10; HA, *Commodus*, 7.2 and 11.3; *Herodian*, 1.13.8; Paul Richard Carey Weaver, *Famila Caesaris* p. 27.
64. HA, *Commodus*, 6.8 and 6.13; *Herodian*, 1.12.3 and 1.13.1; *Dio*, 73.13.5; Hekster, *Commodus* p. 70; F Millar, *A Study of Dio* p. 130; J H Oliver, *Three Attic Inscriptions Concerning the Emperor Commodus* AJPh 71 (1950) 170 on pp. 178–9; AE (1961) 280 = Moretti RFIC 38 (1960) 68; Frank Mclynn, *Marcus Aurelius* p. 434.
65. *Herodian*, 1.12.3–5.
66. F Millar, *Emperor in the Roman World* p. 94; HA, *Commodus*, 7.1; HA, *Pertinax*, 3.7; *The Cambridge Ancient History* Volume XI (Cambridge University Press, 2007) pp. 189–190.
67. *Dio*, 73.13.1; HA, *Commodus*, 9.1; HA, *Pertinax*, 4.1–2.
68. Richard Saller, *Personal Patronage under the Early Empire* pp. 12–14; Gilbert Picard, *Rev Hist. Relig.* 155 (1959) pp. 41–62.
69. *Herodian*, 3.10.6; *Dio*, 74.15.4; A Birley, *Septimius Severus* p. 93.

70. Stephen Benko, *The Virgin Goddess; Studies in Pagan and Christian Roots of Mariology* (Leiden, 2004) pp. 30–35; HA, *Macrinus*, 3.1; Augustine, *Enarratio in Psalmum*, 62.7; Augustine, *City of God*, 7.26; HA, *Commodus*, 14.3; Robert Turcan, *The Cults of the Roman Empire* pp. 58–9, 180–183.

Chapter 6
1. *Dio*, 73. 13.1; Tacitus, *Annals*, 3.54.3; The British Museum, 'Catalogue of the Greek Coins' (*BMC*) Londres 1873–1927 (reimpr 1963–1965); A Bonti and Z Simonetti, 'Corpus Nummorum Romanorum' (*CNR*) (Firenze, 1972–79) no 522.
2. David Kessler and Peter Temin, 'The Organisation of the Grain trade in the Early Roman Empire', *Economic History Review* 60 (2007); Alessandro Cristofori, *Grain Distribution in Late Republican Rome* University of Bologna; Juvenal, *Satires*, 10.81; Tacitus, *Histories*, 1.73.
3. *Herodian*, 1. 12.3; *Dio*, 73.13.3; C R Whittaker, 'The Revolt of Papirius Dionysius AD 190' *Historia* 13 (1964) p. 355.
4. Michael Charles and Neal Ryan, 'The Roman Empire and The Grain Fleets: Contracting out of Public Services' (Queensland University of Technology) pp. 1–22; O W Reinmuth, 'A Working list of the Prefects of Egypt: 30 BC–299 AD' Vol 4, Issue 4, *The Bulletin of the American Society of Papyrologists*, (Michigan Publishing) p. 102; De Ranieri, 'Retroscena Politici' pp. 184–5 as quoted in Hekster, *Commodus* p. 73 note 186 demonstrates that Papirius Dionysius never set foot in Egypt and Cleander's appointment of him as Prefect of the Annona was due to his need for a capable administrator in this post. However Cleander must have been aware of the affront such a recall would cause and the reappointment of a man who resented his demotion from his previous post would not result in an efficient administration. His reappointment must either be due to the fact his successor had not yet been appointed and so he was asked to fill the office until a successor was appointed, or Papirius Dionysius still held the confidence of the emperor despite the *cubicularius'* suspicions . Events seem to support the latter as the conspiracy was directed at Cleander only, Commodus escaping any criticism for the famine.
5. *Herodian*, 1.12.5; *Dio*, 73.13.1–6; C R Whittaker, 'The Revolt of Papirius Dionysius' pp. 348–69 and following; Suetonius, *Caligula*, 55.2; H H Scullard, *Festivals and Ceremonies of the Roman Republic* (Thames and Hudson, 1981) pp. 177–8, 181, 205–7.
6. *Herodian*, 1.12.6 to 1.13. 4.
7. *Dio*, 73.13.4–6; F Millar, *A Study of Cassius Dio* pp. 130–1.
8. Alfody, *Cleanders Sturz* pp. 94–110.
9. HA, *Commodus*, 7.4; *The Cambridge Ancient History* Vol XI (Cambridge University Press, 2007) pp. 189–190.
10. *Herodian*, 1.12.9 note 2 p. 81 of Loeb edition and 1.13.1–4 and 1.17.7 note 2 on p. 116; A Birley, *Septimius Severus* p. 244 note 26.
11. *Dio*, 73. 4.6–7 and 73.13.5; *Herodian*, 1.17.6; HA, *Verus*, 9.7; CIL 10.5918.
12. Hekster, *Commodus* p. 74 note 193; Amanda Claridge, *Rome, An Oxford Archaeological Guide* pp. 434–8; J Humphrey, *Roman Circuses: Arenas for Chariot*

Racing (Berkley, 1986) p. 76 discounts the higher figures for the capacity of the Circus Maximus suggesting a figure of 150,000.

13. HA, *Commodus*, 7.2 and 14.2–2; *Herodian*, 1.13.4–6; *Dio*, 73.13.5–6.
14. HA, *Septimius Severus*, 4.4–5.
15. HA, *Didius Julianus*, 2.3.
16. W Fröhner, *Les Médaillons de l'empire romain, depuis le règne d'Auguste jusqu'à Priscus Attale* (Paris, 1878) pp. 116–46.
17. O Hekster *Commodus* p. 74 citing Alfody, *Cleanders Sturz* pp. 106–122 and Whittaker, 'The Revolt of Papirius Dionysius' p. 369.
18. HA, *Commodus*, 7.4–5.
19. HA, *Pertinax*, 4.4.
20. *Herodian*, 1.13.6.
21. *Ammianus Marcellinus*, 26, 6, 9.
22. Philo, *Legatio*, (Embassy to Gaius) 31.
23. Robert Turcan, *The Cults of the Roman Empire* pp. 78,92–3, 114 -118; HA, *Commodus*, 9.4 and 16.4; HA, *Niger*, 6.8–9; HA, *Caracalla*, 9.11.

Chapter 7
1. *Herodian*, 1.13.7–8; *Dio*, 73.14.1; HA, *Commodus*, 19.7.
2. *Dio*, 73.14.1–3; M Taylor, *Antiochus the Great* (Pen and Sword Books, 2013) p. 59–50; HA, *Commodus*, 8.3–4; A Birley, *Septimius Severus* pp. 70–72, 216–223; HA, *Septimius Severus*, 43–4; Leonardo de Arrizabalaga y Prado, *The Emperor Elagabalus: Fact or Fiction?* (Cambridge University Press) p. 216; Barbara Levick, *Julia Domna: Syrian Empress* (Routledge) p. 34; Royal Huntsman: R Grant, *The Antonines* p. 184 citing RIC III p. 407 no 332, cf p. 357.
3. HA, *Commodus*, 7.4; *Dio*, 73.14.3; CIL VI.31856=ILS 1327 from Rome : career of Lucius Julius Vehilius Gratus Julianus : fought in Parthia and in northern war with vexillations of a legion, awarded financial rewards by Marcus Aurelius and Verus as well as Marcus Aurelius and Commodus thanks to victory in the war against Germans and Sarmatians. Prefect of the fleet at Misenum and Ravenna and by 15 July 190 AD sole Praetorian Prefect. CIL 14. 4378 (Iulio Iulian(o) pr(aefecto) pr(aetorio).
4. *Dio*, 73.4.6–7; *Herodian*, 1.16.4 and 1.13.8.
5. *Herodian*, 2.1.10.
6. AE (1949) 38.11,5–6 cited in Hekster, *Commodus* p. 77; HA, *Commodus*, 9.2.
7. Hekster, *Commodus* p. 116 citing Bergmann, *Strahlen der Herrscher* pp. 248–52,figs 47.1–3 and 48,1–3 who studied the varying hairstyles on the portraiture of Commodus including portrait in the Museo delle Terme in Rome; H M D Parker, *A History of the Roman world AD 138 to 337 AD* (London, 1935) p. 34; Tony Honore, *Ulpian: Pioneer of Human Rights* (Oxford University Press, 2002) p. 12; Athenaeus 12.537.
8. *Dio*, 73.15.6; Hekster, *Commodus* pp. 104–110; Michael Taylor, *Antiochus the Great* p. 111.
9. Seneca, *De Clem*, 1.13.5; R P Saller, *Personal Patronage in the Early Empire* pp. 75–78.
10. *Dio*, 73.16.2; HA, *Commodus*, 16.8 and note 8 p. 303; *Herodian*, 1.13.7 and note 2 p. 87; Hekster, *Commodus* p. 94.

11. *Dio*, 73.17.3; HA, *Commodus*, 2.9, 8.8 and 13.4; M Rostovtseff and H Mattingly, 'Commodus-Hercules in Britain' *JRS* 13, (1923) p. 105.
12. *Herodian*, 1.13.8; *Dio*, 73.13.4 and 73.17.1; HA, *Commodus*, 16. 8–9.
13. Coinage : RIC III, BMCRE 658, Cohen 40; HA, *Commodus*, 85; Hekster, *Commodus* p. 108; Fred S Kleiner, *A History of Roman Art* (Cengage Learning, 2010) p. 192; Eric R Varner, *Monumenta Graeca et Romana: Mutilation and transformation : damnatio memoriae and imperial portraiture*, Monumenta Graeca et Romana No. 10 (Brill Academic Publishing, 2004) p. 141.
14. Hekster, *Commodus* pp. 128–9; Suetonius, *Caligula*, 54.1; *Dio*, 59.5.5; HA, *Hadrian*, 14.10; HA, *Marcus Aurelius*, 8.12; HA, *Commodus*, 2.9, 5.7, 8.5, 11.10–13, 12.11–12, 13.3, 15.4.
15. Hekster, *Commodus* pp. 104–106; Zsuzsanna Varhelyi, *The Religion of Senators in the Roman Empire: Power and Beyond* pp. 197–8; *Dio*, 73.17.4; HA, *Commodus*, 15.8.
16. HA, *Commodus*, 7. 5–8.
17. Zsuzsanna Varhelyi, *The Religion of Senators in the Roman Empire: Power and Beyond* pp. 199–200; CIL vi 1348.
18. E J Champlin, *Miscellanea Testamentaria* Source: Zeitschrift für Papyrologie und Epigraphik, Bd. 69 (1987), pp. 197–206.
19. CIL 8.2366 named in an inscription of 191; see also CIL 3.12487/CIL816530, CIL 22689 SH; 'Commodus' 5.9; *Dio*, 73.4.6.
20. Eric Varner, *Monumenta Graeca et Romana: Mutilation and transformation no 10* pp. 152–3.
21. Hekster, *Commodus* pp. 102–3 and 121–2.
22. Emma Stafford, *Herakles (Gods and Heroes of the Ancient world)* (Routledge, 2011) note 22; Hekster, *Commodus* p. 126; Athenaeus, *Deipn* 12.537f.
23. Z Varhelyi, *The Religion of Senators* p. 97; Amanda Claridge, *Rome; An Oxford Archaeological Guide* p. 288 and 290; HA, *Commodus*, 10.9.
24. Hekster, *Commodus* p. 77 and 102 citing CIL 14.3449 (=ILS 400); A Birley, *Septimius Severus* pp. 83–85; AE 1949,38; HA, *Septimius Severus*, 4.4; HA, *Niger*, 1.5; Edward Champlin, 'Notes on the Heirs of Commodus' *The American Journal of Philology* Vol 100, No 2 (Summer, 1979) p. 303.
25. A Birley, *Septimius Severus* p. 225. The African origins of Petronii are stressed. M Petronius Mamertinus, consul of 150 AD had sons Sura Mamertinus, consul 182 AD and Sura Septimianus, consul 190 AD, who may have been the product of a marriage with a 'Septimia', perhaps a sister of C Septimius Severus, consul 160 AD or P Septimius Aper, consul 153 AD.
26. *Herodian*, 1.16.4; *Dio*, 73.4.7; HA, *Commodus*, 11.9; BMC IV clxxxi in note 2 p. 99 of Loeb edition of *Herodian*.
27. HA, *Albinus*, 2. 1–5.
28. Edward Champlin, 'Notes on the Heirs of Commodus' *The American Journal of Philology* Vol 100, No 2 (Summer, 1979) pp. 290–1.

Chapter 8

1. *Dio*, 73.24.1 attributes the fire as a portent of the eventual death of Commodus at the end of 192 AD suggesting a date in the same year. Eusebius, *Chron* 2.174 who mentioned the previous fire in 188/9 refers to this later fire as being in 192 AD as

well. However Jerome, *Chron* ad XII p. 209 who also refers to the earlier fire gives a date of 191 AD.

2. *Dio*, 73.24.1–2; HA, *Commodus*, 15.7; *Herodian*, 1.14.1–3; Amanda Claridge, *Rome; An Oxford Archaeological Guide* pp. 105–8 and 171–2; *Galen*, 13.362; Steven Rutledge, *Ancient Rome as a Museum of Power and the Culture of Collecting* (Oxford University Press) pp. 164–5.
3. *Herodian*, 1.14.6.
4. *Dio*, 73.15.3–4 and 73.16.3.
5. HA, *Commodus*, 17.6 and 16.5.
6. *Dio*, 73.7.4; Hekster, *Commodus* p. 205.
7. *Dio*, 73.15.6; HA, *Commodus*, 9.3 an/d 18.12; HA, *Pertinax*, 6.10; *Herodian*, 1.14.9; F Millar, *Emperor in the Roman World* p. 303; R Saller, *Personal Patronage under the Early Empire* p. 50; A Winterling, *Politics and Society in Imperial Rome* p. 139.
8. Speidel, *Commodus the God-Emperor* p. 114; *Dio*, 73.15.2 and 73.22.3 and note 1 p. 117; HA, *Commodus*, 9.2, 10.9, 11.4, 15.8 and 17.9–11; *Herodian*, 1.14.8 and 1.15.9 and note 2 p. 107, Hekster, *Commodus* pp. 122–5.
9. Michael Rostovtseff, 'Commodus Hercules in Britain' *JRS* Vol 13 (1923) pp. 91–109; Hekster, *Commodus* pp. 166–171 and 182; F Millar, *The Roman Empire and its Neighbours* pp. 177–8.
10. *Dio*, 73.15.3; HA, *Commodus*, 8.6–7; Hekster, *Commodus*, p. 95; MP Speidel, 'Commodus the God Emperor and the Army' *JRS* Vol 83 (1993) pp. 109–114.
11. *Dio*, 73.15.3–6; BMC IV 751, 846; Arthur M Eckstein, *The Foundation Day of Roman Coloniae California Studies in Classical Antiquity, Volume 12* (University of California) pp. 88–9.
12. *Dio*, 73.15.2–4; HA, *Commodus*, 9.9 and 11.8; Hekster, *Commodus*, pp. 65–6.
13. Hekster, *Commodus* pp. 169–178; Aloys Winterling, *Caligula* p. 149; HA, *Commodus*, 9.9; *Dio*, 73 15.2.
14. *Dio*, 73. 15.5; John F White, *Aurelian: Restorer of the World* (Spellmount, 2005) p. 133; Aloys Winterling, *Caligula* pp. 150–2.
15. Hekster, *Commodus* p. 205; Eusebius, *Chron*, 15.4; Ostia-Topographical Dictionary: regio II-Insula VII-Teatro (II,VII,2) found at www.ostia-antica.org/regio2/7/7–2.htm; HA, *Commodus*, 17.9; Gustav Hermansen, *Ostia: Aspects of Roman City Life* (University of Alberta Press, 1981) p. 9 and 63–4: CSA, (Spring, 2013) Ostia Site Report found at sites.davidson.edu/ostia-site-report/
16. *Herodian*, 1.15.7; BMC IV. clxx (liberalitas VIII and IX); *Dio*, 73.16.2; *Dio*, 73. 17.4; Alison Futrell, *The Roman Games; Historical Sources in Translation* (Blackwell Sourcebooks in Ancient History, 2005) p. 158.
17. Allen Ward, 'Gladiator in the Historical Perspective' in *Gladiator: Film and History* Ed by Martin Winkler (Blackwell, 2005) pp. 31–45; M Grant, *The Antonines* p. 68; Hekster, *Commodus* pp. 138–148; HA, *Commodus*, 15.6; *Gladiators and Caesars* edited by Eckart Kohne, Cornelia Ewigleben and Ralph Jackson (British Museum Press, 2000) p. 26 and 131 citing Cicero's Tusculan Disputations.
18. *Gladiators and Caesars* edited by Eckart Kohne, Cornelia Ewigleben and Ralph Jackson p. 128 citing Seneca, *Letters*, 37.1 f.
19. Suetonius, *Caligula*, 18.3; David Potter, 'Gladiators and Blood Sport' in *Gladiator: Film and History* Ed by Martin Winkler pp. 80–86.

20. David Potter, 'Gladiators and Blood sport' in *Gladiator: Film and History* pp. 73–111; Thomas Wiedemann, *Emperors and Gladiators* (Routledge, 1995) p. 120.
21. Juvenal, *Satires*, VI: 82–113.
22. Hekster, *Commodus* p. 205; *Gladiators and Caesars* edited by Eckart Kohne, Cornelia Ewigleben and Ralph Jackson pp. 40, 59–61.
23. HA, *Albinus*, 6.8.
24. *Dio*, 73.20.1; *Gladiators and Caesars* edited by Eckart Kohne, Cornelia Ewigleben and Ralph Jackson p. 14; A Birley, *Septimius Severus* p. 86; *Zosimus*, 2.5.1; *Herodian*, 1.14.9 to 1.15.2.
25. *Herodian*, 1.15.2 and 1.17.3, *Dio*, 73.17.3 and 73. 20.1–2; HA, *Commodus*, 9.6.
26. A Garzetti, *From Tiberius to the Antonines* p. 541; HA, *Commodus*, 11.9.
27. *Dio*, 73.17.2–3 and 73.20.1–3; *Herodian*, 1.15.3–8; Aurelius Victor, *Caes*, 17.4.
28. *Dio*, 73.21.2.
29. *Dio*, 73.21.3; HA, *Commodus*, 16.6–7; Hekster, *Commodus* pp. 146–8.
30. *Herodian*, 1.15.7.
31. HA, *Commodus*, 15.6.
32. Hekster, *Commodus*, p. 136.
33. Dracontius, *Satisfactio*, pp. 187–190; *Malalas*, 12.1:283; Eusebius, *A History of the Church*, 21.1; Hekster, *Commodus* p. 185.

Chapter 9
1. Hekster, *Commodus* p. 80 note 216 citing Grosso, *Commodo* p. 399–405; *Dio*, 73. 21.3 and 74.1.1; HA, *Pertinax*, 4.4 and 5.2, HA, *Commodus*, 8.7; *Herodian*, 2.1.10; Julian, *Caesars*, 312C.
2. E Champlin, 'The heirs of Commodus' *The American Journal of Philology* Vol 100 no 2 (1979) p. 298 and 302–306; HA, *Pertinax*, 5.2; *Dio*, 53.19 and 54.15.2–4; F Millar, *Cassius Dio* p. 120 and 136.
3. *Herodian*, 1.16. 3– 1.17.6 and note 4 p. 109; F Millar, *Cassius Dio* p. 133; Hekster, *Commodus* p. 80 and note 216.
4. R Turcan, *The Cults of the Roman Empire* p. 152; Macrobius, *Saturnalia* I, 23, 12; *Herodian*, 2.2.9.
5. HA *Pertinax*, 4.4.
6. *Herodian*, 1.17.6.
7. *Dio*, 73.4.6.
8. *Herodian* Loeb edition pp. 110–111 note 1 citing ILS 406 and ILS 1909.
9. HA, *Pertinax*, 13.2–5.
10. E Champlin, 'The Heirs of Commodus' *AJP* Vol 100 (1979) pp. 289–306.
11. *Dio*, 74.3.2–4 and 74.7.2 ; HA, *Pertinax*, 4.10 and note 2 p. 324 in Loeb edition; *Herodian*, 2.3.1–4; E Champlin, 'The Heirs of Commodus' *AJP* Vol 100 (1979) p. 290.
12. *Dio*, 73.22.1 and 74.6.3; *Herodian*, 1.16.5; HA, *Pertinax*, 5.3 and 10.8–10; HA, *Didius Julianus*, 6.2.
13. *Herodian*, 1.17.7–11; Aurelius Victor, *Caes*, 17.8; *Dio*, 73.22.1–6; HA, *Commodus*, 17.1–2; Hekster, *Commodus* p. 184 citing Athenaeus, *Deipnosophistae*, 1.2c and CIL 6.2126.

14. *Herodian*, 1.12.6, 2.1.1–5, 2.4.1 and note 1 pp. 128–9; HA, *Pertinax*, 4.3–4; *Dio*, 74.1.1–5; Hekster, *Commodus* pp. 184–5; ILS 1141; ILS 401.

15. *Dio*, 74.1.4–5, 74.2.4 and 74.3.3; HA, *Pertinax*, 4.7–11 and 5.2; HA, *Commodus*, 18.

16. *Dio*, 74.2.3; E Champlin, 'The Heirs of Commodus' *AJP* Vol 100 No2 (1979) p. 306.

17. *Dio*, 74.2.5–6.

18. HA, *Commodus*, 20.3–5; HA, *Septimius Severus*, 13.9.

19. HA, *Pertinax*, 5.2–4; HA, *Septimius Severus*, 13.1–9; *Dio*, 74.3.4; *Herodian*, 2.3.1 and 2.2.9.

20. *Dio*, 74.4.3–4 and 74.5.4; *Herodian*, 2.3.3–4, 2.4.1 and note 2 p. 153 (Loeb edition); HA, *Pertinax*, 6.1–3.

Chapter 10

1. HA, *Pertinax*, 6.4–5.

2. *Herodian*, 2.4.4.

3. E Champlin, 'The Heirs of Commodus' *AJP* Vol 100 No2 pp. 297–300; *Herodian*.

4. HA, *Pertinax*, 6.6 and 7.6; *Dio*, 74.1.2 and 74.8.2–3; *Herodian*, 2.4.6.

5. *Dio*, 74.5.2 and 74.6.1; HA, *Pertinax*, 7.4, 9.2 and 9.9.

6. HA, *Pertinax*, 7.8 -8.7; *Dio*, 74.5.4–5 and 74.8.5.

7. HA, *Pertinax*, 8.1 and 13.9.

8. *Dio*, 74.6.2; HA, *Pertinax*, 7. 2–7.

9. HA, *Pertinax*, 9.2–8 and 6.10–11; *Dio*, 74.3.4; *Herodian*, 2.4.2.

10. *Dio*, 74.15.4; HA, *Pertinax*, 13.1.

11. *Dio*, 74.6.1; *Herodian*, 2.4.4.

12. HA, *Pertinax*, 10.1–2; *Dio*, 74.8.1–5; E Champlin, 'The Heirs of Commodus' *AJP* Vol 100 No2 pp. 300–305.

13. *Dio*, 74.81–5.

14. HA, *Pertinax*, 11.1.

15. HA, *Pertinax*, 11.3 and 13.7, HA, *Didius Julianus*, 2.6; *Dio*, 74.11.1.

16. HA, *Pertinax*, 11.1–10; *Dio*, 74.9.1–4; *Herodian*, 2.5.2–5.

17. *Dio*, 74.10.1–3; *Herodian*, 2.5.5–9; HA, *Pertinax*, 11.10–13.

18. *Dio*, 74.11.1– 12.5; *Herodian*, 2.6.4–14; HA, *Didius Julianus*, 2.6.

19. *Dio*, 74.13.2; HA, *Pertinax*, 12.8; HA, *Didius Julianus*, 3.8; Hekster, *Commodus* p. 186.

20. HA, *Didius Julianus*, 6.2 and 7.5; *Dio*, 74.16.5; O W Reinmuth, 'A Working List of the Prefects of Egypt 30 BC to 299 AD' in *The Bulletin of the American Society of Papyrologists* p. 101; A Birley, *Septimius Severus* p. 97.

21. CIL VIII.9317.

22. *Dio*, 74.13.2–5; *Herodian*, 2.7.5.

23. HA, *Didius Julianus*, 6.6 and 7.3; *Herodian*, 2.12.4; *Dio*, 74.17.5.

24. *Dio*, 77.7.4–5.

25. *Herodian*, 2.12.1–11; *Dio*, 75.1.1–2.

26. *Dio*, 74.16.5.

27. HA, *Severus*, 11.2–13.9; *Dio*, 76.7.4–8.5; *Herodian*, 3.8.6–8.

28. A Birley, *Septimius Severus* pp. 127–8; *Herodian*, 3.8.4; *Dio*, 76.8.2–5.

29. CIL VIII 9317.

30. A Birley, *Septimius Severus* p. 128; *Herodian*, 3.8.4.

278 The Emperor Commodus

1. *Dio*, 72. 36.4.
2. Philostratus, *Lives of the Sophists*, 2.1.
3. Aloys Winterling, *Politics and Society in Imperial Rome* (Wiley-Blackwell, 2009) pp. 44–5.
4. R P Saller, *Personal Patronage Under the Early Empire* pp. 15–17.
5. R P Saller, *Personal Patronage Under the Early Empire* pp. 66–67; Tacitus, *Annals*, 12.8.
6. Aloys Winterling, *Politics and Society in Imperial Rome* (Wiley-Blackwell, 2009) p. 111.
7. R P Saller, *Personal Patronage under the Early Empire* p. 78; Aloys Winterling, *Politics and Society in Imperial Rome* (Wiley-Blackwell, 2009) pp. 105–6.
8. *Dio*, 74.2.3.
9. Aloys Winterling, *Politics and Society in Imperial Rome* (Wiley-Blackwell, 2009) pp. 114–5; *Dio*, 59.16.3–10 and 76.8.1–4.
10. HA, *Commodus*, 9.1. The biographer adds that if anyone expressed a wish to die Commodus hastened them on their way copying the very words and alleged actions of Caligula.
11. Aloys Winterling, *Politics and Society in Imperial Rome* (Wiley-Blackwell, 2009) p. 109, 116–119; A Garzetti, *From Tiberius to the Antonines* p. 552; Herodian, 1.14.8.
12. HA, *Septimius Severus*, 17.11; Cohen iii p. 234 no 61 (see note in Loeb edition); *Herodian*, 1.17.12.

Bibliography

Picture Credits and Copyright Information
1. By Naughtynimitz (Own work) [CC BY-SA 3.0 (http://creativecommons.org/ licenses/by-sa/3.0)], via Wikimedia Commons.
2. 'Commodus, Kunsthistorisches Museum Vienna - 20100226' by CristianChirita. - Own work. Licenced under CC BY-SA 3.0 via Wikimedia Commons - http:// commons.wikimedia.org/wiki/File:Commodus,_Kunsthistorisches_Museum_ Vienna_-_20100226.jpg#/media/File:Commodus,_Kunsthistorisches_ Museum_Vienna_-_20100226.jpg.
3. By MM (Own work) [CC BY-SA 4.0 (http://creativecommons.org/licenses/by-sa/4.0)], via Wikimedia Commons.
4. I, Sailko [GFDL (http://www.gnu.org/copyleft/fdl.html) or CC BY-SA 3.0 (http://creativecommons.org/licenses/by-sa/3.0)], via Wikimedia Commons.
5. By Dave & Margie Hill / Kleerup from Centennial, CO, USA (Getty Villa - Collection Uploaded by Marcus Cyron) [CC BY-SA 2.0 (http://creativecommons. org/licenses/by-sa/2.0)], via Wikimedia Commons.
6. Wikicommons: © Marie-Lan Nguyen / Wikimedia Commons, via Wikimedia Commons.
7. By Anagoria (Own work) [GFDL (http://www.gnu.org/copyleft/fdl.html) or CC BY 3.0 (http://creativecommons.org/licenses/by/3.0)], via Wikimedia Commons.
8. By Segafredo18 (Own work) [CC BY-SA 3.0 (http://creativecommons.org/ licenses/by-sa/3.0) or GFDL (http://www.gnu.org/copyleft/fdl.html)], via Wikimedia Commons.
9. Shakko/Wikipedia.
10. © Marie-Lan Nguyen/Wikimedia Commons, via Wikimedia Commons.
11. By Ad Meskens (Own work) [CC BY-SA 3.0 (http://creativecommons.org/ licenses/by-sa/3.0) or GFDL (http://www.gnu.org/copyleft/fdl.html)], via Wikimedia Commons.
12. English-speaking Wikipedia user ChrisO [GFDL (http://www.gnu.org/copyleft/ fdl.html) or CC-BY-SA-3.0 (http://creativecommons.org/licenses/by-sa/3.0/)], via Wikimedia Commons.
13. Wikimedia Commons.
14. Public Domain.
15. Classical Numismatic Group, Inc. http://www.cngcoins.com [GFDL (http:// www.gnu.org/copyleft/fdl.html) or CC BY-SA 2.5 (http://creativecommons. org/licenses/by-sa/2.5)], via Wikimedia Commons.
16. Classical Numismatic Group, Inc. http://www.cngcoins.com [GFDL (http://www. gnu.org/copyleft/fdl.html) or CC BY-SA 2.5 (http://creativecommons.org/ licenses/by-sa/2.5)], via Wikimedia Commons.

17. By Wolfgang Sauber (Own work) [GFDL (http://www.gnu.org/copyleft/fdl. html) or CC BY-SA 3.0 (http://creativecommons.org/licenses/by-sa/3.0)], via Wikimedia Commons.
18. Classical Numismatic Group, Inc. http://www.cngcoins.com [GFDL (http:// www.gnu.org/copyleft/fdl.html) or CC BY-SA 2.5 (http://creativecommons. org/licenses/by-sa/2.5)], via Wikimedia Commons.
19. Classical Numismatic Group, Inc. http://www.cngcoins.com [GFDL (http:// www.gnu.org/copyleft/fdl.html) or CC BY-SA 2.5 (http://creativecommons. org/licenses/by-sa/2.5)], via Wikimedia Commons.
20. Classical Numismatic Group, Inc. http://www.cngcoins.com [GFDL (http:// www.gnu.org/copyleft/fdl.html) or CC BY-SA 2.5 (http://creativecommons. org/licenses/by-sa/2.5)], via Wikimedia Commons.
21. Classical Numismatic Group, Inc. http://www.cngcoins.com [GFDL (http:// www.gnu.org/copyleft/fdl.html) or CC BY-SA 2.5 (http://creativecommons. org/licenses/by-sa/2.5)], via Wikimedia Commons.
22. Classical Numismatic Group, Inc. http://www.cngcoins.com [GFDL (http:// www.gnu.org/copyleft/fdl.html) or CC BY-SA 2.5 (http://creativecommons. org/licenses/by-sa/2.5)], via Wikimedia Commons.
23. I, Sailko [GFDL (http://www.gnu.org/copyleft/fdl.html) or CC BY-SA 3.0 (http://creativecommons.org/licenses/by-sa/3.0)], via Wikimedia Commons.
24. I, Sailko [GFDL (http://www.gnu.org/copyleft/fdl.html) or CC BY-SA 3.0 (http://creativecommons.org/licenses/by-sa/3.0)], via Wikimedia Commons.
25. By Lgtrapp (Own work) [CC BY-SA 3.0 (http://creativecommons.org/licenses/ by-sa/3.0)], via Wikimedia Commons.
26. Classical Numismatic Group, Inc. http://www.cngcoins.com [GFDL (http:// www.gnu.org/copyleft/fdl.html), CC-BY-SA-3.0 (http://creativecommons.org/ licenses/by-sa/3.0/) or CC BY-SA 2.5 (http://creativecommons.org/licenses/ by-sa/2.5)], via Wikimedia Commons.
27. By Carole Raddato from FRANKFURT, Germany [CC BY-SA 2.0 (http:// creativecommons.org/licenses/by-sa/2.0)], via Wikimedia Commons.
28. By Carole Raddato from FRANKFURT, Germany [CC BY-SA 2.0 (http:// creativecommons.org/licenses/by-sa/2.0)], via Wikimedia Commons.
29. Public Domain.
30. Public Domain.
31. By Carole Raddato from FRANKFURT, Germany [CC BY-SA 2.0 (http:// creativecommons.org/licenses/by-sa/2.0)], via Wikimedia Commons.
32. By Carole Raddato from FRANKFURT, Germany [CC BY-SA 2.0 (http:// creativecommons.org/licenses/by-sa/2.0)], via Wikimedia Commons.
33. By Carole Raddato from FRANKFURT, Germany [CC BY-SA 2.0 (http:// creativecommons.org/licenses/by-sa/2.0)], via Wikimedia Commons.
34. By Wolfgang Sauber (Own work) [GFDL (http://www.gnu.org/copyleft/fdl. html) or CC BY-SA 3.0 (http://creativecommons.org/licenses/by-sa/3.0)], via Wikimedia Commons.
35. By Carole Raddato from FRANKFURT, Germany [CC BY-SA 2.0 (http:// creativecommons.org/licenses/by-sa/2.0)], via Wikimedia Commons.
36. Classical Numismatic Group, Inc. http://www.cngcoins.com [GFDL (http:// www.gnu.org/copyleft/fdl.html), CC-BY-SA-3.0 (http://creativecommons.org/

licenses/by-sa/3.0/) or CC BY-SA 2.5 (http://creativecommons.org/licenses/by-sa/2.5)], via Wikimedia Commons.
37. [GFDL (http://www.gnu.org/copyleft/fdl.html) or CC-BY-SA-3.0 (http://creativecommons.org/licenses/by-sa/3.0/)], via Wikimedia Commons.

Abbreviations

AA   Antiquites Africaines
AE   L'Annee epigraphique (Paris 1888)
AJPH   American Journal of Philology
BMC   H Mattingly; Coins of the Roman Empire in the British Museum IV. Antoninus Pius to Commodus, London 1940
CIL   Corpus Inscriptionum Latinarum (Berlin 1863)
CNR   Corpus Nummorum Romanorum, A Bonti and Z Simonetti (CNR) Firenze, 1972–79
CSA   Classical Semester Abroad
HA   Historia Augusta
ILS   Dessau, H. Inscriptiones Latinae Selectae (Berlin, 1892–1916)
JRA   Journal of Roman Archaeology
JRS   Journal of Roman Studies
PIR   Prosopographia Imperii Romani (Berlin and Leipzig 1933)
RIC   Roman Imperial Coinage, H Mattingly and R Syndenham etc (London 1923–67)
RIB   Ribchester Inscriptions

Ancient Sources

Aristides, Aelius, *Panathenaic Oration: And In Defence of Oratory* Loeb Classical Library (Harvard University Press, 1973).
Athenaeus, *Deipnosophistai* Book on Demand Pod (2011).
Augustine, *Confessions* translated by R S Pine-Coffin (Penguin Classics, 2002).
Augstine, *City of God* translated by Henry Bettenson (Penguin Classics, 2003).
Augstine, *Enarratio in Psalmum, (Like as the Hart)* (Blackfriars, 1947).
Dio, Cassius, *Roman History* translated by Earnest Cary, Loeb Classical Library (Harvard University Press, 1989).
Dio of Prusa, *Third Discourse on Kingship, Orations* translated by A Russell, Cambridge Greek and Latin Classics - Imperial Library (Cambridge University Press, 1992).
Epictetus, *Discourses* translated by W A Oldfather, Loeb Classical Library (Harvard University Press, 1989).
Eusebius, *The History of the Church* translated by G A Williamson (Penguin Classics, 1989).
Eusebius, *Chronicle*, translations found at http://rbedrosian.com/euseb.html or http://www.attalus.org/translate/eusebius.html.
Eutropius, *Breviarium* translated by H W Bird (Liverpool University Press, 1993).
Fronto, *Correspondence* Loeb Classical Library (Harvard University Press, 1989).
Galen, *Method of Medicine* translated by Ian Johnston and G H R Horsley, Loeb Classical Library (Harvard University Press, 2011).

Galen, *On the Natural Faculties* Loeb Classical Library (Harvard University Press, 1989).

Herodian, *History of the Empire Books 1 - 4* translated by C R Whittaker, Loeb Classical Library (Harvard University Press, 1989).

Historia Augusta, *The Lives of Hadrian, Verus, Marcus Aurelius, Avidius Cassius, Commodus, Pertinax, Didius Julianus, Septimius Severus, Pescennius Niger, Clodius Albinus, Macrinus, Caracalla* translated by David Magie, Loeb Classical Library (Harvard University Press, 1991).

Hyppolitus, *Philosophoumena* translated by Patrice Franois Marie Cruice (Saraswasti Press 2012).

Jerome, *Chronicle* translation found at http://www.tertullian.org/fathers/index.htm#jeromechronicle.

Julian, *Caesars* vol 2 translated by W C Wright, Loeb Classical Library (Harvard University Press, 1989).

Justinian, *Codex Justinianus* translated by S P Scott (Lee Walker, 2013).

Justinian, *The Digest of Justinian* (University of Pennsylvania Press, 2008).

Lucian, *Dialogues of the Dead* translated by A M Harmon, Loeb Classical Library (Harvard University Press, 1989)

Macrobius, *Saturnalia* translated by R A Kaster, Loeb Classical Library (Harvard University Press 2011).

Malalas John, *Chronicle* Australian Centre of Byzantine Studies, (University of Sydney, 1986).

Marcellinus, Ammianus, *History*, translated by J C Rolfe, Loeb Classical Library (Harvard University Press, 1989).

Marcus Aurelius, *Meditations* translated by C R Haines, Loeb Classical Library (Harvard University Press, 1989).

Martial, *Epigrams* volume 2 Loeb Classical Library (Harvard University Press, 1989).

Mattingly, H, *Coins of the Roman Empire in the British Museum IV from Antoninus Pius to Commodus* (London, 1940).

Orosius, *Christian History* The Iberian Fathers: V.3, Fathers of the Church Series, (The Catholic University of America Press, 1999).

Philo, *Embassy to Gaius* vol X translated by F H Colson and G H Whitaker, Loeb Classical Library (Harvard University Press).

Philostratus, *Lives of the Sophists* Loeb Classical Library (Harvard University Press, 1989).

Pliny, *Letters and Panegyricus* translated by B Radice, Loeb Classical Library (Harvard University Press, 1969).

Seneca, *De Beneficii and De Clementia* translated by John W Basore, In Moral

Seneca, *De Ira (Of Anger)* Amazon Media: Kindle Edition.

Essays, Loeb Classical Library (Harvard University Press, 1989).

Statius, *Silvae* translated by D R Shackleton-Bailey, Loeb Classical Library (Harvard University Press, 2003).

Suetonius, *The Twelve Caesars* translated by Robert Graves (Penguin Classics, 2007).

Tacitus, *Annals Of Imperial Rome* translated by M Grant (Penguin Classics, 1996).

Tacitus, The *Histories* translated by Kenneth Wellesley (Penguin Classics, 1982).

Tertullian, *Apologeticus Adversus Gentes Pro Christianis* (Ulan Press, 2012).

Victor, Aurelius, *De Caesaribus* translated by H W Bird (University of Liverpool Press, 1994).

Victor, Auerlius, *Epitome de Caesaribus* online translation found at De Imperatoribus Romanis: http://www.luc.edu/roman-emperors/epitome.htm.

Corpus Medicorum Graecorum/Latinorum, online publications Akademie der Wissenschaften. berlin-brandenburgische.

Zosimus, *New History* translated by J J Buchanan and H T Davis (Trinity University Press, 1967).

Modern Sources

Adams, G, *The Emperor Commodus* (BrownWalker Press, 2013).

Alfoldy, A, *Bellum Desertum in 'Die Krise des romischen Reiches'* (Geschichte, Geschichtsschreibung und Geschichtsbetrachtung, Stuttgart, 1989).

Arrizabalaga, Leonardo de y Prado, *The Emperor Elagabalus: Fact or Fiction?* (Cambridge University Press).

Aymard, J, *La conjuration de Lucilla* translated from http://www.persee.fr/web/revues/home/prescript/article/antiq_07702817_2007_num_76_1_2621 REA 57 1955.

Bagnall, R S, *Women and Society in Greek and Roman Egypt: A Sourcebook* edited by Jane Rowlandson (Cambridge University Press).

Barker, P, *The Empire Stops Here* (Pimlico 2010).

Beckman, M, *Column of Marcus Aurelius: the Genesis and Meaning of a Roman Imperial Monument* (University of North Carolina Press, 2011).

Benko, S, *The Virgin Goddess; Studies in Pagan and Christian Roots of Mariology* (Leiden, 2004).

Bingham, S, *The Praetorian Guard: A History of Rome's Special Forces* (I B Tauris and Co Ltd, 2013).

Birley, A, *Marcus Aurelius: A Biography* (Routledge, 2001).

Birley, A, *Hadrian: The Restless Emperor* (London-New York, 1997).

Birley, A, *Cambridge Ancient History* 2nd Edition Vol XI (2000).

Birley, A, *The African Emperor, Septimius Severus* (Batsford, 1988).

Brassington, M, *Ulpius Marcellus, Britannia* Vol 11 (November, 1980).

Breeze, D, *The Northern Frontiers of Roman Britain* (Book Club Association, 1982).

Breeze, D, *Roman Officers and Frontiers* (Franz Steiner Verlag Wiesbaden GmbH, 1993).

Brill, E J, *Leaders and Mass Movements in Late Antiquity* edited by Irad Malkin and Z W Rubinsohn, studies in honour of Zvi Ya'vets (1995).

Brunt, P A, 'Administration of Roman Egypt', *JRS* 65 (1975).

Brunt, P A, 'The Fall of Perennis', *Classical Quarterly* 23 (1973).

Campbell, B, *The Roman Army; A Sourcebook* (Routledge, 1994).

Cavallini, E, 'Was Commodus Really That Bad?' in *The Fall of the Roman Empire: Film and History* edited by Martin Winker (Wiley-Blackwell, 2009).

Champlin, E, 'Notes on the Heirs of Commodus', *AJPH* 100 (1979).

Champlin, E, *Miscellanea Testamentaria* Source: Zeitschrift für Papyrologie und Epigraphik, Bd. 69 (1987) pp. 197–206.

Champlin, E, *Fronto and Antonine Rome* (Harvard University Press, 1980).

Charles M, and Ryan N, *The Roman Empire and the Grain Fleets; Contracting out public services in Antiquity* (Queensland University of Technology).

Chatr Aryamontri D, Excavation on Commodus' villa at Lanuvium; Montclair University http://www.montclair.edu/chss/center-heritage-archaeological-studies. Claridge, A, *Rome, an Oxford Archaeological Guide* (Oxford University Press).

Cohen, H, *Description historique des monnaies frappees sous l'empire Romain. III. Medailles Imperiales* (Leipzig, 1930).

Crook, J A, *Consilium Principis* (Cambridge, 1955).

Cunha, C B and Cunha B A, 'Great Plagues of the Past and Remaining Questions', in *Paleomicrobiology: Past Human Infections* edited by D Raoult and M Drancourt (Springer-Verlag Berlin Heidelberg, 2008) pp. 12–14.

De Blois L, *The Crisis of the Third Century AD in the Roman Empire: A Modern Myth* www.phil-fak.uni-duesseldorf.de/…/Blois.

De la Bédoyère G, *Roman Britain: a New History* (Thames and Hudson, 2010).

De la Bédoyère G, *People of Roman Britain* http://www.romanbritain.freeserve.co.uk.

De Ranieri C, 'Retoscena politici e lotte dinastiche sullo della vicenda di Aurelio Cleandro', *RSA* 27 (1997).

Dessau, H, *Inscriptiones Latinae Selectae* (1916).

Dobson, B, *Roman Officers and Frontiers* (Franz Steiner Verlag Wiesbaden GmbH, 1993).

Duncan, Jones R P, 'Effects of the Antonine Plague' in *JRA* 9 (1996).

Eck, W, *Cambridge Ancient History* 2nd Edition Vol XI (2000).

Eckstein, A, 'Commodus and the Limits of the Roman Empire' in *Gladiator: Film and History* (Blackwell Publishing, 2005).

Eckstein, A, 'The Foundation Day of Roman Coloniae', *California Studies in Classical Antiquity* Volume 12 (University of California).

Edgar, C C and A S Hunt, *Select Papyri 2* 315, as recorded in columbia.edu/cu/libraries/ins…nput/MiU_apis_20050623.txt; P. Oxy. II 237 (1963).

Elliot, Paul, 'The Legions in Crisis: Transformation of the Roman Soldier AD 192–284' (Fonthill, 2014).

Erdkamp, P, *The Grain Market in the Roman Empire* (Cambridge University Press).

Ewigleben, C and Jackson, R, *Gladiators and Caesars* edited by Eckart Kohne (British Museum Press, 2000).

Fröehner, W, *Les médaillons de l'empire romain, depuis le règne d'Auguste jusqu'à Priscus Attale* (Paris, 1878).

Futrell, A, *The Roman Games; Historical Sources in Translation* (Blackwell Sourcebooks in Ancient History, 2005).

Garzetti, A, *From Tiberius to the Antonines: A History of the Roman Empire AD 14–192* (Methuen and Co Limited, 1974).

Grant, M, *The Antonines: the Roman Empire in Transition* (Routledge, 1996).

Grierson, M, *A Study of the Municipal Aristocracies in the Roman Empire in the West, with Special Reference to North Africa* (1958). Durham e-theses-Durham University found at http://etheses.dur.ac.uk/1980.

Cristofori, A, *Grain Distribution in Late Republican Rome* (University of Bologna).

Grosso, F, *La lotta politica al tempo di Commodo* (Turin, 1964).

Grunewald, T, *Bandits in the Roman Empire: Myth and Reality* (Routledge, 2008).

Hekster, O, *Commodus: An Emperor at the Cross Roads* (J C Gieben, Amsterdam, 2002).

Henig, M, 'The Victory Gem from Lullingstone Roman Villa', *Journal of the British Archaeological Association* 160 (2007).

Hermansen, G, *Ostia: Aspects of Roman City Life* (University of Alberta Press, 1981).

Hojte, J M, *Roman Imperial Statue Bases: from Augustus to Commodus* (Aarhus University Press, Aarhus, 2005).

Honoré, Tony, *Ulpian: Pioneer of Human Rights* (Oxford University Press, 2002).

Humphrey, J, *Roman Circuses: Arenas For Chariot Racing* (Berkley, 1986).

Hunt, A S and C C Edgar, *Select Papyri 2* 315 (1963) as recorded in columbia.edu/cu/libraries/ins…nput/MiU_apis_20050623.txt; P. Oxy. II 237.

Jackson, R and Ewigleben, C, *Gladiators and Caesars* edited by Eckart Kohne (British Museum Press, 2000).

Jarrett, M, *A Study of Municipal Aristocracies of the Roman Empire* a 1958 Durham University e thesis: *etheses.dur.ac.uk/1980/2/1980_v2.pdf (1958)*.

Kessler, D and Peter Temin, 'The Organisation of the Grain trade in the Early Roman Empire', *Economic History Review* 60 (2007).

Kleiner, F S, *A History of Roman Art* (Cengage Learning, 2010).

Klodzinski, C, *Praetorian Prefects of the Emperor Commodus* KLIO PL ISSN 1643–8191, Vol 20 (1) (2012).

Klodzinski, K, *Equestrian cursus honorum based on careers of two prominent officers of the emperor Marcus Aurelius* in www.academia.edu/1872904/Equestrian_cu.

Kovacs, P, 'Burgus Building Instructions of Commodus from Pannonia', in *Sylloge Epigraphica Barcinonensis* (SEBarc) VI (2008).

Kurilic, A, *Ruling Class of Asseria: Magistrates and Benefactors and their Familiae and Families* nrcak.srce.hr/file/59664'.

Levick, B, *Julia Domna: Syrian Empress* (Routledge, 2007).

Linderski, J, *Roman Questions II* (Habes Franz Steiner Verlag Stuttgart, 2007).

Littman, R J and M L, 'Galen and the Antonine Plague', *AJPH* 94 no 3 (The John Hopkins University Press) pp. 243–255.

Mangard, G, *l'inscription dedicatoire du theatre du Blois l'Abbe a eu (siene-maritime)* Gallia 40 (1982).

Mann, J C, *Hermes* 91 iv (1963).

Mattingly, D, *An Imperial Possession; Britain in the Roman Empire* (Penguin, 2007).

Mattingly, H and Rostovtseff M, 'Commodus-Hercules in Britain', *JRS* 13.

McLynn, F, *Marcus Aurelius, Warrior, Philosopher, Emperor* (Vintage, 2010).

Mennen, I, *Power and Status in the Roman Empire 193 -284 AD* (Brill, 2011).

Millar F, *A Study of Cassius Dio* (Oxford, 1964).

Millar F, *The Emperor in the Roman World* (Duckworth, 1977).

Millar F, *The Roman Empire and its Neighbours* (Duckworth, 1981).

Oliver, J H, 'The Sacred Gerusia and the Emperor's Consilium' in *The American* on www.ascsa.edu.gr/pdf/uploads/hesperia/147433.pdf.

Oliver, J H, 'Three Attic Inscriptions Concerning the Emperor Commodus', *AJPH* 71, (1950) p. 170.

Parker, A, *A History of the Roman World* (London, 1935).

Pflaum, H G, *Les carrieres procuratoriennes equestres sous le Haut-Empire romain* Bibliotheque archeologique et historique (P Geuthner, 1982).

Picard, G, *La republique des Pictones n105 555f Dem 'La revolte de Maternus'* n 105.

Potter, D, 'Gladiator: Gladiators and Blood Sport', in *Gladiator: Film and History* (Blackwell, 2008).

Potter, D, *The Roman Empire at Bay: AD 180–395* (Routledge, 2004).

Rathbone, D, *Villages, land and population in Graeco-Egypt* PCPhS n.s. 36 (1990).

Reinmuth, O W, 'A Working list of the Prefects of Egypt: 30 BC–299 AD', Vol 4, Issue 4, *The Bulletin of the American Society of Papyrologists* (Michigan Publishing).

Reynolds, J, *Aphrodisias and Rome* (London, 1982).

Richardson, L, *A New Topographical Dictionary of Ancient Rome* (Hopkins University Press Baltimore, 1992).

Rostovtseff, M and Mattingly, H, 'Commodus-Hercules in Britain', *JRS* 13.

Ruger, C, *Roman Germany* Cambridge Ancient History XI (Cambridge University Press, 2000).

Rutledge, S, *Ancient Rome as a Museum of Power and the Culture of Collecting* (Oxford University Press, 2012).

Ryan, N and Charles, M, *The Roman Empire and the Grain Fleets; Contracting out public services in Antiquity* (Queensland University of Technology).

Saller, R P, *Personal Patronage under the Early Empire* (Cambridge University Press, 2002).

Salway, P, *History of Roman Britain* (Oxford University Press, 1997).

Scheidel, W, *Roman Well Being and the Economic Consequences of the Antonine Plague* (Princeton/Stanford University Press, 2010).

Scullard, H H, *Festivals and Ceremonies of the Roman Republic* (Thames and Hudson, 1981).

Spaul, J E H, *Governors of Tingitana* in AA vol 30 (1994).

Speidel, M P, 'Commodus the God Emperor and the Army', *JRS* Vol 83 (1993).

Stafford, E, *Herakles (Gods and Heroes of the Ancient world)* (Routledge, 2011).

Stein, F J, *Dexippus et herodianus rerum scriptores quatenus Thucydidem secuti sint* Mnemosyne vol14 (Brill, 1961).

Syme, R, *The Roman Revolution* (Oxford University Press, 1939).

Szaivert, 'Munzpragung' no 1072 hosted at *repository.ubn.ru.nl/bitstream/handle/2066/17127/165849.pdf;…2*.

Talbert, R, *The Senate of Imperial Rome* (Princeton, 1984).

Taylor, M, *Antiochus the Great* (Pen and Sword Books, 2013).

Temin, P and Kessler D, 'The Organisation of the Grain trade in the Early Roman Empire', *Economic History Review* 60 (2007).

Traupman, J C, *The Life and Reign of Commodus* PhD thesis (Princeton, 1956).

Turcan, R, *The Cults of the Roman Empire* (Wiley-Blackwell, 1996).

Vahl, J, *Imperial Representations of Clementia: from Augustus to Marcus Aurelius* 2007. MA dissertations DigitalCommons@Master: McMaster University.

Varhelyi, Z, *The Religion of Senators in the Roman Empire: Power and Beyond* (Cambridge University Press, 2010).

Varner, E R, *Monumenta Graeca et Romana: Mutilation and transformation : damnatio memoriae and imperial portraiture* Monumenta Graeca et Romana No. 10 (Brill, 2004).

Ward, A, 'History, Ancient and Modern in The Fall of the Roman Empire' in *The Fall of the Roman Empire: Film and History* edited by Martin Winker (Wiley-Blackwell, 2009).

Ward, A, 'Gladiator in the Historical Perspective' in *Gladiator: Film and History* (Blackwell Publishing, 2005).

Weaver, R P C, *Familia Caesaris, A Social Study of the Emperor's Freemen and Slaves* (Cambridge University Press, 1972).

White, J F, *Aurelian: Restorer of the World* (Spellmount, 2005).

Whittaker, C R, *Cambridge Ancient History* 2nd Edition Vol XI (2000).

Whittaker, C R, *The Revolt of Papirius Dionysius AD 190* Historia 13 (1964).

Wiedemann, T, *Emperors and Gladiators* (Routledge, 1995).

Winterling, A, *Caligula* (University of California Press, 2011).

Winterling, A, *Politics and Society in Imperial Rome* (Wiley-Blackwell, 2009).

Index

Acilius Glabrio, Marcus, xiv, 44, 55, 77, 154–5, 159, 206–207, 214, 217–19, 223, 245

Adrian of Tyre, 2–3, 10, 30

Aelius Aristides, 29, 86, 160, 171–3, 175, 197, 201–205, 207–12, 215–18, 220, 224–7, 230, 240, 242, 263

Aemilius Laetus, Q., 160, 171–3, 175, 197, 201–205, 207–12, 215–20, 224–7, 230, 240, 242, 263

Africa, xvii, 4, 37–8, 41, 43–5, 54–5, 65, 68, 85, 93, 104, 111, 120–1, 124, 129, 132, 136–8, 140–7, 154, 160–1, 172, 175, 182, 185, 187, 224, 248, 261, 274

Agaclytus (Imperial freedman), xiv, 8–9, 107, 138

Agrippus Aelius Memphius Apolaustus, L. (Imperial freedman), 7–9, 107, 139, 154, 160, 267–8

Alexandria, xviii, 12, 19, 28–9, 120, 146, 156, 174, 187, 232, 269

Amicitiae, xv, 47, 70, 109, 126, 128, 130, 134, 143–4, 168, 200, 230

Annia Cornificia, 4, 10, 152, 160, 168, 170, 205, 207, 241

Annia Faustina, xiv, 55, 167, 169–70

Annia Fundiana Faustina, 13, 76

Annius Fabianus, L., 133

Annius Verus, M. (brother of Commodus), 4–5, 13

Antioch, 11, 19, 23, 25, 28–9, 59, 65, 68, 185

Antistius Adventus, Q., 49, 54, 58, 111, 136

Antistius Burrus, Lucius, 4, 54, 68, 111, 136–8, 141–3, 151, 162, 173, 240–2

Antistius Capella, 1

Antonius Antius Lupus, M., 111, 167–70, 216

Antoninus Pius (Emperor), xiii, 1, 10, 17, 33–4, 44–5, 74, 88, 91, 97, 107, 123, 125–6, 136, 138, 165

Aquileia, xvii, 8, 12

Arrius Antoninus, C., xvi, 25, 130, 136–8, 141–3, 146, 155

Ateius Sanctus, 1

Atilius Aebutianus, P., 114

Asellius Aemilianus, 130, 172

Asinius Rufinus, M., 84, 182

Athens, 2–4, 17, 27, 30, 47, 63, 65, 110, 185, 247

Aufidius Victorinus, C., xiv, xvii, 8, 10, 38, 49, 54, 65, 68, 77, 83, 90, 111–12, 133, 136

Augustus (Emperor), vi, xiii, 1, 64, 76, 88, 122, 126, 156, 160, 166, 178, 199, 234, 249–50

Aurelius Agaclytus, L. (Imperial freedman), xiv, 8–9, 107, 138

Aurelius Apolaustus Memphius, L. (Imperial freedman), 9, 107, 139, 154, 160, 268

Aurelius Fulvius Antoninus, Titus (brother of Commodus), 3–4

Avidius Cassius, xviii, xxi, 18–25, 28, 31, 33, 48, 50, 53, 58–9, 63, 66–7, 78–80, 96, 106, 109, 128, 136, 168, 186, 205, 239, 249, 261

Banquets, xv, 5, 7, 69, 71, 83–6, 107, 127, 148, 182, 223, 229, 245, 250, 261

Basilica of Trajan, 22

Bassaeus Rufus, M., 17, 25, 45–6, 55

Baths of Cleander, 123, 187